I. Pink lady's slipper *(Cypripedium acaule)*
J. Old-man-of-the-mountain *(Hymenoxys grandiflora)*
K. California poppy *(Eschscholzia californica)*
L. Baby blue-eyes *(Nemophila menziesii)*
M. Eastern trout lily *(Erythronium americanum)*
N. Sky lupine *(Lupinus nanus)*
O. Scarlet sage *(Salvia coccinea)*

A Garden of Wildflowers

101 Native Species and How to Grow Them

Henry W. Art

Illustrations by Hyla M. Skudder

STOREY COMMUNICATIONS, INC.
POWNAL, VERMONT 05261

Cover design and illustration by Hyla M. Skudder

Edited by Deborah Burns and Tom Rawls

Design by Cindy McFarland and Andrea Gray

Illustrations on pages 4, 9, 10, 13, 14, 24, 28, 41, 47
by Elayne Sears

Typesetting by Quad Left, Burlington, Vermont

Printed in the United States by Alpine Press

First Printing, February 1986

Library of Congress Catalog Card Number: 85-45163

International Standard Book Number: 0-88266-404-2
0-88266-405-0 (pbk.)

Library of Congress Cataloging-in-Publication Data

Art, Henry Warren.
    A garden of wildflowers.

    "A Garden Way Publishing book."
    Includes index.
    1. Wild flower gardening — United States. 2. Wild flowers — United States. I. Title.
SB439.A78   1986   635.9'676'0973   85-45163
ISBN 0-88266-404-2
ISBN 0-88266-405-0 (pbk.)

*This book is dedicated to
Pam, Andrew, Jamie, and Matthew
for the many stops to look along the way.*

*Also in appreciation of B.E. Mahall
and F.H. Bormann for the eastern,
and J.R. Haller for the western perspectives.*

Contents

Acknowledgments

The author and illustrator would like to thank the following people:

Martha M. Storey, for wanting a good book on wildflowers and providing encouragement along the way.

James R. Beall, Sr., for editorial assistance in the preparation of the manuscript.

Chris Skudder for moral support and holding down the fort.

J. Robert Haller, University of California – Santa Barbara for supplying many photographic images helpful in the preparation of the illustrations of California wildflowers.

Michael Canoso and Walter Kittredge for assistance in the use of the Harvard University Herbaria (the Collections of the Gray Herbarium and Arnold Arboretum).

Sarah McFarland, Lee Dalzell, and Barbara Prentice of the Reference Department, Sawyer Library, Williams College for their on-line literature searches and attention to interlibrary loan requests.

Gene Baxter and Penny Logan of the New England Wild Flower Society for assistance in their slide library.

Orville M. Steward, James Taylor, and Kenneth Lodewick of the American Penstemon Society for illustrative material on penstemons.

Tom Viti and Jerry Cirillo of the Westwood, Massachusetts Library, and many folks on the staff of the Morrill Library, University of Massachusetts for their aid in obtaining illustrative material.

Dr. R. Stewart Smith and the Nitragin Company for providing technical information concerning rhizobia and allowing the use of their trademarked name.

Dr. Leonard Moss, Ph.D., for his eternal excitement over the native flora.

The hundreds of people associated with botanic gardens, nature centers, arboreta, wildflower seed companies, native-plant nurseries, native-plant societies, and botanical organizations, who responded to the requests for the information that is contained in the appendices.

Part I

AN INTRODUCTION TO WILDFLOWERS

Why a Garden
of Wildflowers?

With the abundance of new horticultural varieties of garden flowers that each year add to the already crammed pages of seed catalogs, why would anyone want to grow common native plants? A simple question with numerous answers. Some of the answers are found in the pages of this book, but the best answers are found by the gardener in the actual growing of the plants.

There is something rewarding in the cultivation of flowers in general. It is an aesthetic experience, for most plants grown for their flowers have little other economic use. They are cultivated for the pleasure of seeing the blossoms and foliage, or even smelling the scents of perfumes and nectars. The beauty of flowers is no biological accident; their attractiveness ensures the continuation of their species. Flowering plants have evolved from ancestors with rather inconspicuous reproductive systems dependent on wind for pollination. The evolution of more efficient pollination by insects occurred concurrently with the evolution of showy, sweet-smelling flowers to attract the insects. In a real sense we share an appreciation of natural beauty with those insects, which are also ensuring the plant will produce seeds and thereby the next generation of flowers.

This book deals with wildflowers, plants that have the capacity to make it on their own without human assistance. Most wildflowers can be maintained in their native habitats with little effort, once they are established. However, not all plants that are called wildflowers are native to North America. Many weedy wildflowers have been imported from Europe and Asia, either by accident or for their ornamental value. Oxeye daisy, yarrow, Queen Anne's lace, scarlet pimpernel, common St. Johnswort, and many other attractive wildflowers originated in foreign lands but have taken up permanent residence in the New World. Not all of these aliens are welcome guests, for some of them have become aggressive weeds, and each year vast sums of money are spent on their control.

All of the wildflowers in this book are native to North America, and some have been considered garden plants for more than the last three centuries. Early explorers and settlers would frequently send North American native species back to Europe, where many of these newfound plants such as gayfeather, goatsbeard, and false dragonhead became garden favorites. It is ironic that some of the American species have been more popular in European gardens than in those in their native range. Other North American natives such as Virginia bluebells, annual phlox, cosmos, spiderwort, and California poppy have so long been listed in garden catalogs that we may be accustomed to thinking of them as domesticated plants. By expanding your horizons beyond the conventional

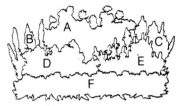

A. Cosmos
B. Gayfeather
C. False dragonhead
D. Purple coneflower
E. Mexican hat
F. Lance-leaved coreopsis

Note: Wildflowers depicted in these and the following sample gardens may not bloom simultaneously.

Cutflower bed, summer.

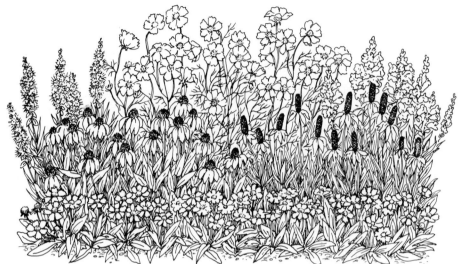

horticultural species to native wildflowers, you can find new and exciting beauty as nearby as your garden.

In creating a garden of wildflowers, you may find a deeper sense of identity with the natural environment and develop a feeling of rootedness that is not possible when cultivating domesticated, horticultural varieties. At the same time, native plants provide a wonderful opportunity for learning through observation. For example, the flowers of Jack-in-the-pulpit have the capacity to change sex from year to year depending upon the growing conditions. Small plants don't flower, medium-sized plants generally have male flowers, and large plants have female flowers. A relatively small number of plants have both male and female flowers. The size of the plant the previous year is the best indicator of the likely sex of the plant the next season.

The pollination of our Lord's candle is another fascinating story. The plant starts to flower as its only pollinator, the yucca moth, *Tegeticula maculata,* emerges in the spring. Individual flowers open in the evening when the moth is most active. A female moth visits a flower and, with her specialized mouth parts, scrapes the pollen, rolls it up into a ball about three times the size of her head, and flies with it to another newly opened flower. She backs down to the base of the pistil, injects her eggs into the ovary of the plant, and then crawls to the stigmatic surface. Here she carefully attaches the mass of pollen, ensuring both the fertilization of the flower and the production of seeds, which the developing moth larvae need for their survival. The growing larvae consume some of the seeds, but burrow out of the fruit and into the ground before the pod shatters and seeds are released. Adult moths emerge from the ground the next spring during flowering season, completing the life cycle. Neither our Lord's candle nor the species of yucca moth that pollinates it can reproduce without the other.

In contrast to many of the domesticated garden plants, locally adapted species can keep us well informed of the seasonal rhythms. Native wildflowers amply reward those who keep track of their life cycles: how they emerge from the soil, how they grow, how the flowers unfold, how pollination occurs, how the fruits develop, and finally how the seeds are dispersed. Wildflowers, be they spring beauties of the eastern woodlands or farewell-to-spring of the western grasslands, become part of the cycles of our lives and our anticipation of one season flowing into the next.

There is a growing interest in the cultivation of native plants, as is exemplified by programs aimed at preserving and restoring wildflowers as part of our natural heritage. With the massive disruption of much of the North American continent over the past three centuries, precious little undisturbed vegetation remains, and all regions of the country are currently troubled to some extent by airborne pollutants. In response to this situation, restoration programs were started at several midwestern sites in the 1960s. These programs on both private and public lands are attempting to reestablish native grasses and wildflowers in areas that were highly disturbed or taken over by alien species. Another program, "Operation Wildflower," a nationwide effort sponsored by the National Council of State Garden Clubs, state highway agencies and the federal government, was started in 1973 to establish native plant species along roads and highways. The program's intent is that the rights-of-way in this country will some day be covered with native plants that are well adapted and can maintain themselves at little or no cost.

What to do With Wildflowers?

The cultivation of native wildflowers adapted to your locale can open new horizons in low-maintenance gardening. A sense of satisfaction comes as well, with the encouragement and reestablishment of plants that might once have grown where gardens are now. The simplest approach is to use wildflowers in existing gardens to complement your ornamental plants. Alternatively, you may desire to establish small gardens of wildflowers with different habitat requirements. You don't have to start out on a grand scale reclaiming vast spaces. A small flower bed at the corner of your house, a small patch of land otherwise unused, or even those areas between the roots of the trees in the front yard can be enhanced by plantings of wildflowers. You can't mow there anyway.

GARDEN THEMES

Conventional flower beds might include such species as Mexican hat, coral-bells, lance-leaved coreopsis, cosmos, false dragonhead, butterfly weed, purple coneflower, gayfeather, and blanketflower, all of which make excellent cut flowers because of their long stems and durable blossoms. Numerous native plants are ideal for sunny or shady borders. Snow-on-the-mountain, scarlet sage, Southwestern verbena, Chinese houses, California poppy, tidy tips, baby blue-eyes, blue-eyed grass, owl's clover, and wind poppy, with their interesting foliage and brilliant-hued flowers, all make superb border plants.

One can also design a garden of wildflowers for specialized purposes. If you are interested in attracting butterflies to your garden, plant flowers with contrasting colors and tubular, nectar-producing flowers. Consider butterfly weed, blanketflower, New England aster, black-eyed Susan, purple coneflower, wild bergamot, lupines, purple prairie clover, Southwestern verbena, Douglas's wallflower, or annual phlox. Hummingbirds are attracted to red plants that point out or hang down. To lure hummingbirds into your garden, try planting cardinal flower, standing cypress, Eastern columbine, Indian pink, scarlet sage, and other species with red flowers.

Perfume Garden. Rather than just planning a garden of wildflowers for visual effects, you may want to design beds with native species known for their delightful scents. Groundnut, Douglas's wallflower, wintergreen, blazing star, partridgeberry, shinleaf, false Solomon's seal, and wind poppy all have exceptionally fragrant flowers.

Edible Garden. Although they make an expensive meal, some native species are edible and a garden could be designed for that purpose. The leaves of yellow clintonia, California poppy, spiderwort, trillium, and meadow beauty can be used as greens. The leaves and bulbs of nodding wild onion and wild leek make an excellent seasoning. Underground parts of other wildflowers are starchy and can be prepared like potatoes. The roots of bitterroot, the tubers of groundnut, and the corms of spring beauty, blue dicks, and trout lily can be cooked and eaten. The fruits of mayapple, wintergreen, and pasture rose can be eaten raw or made into preserves, while teas can be made by steeping the leaves of wintergreen or wild bergamot, and candy can be prepared from the roots of wild ginger. Other species, however, such as white baneberry, larger blue flag, and snow-on-the-mountain, are poisonous, and even some portions of "edible" plants, like the leaves of mayapple, are poisonous.

Ground Covers and Hedges. Some of the native species in this book make excellent ground covers. If you want a low ground cover for acidic soils, then partridgeberry, wintergreen, yellow clintonia, and bunchberry should be considered. If a ground cover a foot or so high is desired, try bloodroot, Canada anemone, or mayapple. Groundnut is an excellent choice for covering stumps or other unsightly areas, since its vines grow rapidly. Banks and steep areas prone to erosion might be planted with New England aster, lance-leaved coreopsis, blanketflower, and Rocky Mountain penstemon, for an attractive, low-maintenance alternative to grass.

Native plants can also be effectively used as seasonal hedges and screens. Once established, pasture rose can be formed into an attractive shrubby hedge, while goatsbeard, cardinal flower, and compass plant can be thickly planted to create attractive living screens.

Rock Garden. No rock garden is truly complete without representative native species. Depending upon your geographic location and the moisture available (in the rock garden), Eastern columbine, pasqueflower, blue-eyed grass, Missouri evening primrose, Colorado columbine, coralbells, bluets, old-man-of-the-mountain, bitterroot, shooting stars, bloodroot, Indian pink, Southwestern verbena, sharp-loped hepatica, sky lupine, linanthus, Douglas's iris, or desert marigolds may be appropriate.

Natural Gardens. A highly successful way to use native plants is to concentrate on the local flora of your region by planting wildflowers in an appropriate natural setting. In the East you might want to try planting Jack-in-the-pulpit, wild ginger, spring beauty, trout lily, Dutchman's breeches, Solomon's seal, bloodroot, and trilliums in a deciduous woodland setting. In the Midwest, prairie species such as leadplant, butterfly weed, rattlesnake master, gayfeather, purple prairie clover, and purple coneflower, mixed with appropriate native grasses, create a stunning natural garden. Likewise the addition of goldfields, tidy tips, Western shooting star, blazing star, golden stars, and blue dicks to grasslands on the West Coast mimics the natural landscape. Often it is prudent to remove small areas of competing vegetation from around the native species

A. Blanketflower
B. New England aster
C. Wild bergamot
D. Butterfly weed
E. Black-eyed Susan
F. Annual phlox

Butterfly garden, summer.

you wish to reestablish in these gardens. Once established, most of these species will maintain themselves with little further attention. In humid climates, however, even in prairie regions, it may be necessary periodically to burn grasslands, to prevent the encroachment of shrubs and trees.

Be Adventuresome and Solve Problems. You might also want to experiment with wildflowers by planting them in different ways. Nearly all of the species described in this book can be grown in a considerably wider area than shown by the maps of their native range. Don't be timid about trying to grow a species from the other side of the continent if local conditions are adequate for the plant's needs. Meadows, depending upon your location, might be planted with black-eyed Susan, wood lily, silky aster, lance-leaved coreopsis, blue flax, wild bergamot, purple coneflower, closed gentian, tidy tips, Eastern columbine, or farewell-to-spring. Or you might like to try naturalizing trout lily, yellow fawn lily, or bluets in your lawn, if you don't use herbicides and are in no rush to mow as soon as possible in the spring.

Wildflowers may also present solutions for problem spots in your gardens. Hot courtyards or areas next to south-facing walls, which tend to be parched during the summer, may be ideal locations to raise Southwestern verbena, desert marigold, desert mallow, and other species from the arid Southwest. In areas that are chronically too wet for conventional garden species try planting iris, turtlehead, meadow beauty, elephantheads, or cardinal flower.

Container Gardening. One way of growing wildflowers, even if your local conditions are quite different from those usually required by a particular species, is by gardening in containers. Many of the small or medium-sized plants

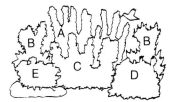

A. Standing cypress
B. Cardinal flower
C. Scarlet sage
D. Eastern columbine
E. Indian pink

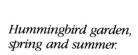

Hummingbird garden,
spring and summer.

described in this book can be grown in pots or other containers. The advantage of container gardening is that as seasons change you can move the plants indoors or out to match the needs of the species. Container gardening may be the easiest way to grow tender species in regions with severe winters and to grow species that require winter chilling in regions that are usually frost-free. Even if you live in a region with cold winters, you might want to try to force wildflowers such as wild ginger, Jack-in-the-pulpit, mayapple, bloodroot, white and purple trilliums, Dutchman's breeches, spring beauty, sharp-lobed hepatica, and even wild bergamot. Simply bury the pot in the fall so the level of the soil inside the container is even with the ground surface, and mark the location. The pots can then be brought indoors in midwinter and kept in a warm, sunny window for late winter flowering. It is a good idea not to try to force the same individual plants in successive years. Allow them to follow the natural seasonal rhythms the following year.

Even species that attain great size in their native habitats can be effectively grown in containers. For example, our Lord's candle, which has leaves approaching three feet in length in its native Southern California, can be grown as an attractive, medium-sized, indoor foliage plant anywhere with a sunny window. Don't be afraid to experiment.

Getting a Start

This book contains descriptions, cultural information, and propagation directions for 101 species native to North America. The species included are drawn from all regions of the country, and while some naturally thrive only where the winters are mild, and others require chilling temperatures to complete their life cycles, most of the plants can be grown easily anywhere if proper cultural attention is given. Even species with restricted natural ranges, such as California poppy, can be grown in gardens coast to coast.

PLANTING STOCK

One of the first questions is where to obtain seeds or plants to start a garden of wildflowers. Where not to obtain plants is easier to answer. *Plants growing in their native habitats should never be dug up for the garden.* Apart from the laws that protect wildflowers in many states, it is unethical to uproot these wildflowers. Although none of the plants in this book are considered rare or endangered, they do tend to become scarce at the edges of their ranges. The propagation instructions given with the 101 species of wildflowers are intended only for gardeners who desire to make divisions of their own plants, not of those plants growing in the wild. The only circumstance in which it is acceptable to dig up wildflowers is when they are imminently threatened by highway construction or development. In those cases, prior approval must be obtained from the proper authorities, and, if possible, plants should be dug while dormant.

Nursery-grown and -packed plant material will yield the best wildflower gardening results. Before ordering plants by mail or from a local retail outlet, you should ask whether the plants have been propagated in a nursery. Do not buy plants that have merely been collected in the wild, since collecting may reduce natural populations of plants deserving protection. You may wish to purchase perennials from a producer who is relatively close by, since there is a greater likelihood that you will receive stock that is adapted to your local conditions.

Live Plants. Since it may take several years for perennial wildflowers to bloom when started from seed, the fastest way to establish them in the garden is to purchase live plants from reputable suppliers. Planning is needed. Perennial wildflowers are best shipped and planted when they are dormant, and therefore most suppliers ship only during the late winter to midspring, and again in the autumn, after plants have become dormant but before the ground freezes. The obvious problems of shipping live material in and out of regions with cold winters are not as difficult in frost-free regions, but you should contact any supplier to determine the seasons of availability and whether there are any other constraints in shipping the specific live wildflowers you wish to plant.

Seeds. Much can be gained by propagating wildflowers by seed, since seeds are available year round, are not as fragile as living plants, and are much less expensive. Raising plants from seed also gives the gardener an opportunity to become familiar with the complete life cycle of plants. Since many of the wildflowers in this book will self-seed once established, it is useful to know from experience what the seedlings of the species look like. Often the leaves of seedlings look different from those of mature plants, and without this knowledge they might be accidently removed as weeds.

You can collect the seeds of most perennials growing in the wild without fear of significantly affecting their populations, if only a small proportion of the seeds are collected. Since annuals reproduce only by seed, you should collect their seeds only in locations where they are abundant. Prior to collecting any seeds, permission of the property owner is essential.

Wildflower seeds are usually available throughout the year from mail-order suppliers. Some species of wildflowers have enhanced germination when their seeds are chilled, or "stratified," for a period of time. If you are interested in growing those species, some suppliers sell seeds that have been pretreated by chilling. Check with the supplier to determine whether its seeds would benefit from additional cold treatment.

SUPPLIERS

There are a growing number of reputable commercial producers and distributors of wildflower plants and seeds. Some commercial sources are listed in Appendix A (although their inclusion here is in no way an endorsement by the author or publisher) and most have catalogs or lists giving prices of seeds, live plants, and other items useful in wildflower gardening. Many of these catalogs are extremely useful sources of information about growing native plants. As is noted in Appendix A, some of the suppliers make a small charge for their catalogs and some refund the charge with the first order. It is a good idea to order catalogs well in advance of your anticipated planting time.

If you are planning to plant large areas with either seed or live wildflowers, some suppliers listed in Appendix A sell large quantities at wholesale prices. While many suppliers give wholesale discounts to the public, some sell at wholesale rates only to registered retailers, so check with the supplier first.

BEWARE OF SEED MIXES

Wildflower gardeners should be cautious about using commercial wildflower seed mixtures, which recently have been gaining popularity. Some suppliers painstakingly formulate mixes that are representative of native wildflowers of specific regions or habitats. More frequently, however, mixes are formulated for broad geographic regions and may contain species not particularly adapted to your local conditions. Furthermore, it is often difficult to know just what species are contained in some of the mixtures and in what proportions. Some producers will vary the composition of the mixture depending upon the temporary

A. Groundnut
B. Blazing star
C. Douglas's wallflower
D. False Solomon's seal
E. Wind poppy

Perfume garden, late spring and summer.

availability of seeds, so there is no guarantee that the product will be uniform from year to year.

A further difficulty with some of the mixes is the inclusion of weedy, non-native wildflower species which, while attractive, may become aggressive. The following are non-native species that have been found in various "wildflower" mixes:

SPECIES	PLACE OF ORIGIN	SPECIES	PLACE OF ORIGIN
Ox-eye daisy	Europe	Dame's rocket	France
Corn poppy	Europe	African daisy	South Africa
Sweet alyssum	Europe-W. Asia	Foxglove	Europe
White yarrow	Europe	Candytuft	SE Europe-W. Asia
Baby's breath	S. Europe	4 O'Clock	Peru
Purple loosestrife	N. Europe	Queen Anne's Lace	Europe
St. Johnswort	Europe-Africa		

MORE INFORMATION

This book may be just a beginning for you. Further information is available from many sources.

Botanical gardens, nature centers, and arboreta are excellent sources of information about gardening with native plants. A state-by-state listing of such institutions is given in Appendix B. This listing includes the admission fee, if any, the season of operation, and the phone numbers. The resources of these gardens and centers usually extend beyond their collections of living native plants. Many offer workshops, symposia, or lecture series on wildflower gardening. Some publish magazines, newsletters, and brochures that include information on native plants, and they often have shops that sell books on wildflowers and also wildflower seeds and live plants.

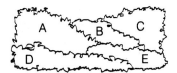

A. Yellow clintonia
B. Wild ginger
C. Bunchberry
D. Wintergreen
E. Partridgeberry

Ground covers, late spring.

Many botanical gardens offer memberships that entitle members to use library facilities, attend special events at reduced prices, go on field trips, consult with the horticultural staff, call a "gardening hotline," and other benefits. If you become interested in the institution's activities, you may find a program in which you could become a volunteer.

There are numerous other places, not listed in Appendix B, to observe wildflowers. Many local, regional, state, and national parks have preserved areas of native vegetation. The National Forests and National Wildlife Refuges are also ideal places to see native wildflowers, as are lands owned by various chapters of the Audubon Society and the Nature Conservancy.

Native plant societies and some horticultural organizations are excellent sources of information about native plants. Appendix C lists botanical organizations that are concerned with wildflowers. The activities of these societies are quite varied, ranging from projects to conserve rare and endangered plants to field trips and lecture series. Many of the native plant societies periodically publish newsletters or bulletins and have smaller local chapters that hold regular meetings. Some of the societies are affiliated with specific botanical gardens or arboreta, while others have a more regional or national focus.

An annotated bibliography of books and published resources on wildflower gardening is contained in Appendix D.

Plant Descriptions

The technical terminology used in the descriptions of the flowers, leaves, shoots, and roots for the 101 species of plants in this book has been kept to a minimum. However, the knowledge of some botanical terms is helpful and relatively painless to acquire.

The illustrations below show two typical flowers with all the parts that are usually present. *Complete flowers* consist of all the parts illustrated, but some of the wildflowers in the book may be missing one or more, or the parts may be fused together in different arrangements. The trillium (below left) is a *simple flower.* Tidy tips (below right) has a *composite flower head* typical of members of the aster family.

FLOWERS

In simple flowers, a flower stalk or *peduncle* terminates in a fleshy pad (the *receptacle*) to which other flower parts are attached. The outermost parts of the flower are the *sepals,* which are usually small green leaflike structures that cover and protect the flower while it is in the bud. Collectively, all of the sepals are called the *calyx,* which is Latin for "cup." In some species the sepals are fused together forming a tubular calyx, and in other species they resemble petals. Immediately inside the sepals are the *petals,* which may take on a variety of forms, some species having petals fused together into a tube, and others having petals that are free and unattached. On some flowers, all the petals are

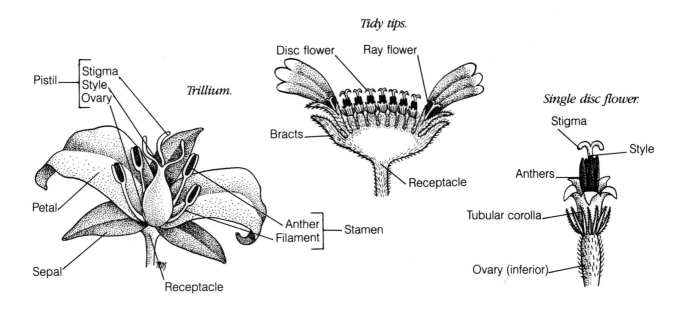

Tidy tips.

Trillium.

Single disc flower.

symmetrical, but on others, the petals take irregular forms. Collectively the petals are called the *corolla,* which means "small crown" in Latin.

In the center of the flower are the sexual parts, the male *stamens* and the female *pistil.* There may be one or several pistils depending upon the species, but most flowering plants have more than one stamen. The stamen consists of a slender stalk, the *filament,* to which the pollen-bearing sacks, the *anthers,* are attached. The pistil has three major components, whose shapes may vary widely among species. The upper surface of the pistil, which receives pollen grains, is the *stigma.* The stigma is attached to the *ovary* at the base of the pistil by a usually slender tissue known as the *style.* Inside the ovary is a chamber containing the *ovules,* the female sex cells which, following fertilization, mature into seeds. After pollen grains are deposited on the stigma, they germinate, sending microscopic tubes down through the style, through portions of the ovary, and finally into the ovules. As the ovules develop into seeds, the ovary matures into the fruit of the plant.

Species of plants in the aster family, such as tidy tips, have a more complex structure to their flowers. These species usually have two types of small flowers clustered together in a composite *flower head.* The small flowers or *florets* share a common, broad receptacle, which is usually enclosed from below by many leafy *bracts.* The *ray flowers* usually form a ring around the outside of the head. Each ray flower has a relatively long, straplike petal, which upon close inspection can be seen to be several small petals fused together. In the center of the flower head are the even smaller *disc flowers,* with minute, tubular corollas. The stamens and the pistils in these flowers are surrounded by the petals, but they are usually so small that magnification is required to see them clearly. Many species in the aster family have sterile ray flowers that lack stamens and pistils entirely.

COLOR AND HEIGHT

The color of the flower and the height of the plant are two important concerns when the gardener is deciding how to lay out a garden. To aid in planning, the 101 species of plants described in this book are listed on pages 18–19 by flower color and pages 20–21 by height. You should keep in mind that some species, such as butterfly weed and Colorado columbine, vary in color depending upon their geographic origins. Also, the height of a plant depends to some extent on the conditions in which it is grown, so use the information in these charts as a rough guide. Further information concerning flower color and plant height is given in the descriptions of individual species.

ROOT SYSTEMS

The nature of the underground parts of the 101 wildflowers described in this book varies greatly and may influence the types of habitats in which they can be grown. The root system also affects the ease with which a plant can be propagated. Six of the eight most common "root types" illustrated on page 17 are actually the underground stems, or "rootstocks," of perennials. The remaining two are true roots and lack leaf buds.

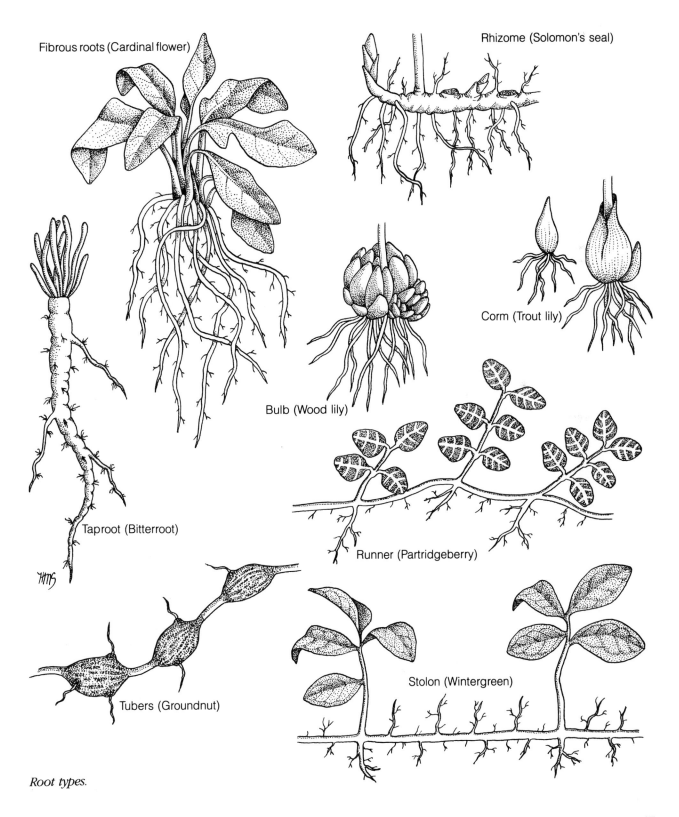

Fibrous roots (Cardinal flower)

Rhizome (Solomon's seal)

Corm (Trout lily)

Bulb (Wood lily)

Taproot (Bitterroot)

Runner (Partridgeberry)

Tubers (Groundnut)

Stolon (Wintergreen)

Root types.

FLOWER COLOR

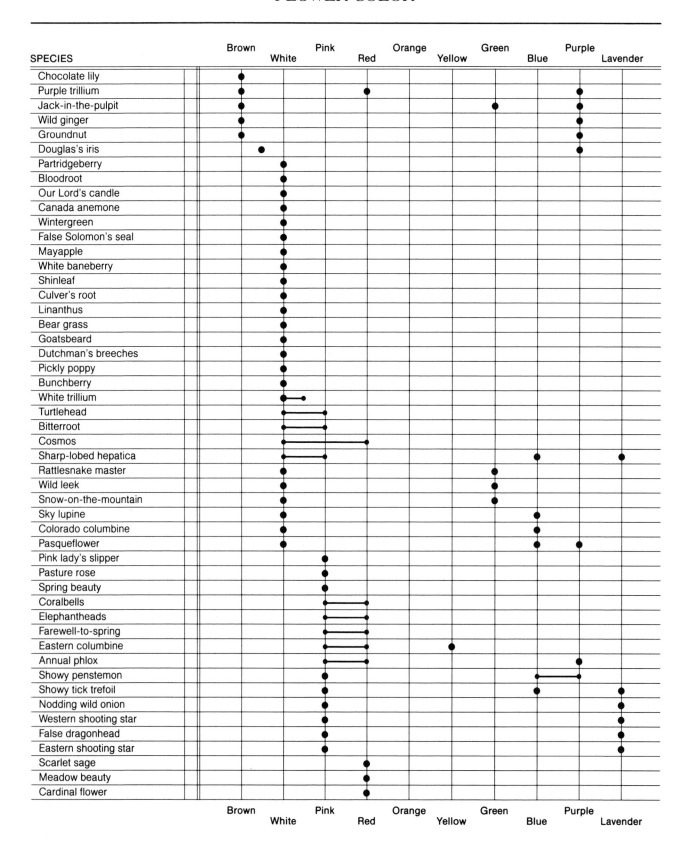

SPECIES	Brown	White	Pink	Red	Orange	Yellow	Green	Blue	Purple	Lavender
Chocolate lily	●									
Purple trillium	●			●					●	
Jack-in-the-pulpit	●						●		●	
Wild ginger	●								●	
Groundnut	●								●	
Douglas's iris		●							●	
Partridgeberry		●								
Bloodroot		●								
Our Lord's candle		●								
Canada anemone		●								
Wintergreen		●								
False Solomon's seal		●								
Mayapple		●								
White baneberry		●								
Shinleaf		●								
Culver's root		●								
Linanthus		●								
Bear grass		●								
Goatsbeard		●								
Dutchman's breeches		●								
Pickly poppy		●								
Bunchberry		●								
White trillium		●—●								
Turtlehead		●——●								
Bitterroot		●——●								
Cosmos		●————————●								
Sharp-lobed hepatica		●——●						●		●
Rattlesnake master		●					●			
Wild leek		●					●			
Snow-on-the-mountain		●					●			
Sky lupine		●						●		
Colorado columbine		●						●		
Pasqueflower		●						●	●	
Pink lady's slipper			●							
Pasture rose			●							
Spring beauty			●							
Coralbells			●——●							
Elephantheads			●——●							
Farewell-to-spring			●——●							
Eastern columbine			●——●		●					
Annual phlox			●——●						●	
Showy penstemon			●					●——●		
Showy tick trefoil			●					●		●
Nodding wild onion			●							●
Western shooting star			●							●
False dragonhead			●							●
Eastern shooting star			●							●
Scarlet sage				●						
Meadow beauty				●						
Cardinal flower				●						

FLOWER COLOR
(continued)

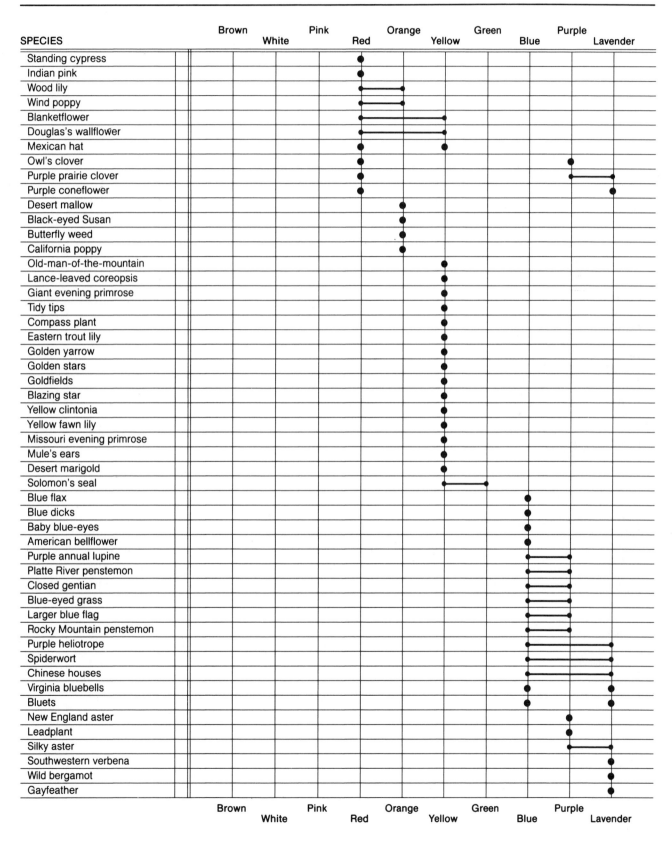

SPECIES	Brown	White	Pink	Red	Orange	Yellow	Green	Blue	Purple	Lavender
Standing cypress				●						
Indian pink				●						
Wood lily				●—————●					
Wind poppy				●—————●					
Blanketflower				●———————————●				
Douglas's wallflower				●———————————●				
Mexican hat				●		●				
Owl's clover				●					●	
Purple prairie clover				●					●—————●
Purple coneflower				●						●
Desert mallow					●					
Black-eyed Susan					●					
Butterfly weed					●					
California poppy					●					
Old-man-of-the-mountain						●				
Lance-leaved coreopsis						●				
Giant evening primrose						●				
Tidy tips						●				
Compass plant						●				
Eastern trout lily						●				
Golden yarrow						●				
Golden stars						●				
Goldfields						●				
Blazing star						●				
Yellow clintonia						●				
Yellow fawn lily						●				
Missouri evening primrose						●				
Mule's ears						●				
Desert marigold						●				
Solomon's seal						●————●			
Blue flax								●		
Blue dicks								●		
Baby blue-eyes								●		
American bellflower								●		
Purple annual lupine								●——————●	
Platte River penstemon								●——————●	
Closed gentian								●——————●	
Blue-eyed grass								●——————●	
Larger blue flag								●——————●	
Rocky Mountain penstemon								●——————●	
Purple heliotrope								●———————————●
Spiderwort								●———————————●
Chinese houses								●———————————●
Virginia bluebells								●		●
Bluets								●		●
New England aster									●	
Leadplant									●	
Silky aster									●—————●
Southwestern verbena										●
Wild bergamot										●
Gayfeather										●

PLANT HEIGHT

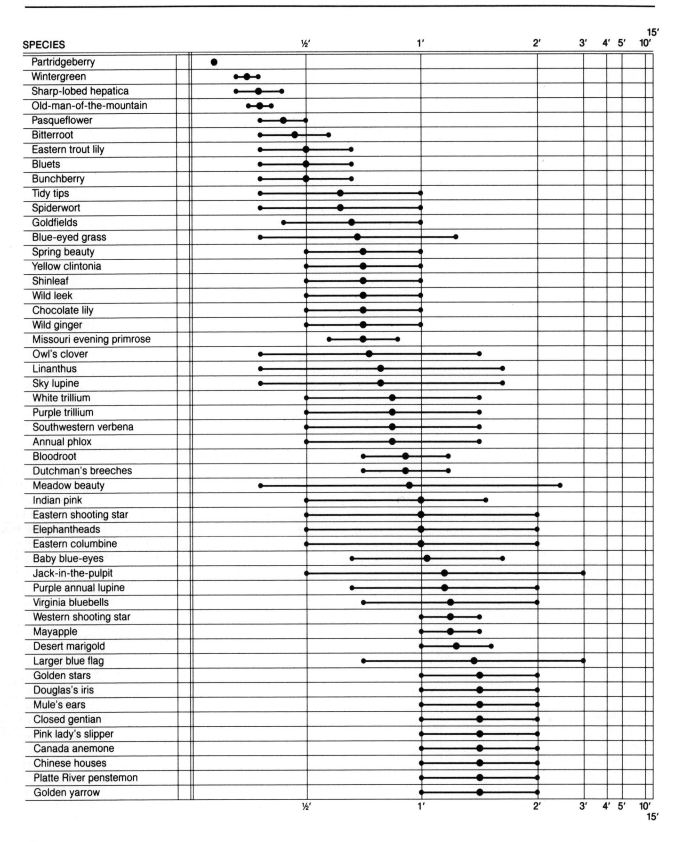

| SPECIES | ½' | 1' | 2' | 3' | 4' 5' | 10' 15' |

Partridgeberry
Wintergreen
Sharp-lobed hepatica
Old-man-of-the-mountain
Pasqueflower
Bitterroot
Eastern trout lily
Bluets
Bunchberry
Tidy tips
Spiderwort
Goldfields
Blue-eyed grass
Spring beauty
Yellow clintonia
Shinleaf
Wild leek
Chocolate lily
Wild ginger
Missouri evening primrose
Owl's clover
Linanthus
Sky lupine
White trillium
Purple trillium
Southwestern verbena
Annual phlox
Bloodroot
Dutchman's breeches
Meadow beauty
Indian pink
Eastern shooting star
Elephantheads
Eastern columbine
Baby blue-eyes
Jack-in-the-pulpit
Purple annual lupine
Virginia bluebells
Western shooting star
Mayapple
Desert marigold
Larger blue flag
Golden stars
Douglas's iris
Mule's ears
Closed gentian
Pink lady's slipper
Canada anemone
Chinese houses
Platte River penstemon
Golden yarrow

PLANT HEIGHT
(continued)

SPECIES	½'	1'	2'	3'	4'	5'	10'	15'
Lance-leaved coreopsis		●——●——●						
Silky aster		●——●——●						
Nodding wild onion		●——●——●						
Wind poppy		●——●——●						
Scarlet sage		●——●——●						
Coralbells		●——●——●						
White baneberry		●——●——●						
Yellow fawn lily		●——●——●						
California poppy		●——●——●						
Groundnut		●——●——●						
Colorado columbine		●——●——●						
Rocky Mountain penstemon		●———●———●						
Blue flax		●————●————●						
Butterfly weed		●————●————●						
Turtlehead		●————●————●						
Pasture rose		●————●————●						
Solomon's seal		●————●————●						
Wood lily		●————●————●						
Douglas's wallflower		●————●————●						
Snow-on-the-mountain		●————●————●						
Farewell-to-spring		●————●————●						
False Solomon's seal		●————●————●						
Purple prairie clover		●——●——●						
Black-eyed Susan		●——●——●						
Purple heliotrope		●——●——●						
Prickly poppy		●——●——●						
Blazing star		●———●———————●						
Cardinal flower		●———●————————●						
Gayfeather		●———●————————●						
Rattlesnake master		●———●——————————●						
Desert mallow		●——●——●						
Mexican hat		●——●——●						
Leadplant			●—●—●					
Blue dicks			●—●—●					
Wild bergamot			●—●——●——●					
False dragonhead			●—●——●——●					
Blanketflower			●—●——●——●					
Showy penstemon			●—●——●———●					
New England aster			●—●——●———●					
Purple coneflower			●—●——●———●					
Standing cypress			●—●——●———●					
Bear grass			●—●——●———●					
American bellflower			●——●————●————●				
Culver's root			●——●————●————●				
Showy tick trefoil			●——●————●————●				
Giant evening primrose					●—●—●			
Cosmos					●—●—●			
Compass plant					●—●—●			
Goatsbeard					●—●—●			
Our Lord's candle					●————————————●			

True Roots. True roots (illustrated on page 17) may be either diffuse and fibrous, as is the case with many garden plants like the cardinal flower, or they may be a strongly vertical, carrotlike taproot as is seen in the bitterroot. Some species of wildflowers have root systems that are intermediate between the two basic types.

Runners and Stolons. Underground stems take on a variety of forms. The simplest rootstock has thin horizontal branches that give rise to new plants. These branches are usually called "runners" if they are above ground, as with strawberries, and "stolons" if they are below ground, as with mint. Partridge-berry and wintergreen are good examples of wildflowers with runners and stolons respectively.

Tubers. If the tip of a stolon produces a swollen, fleshy storage organ, it is called a "tuber." The leaf buds of tubers are frequently called "eyes." The potato is probably the most familiar example of a tuber, but wildflowers such as groundnut also have this type of rootstock.

Rhizomes. Thick, fleshy, horizontal, underground stems with buds on their top surfaces and roots on their bottom surfaces are called "rhizomes." Rhizomes, like those of iris and Solomon's seal, accumulate rich stores of starch, which are used by the shoots and flowers as the perennials emerge from dormancy.

Corms and Bulbs. Rootstocks may also be round and bulbous. If such a rootstock is formed from the swollen, solid base of the stem, as it is for gladiolus, it is called a "corm." Corms may look similar to true "bulbs," which are formed by fleshy leaves that surround a bud atop a short stem, as in onions and tulips. Jack-in-the-pulpit and trout lily have corms, while wood lily and chocolate lily have true bulbs. The corms and bulbs of mature plants of some species form small offsets called "cormlets" or "bulblets" depending upon the plant's structure.

Flowering Season

A great number of factors, some genetic and some environmental, affect the onset and length of the flowering season of wildflowers. There may be complex interactions between climatic factors, such as amount of sunlight, length of day, moisture, and temperature of air and soil, that determine exactly when plants start flowering.

Annual species usually have longer flowering seasons than perennials and will of course flower in a single growing season. There are, however, few annuals that will flower in the springtime in regions with cold winters, and even though perennials may require several or many years to reach maturity and flower, once established they generally require little maintenance, reliably reappearing year after year.

CLIMATE

The overall climatic patterns of temperature and precipitation have a considerable effect on the flowering of wildflowers. In general, spring progresses from south to north at about 20 miles per day and from the center of the continent toward the ocean-moderated coasts at about 65 miles per day. In eastern North America, where there are cold winters, warm summers, and even distribution of precipitation throughout the year, the succession of wildflowers starts in woodlands in the early spring and progresses into fields during the summer and fall. As one progresses toward the Midwest and Great Plains, the total amount of precipitation decreases and the summers become increasingly dry and hot. On the prairies, spring and midsummer are the time of greatest flowering. On the Pacific Coast, the overall pattern is of wet and mild winters, followed by summers that are either hot and dry in the Southwest or more moderate in the Northwest. The flowering season in much of California starts in late winter and is over by early summer, when much of the landscape turns brown. So as spring is just arriving in Maine, many species are in full bloom in Iowa, and the show is nearly over in California. As a result, some species are best planted in the fall in the West but in the spring in the East.

The emergence of perennials from a winter dormancy is often induced by warm temperatures in the spring. For many species the date of emergence or flowering is closely related to "growing degree days." Growing degree days, like "heating degree days" used to calculate the heating needs of buildings, are a measure of the total accumulation of temperatures above a critical air temperature. Growing degree days are calculated by adding the daily average temperatures above either 40°F for cool-season plants or 50°F for warm-season plants. These base temperatures are used because they appear to be the temperatures critical to induce plant growth or flowering in the spring.

A. Coralbells
B. Eastern shooting star
C. Pasqueflower
D. Bitterroot
E. Old-man-of-the-mountain
F. Missouri evening primrose

Rock garden, spring and early summer.

Perennial species vary widely in the number of degree days required for their emergence and flowering, and there may be as much as a month's difference in the date of flowering of a given species because of year-to-year variation in degree days. Years with an above-average number of cloudy days or heavier-than-normal precipitation will tend to have slower accumulation of growing degree days than usual.

The relative order of flowering of wildflower species, however, tends to be consistent from year to year. The general seasonal progression of flowering of the perennial wildflowers in this book is shown on pages 26–27. The seasons of flowering are given, rather than calendar months, because the number of growing degree days will vary from one locale to the next and from year to year. The seasons refer to the flowering of a given species in its native range, and the gardener may find that the flowering sequence may be slightly different when a plant is grown in other parts of the country. For example, California poppy blooms from late winter to early summer when grown as a perennial along the Pacific coast, but when grown as an annual elsewhere it may flower later and longer.

LOCAL CONDITIONS

The exact time of flowering in your garden may also be influenced by a number of local factors such as slope, elevation, soil type, and mulch. If your garden slopes to the south, it will be warmer and spring will arrive sooner than if it slopes to the north. The warmest slopes are those on which the sun's rays strike perpendicularly, but even a 5-degree, south-facing slope may have a microclimate equivalent to that of a flat surface 300 miles south. A similar slope facing north would be equivalently cooler. Therefore, flowering dates may vary by as much as several weeks depending upon the local topography.

The elevation of a garden will also influence how rapidly growing degree days accumulate. At a given latitude, air temperatures generally decrease 3°F per 1,000 feet of rise. For each 100-foot increase in elevation, the air temperature is only three-tenths of a degree cooler, but flowering is delayed by about one day.

Soil conditions may advance or retard the progression of flowering. Sandy soils generally warm up more rapidly in the spring than do peaty or clayey soils. Dark-colored soils will warm more rapidly than light soils. Heavy mulches, while keeping soils warmer in the winter, provide an insulating layer that may both slow the warming in the spring and maintain cooler soils in the summer.

GENETIC FACTORS

Some, but not all, plants are genetically programmed to flower in response to specific day lengths or hours of darkness. The stimulation of flowering by various critical day lengths is found in a wide variety of wildflowers, ranging from annuals to biennials and perennials. Some plants, such as blanketflower, blue flax, black-eyed Susan, and annual phlox, flower only when the days are long and the nights are short. They are known as "long-day" plants, although they are actually responding to the short nights associated with late spring and early summer. The northern regions of North America, with relatively shorter spring and summer nights, tend to have a greater proportion of so-called long-day plants than do southern regions. The southern limits of some long-day species are determined by the day length (short nights) needed for their flowering.

Other species, such as cosmos and many of the asters, are "short-day" plants and flower when the days are short and the nights are long. These species are stimulated to flower by the long nights of early spring, late summer, and fall.

Regional differences in climatic patterns and day lengths have led to the evolution of genetically distinct varieties in some wildflower species. These varieties, known as "ecotypes," are well adapted to local conditions. When individuals of different ecotypes are planted together in the same garden, they will frequently flower at different times. For instance, bloodroots from Vermont flower about one week earlier than bloodroots from West Virginia when they are grown together, while hepaticas from southern regions tend to flower sooner than those from northern regions.

EXTENDING THE FLOWERING SEASON

There are several ways in which the flowering season can be prolonged. With some species, like butterfly weed, trim some of the plants just before they set flower buds. That will delay their flowering for several weeks, and the clipped plants will come into bloom as the flowers on the untrimmed plants are fading. Many species will have extended flowering if the withering blooms are removed (deadheaded) before the fruits and seeds start to mature. The only drawback of this technique is that you sacrifice production of seed that could be used for further propagation.

Many of the southwestern species, those like purple heliotrope and desert marigold that are native to the desert or the Southern California coast, flower

FLOWERING PROGRESSION

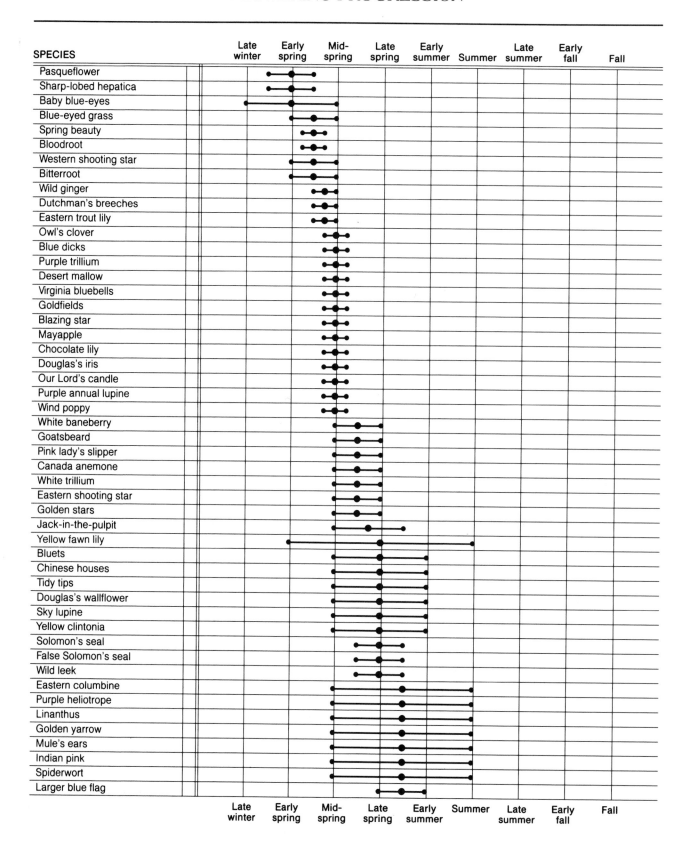

SPECIES	Late winter	Early spring	Mid-spring	Late spring	Early summer	Summer	Late summer	Early fall	Fall
Pasqueflower		•—•—•							
Sharp-lobed hepatica		•—•—•							
Baby blue-eyes	•———•———•								
Blue-eyed grass		•——•							
Spring beauty		•—•							
Bloodroot		•—•							
Western shooting star		•———•							
Bitterroot		•———•							
Wild ginger		•—•							
Dutchman's breeches		•—•							
Eastern trout lily		•—•							
Owl's clover		•—•							
Blue dicks		•—•							
Purple trillium		•—•							
Desert mallow		•—•							
Virginia bluebells		•—•							
Goldfields		•—•							
Blazing star		•—•							
Mayapple		•—•							
Chocolate lily		•—•							
Douglas's iris		•—•							
Our Lord's candle		•—•							
Purple annual lupine		•—•							
Wind poppy		•—•							
White baneberry			•—•—•						
Goatsbeard			•—•—•						
Pink lady's slipper			•—•—•						
Canada anemone			•—•—•						
White trillium			•—•—•						
Eastern shooting star			•—•—•						
Golden stars			•—•—•						
Jack-in-the-pulpit			•——•——•						
Yellow fawn lily	•———————•———————•								
Bluets			•——•——•						
Chinese houses			•——•——•						
Tidy tips			•——•——•						
Douglas's wallflower			•——•——•						
Sky lupine			•——•——•						
Yellow clintonia			•——•——•						
Solomon's seal			•—•—•						
False Solomon's seal			•—•—•						
Wild leek			•—•—•						
Eastern columbine			•————•————•						
Purple heliotrope			•————•————•						
Linanthus			•————•————•						
Golden yarrow			•————•————•						
Mule's ears			•————•————•						
Indian pink			•————•————•						
Spiderwort			•————•————•						
Larger blue flag				•—•—•					

	Late winter	Early spring	Mid-spring	Late spring	Early summer	Summer	Late summer	Early fall	Fall

FLOWERING PROGRESSION
(continued)

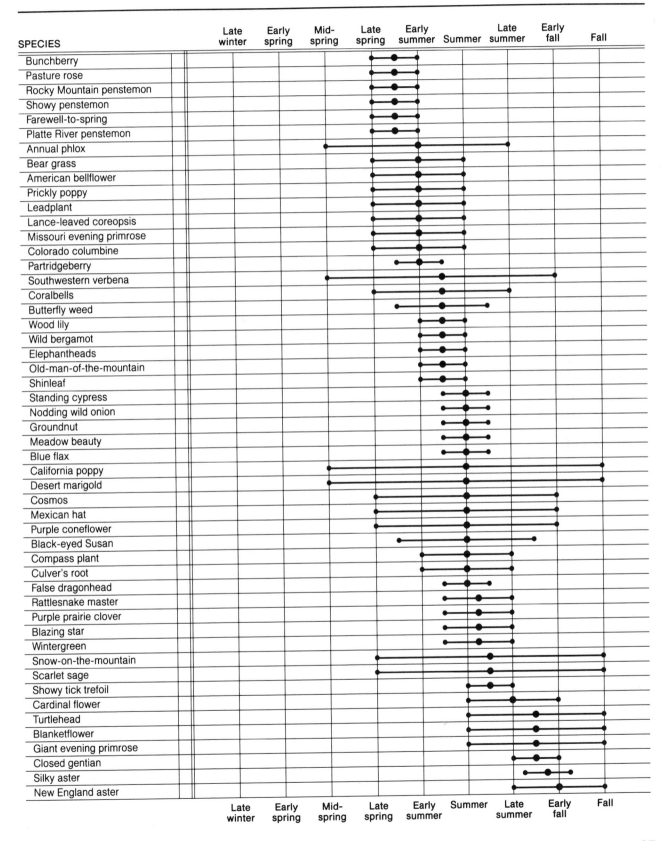

SPECIES	Late winter	Early spring	Mid-spring	Late spring	Early summer	Summer	Late summer	Early fall	Fall
Bunchberry									
Pasture rose									
Rocky Mountain penstemon									
Showy penstemon									
Farewell-to-spring									
Platte River penstemon									
Annual phlox									
Bear grass									
American bellflower									
Prickly poppy									
Leadplant									
Lance-leaved coreopsis									
Missouri evening primrose									
Colorado columbine									
Partridgeberry									
Southwestern verbena									
Coralbells									
Butterfly weed									
Wood lily									
Wild bergamot									
Elephantheads									
Old-man-of-the-mountain									
Shinleaf									
Standing cypress									
Nodding wild onion									
Groundnut									
Meadow beauty									
Blue flax									
California poppy									
Desert marigold									
Cosmos									
Mexican hat									
Purple coneflower									
Black-eyed Susan									
Compass plant									
Culver's root									
False dragonhead									
Rattlesnake master									
Purple prairie clover									
Blazing star									
Wintergreen									
Snow-on-the-mountain									
Scarlet sage									
Showy tick trefoil									
Cardinal flower									
Turtlehead									
Blanketflower									
Giant evening primrose									
Closed gentian									
Silky aster									
New England aster									

Late winter / Early spring / Mid-spring / Late spring / Early summer / Summer / Late summer / Early fall / Fall

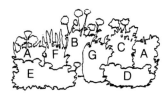

A. California poppy
B. Blue dicks
C. Blazing star
D. Goldfields
E. Tidy tips
F. *Stipa pulchra*
G. *Poa scabrella*

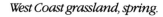

West Coast grassland, spring.

in response to rainfall. Simply by providing adequate moisture, the flowering season of these species can be prolonged.

If you have a number of different garden sites with varying slopes and exposures, the differences in microclimates may be sufficient to accelerate flowering in some plants and delay it in others. Another means of extending the flowering season of a given species is to purchase seeds or plants from several different geographic regions so that different ecotypes are represented in the garden. The differences in the flowering times may be sufficient to prolong the season of even those species with short-lived flowers.

Wildflower Culture

LIGHT CONDITIONS

While the vast majority of domesticated horticultural species planted in the garden require full sunlight for their optimum growth, different native plants have evolved to survive in a wide variety of light conditions, from full sun to deep shade. Therein lies an opportunity in gardening with wildflowers. The light preferences of the 101 species of native plants included in this book are given on pages 30–31.

While some species are successfully grown only in a rather restricted range of light conditions, others can be cultivated in habitats that are either sunny or shady. Often the form of the plant is different when grown in the sun or shade. Typically the leaves of a plant will be thinner and larger when grown in the shade than when grown in the open. Some species, such as white baneberry and shinleaf, are adapted to deep shade and suffer leaf scorching if grown in full sun. Other species, purple heliotrope or lance-leaved coreopsis, for example, need full sunlight or they become scraggly and "leggy." Still other species, like bunchberry, prefer partial shade and produce smaller plants when grown in full sun. Sun-loving species, such as New England aster, produce the largest plants in full sun.

The light conditions in deciduous forests change dramatically through the year, and various species of wildflowers have evolved flowering and growth patterns in response to these changes. In the early spring there are some perennial wildflowers, such as spring beauty, trout lily, and Dutchman's breeches, that emerge from the soil, grow rapidly, flower, and produce seed in that brief period of warm, sunny weather before the trees overhead have leafed out. As the dense forest shade develops, these plants go into dormancy until the following spring. Although they are woodland plants, they need full sunlight for their optimum growth and should be cultivated in sites that are sunny during the spring. Other woodland species, such as shinleaf, are tolerant of deep shade and can even be grown in permanently shaded gardens on the north sides of buildings.

TEMPERATURE

While most of the annual plants included in this book can be grown in any garden, perennial wildflowers usually have northern or southern limits that are determined by winter temperatures. Most gardeners are familiar with hardiness zones, which indicate the relative mildness or severity of winter temperatures. (See page 33, U.S.D.A. Hardiness Zone Map.) The higher the hardiness zone number, the milder the winter climate.

Most perennials have a limited range of hardiness zones in which they can survive. Some wildflowers native to warm climates, such as blue dicks and our Lord's candle, cannot tolerate prolonged periods of subfreezing temperatures

LIGHT CONDITIONS

SPECIES	Open, full sun	Filtered sun, partial shade	Light shade	Heavy shade
Blazing star	●—●			
Nodding wild onion	●—●			
Southwestern verbena	●—●			
Leadplant	●—●			
Giant evening primrose	●—●			
Missouri evening primrose	●—●			
Owl's clover	●—●			
Elephantheads	●—●			
Platte River penstemon	●—●			
Prickly poppy	●—●			
Rocky Mountain penstemon	●—●			
Purple prairie clover	●—●			
Purple heliotrope	●—●			
Butterfly weed	●—●			
Annual phlox	●—●			
Purple annual lupine	●—●			
Bitterroot	●—●			
Desert marigold	●—●			
Golden stars	●—●			
Blue dicks	●—●			
Golden yarrow	●—●			
Rattlesnake master	●—●			
Scarlet sage	●—●			
Desert mallow	●—●			
Our Lord's candle	●—●			
Compass plant	●—●			
Lance-leaved coreopsis	●—●			
Blue flax	●—●			
Cosmos	●—●			
Sky lupine	●—●			
Douglas's wallflower	●—●			
Mule's ears	●—●			
Tidy tips	●—●			
California poppy	●—●			
Old-man-of-the-mountain	●—●			
Mexican hat	●—●			
Blanketflower	●—●			
Blue-eyed grass	●—●			
Snow-on-the-mountain	●—●			
Linanthus	●—●			
Showy penstemon	●—●			
Pasqueflower	●——●——●			
Purple coneflower	●——●——●			
Closed gentian	●————●———●		
Coralbells	●————●————●		
Indian pink	●————●————●		
Wild bergamot	●————●————●		
Bluets	●————●————●		
Yellow fawn lily	●————●————●		
Black-eyed Susan	●————●————●		

LIGHT CONDITIONS
(continued)

SPECIES	Open, full sun	Filtered sun, partial shade	Light shade	Heavy shade
Cardinal flower	●————	●		
Showy tick trefoil	●————	●		
New England aster	●————	●		
Spring beauty	●————	●		
Gayfeather	●————	●		
Farewell-to-spring	●————	●		
Meadow beauty	●————	●		
Baby blue-eyes	●————	●		
Standing cypress	●————	●		
Silky aster	●————	●		
Larger blue flag	●————	●		
Groundnut	●————	●		
Bear grass	●————	●		
Canada anemone	●————	●		
Goldfields	●—●			
Pasture rose	●————	●————		
Virginia bluebells	●————————	●	●	
Bunchberry	●————————	●	●	
Eastern columbine	●————————	●	●	
Douglas's iris	●————————	●	●	
Eastern shooting star	●————————	●	●	
False dragonhead	●————————	●	●	
Colorado columbine	●————————	●	●	
Turtlehead	●————————	●	●	
American bellflower	●————————	●		
Culver's root	●————————	●		
Chocolate lily		●————●		
Wood lily		●————●		
Wild leek		●————●		
Wintergreen		●————●————	●	
Spiderwort	●————————	●	————	●
Yellow clintonia	●————————	●	————	●
Bloodroot	●————————	●	————	●
Eastern trout lily	●————————	●	————	●
Mayapple	●————————	●	————	●
Solomon's seal	●————————	●	————	●
Goatsbeard	●————————	●	————	●
Wind poppy	●————————	●	————	●
Pink lady's slipper	●————————	●	●	
Chinese houses		●————●	●	
Sharp-lobed hepatica		●————●	————	●
False Solomon's seal	●————————	●	————	●
Western shooting star	●————————	●	————	●
Jack-in-the-pulpit		●————	●	———●
Partridgeberry		●————	●	———●
Wild ginger		●————	●	———●
Dutchman's breeches		●————	●	
Purple trillium			●————●	———●
White trillium			●————●	———●
White baneberry			●————	●———●
Shinleaf				●——●

	Open, full sun	Filtered sun, partial shade	Light shade	Heavy shade

and therefore are limited to year-round gardens in warm hardiness zones. Other species, such as elephantheads and pasqueflower, can survive even arctic winters. The approximate range of hardiness zones for the species of wildflowers in the book are given on pages 34–35 and are shown on the individual range maps. The hardiness ranges indicated are approximate. Perennials can usually be cultivated in colder hardiness zones if insulation is provided by a heavy over-winter mulch to prevent frost penetration into the soil. Be careful to remove the mulch in the spring and to choose a mulching material that will not alter the desired acidity/alkalinity conditions for pH-sensitive species, as is explained in the section to follow concerning soils.

Cold wintertime temperatures influence not only the northern range of perennials, but the southern limits as well. Many species that have evolved to survive in colder areas enter a period of dormancy in the late summer or fall, while temperatures are relatively mild, and then actually require cold winter temperatures for continuation of their life cycles the following spring. It has long been known that some horticultural fruit crops can be grown only in regions with sufficiently cold winters. For example, peaches require 400 to 800 hours or more of exposure to temperatures below 45°F to break their dormancy, and apple trees require about twice that length of chilling time. Likewise, many northern native wildflowers, such as wild leek, spring beauty, and trout lily, enter a dormancy in the fall that is broken by exposure to cold temperatures over the winter months. Without this chilling, they would simply remain dormant or would grow more slowly and not have proper floral development the following spring.

Many plants require winter chilling of their seeds as well. As is discussed in the following section on propagation, the breaking of dormancy and proper germination of some seeds require or are enhanced by exposure to weeks or months of temperatures of 40°F or below.

Some wildflowers are sensitive to summertime temperatures as well. For example, yellow clintonia and bunchberry require relatively cool temperatures during the summer growing season and cannot be successfully grown in regions with hot summer temperatures. Even goldfields, a plant of the Southwest, requires relatively cool nighttime temperatures to continue flowering.

MOISTURE CONDITIONS

Just as wildflowers have adapted to different temperature and light conditions, they have evolved to survive under different moisture conditions, ranging from arid deserts to humid forests. On a local scale, the gardener has a choice of wildflowers that grow in just about any soil-moisture condition that might be encountered, as is shown in the chart on pages 36–37.

Some species, such as larger blue flag, cardinal flower, Douglas's iris, turtlehead, and meadow beauty, thrive in soils that are continually wet. However, these wildflowers can also be easily cultivated in well-drained soils of moderate moisture, conditions that are typical of most flower gardens. Other species such

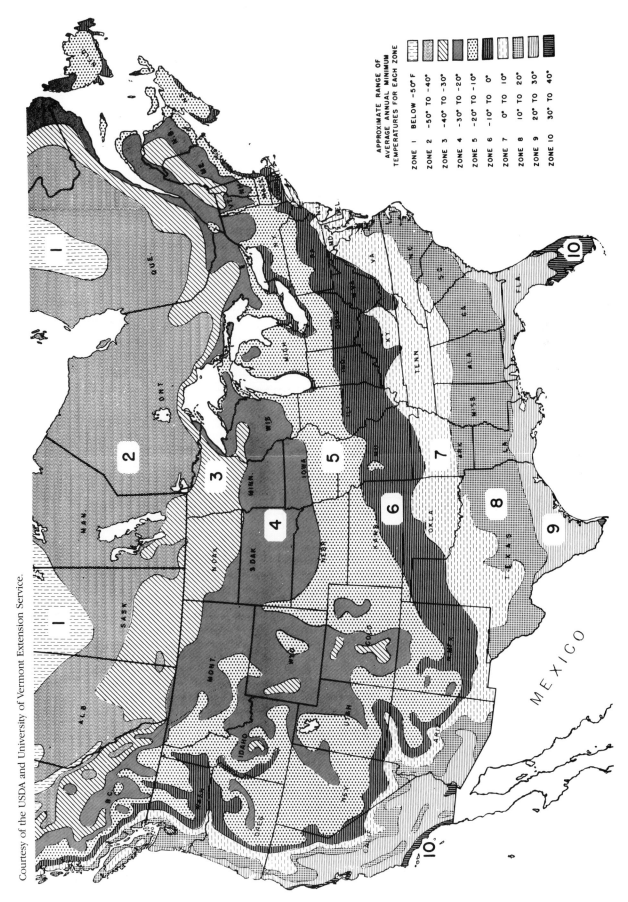

Courtesy of the USDA and University of Vermont Extension Service.

HARDINESS ZONES

SPECIES	Zone Range
Blue flax	1–10
Bunchberry	1–6
Pasqueflower	1–6
Elephantheads	2–5
Canada anemone	2–6
Shinleaf	2–6
Pink lady's slipper	2–7
Larger blue flag	2–7
Purple trillium	2–7
False Solomon's seal	2–8
Blanketflower	2–8
False dragonhead	2–8
Cardinal flower	2–9
Platte River penstemon	2–9
Old-man-of-the-mountain	3–5
Yellow fawn lily	3–6
Closed gentian	3–6
Showy tick trefoil	3–6
Leadplant	3–6
Yellow clintonia	3–7
Colorado columbine	3–7
Wild ginger	3–7
New England aster	3–7
Dutchman's breeches	3–7
White baneberry	3–7
Sharp-lobed hepatica	3–7
Black-eyed Susan HA	3–7
Purple coneflower	3–8
Mayapple	3–8
Purple prairie clover	3–8
Bloodroot	3–8
Culver's root	3–8
Compass plant	3–8
Wintergreen	3–8
Jack-in-the-pulpit	3–8
Eastern columbine	3–8
Turtlehead	3–8
Silky aster	3–8
White trillium	3–8
Gayfeather	3–9
Wild bergamot	3–9
Groundnut	3–9
Virginia bluebells	3–9
Butterfly weed	3–10
Eastern trout lily	4–7
Wood lily	4–7
Wild leek	4–8
Rocky Mountain penstemon	4–8
Bear grass	4–10
Giant evening primrose	4–10
Bitterroot	4–10
Mule's ears	4–10

Zone scale: 1 2 3 4 5 6 7 8 9 10

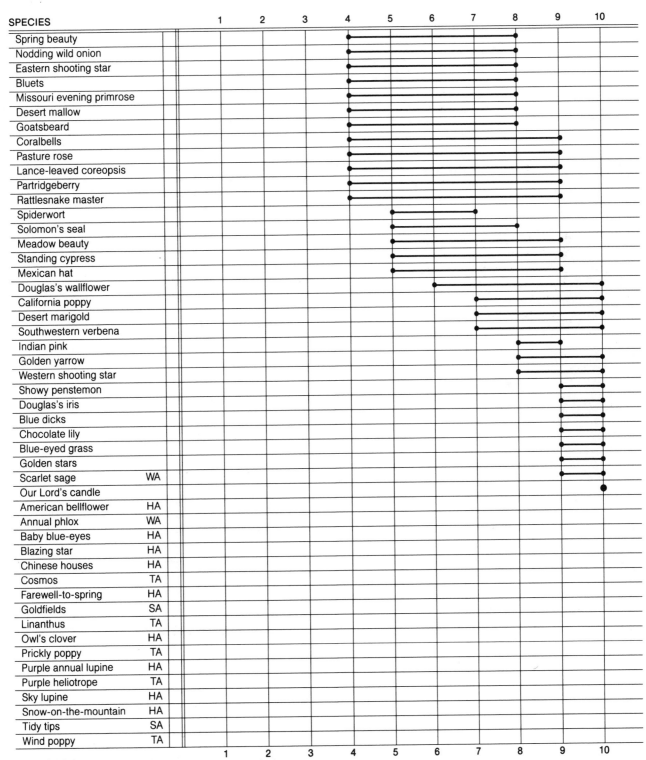

SPECIES		1	2	3	4	5	6	7	8	9	10
Spring beauty					●──────────●					
Nodding wild onion					●──────────●					
Eastern shooting star					●──────────●					
Bluets					●──────────●					
Missouri evening primrose					●──────────●					
Desert mallow					●──────────●					
Goatsbeard					●──────────●					
Coralbells					●─────────────────●				
Pasture rose					●─────────────────●				
Lance-leaved coreopsis					●─────────────────●				
Partridgeberry					●─────────────────●				
Rattlesnake master					●─────────────────●				
Spiderwort						●────────●			
Solomon's seal						●────────────●			
Meadow beauty						●──────────────────●			
Standing cypress						●──────────────────●			
Mexican hat						●──────────────────●			
Douglas's wallflower							●────────────────────●	
California poppy							●──────────────●	
Desert marigold							●──────────────●	
Southwestern verbena							●──────────────●	
Indian pink								●────────●	
Golden yarrow								●────────●	
Western shooting star								●────────●	
Showy penstemon									●────●
Douglas's iris									●────●
Blue dicks									●────●
Chocolate lily									●────●
Blue-eyed grass									●────●
Golden stars									●────●
Scarlet sage	WA									●────●
Our Lord's candle										●
American bellflower	HA									
Annual phlox	WA									
Baby blue-eyes	HA									
Blazing star	HA									
Chinese houses	HA									
Cosmos	TA									
Farewell-to-spring	HA									
Goldfields	SA									
Linanthus	TA									
Owl's clover	HA									
Prickly poppy	TA									
Purple annual lupine	HA									
Purple heliotrope	TA									
Sky lupine	HA									
Snow-on-the-mountain	HA									
Tidy tips	SA									
Wind poppy	TA									

WA (Winter Annual): Planted in fall, flowers next spring or summer.
HA (Hardy Annual): Planted in fall or spring, grows early spring to early fall.
SA (Semi-hardy Annual): Planted in early spring, grows spring to summer.
TA (Tender Annual): Planted in mid- or late spring, grows summer.

SOIL MOISTURE CONDITIONS

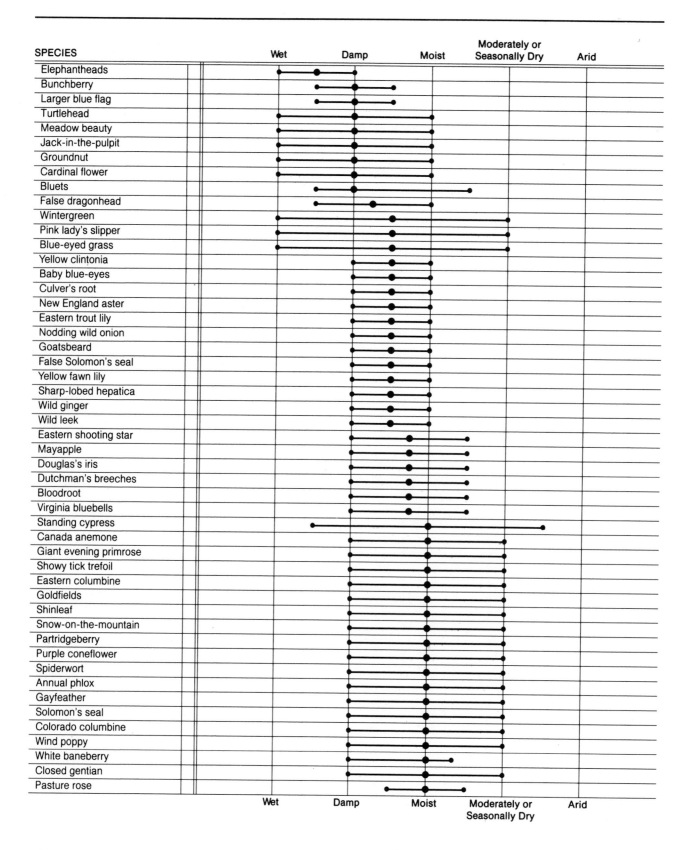

SPECIES	Wet	Damp	Moist	Moderately or Seasonally Dry	Arid
Elephantheads					
Bunchberry					
Larger blue flag					
Turtlehead					
Meadow beauty					
Jack-in-the-pulpit					
Groundnut					
Cardinal flower					
Bluets					
False dragonhead					
Wintergreen					
Pink lady's slipper					
Blue-eyed grass					
Yellow clintonia					
Baby blue-eyes					
Culver's root					
New England aster					
Eastern trout lily					
Nodding wild onion					
Goatsbeard					
False Solomon's seal					
Yellow fawn lily					
Sharp-lobed hepatica					
Wild ginger					
Wild leek					
Eastern shooting star					
Mayapple					
Douglas's iris					
Dutchman's breeches					
Bloodroot					
Virginia bluebells					
Standing cypress					
Canada anemone					
Giant evening primrose					
Showy tick trefoil					
Eastern columbine					
Goldfields					
Shinleaf					
Snow-on-the-mountain					
Partridgeberry					
Purple coneflower					
Spiderwort					
Annual phlox					
Gayfeather					
Solomon's seal					
Colorado columbine					
Wind poppy					
White baneberry					
Closed gentian					
Pasture rose					

Wet Damp Moist Moderately or Seasonally Dry Arid

SOIL MOISTURE CONDITIONS
(continued)

SPECIES	Wet	Damp	Moist	Moderately or Seasonally Dry	Arid
White trillium			●		
Purple trillium			●		
Spring beauty			●		
Chinese houses			●		
American bellflower			●		
Western shooting star			●	—	
Black-eyed Susan		—	●	—	
Compass plant		●	—	—	
Wood lily			●	—	
Wild bergamot			●	—	
California poppy			●	—	
Old-man-of-the-mountain			●	—	
Tidy tips			●	—	
Rattlesnake master			●	—	
Coralbells			●	—	
Mule's ears			●	—	
Cosmos			●	—	
Farewell-to-spring			●	—	
Rocky Mountain penstemon			●	—	
Owl's clover			●	—	
Platte River penstemon			●	—	
Blazing star			●	—	
Showy penstemon			●	—	
Silky aster			—	●	—
Purple heliotrope			—	●	—
Lance-leaved coreopsis			—	●	—
Blanketflower			—	●	—
Douglas's wallflower			—	●	—
Linanthus			—	●	—
Mexican hat			—	●	—
Bear grass			—	●	—
Blue flax			—	●	—
Southwestern verbena			—	●	—
Leadplant				●	
Pasqueflower				●	
Golden stars				●	
Butterfly weed				●	
Our Lord's candle				●	
Scarlet sage				●	
Chocolate lily				●	
Sky lupine				●	
Golden yarrow				●	
Purple annual lupine				●	
Prickly poppy				●	
Indian pink				●	
Purple prairie clover				●	
Blue dicks				●	
Missouri evening primrose				●	
Desert mallow				●	—
Desert marigold				●	—
Bitterroot				●	—

	Wet	Damp	Moist	Moderately or Seasonally Dry	Arid

as lance-leaved coreopsis, purple heliotrope, and desert marigold may need moisture while they are becoming established in the garden, but then grow better if the soil is dry.

Many of the species that are native to regions with wet winters and springs but dry summers, such as Indian pink, golden stars, and blue dicks, need moisture during part of the year, but should be allowed to dry out during their period of summer dormancy. Wildflower gardeners should be judicious with the hose; western penstemons and lupines and even species like wild bergamot that grow in relatively humid regions have problems with leaf mildew if there is too much moisture. Seedlings of most wildflowers are especially sensitive to fungal attack when soils are cold and wet.

The cultivation of wildflowers is easiest when you match a species' optimal requirements with naturally occurring conditions in the gardens, so consider your soil before selecting seeds and plants. If your soil is sandy, it will drain quickly, and you should consider planting species that do well in drier conditions. Clayey and peaty soils are often poorly drained, making them suitable for species preferring plenty of soil moisture.

However, if your soil conditions are not quite suitable for a particular species, you may be able to rectify the situation by adding the proper soil amendments before planting. A little extra time and energy invested in site preparation will pay large dividends in the future, so do not rush your wildflowers into soils to which they are ill adapted. While the root systems of most wildflowers are relatively shallow, soils should be prepared to a depth of several feet for maximum success. Avoid merely piling soil amendments on the top of the soil where they will have a marginal effect; instead work them thoroughly into the soil. For example, organic matter well mixed into the soil tends to aerate it and increase its water-holding capacity. Organic matter left as a mat on the surface of the soils may, however, become excessively dry when rain is scant.

If your soil is too dry, it is obviously easy to increase soil moisture by watering. The addition of clay, humus, or even coarse organic matter may, however, be a more effective way of assuring the long-term retention of moisture. If you need to create an even wetter habitat for growing plants like elephantheads, remove the surface 18 inches of soil, pack the bottom of the depression with a layer of clay several inches thick (or use thick plastic sheeting), and fill the depression with the original soil. The clay or plastic liner will slow the downward movement of water, thereby creating a wetland.

If the soil is too wet because of an overabundance of clay, drainage can be improved by the addition of sand or gravel mixed with copious amounts of compost or other organic matter. The organic matter creates additional air spaces in clayey soil and helps to prevent the clay from merely coating the grains of sand. Alternatively, gypsum (calcium sulfate) can be added to clayey soil to improve drainage. Since gypsum is an acidifying agent, it should only be used where you will be planting wildflowers that thrive in acid soil, with a pH 5.5 and below. Gypsum has the additional benefit of helping to conserve nitrogen compounds in the soil. Gypsum is available at many garden or building-supply centers.

In humid regions the cultivation of wildflowers that require summer drought presents a problem, since the roots of species like bitterroot, chocolate lily, blue dicks, and golden stars are susceptible to rot if the soils are too wet. One solution to this problem is to cover the surface of the soil with a pane of glass or plastic sheeting just after these wildflowers have gone into their summer dormancy. The soil directly under the covering will receive less rain and should be considerably drier unless your garden is on a slope.

The specific soil requirements of each of the 101 native plants is given on the page describing each species. Some species thrive where nutrient levels are high and the soil has an abundance of humus in the soil. Other species do best where there is little organic matter and the soil fertility is low.

pH AND OTHER SOIL CONDITIONS

One of the most important soil factors in the cultivation of many wildflowers is the acidity/alkalinity, or "pH," of the soil. The pH is simply a measure of relative acidity or alkalinity on a scale from 0 (most acidic) to 14 (most alkaline), with a value of 7 indicating neutral conditions. The pH units are based on multiples of ten, so a soil with a pH of 4.0 is 10 times more acidic than a soil with a pH of 5.0, and 100 times more acidic than a soil with a pH of 6.0. Likewise, a pH of 9 is 10 times more alkaline than a pH of 8, and so forth.

The pH of the soil is important because it directly and indirectly influences the availability of nutrients essential for plant growth. Nutrients such as phosphorus, calcium, potassium, and magnesium are most available to plants when the soil pH is between 6.0 and 7.5. Under highly acidic (low pH) conditions, these nutrients become insoluble and relatively unavailable for uptake by plants. However, iron, trace minerals, and some toxic elements such as aluminum become more available at low pH. High soil pH may also decrease the availability of nutrients. If the soil is more alkaline than pH 8, phosphorus, iron, and many trace minerals become insoluble and unavailable for plant uptake.

The availability of nitrogen, one of plants' three basic nutrients, is influenced by pH as well. Much of the nitrogen that plants eventually use is bound within organic matter, and the conversion of this bound nitrogen to forms available to plants is accomplished by several species of bacteria that live in the soil. When the pH of the soil drops below 5.5, the activity of these bacteria is inhibited, and little nitrogen is made available to the plants. At about the same pH levels there is a general decline in most forms of bacterial activity and an increase in the activity of soil fungi. This shift in soil biology may further influence which plants can survive and which cannot.

The usual pH range of soils is from about 4 to about 8. Typically in the humid East, the precipitation has been sufficient to have removed large amounts of potassium, calcium, magnesium, and other alkaline nutrients. As a result the soils in humid regions tend to be acidic with pH values below 7. In the arid West the situation is quite different. There substantially less precipitation falls, and as a result, the alkaline constituents may maintain soil pH significantly higher than 7.

Local soil acidity/alkalinity may vary because of differences in bedrock geology or the vegetation present. In general, regardless of the geographic region, locations with limestone or marble bedrock have soils with increased alkalinity, and locations with granite bedrock have acidic soils. Certain species of plants may also increase the acidity of the soil through the addition of organic matter with a low pH. The dead foliage of pines, spruce, fir, oaks, and many of the heath plants may acidify the soil as it decomposes. In cool, wet areas, the growth of sphagnum and other mosses may also create acidic conditions.

Some species of wildflowers are relatively insensitive to soil acidity/alkalinity, while others survive only over a narrow pH range. Most often, pH preferences are more related to the balance of various nutrients required by particular species, or changes in the biological activity of soil organisms, rather than to the acidity or alkalinity itself. On pages 42–43 is a guide to the pH preferences of those species of wildflowers that have specific pH requirements.

HOW TO MEASURE pH

Before deciding which wildflowers to cultivate and where to plant them, it is essential to know something about the pH of your soils. The measurement is actually quite simple and there are a number of commercial products readily available from most garden suppliers. The pH is measured by taking several samples of the soil from the root zone at several different spots in the garden. Using a plastic spoon, place the soil in a clear plastic or glass vial and add an equal volume of water. The combined sample is then shaken or stirred to mix the soil and water thoroughly, and then left for a moment, allowing the soil to settle. Then the pH of the liquid in the top of the vial can be determined by any one of several means.

The least expensive way to measure pH is with "indicator paper," which can be purchased in short strips or long rolls. This is like litmus paper, but rather than telling you whether a solution is merely acid or alkaline, it produces a range of colors to indicate the pH value. Just stick the strip of paper into the liquid mixed with the soil and compare the color of the dampened paper with the reference chart provided.

A slightly more accurate method, although usually more expensive, is the use of indicator solutions, which are frequently sold in pH kits. A small amount of the liquid extracted from the soil-and-water mix is placed in a ceramic dish, and a few drops of indicator solution are added. As with the indicator papers, the color produced is compared with a pH reference chart.

Another means of measuring pH is with a pH meter. One type operates without batteries and measures pH based on the conductivity of moistened soil. This type of meter is neither more accurate nor faster than the color-indicator

A. Jack-in-the-pulpit
B. Dutchman's breeches
C. Purple trillium
D. Bloodroot
E. Eastern trout lily
F. Spring beauty

Eastern woodland garden, spring.

methods using solutions or paper. All provide a rough, but useful, estimate of soil pH.

The most accurate measurements of soil pH use electronic meters with one or several electrodes. These instruments are quite expensive and are used by soil testing laboratories for determining soil pH. Most state Agricultural Experiment Stations, usually located at land-grant universities, will test soil samples for a nominal charge. To arrange for such pH testing, contact your state's land-grant university or your county's Agricultural Extension Service Agent.

CHANGING THE pH OF SOILS

You may find that the pH of your soil is not suitable to cultivate a particular species, even though all other environmental conditions seem perfect. The acidity or alkalinity of soils can be altered to a limited extent through the addition of various soil amendments. It may take several years to change permanently a soil's pH, so be patient.

Pine, spruce, and fir needles are naturally occurring acidic organic materials, which can be added to garden soils to lower the pH. If none of these is locally available, peat moss works well in acidifying soils. Powdered gypsum and sulfur powder can also be used to lower soil pH, but they should be used with some caution, since they act more rapidly than the organic materials.

Ground limestone is the amendment of choice to raise the pH of the soil. Medium-ground limestone may give better results than very coarse limestone (which may be slow to neutralize soil acids) or fine limestone (which may be too quickly lost from the soil). Wood ashes can also be used to increase soil alkalinity, but keep in mind that they are more concentrated than limestone and may even "burn" wildflowers if too much is applied.

pH PREFERENCES

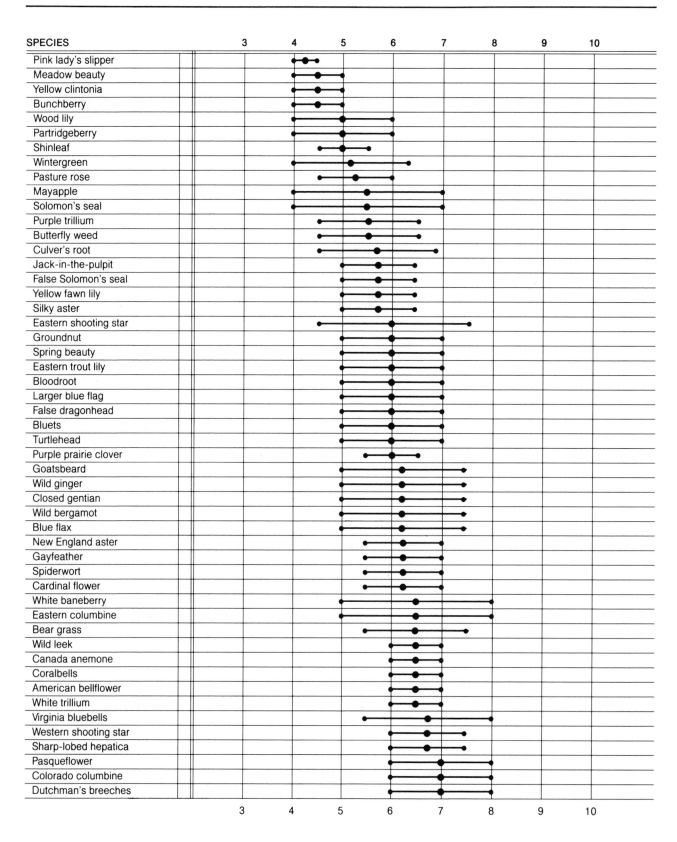

SPECIES	3	4	5	6	7	8	9	10
Pink lady's slipper								
Meadow beauty								
Yellow clintonia								
Bunchberry								
Wood lily								
Partridgeberry								
Shinleaf								
Wintergreen								
Pasture rose								
Mayapple								
Solomon's seal								
Purple trillium								
Butterfly weed								
Culver's root								
Jack-in-the-pulpit								
False Solomon's seal								
Yellow fawn lily								
Silky aster								
Eastern shooting star								
Groundnut								
Spring beauty								
Eastern trout lily								
Bloodroot								
Larger blue flag								
False dragonhead								
Bluets								
Turtlehead								
Purple prairie clover								
Goatsbeard								
Wild ginger								
Closed gentian								
Wild bergamot								
Blue flax								
New England aster								
Gayfeather								
Spiderwort								
Cardinal flower								
White baneberry								
Eastern columbine								
Bear grass								
Wild leek								
Canada anemone								
Coralbells								
American bellflower								
White trillium								
Virginia bluebells								
Western shooting star								
Sharp-lobed hepatica								
Pasqueflower								
Colorado columbine								
Dutchman's breeches								

pH PREFERENCES
(continued)

SPECIES	3	4	5	6	7	8	9	10
Mexican hat				●——————●——————●		
Golden yarrow*			●————————————————————●			
Prickly poppy			●————————————————————●			
Farewell-to-spring			●————————————————————●			
Lance-leaved coreopsis			●————————————————————●			
Chocolate lily			●————————————————————●			
Bitterroot			●————————————————————●			
Douglas's iris			●————————————————————●			
Douglas's wallflower			●————————————————————●			
Sky lupine			●————————————————————●			
Purple annual lupine			●————————————————————●			
California poppy			●————————————————————●			
Snow-on-the-mountain			●————————————————————●			
Standing cypress			●————————————————————●			
Leadplant			●————————————————————●			
Baby blue-eyes			●————————————————————●			
Giant evening primrose			●————————————————————●			
Tidy tips			●————————————————————●			
Owl's clover			●————————————————————●			
Elephantheads			●————————————————————●			
Linanthus			●————————————————————●			
Showy penstemon			●————————————————————●			
Rocky Mountain penstemon			●————————————————————●			
Blanketflower			●————————————————————●			
Purple heliotrope			●————————————————————●			
Annual phlox			●————————————————————●			
Blazing star			●————————————————————●			
Chinese houses			●————————————————————●			
Old-man-of-the-mountain			●————————————————————●			
Desert marigold			●————————————————————●			
Golden stars			●————————————————————●			
Blue dicks			●————————————————————●			
Missouri evening primrose			●————————————————————●			
Black-eyed Susan			●————————————————————●			
Scarlet sage			●————————————————————●			
Platte River penstemon			●————————————————————●			
Indian pink			●————————————————————●			
Compass plant			●————————————————————●			
Blue-eyed grass			●————————————————————●			
Cosmos			●————————————————————●			
Desert mallow			●————————————————————●			
Wind poppy			●————————————————————●			
Showy tick trefoil			●————————————————————●			
Goldfields			●————————————————————●			
Nodding wild onion			●————————————————————●			
Southwestern verbena			●————————————————————●			
Purple coneflower			●————————————————————●			
Mule's ears			●————————————————————●			
Rattlesnake master			●————————————————————●			
Our Lord's candle			●————————————————————●			

* This and the following species appear to have no strong pH preferences.

After measuring the pH, add the soil amendment, taking care to mix thoroughly and incorporate it uniformly in the top 6–12 inches of soil. Spread the amendment thinly on the surface and then work it into the soil with a spading fork or shovel. Then add another layer, mixing it into the soil. Without an even mixing of the amendment you may find pockets of soil with enormously different pH values. Moisten the soil and then allow the soil to rest for a day or so before again measuring the pH at several spots. Repeat the process until you have the desired pH conditions. A rough rule of thumb is that for a 100-square-foot area of most soils it takes about 2–6 pounds of limestone to raise the pH one unit, and 2½–7 pounds of gypsum, or ½–2 pounds of sulfur, to lower the pH one unit. Clay soils require more of an amendment to change the pH; sandy soils, less. It is strongly recommended that organic matter acidifiers be used before resorting to gypsum or sulfur. It is better to try to change the pH of the soil slowly than to overdo it one way and then the other.

After the appropriate pH is attained, check it periodically. Since the natural processes at work in your garden will be altering the pH through rainfall, bacterial activity, and the uptake of nutrients by plants, you may occasionally have to make further additions of soil amendments. With wildflowers in place, be especially careful to add the amendments in small amounts directly on the surface of the soil, and to work them in without disturbing the plants' roots.

A WORD ABOUT WEEDS & PESTS

The wildflowers of your region are obviously well adapted for survival under the prevailing local conditions. You may, however, find that a modest investment of time spent weeding while your wildflowers are first becoming established will pay large dividends. Many wildflowers are particularly sensitive to the effects of herbicides, so weeding by hand is the only choice.

You will from time to time find that various insects will visit your wildflowers. While some of these may be there for an attractive meal, they usually have an abundance of natural predators that will keep their populations in check, so almost no damage occurs. The use of pesticides is also to be avoided in the cultivation of wildflowers since many of these plants are pollinated by insects, and without the pollinators, there is no fruit and seed production.

When you are trying to establish a garden of wildflowers, slugs, household pets, and, in rural areas, deer may be more of a problem than insects. If dogs, cats, or deer become a nuisance, fencing may be the only reasonable solution. Slugs relish certain species of wildflowers, especially those in the lily family. They feed at night when the humidity is high, and they can do considerable damage by chewing holes in the leaves. Slugs can be effectively controlled by setting out shallow dishes filled with an inch or so of stale beer. Aluminum pie pans with the top lip bent up vertically make ideal slug traps. The slugs prefer the beer to your wildflowers, and once they are swimming in it they drown.

Wildflower Propagation

O ne of the pleasures of growing wildflowers is the opportunity to propagate them and thereby increase their numbers in your garden. As already pointed out, the digging of wildflowers from their native environments, apart from being unethical, is frequently illegal. The best way to obtain wildflowers for your garden is to purchase seeds, plants, or planting stock from reputable suppliers who sell nursery-propagated material (see Appendix A). Once these wildflowers are established, they can serve as stock for further propagation.

SEEDS

Seeds are by far the cheapest means of propagating large numbers of wildflowers, even though some perennials grown from seeds may take a long time before they are mature enough to flower. Usually seeds are collected when the fruits are mature. Many species disperse seed in ways that make it difficult to find plants with the fruits present when you would like to harvest them. One way to capture the seeds before they are released from the plant is to cut off a foot-long section of a discarded nylon stocking and make a sleeve, tying off one end with a string or wire closure. The sleeve is then slipped over the developing fruit, after the flower petals have withered but before the fruit is fully ripe. The open end is then firmly, but gently, tied closed so that the seeds can't fall to the ground, being careful that the stems are not crushed or broken in the process. When the fruits are fully ripe, the stem can be snipped just below the nylon bag, which then can be put in a labeled paper sack and brought indoors for further processing.

Some seeds should be planted fresh and not allowed to dry out, otherwise germination is delayed. Other seeds will not germinate immediately and have to undergo "after-ripening" before they are ready to sprout. Seeds of fleshy fruits should generally be separated from the pulp prior to their storage or planting. If seeds are not the type that need to be planted immediately, and you want to store them for a while, allow them to air dry thoroughly and then store them in small manila envelopes or 35mm film canisters.

The seeds of some species will remain dormant unless they are subjected to chilling temperatures, have their coats mechanically scratched, are subjected to light or darkness, or undergo a combination of these treatments. The specific treatments required to germinate various seeds are detailed on the descriptive pages following this chapter. The treatments fall into four categories: (1) seed chilling, or stratification, (2) seed-coat scratching, or scarification, (3) hot-water treatment, (4) light or dark treatment.

(1) Stratification. Many plants that live in environments with warm or hot summers and cold winters have evolved to have seeds that are dormant the first fall after they have been produced. This adaptation prevents tender seedlings from coming up and being subjected to freezing temperatures when they would be only a month or so old. Breaking dormancy actually requires the seeds to be subjected to cold temperatures for a period of time (a process called stratification), followed by a period of warm temperatures, conditions that are met by the natural progression of seasons. Usually a temperature of only 40°F is sufficient to break the dormancy or enhance germination. The length of stratification varies widely among different native species. Germination of some seeds is improved if they are stratified under moist conditions in addition to the cold temperatures.

The easiest way to stratify seeds, if you live in a region with sufficiently cold winters, is simply to plant the seeds in the fall. Seeds can be planted directly in the garden where desired or in flats that are left outdoors. In regions with warm winters, or if you don't desire to plant the seeds in the fall, it is necessary to refrigerate the seeds for the appropriate period of time. If moist stratification is required, the seeds can be placed in a lightly dampened paper towel that is rolled up and placed in a screw-top jar until planting time.

(2) Scarification. In order for seeds to germinate they have to take up water and oxygen from the outside environment. These substances move through the outer covering of the seed called the "seed coat." Some native species, especially those in the bean family, have seed coats so tough that water and oxygen are prevented from entering, and the seed remains in dormancy unless the seed coat is scratched, or "scarified." This occurs naturally when seeds are moved around in the soil, especially following rainstorms, but in the home garden better results are obtained if the seeds are scarified before planting.

The easiest way to accomplish this with medium-size seeds, such as those of the lupines and leadplant, is to rub the seeds between two sheets of medium-grit sandpaper. You don't want to rub them so hard that you pulverize the seeds, just hard enough to scratch the surface so moisture can penetrate to the seed inside. Large seeds, such as those of compass plant, can be scarified by nicking their coats with a razor blade or, better yet, a sharp pocket knife.

(3) Hot Water Treatments. Some seeds, such as those of lupines, have enhanced germination if dunked in hot water prior to planting. Place the seeds in a jar and fill it halfway with tap water that is hot to the touch, but not scalding. Allow the seeds to remain in the water as it cools overnight. The seeds can then be planted the next day.

(4) Light or Dark Treatments. A few species of wildflowers have seeds that are either stimulated or inhibited by light. If the seeds are stimulated by light, they should be planted shallowly, so sunlight penetrating through the surface of the soil can have its desired effect. If the seeds are inhibited by light, they should be planted at sufficient depth to prevent light from slowing germination.

One of the most efficient ways of propagating wildflowers from seed is to use flats or nursery beds for rearing seedlings for the first year or until they become established. The advantage of flats is that you can transplant seedlings to holding beds and maintain an optimum density of plants more easily than if you were to plant the seed directly in the desired location. Also, some species have seeds that are slow to germinate, and it may take several years for all the viable seeds that were planted to produce seedlings. The soil can be kept in the flats until the seeds have had sufficient time to germinate completely.

If the seeds you are planting are scarce, small pots can be used for raising seedlings. If the species is one that thrives in slightly acidic conditions, peat pots are a real convenience. When the seedlings are sturdy they can be transplanted to a nursery bed, where they can grow without competition from other plants, or to permanent locations. Be careful not to disturb the roots or break off the shoots when removing the seedlings and soil from pots. If you are using peat pots, simply tear off the bottom of the pot and plant the container with its contents so the surface level of the soil is the same as that inside the pot. (Unlike many gardeners, I do tear off the bottom of the peat pot, because I have found the plant makes better contact with the soil if I do.)

A Special Note on Planting Legumes. Members of the bean family often require the presence of certain microorganisms, known as rhizobia, in the soil to ensure their survival. These microbes lead a symbiotic existence with these plants, inhabiting nodules formed on the root systems and fixing atmospheric nitrogen, which the plants eventually use. Not all soils have abundant populations of the microbes needed by leadplant, purple prairie clover, groundnut, lupines, showy tick trefoil, and other leguminous wildflowers. If you have difficulty propagating these wildflowers, you may need to purchase a

A. Leadplant
B. Rattlesnake master
C. Purple prairie clover
D. Gayfeather
E. Nodding wild onion
F. Big bluestem
G. Little bluestem

Midwest prairie, summer.

47

commercially produced "inoculant" and add it to the soil at the time the seeds are planted. Different species require several different strains of microbial inoculants, so the addition of "pea" or "soybean" inoculants would not be effective for wildflowers. Make sure you get the right strain of rhizobia for the species that you plan to cultivate.

Rhizobia inoculants can be ordered directly from The Nitragin Company, Inc., 3101 W. Custer Avenue, Milwaukee, WI 53209, or Kalo, Inc., P.O. Box 12567, Columbus, OH 43212. You will need to indicate the scientific name of the species to be inoculated and the amount of seed you intend to treat. It may take two to four weeks for these companies to prepare special rhizobia if they are not in stock.

ROOTSTOCK DIVISIONS

One of the quickest ways to propagate perennials is by divisions of rootstocks. Rootstocks are best dug up and divided while the plant is in a dormant state, usually in the early spring or fall. In general, perennials that flower in the spring can be most safely divided in the fall, and those that flower in the fall are best divided in the early spring. For those plants with shoots that wither and go into dormancy early in the growing season, like trout lily or Virginia bluebells, the location of the plants should be marked with a stake or other convenient marker so that the rootstocks can be located later in the fall for propagation. In regions with cold winters, there is an advantage to spring division of perennials that flower in summer, since plants will then have a chance to establish a more vigorous root system before the next winter. This spring division may be especially important in soils prone to frost heaving.

Regardless of the type of rootstock (see page 17), the principal technique is quite similar (see page 49). With a sharp knife (a pocket knife will do splendidly), cut the rootstock so that the divided pieces have at least one vegetative bud or "eye" attached. Since the size of the resulting plant will to a large extent be determined by the size of the divided piece, don't make the divisions too small (unless you want lots of tiny plants).

Runners and stolons are easily divided by cutting the horizontal stem between adjacent plants, which can then be dug up and transplanted when dormant. The division of tubers is also easily accomplished. Cut tubers into pieces, each with a bud or two, and plant them with the buds pointing up. Do this the same way you would plant pieces of potato. New shoots and roots will be produced as the plant draws upon the energy reserves of the tuber flesh. Similarly, rhizomes can be divided into pieces, each with buds and associated roots. Replant the segments at the appropriate depth and spacing.

Corms and bulbs of perennial wildflowers can be divided in a manner similar to other garden perennials. The small offsets that develop on the sides of mature corms and bulbs can be removed with a knife during the dormant season and planted at an appropriate depth. These cormlets and bulblets will usually take several years to develop into plants capable of flowering. If not cut

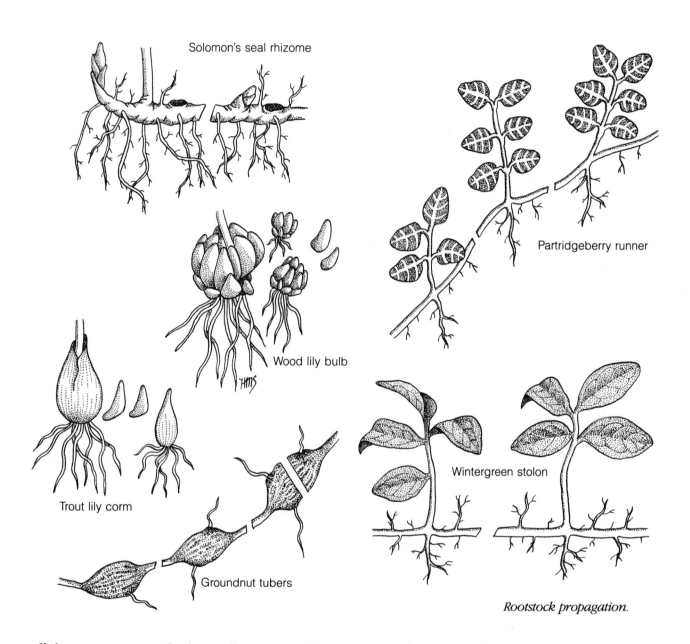

Solomon's seal rhizome

Partridgeberry runner

Wood lily bulb

Trout lily corm

Groundnut tubers

Wintergreen stolon

Rootstock propagation.

off the parent rootstock, these offsets eventually mature into large, densely crowded plants, which may benefit from being divided and given wider spacing.

The fleshy scales of bulbs such as the chocolate lily and wood lily can be divided and planted like seeds in flats to produce large quantities of seedlings. Break off the individual scales from dormant bulbs, and in a flat containing a mixture of sand and compost, plant them with the tips of the scales pointing upward, positioned just at the soil surface. Provide a light shade and keep the soil moist, but not overly wet, until the resulting small plants are sturdy enough to transplant into a nursery bed or permanent location.

After replanting the rootstock divisions be especially careful not to over-water the soil. The soil should be prevented from drying out, but wet soils invite problems. Rootstocks have carbohydrate-rich stores of energy the plant draws upon during its period of most rapid growth. If the soil is too wet, bacterial and fungal rots may attack the newly divided pieces of rootstock and even kill the plants. For this reason, it is a good idea to plant rootstock divisions in a nursery or holding bed that has well-drained soil, and to transplant the stock when dormant the following year.

STEM CUTTINGS

Another means of propagating certain perennials, like scarlet sage, spiderwort and some of the penstemons, is by making cuttings of stems. These cuttings should be made when the shoots are growing vigorously, and they are most successful if the shoot lacks flower buds. The best time to make a cutting is when the plant has been well watered, by rain or artificial irrigation, especially in the early morning before the sun has evaporated the water from the leaf surfaces.

Before making the cuttings, prepare a flat with a mixture of coarse compost or peat moss and builder's sand (don't use beach sand from the ocean — the salt might kill the cuttings). Moisten the soil, poke holes 2–3 inches deep and 5 inches apart with your little finger, and take the flat to the garden. Cut 6-inch pieces of rapidly growing shoots by making a diagonal slice through the stem with a razor blade. Remove any flower buds and the leaves from the bottom 3 inches of the stem, gently place the cutting into the hole, and firmly press the soil around the base to assure good contact between the cutting and the soil. Moisten the soil again.

Since the cuttings initially have no root systems, it is difficult for them to take up water. The flats should be kept in the shade, and the soil should be kept

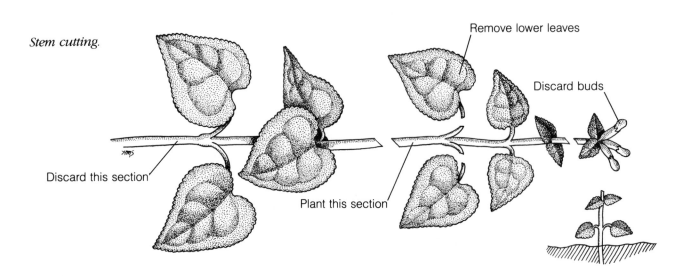

Stem cutting.

Remove lower leaves

Discard buds

Discard this section

Plant this section

moist but not wet. Soils that are too wet will prevent oxygen from getting to the developing roots and also encourage rotting diseases. Protect the cuttings from the effects of drying winds, and mist the plants if the humidity is low. Allow the cuttings to remain in the flat until they go into dormancy at the end of the growing season, and then transplant them to holding beds or permanent locations.

Whether by collecting your own seeds or by dividing or cutting live plants, wildflower propagation can give you satisfactions beyond the considerable cost savings. Many perennials should be divided every several years, and they respond to the treatment by flowering more abundantly and adding even greater beauty to the garden. Perhaps one of the most important benefits of propagating plants yourself is the increased familiarity with wildflowers you gain in the process.

Part II

SPECIES OF WILDFLOWERS

The following pages give detailed information about 101 species of wildflowers. In the tradition of herbals and most wildflower seed catalogs, the plants appear in alphabetical order by scientific name. This should prevent confusion, since although an individual species may have several common names, it usually has only one scientific name.

Each species description starts with a general description of the wildflower and its ecology. Then comes a discussion of its culture and growth requirements and specific directions for its propagation. A few "companions" that grow under similar conditions are listed; often, however, many other species could be included, so browse through the pages and experiment with different combinations of wildflowers.

Each species is illustrated. A scale shows the approximate size of the plant, and a quick reference box shows plant family, flower color, flowering and fruiting times, growth cycle (annual, biennial, or perennial), and hardiness zones where the species can be grown. The map shows the wildflower's native distribution, but most species can be successfully grown over a much wider area.

White baneberry
(Doll's-eyes, white cohosh)

Actaea pachypoda

This 1–2-foot-high hardy perennial is grown more for its clusters of porcelain-white berries than for its flowers. The white flowers have between 4 and 10 thin petals, which are shorter than the numerous stamens in the center. The white fruits are about ⅓ inch in diameter, are borne on a fleshy, pink stalk, and have a dark spot on their centers from which the plant gets one of its common names, "Doll's-eyes." All parts of this plant are poisonous to humans, although birds and small mammals eat the seeds. The compound leaves remain deep green throughout the summer.

CULTURE White baneberry does best in shaded locations that remain moist throughout the growing season. If the soil becomes too dry during the summer, the plant will go into an early dormancy. While complete shade is not necessary, partial shade should be provided. The acidity of the soil is not particularly crucial; baneberries grow well in moderately acid to slightly alkaline soils (pH 5–8). The plant grows naturally in soils that are rich in humus, and annual additions of compost and a light winter mulch of leaves left on in the spring are beneficial.

PROPAGATION Both seeds and root division are successful. Remove the ⅛-inch, brown, half-heart-shaped seeds from the white berries in the early fall. Sow the seeds in flats, cover with ¼ inch of soil, and leave outdoors over winter so that seeds can stratify. Most will germinate in the spring, and seedlings can be carefully transplanted when sturdy. It will take about three years for these plants to reach maturity and produce flowers.

Root division is usually done in the fall just after the leaves have withered. Select rootstock with prominent buds, and divide them into pieces with at least one bud each. Plant the pieces 2 feet apart with the buds about 1 inch below the soil surface. Mulch with deciduous leaves over winter. Propagation by root division usually gives quicker results than propagation from seed.

COMPANIONS Bloodroot, Solomon's seal, columbines, Jack-in-the-pulpit, and other moist-shade-loving plants.

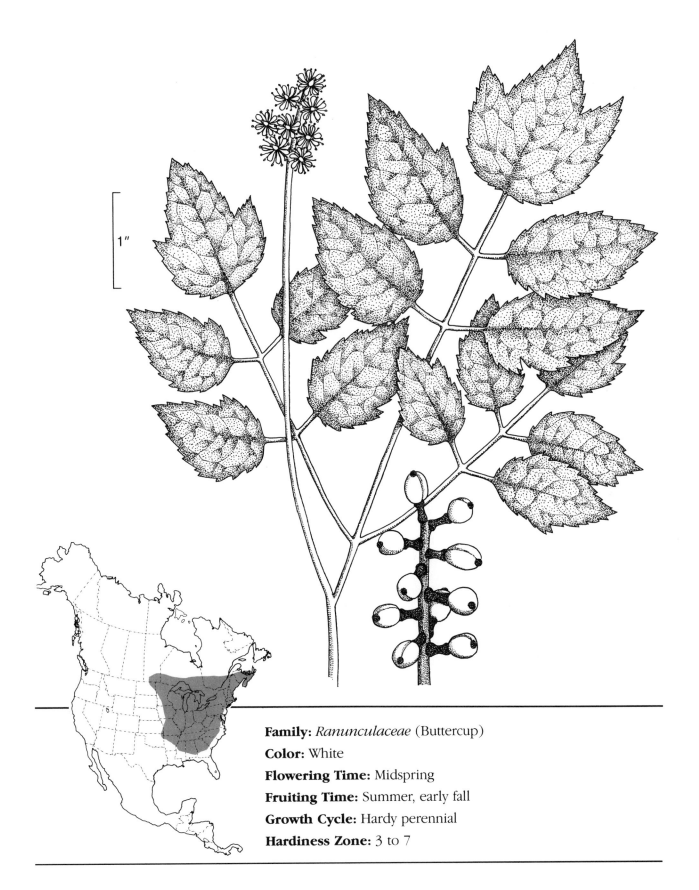

Family: *Ranunculaceae* (Buttercup)

Color: White

Flowering Time: Midspring

Fruiting Time: Summer, early fall

Growth Cycle: Hardy perennial

Hardiness Zone: 3 to 7

1"

WHITE BANEBERRY *(Actaea pachypoda)*

55

Nodding wild onion

Allium cernuum

The wild onion adds a touch of light lavender to moist prairies and woodlands in the eastern U.S. during midsummer. The French explorer La Salle allegedly marked the Algonquian name for this plant, "chigagou," on an early map of the southwest shore of Lake Michigan, and the settlement that eventually developed there took on the name "Chicago." The soft, grasslike leaves and 1–2 foot-high flower stalk arise from bulbs, which look like miniature versions of their cultivated relative. The flowers are borne in a cluster atop the stalk which is bent over so that the flowers nod toward the ground. Individual flowers have 3 petals and 3 petallike sepals, all of which are joined together at their bases. They range in color from white to pink to lavender. The fruit is a 3-part capsule containing small, black seeds. All parts of this plant have a pleasant, pungent oniony scent.

CULTURE

Nodding wild onion grows best in open, moist habitats. It responds well to additions of organic matter to the soil. With little care, nodding wild onion is easy to grow in the garden. It will also naturalize effectively in grasslands, if the grass is not too thick.

PROPAGATION

This plant can be easily propagated by seed or by bulb division. Plant the seeds, when ripe in the fall, ¼ inch deep in soil that is free from competing plants and relatively rich in organic matter. If planted in deep flats, they should be left out over winter, since the seed from at least the northern part of its range requires moist stratification for proper germination. Seed from southern regions may not require such treatment.

The offset bulblets, which form around the base of the larger bulbs, can be divided in the first fall and planted ½–1 inch deep. These are most effectively planted in small groups. Some of these bulblets will produce flowers the next spring, and many will flower the following year.

COMPANIONS

Spiderwort, purple prairie clover, Eastern shooting star, and false dragonhead.

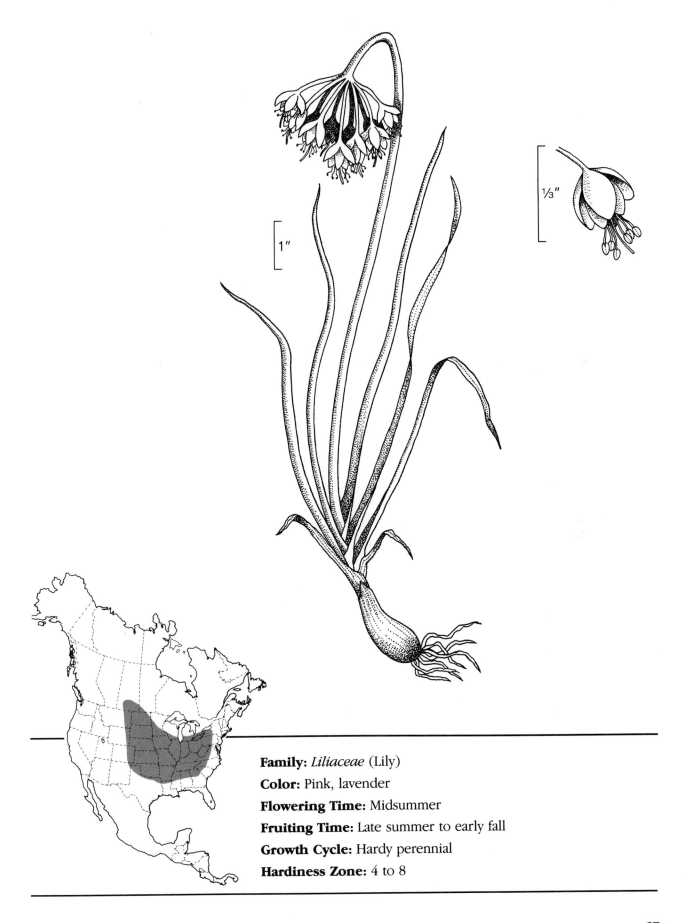

Family: *Liliaceae* (Lily)

Color: Pink, lavender

Flowering Time: Midsummer

Fruiting Time: Late summer to early fall

Growth Cycle: Hardy perennial

Hardiness Zone: 4 to 8

NODDING WILD ONION *(Allium cernuum)*

Wild leek

Allium tricoccum

Wild leek is a favorite of edible-wild-plant fanciers. Groups of 2–3 fleshy, spatula-shaped leaves, some up to a foot long, emerge in the early spring. Often one encounters dense carpets of wild leeks covering the forest floor. The leaves, as well as the 1–2-inch edible bulbs, have a strong oniony flavor. The leaves remain green for about a month and then wither as flowering begins. As the leaves disappear, a hooded flower stalk emerges from the ground and reaches 6–12 inches in height. A hemispherical cluster of small, greenish white, 6-petaled flowers bursts forth at the top of the stalk. The fruit of the wild leek is a ⅓-inch papery capsule which contains 3 shiny, black, ⅛-inch seeds.

CULTURE

Wild leek is a plant of rich woods and thickets. It is adapted to survive in shady conditions by having leaves that go into dormancy as the forest leaves overhead are reaching full size, but it grows best in locations that are sunny at least during the early spring. Plant wild leeks in soil that is rich in humus, or work ample amounts of compost 6 inches into the surface of the site. Wild leek grows best in neutral to mildly acidic soil, so adjust the pH to 6–7. The soil should be moist at least during the spring and early summer, when the wild leek is in leaf and flower.

PROPAGATION

Wild leeks are easily propagated from seeds and divisions of bulb offsets. The black, shiny seeds should be collected when they are exposed in the summer as fruits ripen. Plant them ½ inch deep in outdoor flats containing a mixture of loam and compost. Carefully transplant the small bulbs the following summer, setting them 1–1½ inches deep. Bulbs more than 1 inch in diameter frequently produce small offset bulbs, which can be divided in the summer as the fruits are maturing. Since the conspicuous leaves will have disappeared by the time you will want to divide the offsets, it is a good idea to mark the location of choice plants before the leaves wither. Plant the offsets 1½ inches deep, and give them a good top dressing of compost.

COMPANIONS

Trillium, wild ginger, spring beauty, Dutchman's breeches.

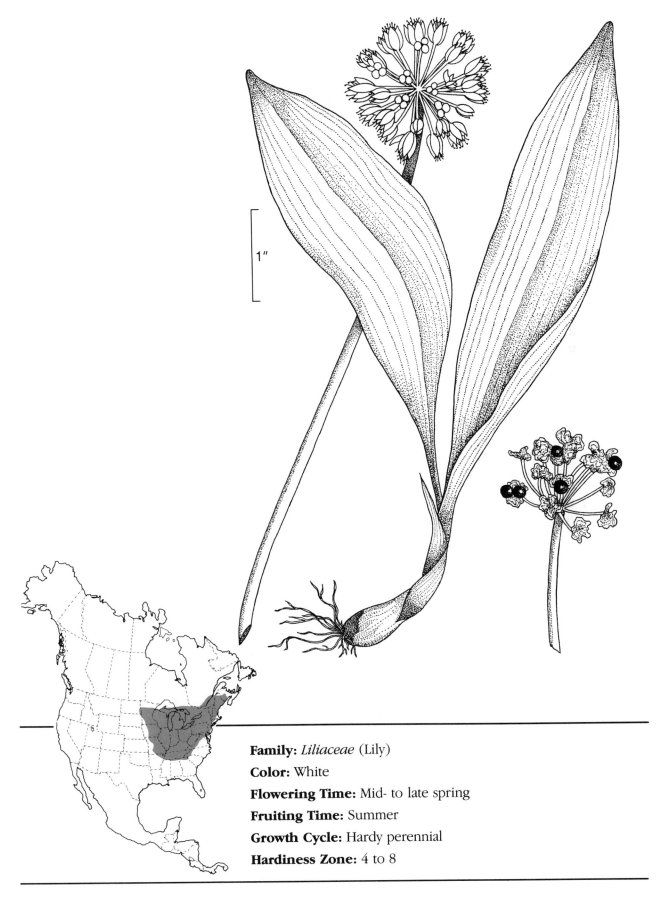

Family: *Liliaceae* (Lily)

Color: White

Flowering Time: Mid- to late spring

Fruiting Time: Summer

Growth Cycle: Hardy perennial

Hardiness Zone: 4 to 8

WILD LEEK *(Allium tricoccum)*

Leadplant

Amorpha canescens

Leadplant is a hardy, semi-woody perennial of the prairies. Its ½-inch-long, compound leaflets are densely covered with short, woolly hairs giving the foliage a grayish color and its common name. The small flowers are clustered together in 4–6-inch spikes atop the 2–3-foot robust stems. While leadplant is a member of the pea family, its violet-gray flowers don't look pealike. The flowers have a single petal, from which the golden yellow stamens protrude. The fruits are small, fuzzy, beanlike pods containing 1 or 2 seeds. Leadplant has a deep, branching taproot, which gives it an advantage in dry prairies, especially those periodically swept by fires.

CULTURE   Leadplant should be cultivated in open, sunny locations, with light shade at most. It does best in relatively dry, well-drained soils with moderate amounts of humus. Like other members of the pea family, leadplant has nitrogen-fixing microorganisms that attach to its roots. If the proper microorganisms are not present in the soil when you first put in leadplant, a commercially available soil inoculant should speed their establishment, and eventually the nitrogen content of the soil around the plants will increase. If inoculation of seeds is needed, use *Amorpha*-type rhizobia (Nitragin-type EL). Leadplant is hardy as far north as zone 4 and half-hardy in colder regions.

PROPAGATION   Leadplant is usually propagated by seed, although making green-wood cuttings of the young stems is also possible. The seeds should be scarified to allow water to enter, and since the plant requires cold winter temperatures for its seeds to germinate, seeds planted in regions warmer than zone 8 should be artificially stratified first (10 weeks of damp stratification at 40°F). Plant the scarified seeds ⅓ inch deep in a nursery bed or deep flat filled with sandy loam mixed with compost. If planted in the fall and left in place during winter, the seeds will germinate over several weeks in the spring when temperatures reach 65–70°F. Allow the seedlings to grow for the summer in nursery bed or flat, and then transplant them in the fall to a permanent location. The buds at the top of the root should be set about 2 inches below the soil surface. If the top of the plant is accidently damaged, the root usually will resprout. Once established, leadplant requires little care, but it takes about 4 years for the plants to reach maturity and flower.

COMPANIONS   Butterfly weed, pasqueflower, purple prairie clover, nodding wild onion, black-eyed Susan.

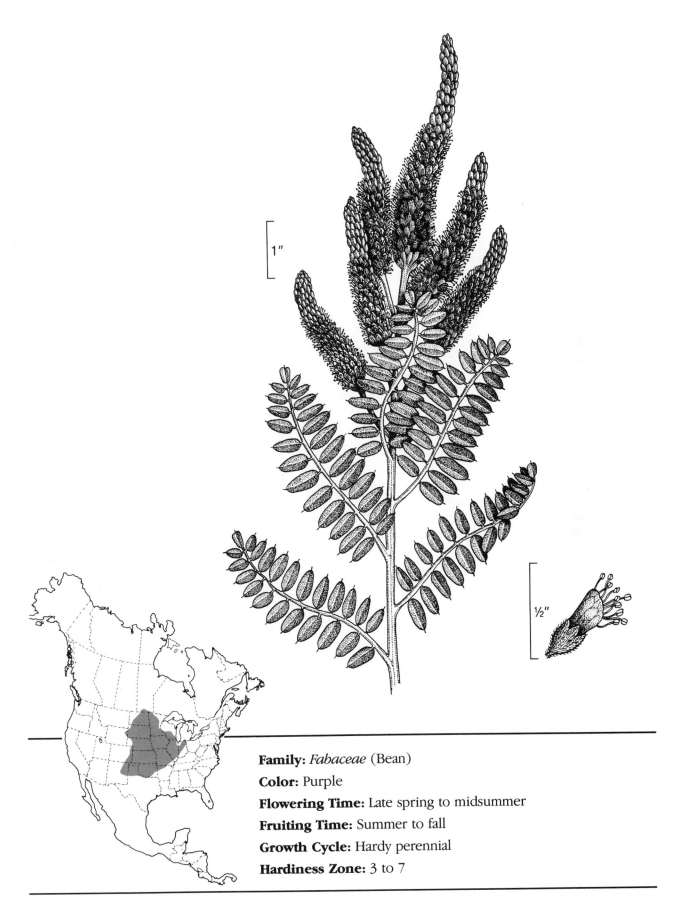

1"

½"

Family: *Fabaceae* (Bean)

Color: Purple

Flowering Time: Late spring to midsummer

Fruiting Time: Summer to fall

Growth Cycle: Hardy perennial

Hardiness Zone: 3 to 7

LEADPLANT *(Amorpha canescens)*

Canada anemone

Anemone canadensis

This is one of the easiest of the northeastern wildflowers to grow and is an excellent plant to fill in open or partially shaded areas. Canada anemone is a hardy perennial which grows 1–2 feet tall. The stalkless leaves surround the stems, and the long-stemmed single flowers have 5 white, unequal-sized, petallike sepals, which surround the rich yellow stamens and pistils in the center. The flowers are usually 1–2 inches in diameter and produce a burrlike cluster of flattened, ¼-inch fruits with long beaks. The root system of the plant is extensive and was used medicinally by Native Americans.

CULTURE Canada anemone grows best in open, sunny locations or in partial shade. While it grows most robustly in soils with moderate moisture and neutral conditions (pH 6–7), it is not at all choosy about soils and can even be found growing along roadsides in the northeastern U.S. Often Canada anemone will naturalize too easily and quickly crowd out other wildflowers in the garden. It is usually prudent to confine the plant with 6-inch plastic or metal strips buried at the soil surface. As clumps of anemone become crowded, flowering may decrease. If this occurs, divide the plants in the fall.

PROPAGATION Canada anemone has no difficulty propagating itself once established. The easiest way to start the plant is to obtain a division of the rhizome in the early spring or fall when it is dormant. Each piece of rhizome should be several inches long and have good roots and buds visible. Plant the segments a foot apart and no more than ½ inch deep, with the bud just at the soil surface. Seeds should be gathered when mature in the summer and planted in the location in which you desire the plants to become established. Usually the seedlings will mature and produce flowers within two years.

COMPANIONS Grow it alone!

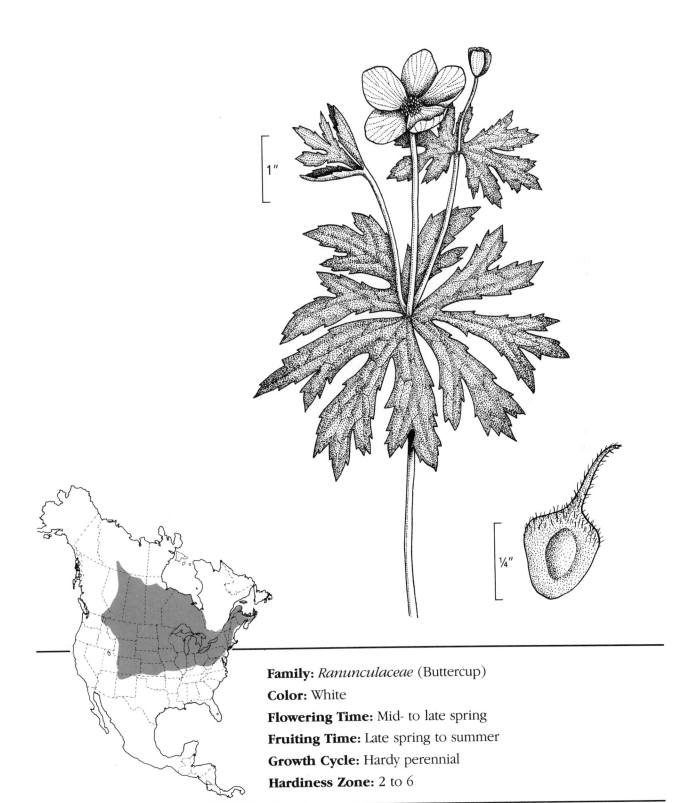

1"

¼"

Family: *Ranunculaceae* (Buttercup)

Color: White

Flowering Time: Mid- to late spring

Fruiting Time: Late spring to summer

Growth Cycle: Hardy perennial

Hardiness Zone: 2 to 6

CANADA ANEMONE *(Anemone canadensis)*

Pasqueflower
(Prairie smoke, windflower)

Anemone patens

A harbinger of spring on the North American prairies and tundra, the pasqueflower blooms are often seen in the matted remains of the previous year's foliage. They are low plants, rarely exceeding 6 inches in height. The finely divided, deeply lobed leaves are covered by long, silky hairs, which give the plant a silvery sheen. The leaves arise from a brown root crown and expand after the flower is open. The solitary, 2–3-inch flowers have 5–7 pointed, petal-like sepals, which range in color from lavender to pale blue to white and surround the many golden stamens and pistils in the center of the flower. The long plumes of the seedlike fruits give rise to one of pasqueflower's other common names, prairie smoke. Pasqueflower's root system is fibrous and possesses enormous regenerative capacity. Both roots and foliage contain an acrid, alkaloid substance, anemonine, which is poisonous to livestock.

CULTURE This hardy perennial grows well in full sun to very light shade, and although it inhabits areas that may become very hot during the summer, it achieves most of its growth during the cool of the spring and fall. Pasqueflower requires a well-drained soil, and once established it can tolerate fairly dry conditions during the summer by becoming dormant. Sandy loams are perfect; the pH should be close to neutral, between 6 and 8.

PROPAGATION Pasqueflower is best propagated from seed. The seeds benefit from a short period of cold, damp stratification, but will germinate without the treatment. This plant is a bit difficult to establish directly in prairies that already support dense stands of grass, but it can easily be raised in a nursery bed for the first year and then transplanted to the desired location. In the fall, place mature seeds in flats filled with sand or sandy loam. Cover the seeds with ⅛ inch of sand, cover with mulch, keep moist, and leave out for the winter. Remove the mulch in the early spring. Stratified seeds planted in the spring will germinate in 1–2 weeks, and plants will reach 3–4 inches by summer. Keep the seedlings under nursery conditions, free from competition with other plants, for the first year. Mulch well each fall and remove some of the mulch in the spring. Seedlings usually take 2–3 years to mature and flower.

Pasqueflower can also be propagated by divisions or cuttings of the roots made in the early spring or late fall. Root segments should be several inches long, planted 1 inch deep, and kept moist until young plants emerge and become established.

COMPANIONS Leadplant, butterfly weed, rattlesnake master, bitterroot.

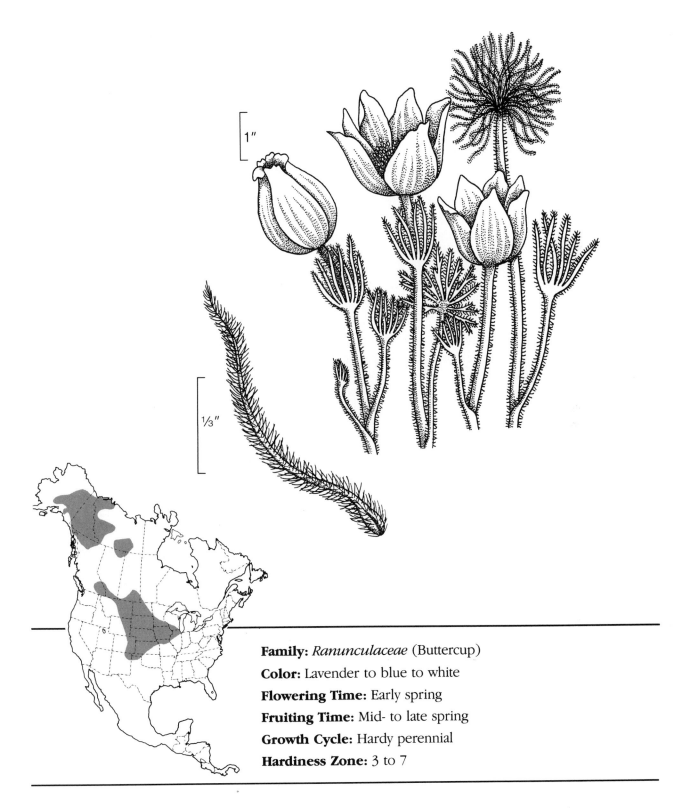

1"

⅓"

Family: *Ranunculaceae* (Buttercup)

Color: Lavender to blue to white

Flowering Time: Early spring

Fruiting Time: Mid- to late spring

Growth Cycle: Hardy perennial

Hardiness Zone: 3 to 7

PASQUEFLOWER *(Anemone patens)*

Groundnut
(Wild bean)

Apios americana

The groundnut, a member of the pea family, is a hardy perennial climbing vine. Since the 1600s it has been grown in Europe for food and for bees, but is infrequently cultivated in its native North America. The stems are long and twining and may reach a height of 1–2 feet as they climb along the ground or over shrubs in their path. Groundnut has compound leaves, with 5–7 leaflets, and compact clusters of fragrant, nectar-rich, pealike, brownish purple flowers. The flowers develop into 2–3-inch pod fruits which contain ¼-inch, black, rectangular seeds. Since this species tends, in New England and to the north, to have 3 sets of chromosomes rather than the usual pair, it does not produce viable seeds in the northern part of its range. Its reproduction in this region is solely by vegetative means from its tubers, which frequently are transported by rivers. The numerous walnut-sized tubers are edible and taste like green peas, giving this plant its common name. In the autumn the top of the plant dies back as the tubers enlarge.

CULTURE

The groundnut spreads rapidly from underground stems and may need to be contained if it encroaches on other plants in a wild garden. Its habit of quickly climbing over low shrubs makes it an ideal plant for the edges of clearings, trellises, or areas that need to be covered in a hurry. It grows best in open to partially shaded locations with soils that are moist during the growing season. Groundnut will grow under a variety of soil conditions, ranging from moderately acidic to neutral (pH 5–7), as long as moisture is available.

PROPAGATION

The best way to propagate groundnut is from divisions of the tubers in the fall. Dig up underground stems and separate the tubers, or obtain nursery planting stock. Plant 2 or 3 tubers together in holes that are 3–4 inches deep and spaced 2 feet apart. Seeds can be planted in either the fall or the spring, about ¾ inches deep in the permanent location where the plants are desired. Since the seeds from the northern part of the range are sterile, make sure you obtain seed from plants grown south of New York. Plant the seeds in clusters of 4–5, and keep them moist but not wet until the seedlings become established. Groundnut usually has little difficulty in forming nitrogen-producing nodules when propagated by tuber division. If inoculation of seeds is required, use cowpea *(Vigna)* rhizobia (Nitragin-type EL).

COMPANIONS

Not for this one!

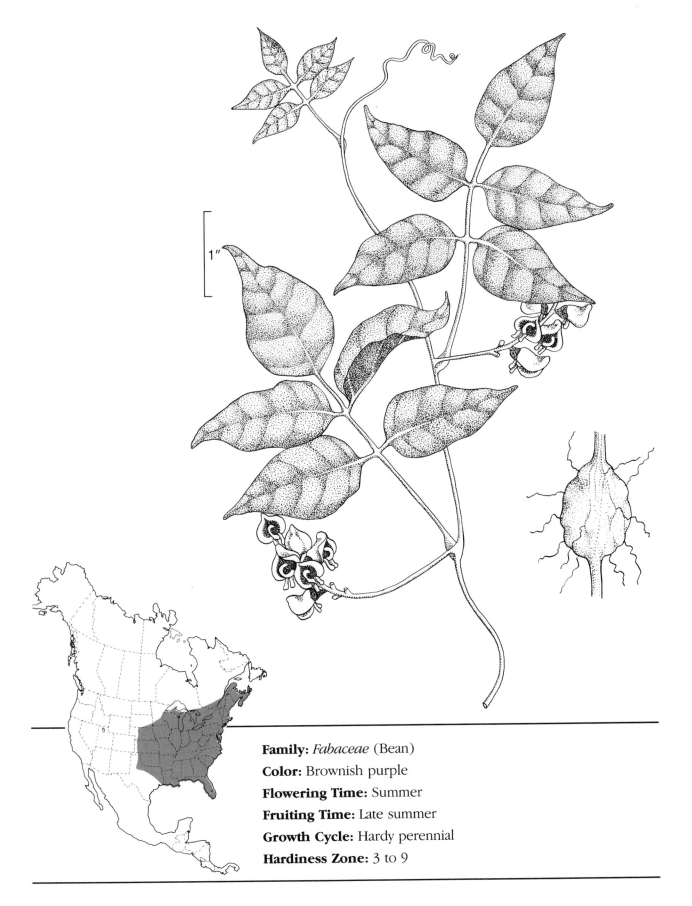

Family: *Fabaceae* (Bean)

Color: Brownish purple

Flowering Time: Summer

Fruiting Time: Late summer

Growth Cycle: Hardy perennial

Hardiness Zone: 3 to 9

GROUNDNUT *(Apios americana)*

Colorado columbine
(Rocky Mountain columbine)

Aquilegia caerulea

The state flower of Colorado, this columbine is a plant of moist aspen and pine groves. It has 1 or 2 divided, smooth, 6-inch-tall stems; these support the 3-part leaves with rounded, indented leaflets typical of columbines. The wild columbine's flowers are more elegant than those of any garden-variety columbine. Nodding while in bud, the 2–3-inch flowers point slightly upward as they blossom. The most common variety of Colorado columbine has sky blue sepals and white petals, while other varieties are all white or all light blue. The flowers have 5 fused, hooded, blue, petallike sepals with 2-inch-long, knobbed spurs. Inside the sepals are 5 white petals, each with 2 rounded lobes. The petals surround the cluster of many bright yellow stamens and pistils in the center of the flower. This columbine is pollinated primarily by hawkmoths and bumblebees, although some bumblebees take a shortcut. They chew off the knob at the end of the spur on the sepal and consume the nectar at the tip of it without pollinating the flower. The fruit consists of 5 connected pods containing small, round seeds.

CULTURE

Although it is a hardy perennial of the Rockies, this columbine can be easily grown in hardiness zones 2 to 7. It should be planted in full sun to partial shade in locations receiving at least several hours of sun each day. The soil may range from rocky to sandy to loamy and should be moist but not overly wet during the growing season. Colorado columbine does best in neutral soils (pH 6–8) that have ample organic matter. Before planting, work compost 6 inches into the soil—but don't add so much that you make the soil spongy and slow to drain.

PROPAGATION

Propagation of Colorado columbine is best from seed. Fresh seed should be scratched lightly into the soil in permanent locations, nursery beds, or flats. Since germination is stimulated by light, locate flats in a sunny location and do not plant the seeds deeply. Stratification is not necessary, but chilling (40°F) in moist sand for 2 months will accelerate germination. Germination may take about a month in the spring. Keep the seeds moist until seedlings become established. Some plants from seed may flower the first year, but most hold off until the second year. Colorado columbine may be short-lived and die out after several years. It is wise to treat it as a biennial and plant seeds for two consecutive years. Once established, Colorado columbine will self-seed.

COMPANIONS

Coralbells, wild leek, white baneberry, chocolate lily, Eastern columbine, Virginia bluebells.

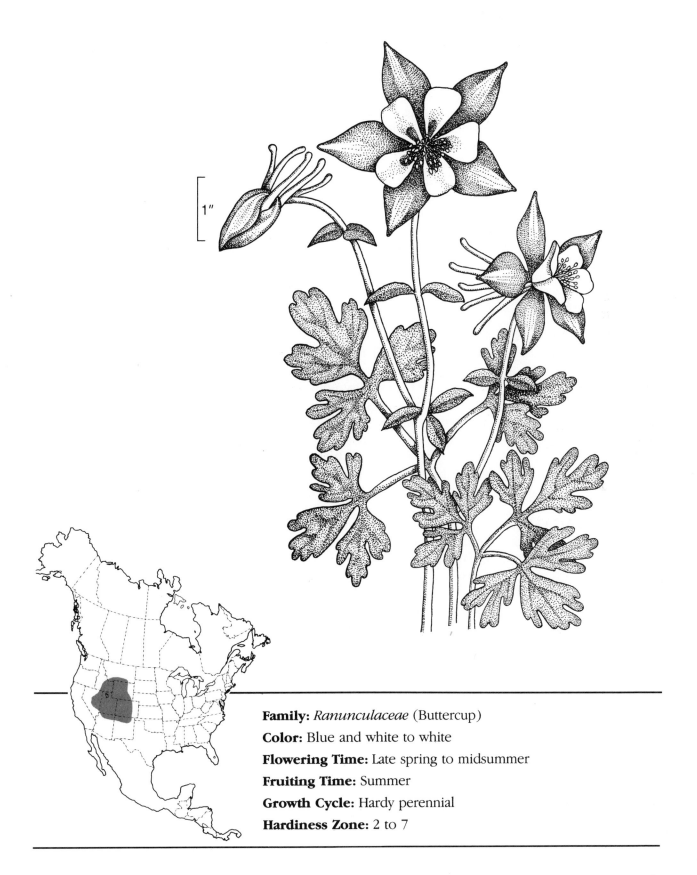

1"

Family: *Ranunculaceae* (Buttercup)

Color: Blue and white to white

Flowering Time: Late spring to midsummer

Fruiting Time: Summer

Growth Cycle: Hardy perennial

Hardiness Zone: 2 to 7

COLORADO COLUMBINE *(Aquilegia caerulea)*

Eastern columbine
(Wild columbine)

Aquilegia canadensis

The Eastern columbine is one of the easiest and most beautiful plants to grow in a native-plant garden. A slender, hardy perennial, it reaches up to 2 feet in height. The attractive, rounded, compound leaves are a dull grayish green and divided into threes. The showy, nodding flowers, which may be up to 2 inches across, are borne on leafy stems at the top of the plant and have 5 spurred scarlet petals covering their yellow centers. Inside the spurs are drops of sweet nectar, extracted by bumblebees as they hang upside-down pollinating the flowers. Hummingbirds also frequent Eastern columbine. Some naturally occurring varieties of the species have salmon, pink, or yellow flowers. The fruit is a capsule that becomes erect as it matures; inside its 5 chambers are many small, glossy, black seeds. The gnarled rootstocks of the Eastern columbine tend to be deep-seated.

CULTURE

Eastern columbine is an ideal plant for rocky slopes and a variety of light conditions, from full sun to full shade. This columbine can be grown in prairies and grasslands, if the grass is not too thick, although it is usually grown in woodlands. While the plant is frequently found in limestone-rich soils in the eastern U.S., it can be successfully grown in moderately acid soils; soil pH between 8 and 5 is acceptable. Although moisture is needed for seedlings to become established, the deep rootstock of mature plants enables the Eastern columbine to endure dry spells well. It is an attractive plant for rock gardens, especially where the winters are relatively mild and the foliage remains green.

PROPAGATION

Eastern columbine is most easily propagated from seed; mature rootstocks are difficult to divide and transplant. For seeds to germinate properly, they must be stratified in moist soil for 3–4 weeks at 40°F or below. Germination will then occur in 3–4 weeks if seeds are held at 70–80°F temperatures. Perhaps the easiest way of planting the seed is to clear a small area where you want the plants to become established and to scratch the seed into the soil with a garden rake. Then cover the area with a light mulch of maple, birch, ash, or other deciduous leaves. Or in the fall, seeds can be sown ¼ inch deep in flats, covered with a thin layer of light soil and mulch, and then left outdoors for the winter. After seedlings have become sturdy the following spring, they may be carefully transplanted to permanent locations. Plants will usually produce flowers the second year. Once established, columbine will self-seed readily and require little further care.

COMPANIONS

Bloodroot, wild ginger, hepatica, wild leek, Colorado columbine, spring beauty.

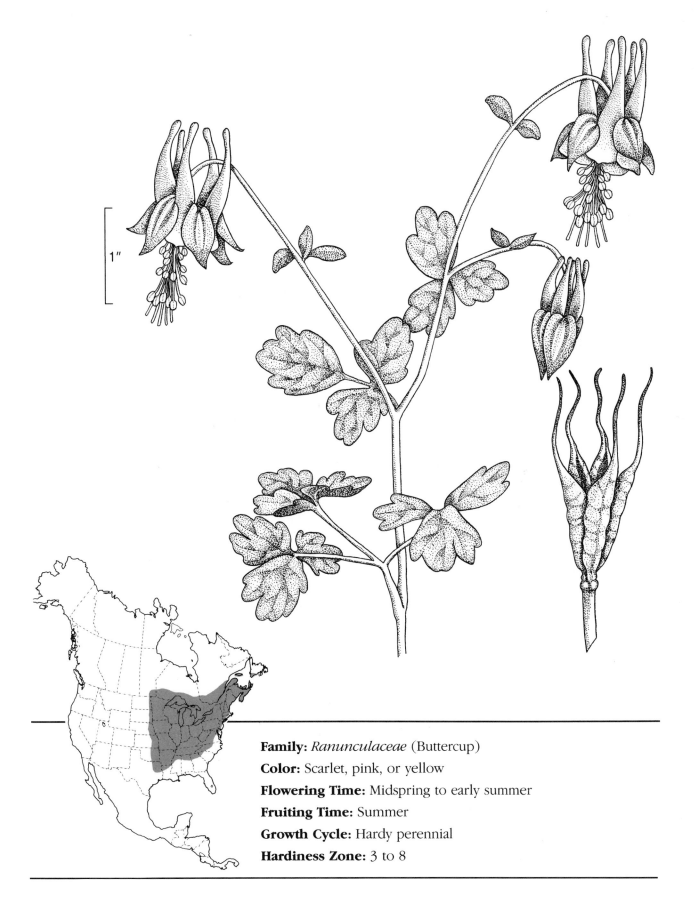

1"

Family: *Ranunculaceae* (Buttercup)

Color: Scarlet, pink, or yellow

Flowering Time: Midspring to early summer

Fruiting Time: Summer

Growth Cycle: Hardy perennial

Hardiness Zone: 3 to 8

EASTERN COLUMBINE *(Aquilegia canadensis)*

Prickly poppy

Argemone munita

Ranchers might think it odd to include in this book a poisonous "weed" that invades dry rangelands in the Southwest. The 1–3-foot, sometimes purplish, branched stems and their clasping, lobed leaves have a yellow sap containing a toxic alkaloid, isoquinolin. However, the plant's foliage and stems are covered with stiff yellow spines, making them unlikely to be eaten. The many showy flowers, each borne at the tip of a branch, are reason enough for including this plant in the garden rather than leaving it in its home on the range. Although the flower buds and sepals are spiny, the 2–5-inch flowers have 6 white petals the texture of crepe paper. In the center of the flower are numerous yellow stamens surrounding the pistil, with its brown-purple, scallop-edged stigma. The fruit is a bristly capsule, which contains many small (¹⁄₁₆-inch) seeds. At maturity the seeds shake out through the holes in the top of the capsule as the fruit sways in the wind.

CULTURE

Prickly poppy should be grown on dry, sandy to gravelly soils in locations with full sun. It will grow well on better soils as long as they are well drained, and the plant is well adapted to gardens nearly anywhere. While weedy in the Southwest, prickly poppy is usually better behaved in other parts of North America.

PROPAGATION

Propagate prickly poppy from seed. This plant grows as an annual or perennial, depending upon its variety and the growing conditions, but it flowers the first year from seed and can be grown as an annual. No cold treatment of the seeds is needed; simply plant them in the spring ⅛ inch deep where desired. In regions with short growing seasons, seeds can be started in flats indoors in the early spring and transplanted to permanent locations when the seedlings are robust. Once established, prickly poppy may self-seed.

COMPANIONS

Cosmos, blanketflower, standing cypress, showy penstemon, annual phlox.

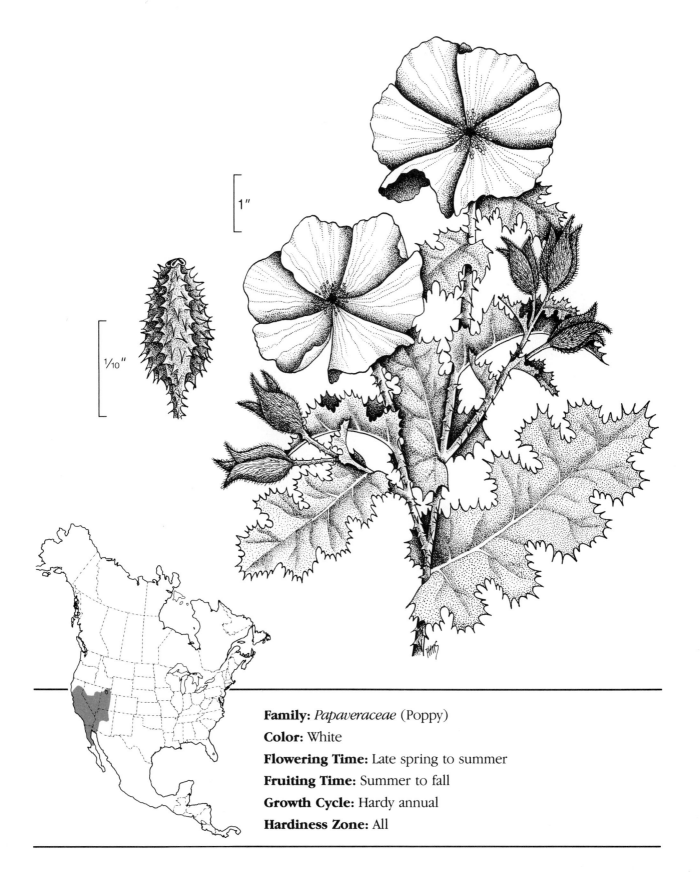

1"

1/10"

Family: *Papaveraceae* (Poppy)

Color: White

Flowering Time: Late spring to summer

Fruiting Time: Summer to fall

Growth Cycle: Hardy annual

Hardiness Zone: All

PRICKLY POPPY *(Argemone munita)*

73

Jack-in-the-pulpit
(Indian turnip)

Arisaema triphyllum

Jack-in-the-pulpit not only has one of the most intriguing flowers, but it also has spectacular clusters of bright orange fruits. With adequate shade and moisture, this hardy perennial may reach a height of 3 feet, although 6–24 inches is more common. The flower consists of a central column, commonly called a "Jack," but botanically referred to as a "spadix." Bearing small male flowers toward the top or small female flowers at the base, the spadix is enveloped by a purple-and-white-striped, hooded petal, called a spathe. The common name is derived from the spathe, which looks like a pulpit in which the spadix, or "Jack," is standing. Jack-in-the-pulpit flowers sometimes change sexes, as mentioned on page 4. As the fruits start to develop, the spathe withers and frequently enshrouds them. The fruits turn from a bright green to red-orange as they mature in the late summer and early fall. The root of the Jack-in-the-pulpit is a 1–2-inch corm that looks like a gladiolus bulb. The corm is edible only after processing to remove the toxic compound calcium oxalate; however, its use by Native Americans as a food plant inspired its common name, Indian turnip.

CULTURE   Jack-in-the-pulpit will grow most vigorously in moist, shady locations, in soils that are seasonally wet. When grown in full sun, the plants tend to be small and stunted. Best results are attained by growing this species in moderately to slightly acidic soils (pH 5–6.5). If you desire female plants, which produce the attractive fruits, keep the soil moist and top-dress annually with compost.

PROPAGATION   Jack-in-the-pulpit is successfully propagated both from seed and by root divisions. Collect fruits in the fall when the berries are red. Remove the ⅛-inch brown seeds from the pulp and plant them ½ inch deep where plants are desired or in flats to be left out over winter. For proper germination the following spring, the seed must be moist-stratified for 6–12 weeks at temperatures below 40°F. Seedlings will mature and produce flowers the second year.

Root divisions can be made in the fall, and the segments planted at depths 3 times their diameters. It is prudent either to wear gloves or to wash your hands immediately after handling the corms since some people develop skin rashes upon touching them.

COMPANIONS   Larger blue flag, turtlehead, trilliums, false Solomon's seal.

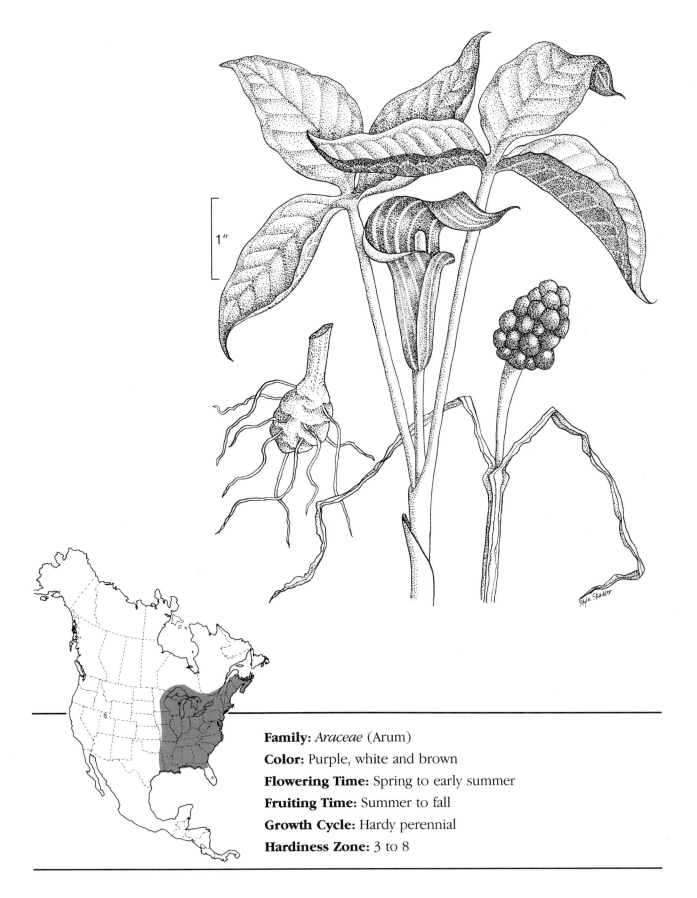

Family: *Araceae* (Arum)

Color: Purple, white and brown

Flowering Time: Spring to early summer

Fruiting Time: Summer to fall

Growth Cycle: Hardy perennial

Hardiness Zone: 3 to 8

JACK-IN-THE-PULPIT *(Arisaema triphyllum)*

Goatsbeard

Aruncus dioicus

Goatsbeard is an herbaceous, hardy perennial that typically grows 4–7 feet tall. Although a member of the rose family, this plant does not look much like a rose. Numerous clusters of tiny male or female flowers are borne on separate plants in spiked plumes at the tops of the main stems. Both the male and female flowers are creamy white, fragrant, and attractive to bees in the late spring. Even after the flowers have shriveled in the early summer, the dense, deep green, compound leaves persist, forming a hedge until the fall when the top of the plant dies back to the roots. Goatsbeard has both rhizomes and a fibrous root system. The seeds are small (less than $\frac{1}{16}$-inch) and contained in small, oval, woody fruits called "follicles," which of course are found only on the female plants. Goatsbeard was introduced into England in the 1600s as a garden flower and is still popular there.

CULTURE

Goatsbeard naturally grows in moist, shady, wooded ravines and limestone bluffs. It can, however, be grown without difficulty in full sunlight and on a variety of soils ranging from moderately acidic to slightly alkaline (pH 5–7.5). The plant needs periodic moisture, and it should be planted in soils that never dry out completely during the summer. Because of its erect form, dense foliage, and large size, goatsbeard makes an ideal plant for low, seasonal screening of locations you'd like to hide or for the backs of gardens. Once established, goatsbeard responds well to thinning every several years. It is hardy to zone 2.

PROPAGATION

Propagation from seeds is quite easy — scratch them into the soil where you want the plant to grow. Root division is an even quicker and easier means of propagation. Roots may be divided when the plant is dormant, either in the early spring or in the fall. The root segments should be placed several inches deep, with the buds barely at the soil surface. The root system of goatsbeard is quite sturdy and benefits from periodic division.

COMPANIONS

If grown in full sun, black-eyed Susan and New England aster. If grown in shade, turtleheads and Solomon's seal. In either case, goatsbeard should be planted behind its companions.

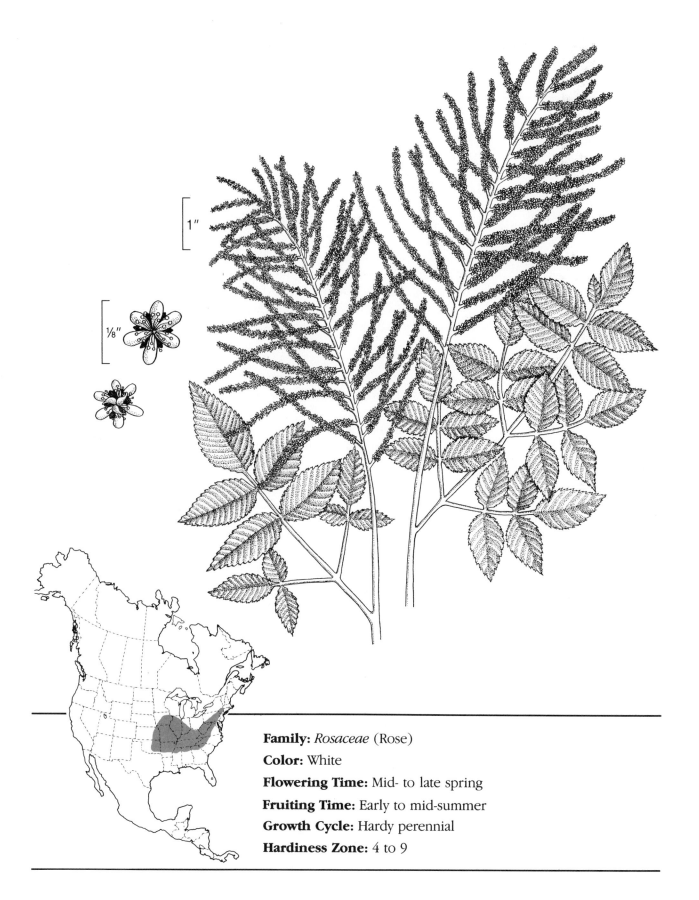

1"

1/8"

Family: *Rosaceae* (Rose)

Color: White

Flowering Time: Mid- to late spring

Fruiting Time: Early to mid-summer

Growth Cycle: Hardy perennial

Hardiness Zone: 4 to 9

GOATSBEARD *(Aruncus dioicus)*

Wild ginger

Asarum canadense

The wild ginger gets its name from the pungent ginger flavor of the edible roots of this hardy, stemless perennial. Wild ginger is far more valued as an ideal ground cover, however, than as an ingredient for making candy. The heart-shaped leaves are a rich medium green and persist throughout the summer. The leaves are quite broad, 7 inches at maturity under ideal conditions, stand 6–12 inches high, and have a velvety texture. The flowers of wild ginger are quite unusual in that they lack petals. The 3 purple-brown, bud-covering sepals open before the leaves have unfurled. Each plant has a single flower, which lies horizontally along the soil surface. Wild ginger is pollinated by beetles that crawl along the ground and into the throat of the blossom, and deposit pollen on the stigma. The fleshy fruit that develops contains several ¼-inch, oval, gray-brown seeds. The seeds are usually picked up by ants, which eat a portion of the seed coat prior to burying the seed.

CULTURE

Wild ginger is usually found growing in rich woods and on limestone ledges. It grows best in partial to full shade, in soils that remain moist but not wet through the growing season. Wild ginger is easily cultivated on a wide range of soils from moderately acidic to alkaline (pH 5–7.5). It can be brought indoors and forced, but requires cold treatment to break the dormancy it enters in the fall.

PROPAGATION

Though wild ginger can be raised from seed, it is often difficult to locate the fruits and seeds among the leaf litter. If you are successful in finding the fruits, collect the seeds as the fruits mature and start to split open. Immediately plant the seeds ½ inch deep where you desire the plants to become established. An easier method of propagation is from the division of the creeping, forking rhizomes. In the fall after the leaves have withered, plant the pieces of rhizomes about ½ inch deep with the bud tip just below the surface of the soil. Mulch with deciduous leaves. Rhizomes can also be divided in the spring, if you can remember where the plants are.

COMPANIONS

Bloodroot, trillium, wild leek, hepatica, columbines.

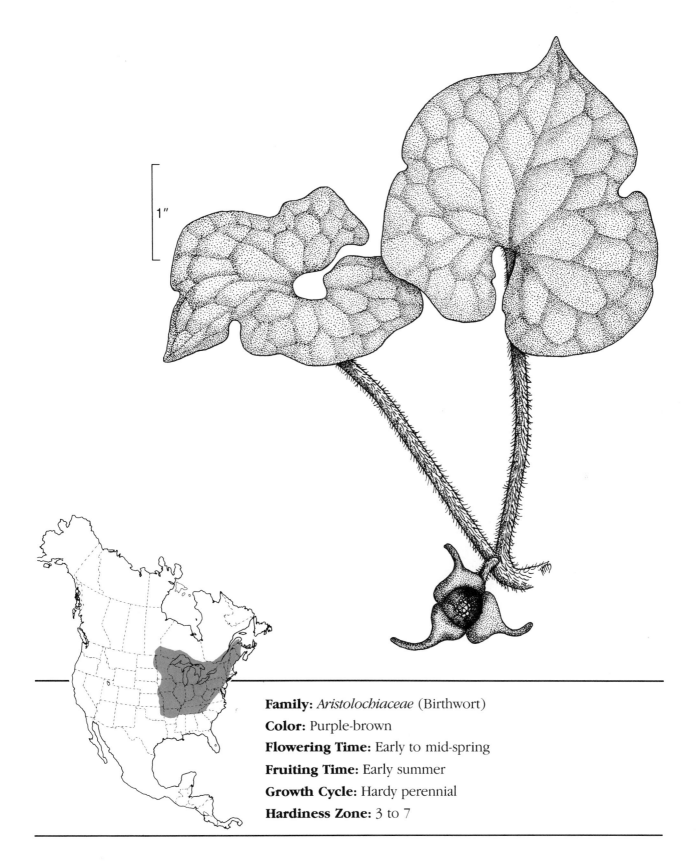

1"

Family: *Aristolochiaceae* (Birthwort)

Color: Purple-brown

Flowering Time: Early to mid-spring

Fruiting Time: Early summer

Growth Cycle: Hardy perennial

Hardiness Zone: 3 to 7

WILD GINGER *(Asarum canadense)*

Butterfly weed

Asclepias tuberosa

(Orange milkweed, butterfly plant, pleurisy root)

The orange, flat-topped clusters of butterfly weed flowers are one of the most striking summer sights in North American prairies. With relatively little effort, this stunning plant can add brilliant color to the gardens of most regions. This hardy perennial is a member of the milkweed family, but differs from many of its relatives by having rough hairy leaves and stems, leaves that are scattered along the stem rather than set in pairs, and the absence of white, milky sap. The 3–5-inch clusters of yellow to orange to red-orange flowers are near the top of the 1–3-foot-high stems. The fused petals of butterfly weed form a crown with 5 projecting horns, and between the horns is sticky pollen, which attaches to the feet of butterflies and other insects that visit the fragrant flowers. Usually fewer than 1 flower in 100 will mature into the fruit, a long pod containing typically flat milkweed seeds with tufts of long, silky hairs to catch the wind. The root system consists of a tuberous rhizome from which smaller fibrous roots extend. The rhizome may become enormous with age. The roots were used as a folk remedy for pleurisy and other lung diseases, thus the common name pleurisy root. Butterfly weed makes a delightful cut flower.

CULTURE Plant butterfly weed in sunny locations with well-drained soils. A sandy loam is ideal, and, once established, the plant endures drought well. Butterfly weed is adaptable to soils ranging between pH 4.5 and 6.5. Pruning the first flower clusters of the summer will provide elegant flowers, prolong the flowering season by 5–6 weeks, and give the plant a pleasant shrubby appearance. Butterfly weed is hardy to zone 3, but protect it in winter in regions colder than zone 6.

PROPAGATION Butterfly weed can be propagated by both seed and root cuttings. Seeds are less work and take about the same amount of time to produce mature plants. Gather seeds in the late summer or early fall. Plant then ½ inch deep in 4-inch-deep pots or deep flats filled with sandy loam, mulch lightly, and leave out over winter. Germination of butterfly weed seeds is enhanced by moist stratification (3 months at 40°F), but there is some germination even without cold treatment. Germination is relatively rapid in the spring when air temperatures rise above 75°F. The seedlings will quickly develop taproots and should not be transplanted to permanent locations until they are dormant in the fall. Many of the plants from seed should bloom the second year. Cuttings of the tuberous rhizome can be made in the fall or early spring. Cut 2-inch sections of the rhizome, each with at least one bud, and plant them 2–3 feet apart with buds 2 inches below the soil surface. Keep the soil slightly moist while young plants are becoming established, but do not overwater, especially in cool weather. If planting in an established grassland or meadow, clear a patch 1 foot in diameter; but once established, butterfly weed will have no problems holding its ground.

COMPANIONS Silky aster, leadplant, purple prairie clover, pasqueflower, black-eyed Susan, rattlesnake master, wild bergamot.

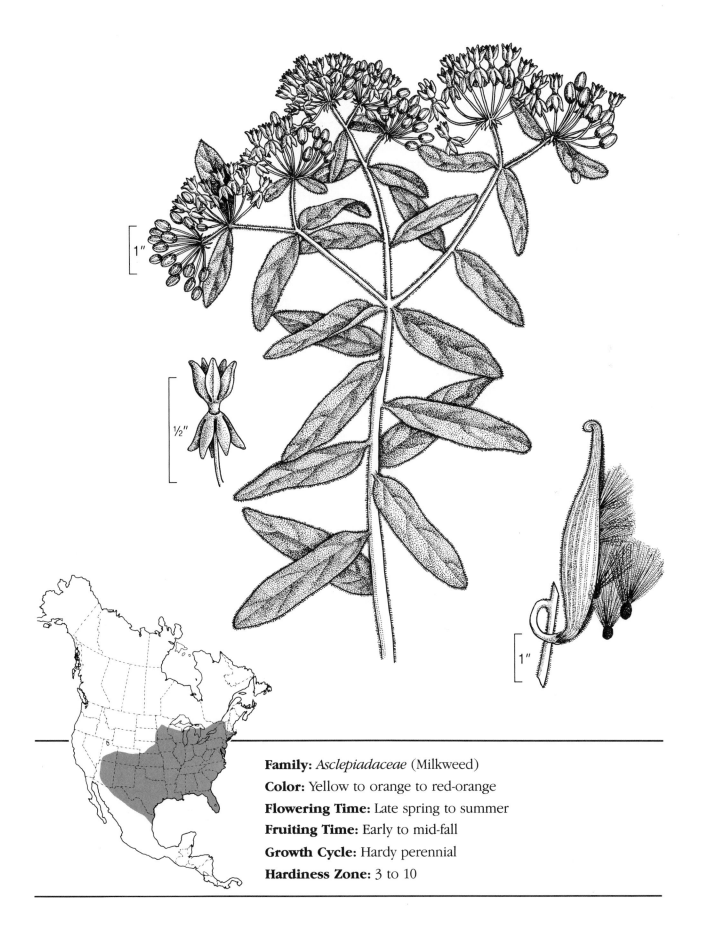

Family: *Asclepiadaceae* (Milkweed)

Color: Yellow to orange to red-orange

Flowering Time: Late spring to summer

Fruiting Time: Early to mid-fall

Growth Cycle: Hardy perennial

Hardiness Zone: 3 to 10

BUTTERFLY WEED *(Asclepias tuberosa)*

New England aster

Aster novae-angliae

Why bother planting a common garden variety of aster when there is this stunning native species? New England asters hardly confine themselves to New England, for they can be found growing in fields from Maine to Colorado and from North Carolina to Kansas, and can be cultivated as a perennial north to hardiness zone 3. This species is the stock from which many of the horticultural varieties of hardy asters have been bred. Usually reaching a height of 2–4 feet, the New England aster has dense leaves covered with bristly hairs and bears clusters of flowers at the tips of leafy branches. The flower-heads have violet-purple ray flowers surrounding the golden yellow disc flowers in the center. The disc flowers develop into ⅛-inch-long fuzzy seeds.

CULTURE

Grow New England asters in full sun to partial shade. They will not grow well if too densely shaded, but are easy to grow in fields and grasslands. While they will grow nicely in soil with acidity ranging from slightly acid to neutral (pH 5.5–7), they grow best where there is ample soil moisture throughout the summer. New England asters can be pruned in the late spring for a more bushy form, and, regardless of shape, they make attractive cut flowers in the fall.

PROPAGATION

If the seeds are sown in the fall, New England asters will usually flower the next fall. They can be grown as annuals in areas lacking a sufficiently cold winter if seeds are cold-damp stratified for 4–6 weeks prior to planting. Stratified seeds have three times the germination rate of non-stratified seeds and can be expected to germinate in 1–2 weeks. The seeds should be planted about ¼ inch deep in mineral soil with no mulch. The best time to propagate by root division is in the late fall. You should divide the roots every few years to keep the plants growing vigorously anyway, so you might as well put the surplus material to good use. Space root divisions a couple of feet apart with the tops of the rhizomes just at the surface of the soil. Once established, New England asters will self-sow, if bare mineral soil and sufficient moisture are available.

COMPANIONS

Black-eyed Susan, Culver's root, spiderwort, butterfly weed.

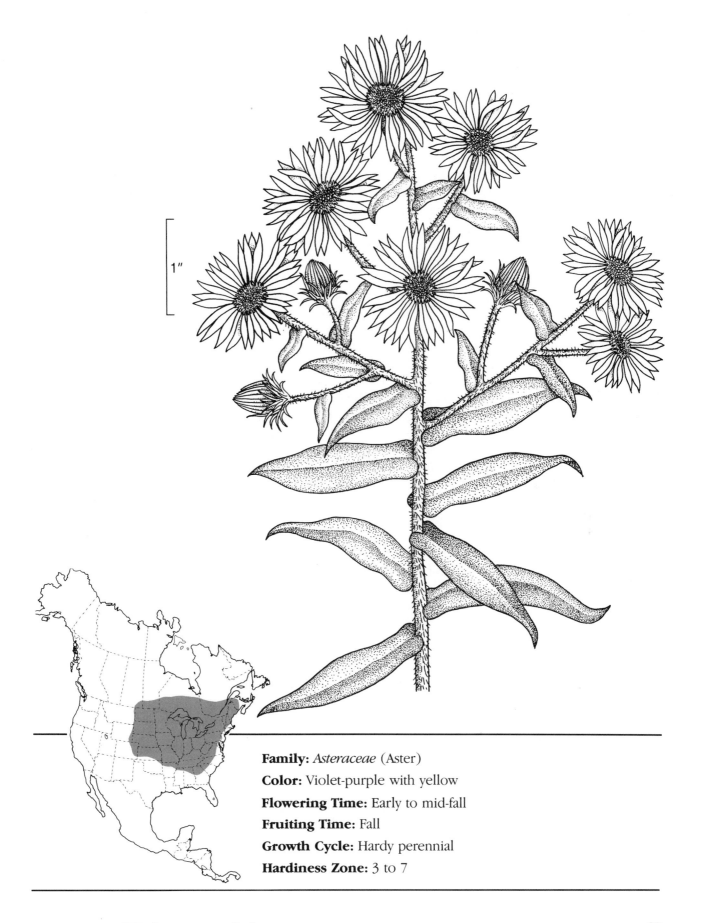

Family: *Asteraceae* (Aster)

Color: Violet-purple with yellow

Flowering Time: Early to mid-fall

Fruiting Time: Fall

Growth Cycle: Hardy perennial

Hardiness Zone: 3 to 7

NEW ENGLAND ASTER *(Aster novae-angliae)*

Silky aster
(Western silvery aster)

Aster sericeus

The silky aster gets its name from the hairy surfaces of its leaves. It is a hardy perennial of the dry prairies, yet it is a pleasant addition to gardens for both its flowers and its attractive foliage. The numerous 1-inch leaves are silvery during the summer and frequently turn bright red in the fall. Small clusters of ½-inch flower heads are borne atop the branched, 1–2-foot-high, smooth stems. The ray flowers are a deep lavender to light blue and surround the yellow disc flowers.

CULTURE

Silky aster grows best in full sun although it can be planted in light shade. Its natural habitat is dry grasslands and woods, where it grows best, yet it can be successfully grown in moderately moist gardens as well. It thrives on soils that are rich in organic matter and slightly acidic (pH 5–6.5). Once established, silky aster competes well with native prairie grasses.

PROPAGATION

Silky aster is usually propagated by seeds, although its roots can also be divided in the fall or spring when the plant is dormant. Collect seeds in midfall when they are ripe, and plant them thickly on the surface of flats filled with a mixture of sand, compost, and peat moss. Cover seeds with ⅛ inch of sand, keep moist, and leave outdoors for the winter. Silky aster seeds benefit from moist stratification (10 weeks at 40°F) and will germinate faster if given a cold treatment. The seeds will quickly germinate as soon as spring has warmed the soil. Thin the seedlings when they are about 1 month old, and carefully transplant them to permanent locations a month later. Some plants may flower the first year; most will wait till their second year. Once established, silky aster tends both to form clumps and to self-seed.

COMPANIONS

Leadplant, purple prairie clover, butterfly weed, pasqueflower, rattlesnake master.

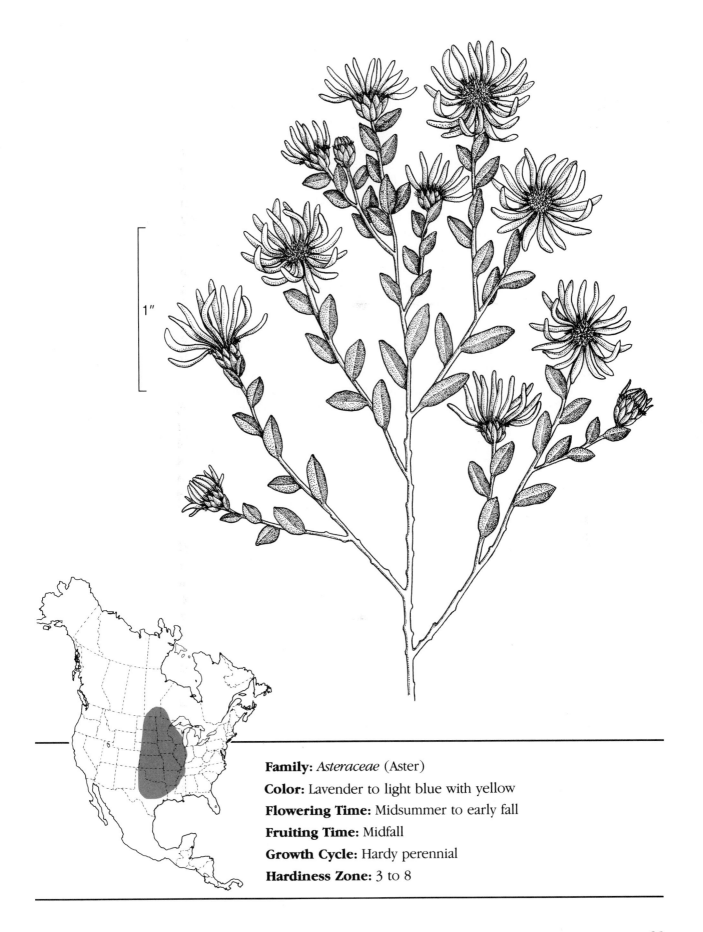

1"

Family: *Asteraceae* (Aster)

Color: Lavender to light blue with yellow

Flowering Time: Midsummer to early fall

Fruiting Time: Midfall

Growth Cycle: Hardy perennial

Hardiness Zone: 3 to 8

Desert marigold
(Desert baileya, wild marigold)

Baileya multiradiata

This woolly plant of the southwestern deserts fills the garden with mounds of brilliant yellow for almost the entire growing season. Both the stems and the broadly lobed, 1½–3-inch-long, gray-green leaves are densely covered with silky hairs. Most of the leaves are toward the base of the stems, the top half of the scape lacking foliage entirely. Single 1–2-inch flower heads top the 12–16-inch stems. The numerous (25–50), yellow, ½-inch-long ray flowers have 3 to 5 teeth on their blunt tips and overlap each other in several layers. As the equally bright yellow disc flowers produce small, grooved, columnar, seedlike fruits, the ray flowers lose their brilliance, droop, and turn papery white. Desert marigold is poisonous to sheep and goats.

CULTURE Desert marigold, being a desert species, must be planted in open, sunny locations on dry, well-drained soils. In humid regions, gritty sands are preferable to clayey loams, though the latter are acceptable in arid areas. This is an excellent plant for rock gardens, providing flowers for many months.

PROPAGATION While desert marigold grows as a biennial or perennial in its native habitat, it should be grown as an annual from seed elsewhere. Plant the seeds ¼ inch deep in the garden in spring, or start them indoors in peat pots filled with sandy loam and transplant them outdoors when all danger of frost has passed. The seeds do not require cold treatment in order to germinate.

COMPANIONS Bitterroot, Missouri evening primrose, Southwestern verbena, pasqueflower, purple heliotrope.

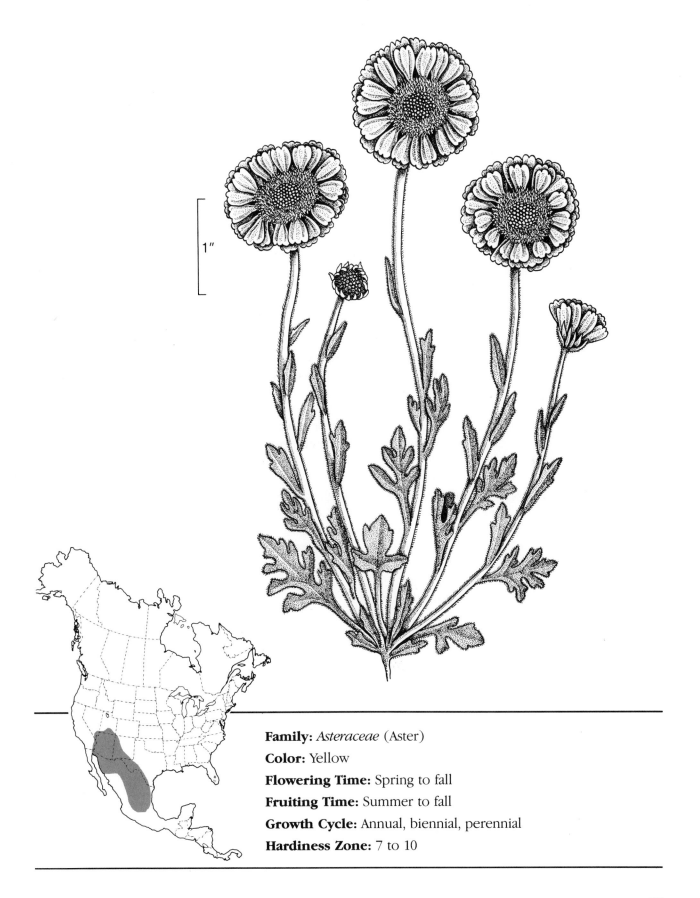

Family: *Asteraceae* (Aster)

Color: Yellow

Flowering Time: Spring to fall

Fruiting Time: Summer to fall

Growth Cycle: Annual, biennial, perennial

Hardiness Zone: 7 to 10

1"

DESERT MARIGOLD *(Baileya multiradiata)*

Golden stars

Bloomeria crocea

These stars come out in the late spring as the coastal grasslands of southern California start to become parched. Golden stars have a single, 4–12-inch, grass-like leaf, which emerges along with the scape from a ⅝-inch-long, crocuslike, fiber-covered, flattened corm. Atop the slender, 1–2-foot-high stem is a loosely domed cluster of 15–60 golden flowers and several leafy bracts. Each of the ½–1-inch-wide, starlike flowers has 6 yellow to orange petals with dark lines running down their centers. The 6 stamens have green anthers and a characteristic cuplike structure at their bases. The pistils have a 3-part ovary and a 3-lobed stigma, features common among members of the amaryllis and lily families. Fruits of golden stars are globular, ¼-inch-long capsules containing ¹⁄₁₆-inch, black, wrinkled seeds.

CULTURE

Grow golden stars in the full sun. The soil can be sandy, gravelly, or clayey as long as it is warm and dry. In humid regions, you may need to increase the drainage of the soil by adding sand, and then keep the soil on the dry side since too much moisture may rot the corm. This perennial is hardy without any additional precautions in zones 9 and warmer. In colder regions, either mulch the plants heavily for the winter or carefully dig up the corms in the late fall, as is commonly done with half-hardy bulbs.

PROPAGATION

Golden stars are best propagated by seed. Even though this plant has a corm, it rarely produces offsets that could be used for propagation. Instead plant the seeds ¼ inch deep in permanent locations, flats, or small pots in the late fall or early spring. No stratification treatment is needed for germination. The seeds germinate readily in the spring, and the mature plants will flower in 3–4 years. To naturalize golden stars in a meadow or grassland, grow them in flats or holding beds for the first year or so and then transplant them as dormant corms 2 inches deep in permanent locations.

COMPANIONS

Sky lupine, purple heliotrope, blue dicks, California poppy, golden yarrow, blazing star, purple annual lupine, owl's clover.

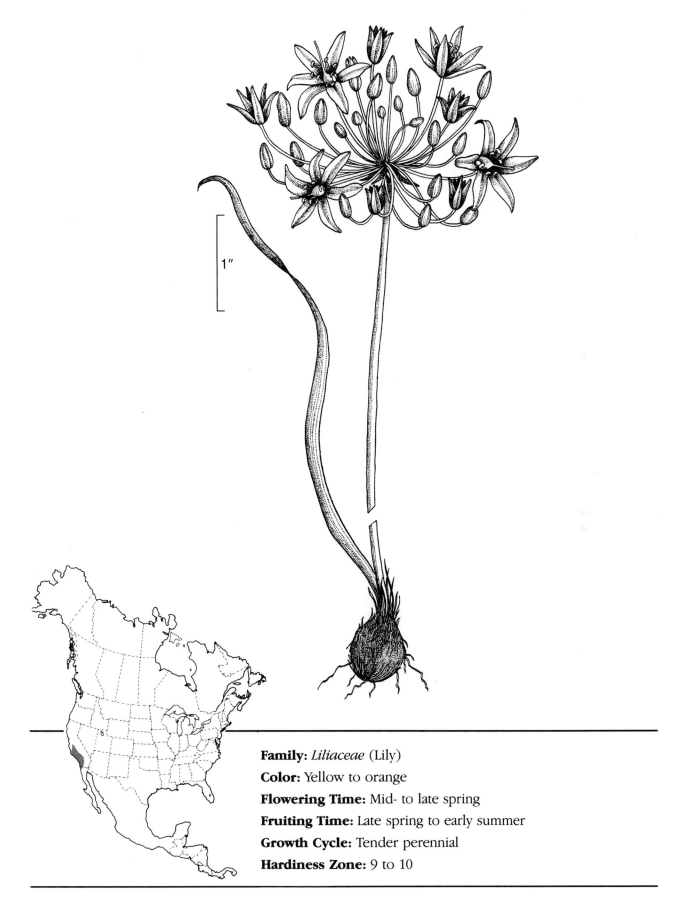

1"

Family: *Liliaceae* (Lily)

Color: Yellow to orange

Flowering Time: Mid- to late spring

Fruiting Time: Late spring to early summer

Growth Cycle: Tender perennial

Hardiness Zone: 9 to 10

GOLDEN STARS *(Bloomeria crocea)*

Blue dicks
(Wild hyacinth)

Brodiaea pulchella
(Dichelostemma pulchellum)

Blue dicks is a spring-flowering perennial common on plains and dry lowlands in California. In many respects it resembles a tall blue version of golden stars. Grasslike, 6–16-inch-long leaves and a smooth, round 2–3-foot-high stem arise from a scaly corm. These corms were eaten both raw and cooked by Native Americans. Up to a dozen violet-blue, ½–¾-inch flowers cluster tightly in a roundish head at the top of the scape, and just below them are several short leafy bracts, sometimes purple. The bases of the 6 petals are fused together to form a ball-like tube. Blue dicks makes an excellent, long-lasting cut flower. Its fruits are ¼-inch-long capsules containing many ⅛-inch seeds. After the fruits have matured in early summer, the leaves wither, and the plant enters dormancy until the following spring.

CULTURE

Blue dicks thrives in dry soils in sunny locations. In its native habitat, this half-hardy perennial is frequently found growing on heavy, gritty clay soils. However, as long as the soil is very well drained, blue dicks is adaptable to normal moisture conditions. If moisture-related problems such as root rot occur, cover the surface of the soil above the dormant corms with plastic sheeting or panes of glass. Although blue dicks does well in hardiness zone 9 and warmer regions, it should be heavily mulched in hardiness zones 7 and 8. In colder regions the corms should be dug up for the winter and stored in a cool, dry place.

PROPAGATION

Blue dicks can be propagated easily by seed or corm divisions. The seed requires no treatment for germination. Plant seeds ¼ inch deep in a sandy loam, and keep moist but not wet. If seeds are sown in permanent locations, the plants should be thinned to 3–5 inches apart by digging up the dormant cormlets and spacing them properly. If flats or nursery beds are used, transplant the dormant cormlets with the same spacing, 2–2½ inches deep. Plants from seed require 2–3 years to flower. Every few years, dig up the mature corms in the fall and carefully divide the offset corms. Plant the divided corms 3–5 inches apart and 3–4 inches deep.

COMPANIONS

Golden yarrow, California poppy, blue-eyed grass, showy penstemon, golden stars.

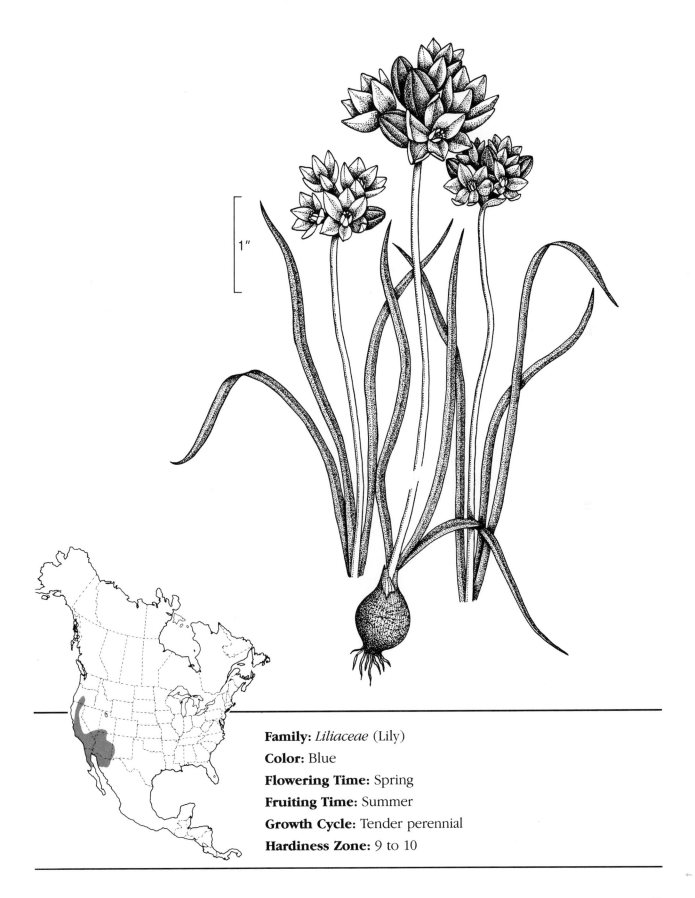

Family: *Liliaceae* (Lily)

Color: Blue

Flowering Time: Spring

Fruiting Time: Summer

Growth Cycle: Tender perennial

Hardiness Zone: 9 to 10

BLUE DICKS *(Brodiaea pulchella)*

American bellflower
(Tall bellflower, American bluebell)

Campanula americana

American bellflower is a relative of the garden species of bluebells and campanulas, but lacks bell-shaped flowers. Instead, this stately annual has flat, 5-petal flowers rising from the axils of leafy bracts and scattered along the top foot or 2 of the unbranched stem. The lowest flowers are the first to open, and blooming then progresses up the stem. The 1-inch flowers are a lovely light blue with white rings in the center and a long style, curved in a subtle S-shape. The bellflower fruit is a capsule with a hole at the tip. When the fruit is fully ripe, the seeds are flung from the capsule whenever the 2–6-foot-high stem sways in the wind. The seeds are elliptical, dark brown, and only $\frac{1}{16}$ inch long. The leaves, lance-shaped with toothed edges, decrease in size up the stem.

CULTURE

Partial or light shade is ideal for the American bellflower, but it will grow in full sun if the soil is not too dry. No special soil conditions are required, although it grows best in soils that are moist, rich in organic matter, and slightly acidic (pH 6–7).

PROPAGATION

Plant the small seeds in the fall or spring by scratching them lightly into the surface of bare mineral soil. The seeds require no chilling, and germination should occur a week or two after the seeds are planted. Keep the soil moist until the seedlings become established.

COMPANIONS

Cardinal flower, Virginia bluebells, showy tick trefoil.

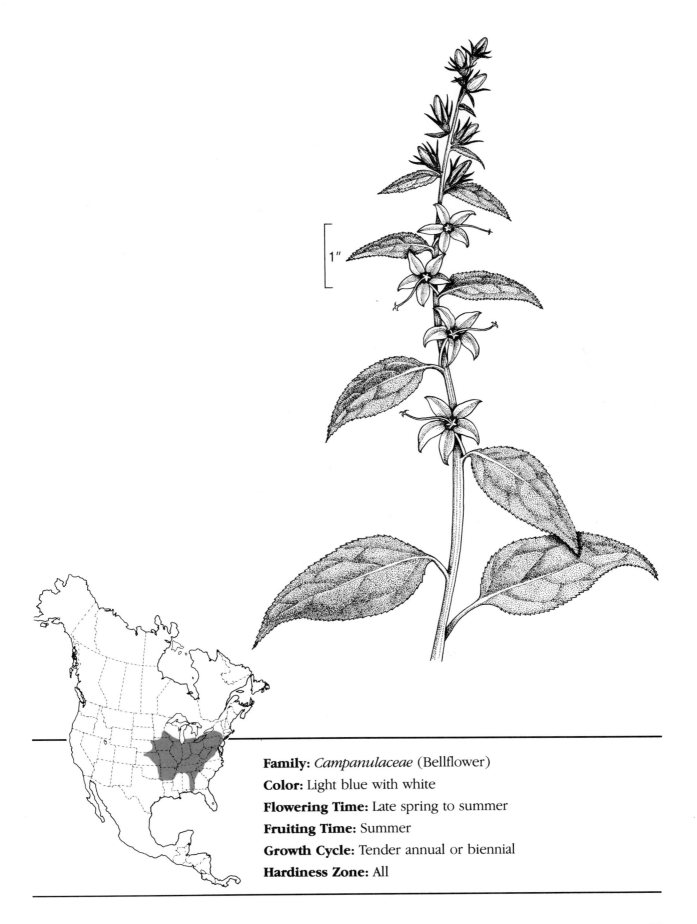

Family: *Campanulaceae* (Bellflower)

Color: Light blue with white

Flowering Time: Late spring to summer

Fruiting Time: Summer

Growth Cycle: Tender annual or biennial

Hardiness Zone: All

AMERICAN BELLFLOWER *(Campanula americana)*

Turtlehead

Chelone glabra

The name turtlehead refers to the terminal spike of puffy-lipped white flowers, which look like the gaping mouths of turtles. Hardy perennials, turtleheads generally grow 1–3 feet high, but may reach 4 feet with ample light and moisture. Pairs of dark green lance-shaped leaves about 5 inches long clasp the smooth stems. The root system is quite fibrous. The 1-inch white flowers, sometimes tinged with pink or yellow-green, are long lasting, and the flowering season frequently lasts into fall. Bees and bumblebees pollinate the flowers, disappearing inside in search of the very sweet nectar. The flower withers late in the season, revealing a green, ½-inch, capsular fruit containing many small, flattened, winged seeds.

CULTURE

The usual habitat of turtlehead is meadows and margins of ditches where the soil is moderately moist or wet. However, this species makes a nice addition to any garden as long as the soil is not excessively dry. Ample applications of compost or rotted manure around the root zone of the plant will provide needed nutrients and conserve moisture during the summer flowering period. Turtleheads are adaptable to a variety of light conditions ranging from full sun to partial shade. The plant is not especially particular about soil conditions, but grows best in moderately to slightly acid soils (pH 5–7).

PROPAGATION

Seeds, root divisions, and cuttings are all successful means of propagating turtlehead. Seeds need cold, damp stratification in order to germinate. If you collect the seeds in the fall, moisten them, place them in a plastic bag, and refrigerate them for 4 months prior to planting in the spring. Direct seeding or seeding in flats in the fall is preferred. Plant about ⅛ inch deep in soil, cover with ⅛ inch sifted compost, and moisten. Plants will germinate in the spring and bloom the second year. Turtleheads self-seed if the soil is moist in the late summer and early fall. The best time to divide roots is early spring or late fall while the plants are dormant. With care, however, the rootstocks can be divided even in early summer. Space root divisions about 18 inches apart and about 1 inch deep with the shoot buds at the soil surface. Make stem cuttings in the summer prior to flowering, being careful to prevent the slip from drying out. Place a 6-inch cutting of the stem into moist sand and provide both support and moisture until the top withers in the fall. Then transplant newly formed rootstock to a permanent location.

COMPANIONS

Cardinal flower, larger blue flag, closed gentian, false dragonhead, Culver's root.

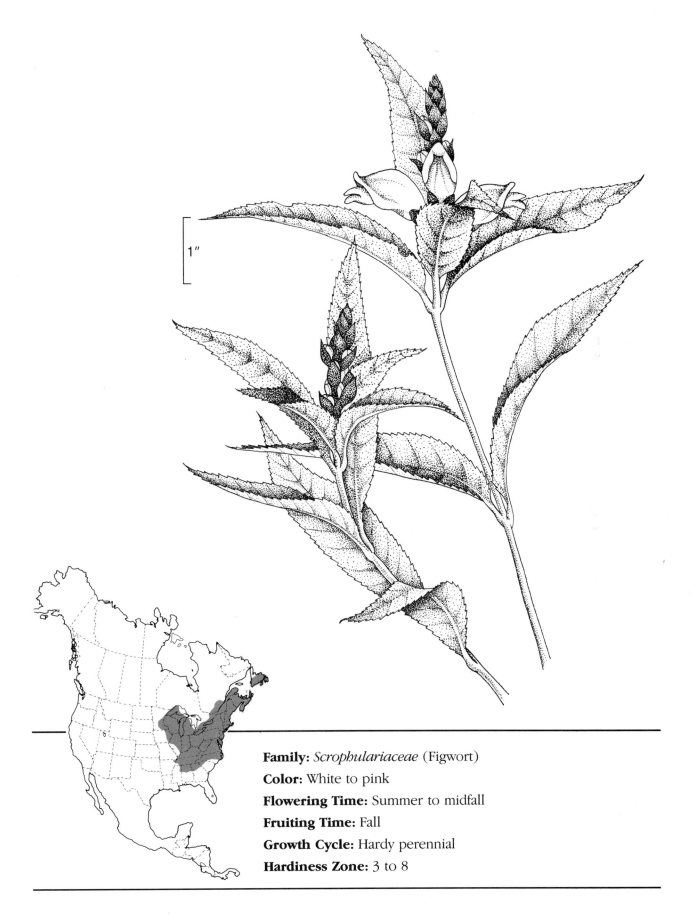

1″

Family: *Scrophulariaceae* (Figwort)

Color: White to pink

Flowering Time: Summer to midfall

Fruiting Time: Fall

Growth Cycle: Hardy perennial

Hardiness Zone: 3 to 8

TURTLEHEAD *(Chelone glabra)*

Farewell-to-spring

(Summer's darling, herald-of-summer, godetia)

Clarkia amoena

Many of this plant's common names, such as farewell-to-spring, herald-of-summer, and summer's darling, refer to its flowering at the end of the spring and beginning of the summer. This annual, native to coastal California and Oregon, is named in honor of Captain William Clark, and not long after the Lewis and Clark Expedition, *Clarkias* were introduced into Europe as garden flowers. Farewell-to-spring stands 1–3 feet tall and has linear, 1–3-inch-long leaves scattered along its stem. In the notches of several of the uppermost leaves are 2–4-inch, pink, cup-shaped flowers with 4 fan-shaped petals, blotched with dark red at their bases. White and lavender forms of this species also occur. Below the flowers are 4 reddish sepals, which often remain attached by their tips even after the flower bud has opened. In the center of the flower a 4-part white stigma tops the pistil, and 8 stamens rest against the petals. The flowers usually open during the day and close at night. The tapering, 1–2-inch-long capsular fruit with 4 grooves contains many tiny brownish seeds.

CULTURE

Farewell-to-spring can grow in full sun to light shade. The soil should be moist but not wet until flowering starts, and then it can be quite dry. Warm, light, sandy loams are best, although heavier soils are tolerated if they are well drained.

PROPAGATION

This hardy annual can only be propagated by seed, but it is easy and generally takes less than 90 days from seed to flowering plant. In its native range seeds can be planted in the fall, but elsewhere they should be planted in the spring as soon as the soil starts to warm. Scratch the seeds into the soil surface in the desired location, and keep the soil moist until seeds germinate a week or two later. No chilling treatment is needed, but germination tends to be most rapid when the temperature is not excessively high. Thin seedlings to 6–9 inches apart.

COMPANIONS

Chinese houses, Douglas's wallflower, sky lupines, owl's clover, purple annual lupine.

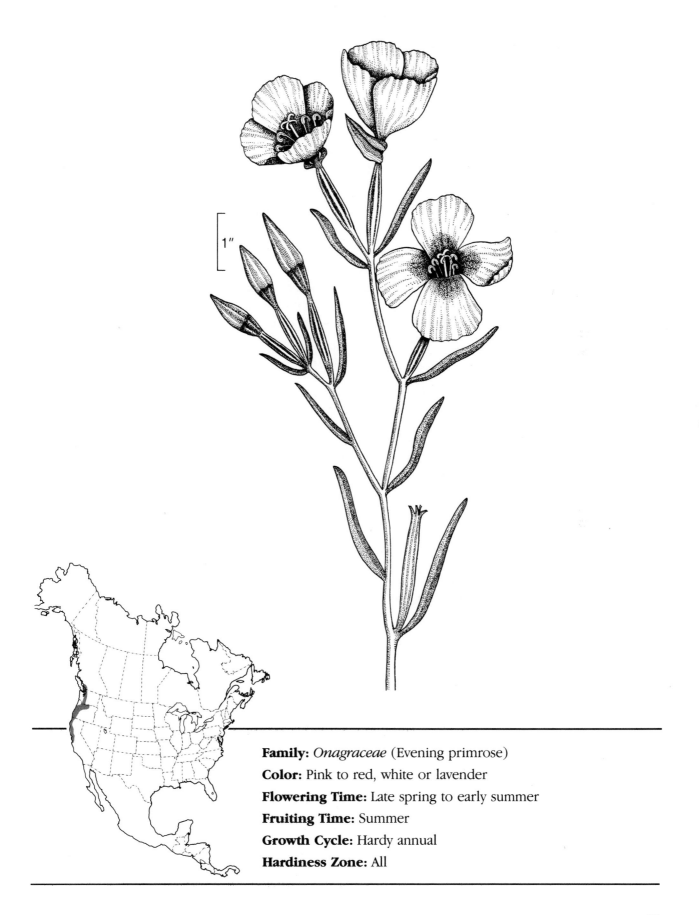

Family: *Onagraceae* (Evening primrose)

Color: Pink to red, white or lavender

Flowering Time: Late spring to early summer

Fruiting Time: Summer

Growth Cycle: Hardy annual

Hardiness Zone: All

FAREWELL-TO-SPRING *(Clarkia amoena)*

Spring beauty

Claytonia virginica

Spring beauties are some of the earliest spring wildflowers to appear in the woods and forests in the East, and they disappear from view just as the forest leafs out fully overhead. The common name is well deserved since this is one of the loveliest, though smallest, of the spring ephemeral plants. The root system of the spring beauty is a deeply buried tuberous corm which looks like a miniature potato an inch or 2 thick. The corm sends up between 2 and 40 succulent shoots, each 5–12 inches high, bearing 2 narrow, fleshy leaves and clusters of showy flowers. The ½-inch flowers have 5 rose-pink petals with darker veins, and last for about 3 days, opening on sunny days and closing at night and on cloudy days. A variety of insects help transfer pollen from the male to the female parts of the same flower and between flowers. The capsulelike fruit matures as the leaves wither in the late spring, and when ripe contains many small, glossy black seeds.

CULTURE   While usually a plant of the woods and forests, occasionally spring beauties are found on lawns and in other grassy locations. During the month or so that they are above ground, spring beauties require full sun or their growth is limited and they lack sufficient energy to produce viable seed. They tolerate a variety of soil conditions (pH 5–7) but do best where there is abundant humus and the soil remains moist rather than dry or wet. While this is a hardy perennial, which can complete its entire life cycle at temperatures between 32° and 40°F, it does not require cold treatment to germinate, to grow, or to flower. When grown in mild climates, however, its growth and flowering tend to be delayed.

PROPAGATION   Since spring beauty is above ground for only 30–40 days a year, it is a good idea to mark the location of the plants so they can be found when you want to propagate them. They are easily grown from seeds, but finding the fruits may be a challenge. Sow seeds in pots or flats at ¼–⅓ inch deep and cover with an equal amount of mulch. Keep the soil moist. Transplant pea-sized corms to their permanent locations, planting them 2 inches deep. Tuberlike corms can be divided in the dormant season. Set pieces, each with at least one bud, in clusters 2–3 inches deep. Mulch well and remove most of the mulch in early spring. Once established, spring beauties will tend to form small colonies through self-seeding and spreading root systems.

COMPANIONS   Hepatica, trout lily, wild ginger.

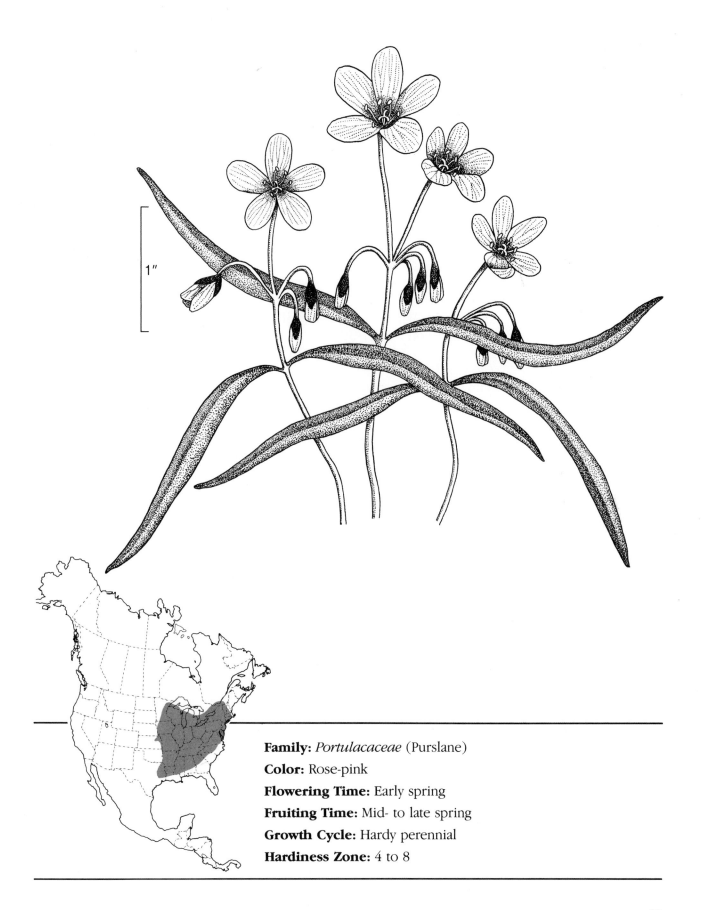

Family: *Portulacaceae* (Purslane)

Color: Rose-pink

Flowering Time: Early spring

Fruiting Time: Mid- to late spring

Growth Cycle: Hardy perennial

Hardiness Zone: 4 to 8

SPRING BEAUTY *(Claytonia virginica)*

Yellow clintonia
(Corn lily, Bluebead lily)

Clintonia borealis

This perennial has attractive features from spring until fall. Once established, it makes a stunning ground cover punctuated by yellow flowers in the late spring and iridescent blue fruits in the summer. Yellow clintonia has 2–4 oval leaves which are usually 6 inches long but may be as large as 10 inches under optimum conditions. These clusters of leaves arise from creeping rhizomes that branch out each summer as they grow along just under the soil surface. The leaves remain green until they wither in midfall, when the next year's shoots extend to the surface of the soil. Clusters of 1–8 flowers are borne on a 6–15-inch stem overtopping the leaves. Each flower has attractive brown anthers and 6 yellow, lilylike divisions. The flowers last for about 2 weeks, after which the developing berry fruit matures to a brilliant cobalt blue, giving rise to the common name bluebead lily. While the young leaves, which taste like cucumber, are edible, the berries are not.

CULTURE Yellow clintonia are difficult to grow at elevations below 1000 feet or where average summer temperatures are substantially above 75°F. They require cool, moist, acid (pH 4–5) conditions in order to flourish. They also thrive in partial to full shade at lower elevations, although in mountain environments they are frequently found growing in full sun. Apply a heavy mulch of mixed pine and deciduous leaves in the fall and leave on during the spring.

PROPAGATION The easiest method of propagating clintonia is from seed. Collect ripe fruit in the late summer or early fall and separate the ⅛-inch, glossy brown, elliptical seeds from the pulp. Plant ¼ inch deep in permanent locations or in flats that are left outdoors over winter. Seeds must be given a cold treatment in order to germinate. Although some seeds may take more than one year, most should germinate the first spring. Seedlings will have a single leaf at first, but with time the leaves will increase in number and size. The young plants take several years to mature and produce flowers. Root division should be done in the early summer as soon as flowering has been completed or in the late fall after the next season's shoots have been formed. Be careful when handling rhizomes and roots, because they are brittle. Plant root section about 1 inch deep with the new shoot tip just at the surface of the soil.

COMPANIONS Trillium, trout lily, yellow fawn lily, bunchberry, elephantheads, shinleaf.

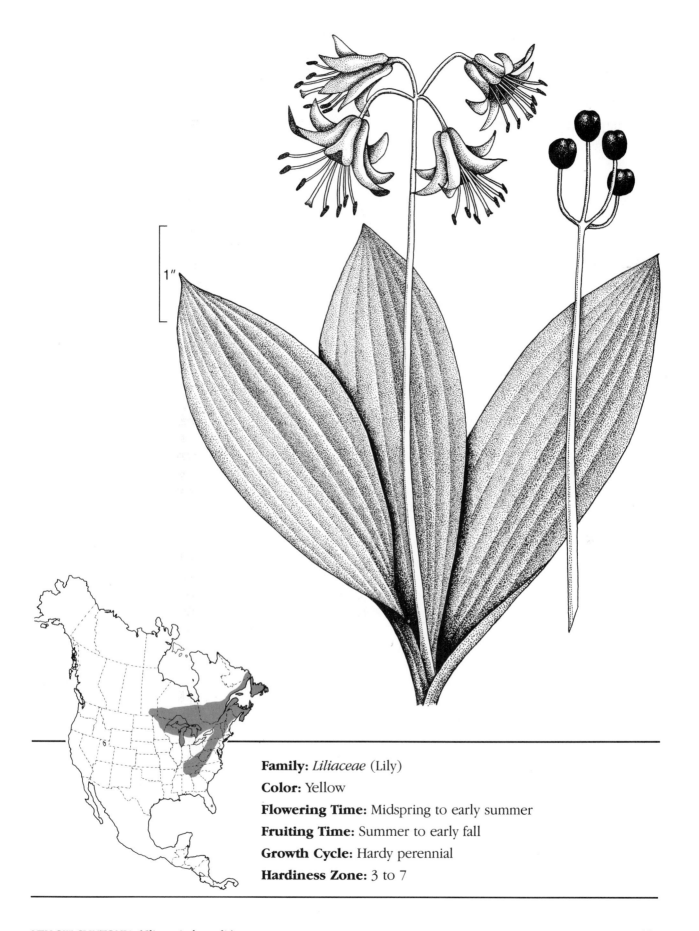

Family: *Liliaceae* (Lily)

Color: Yellow

Flowering Time: Midspring to early summer

Fruiting Time: Summer to early fall

Growth Cycle: Hardy perennial

Hardiness Zone: 3 to 7

YELLOW CLINTONIA *(Clintonia borealis)*

Chinese houses
(Innocence, collinsia)

Collinsia heterophylla

The common name Chinese houses refers to the whorled pagoda effect of the tiers of blue and white flowers encircling the top of this plant's stem. Each of the individual ¾-inch-long flowers has a 2-lobed upper lip of pale blue to white and a 3-lobed, violet to purple lower lip. All the upper lobes have maroon dots at their bases. The middle lobe of the lower lip is more or less folded into a pouch containing the 4 stamens, the long style, and the nectar-producing glands. Chinese houses bear a ¼-inch, round, capsular fruit containing many brown, ¹⁄₁₆-inch ovoid seeds. The bright green, 1–2-inch-long, lance-shaped leaves have toothed edges and clasp the 1–2-foot-high stem. A velvety fuzz often covers the entire plant, including the flowers.

CULTURE Chinese houses grow best in light shade and moist, well-drained soils, although they will tolerate light conditions ranging from full sun to shade. Be sure to provide moderate moisture and shade from the heat of the day if growing this plant in zones 9 or 10. Elsewhere this plant will do quite well under normal garden soil, moisture, and light conditions. In fact, this species used to be a popular garden plant in the East and was called "innocence" even though it frequently escaped the garden and became naturalized far beyond its natural range. A hardy annual, it is ideal for rock gardens, shaded borders, and cut flowers. You can prolong the flowering season by removing the withering flowers before the fruit has set, or by staggering the planting dates.

PROPAGATION Sow seeds in early spring in the East or late fall in the West. If moisture is provided in western gardens, by planting in both the spring and the fall one can get a prolonged season of flowering. Plant the seeds ⅛–¼ inch deep in the desired location and keep moist, but not wet, until flowering is completed.

COMPANIONS Farewell-to-spring, purple annual lupine, coralbells, columbines, Western shooting star.

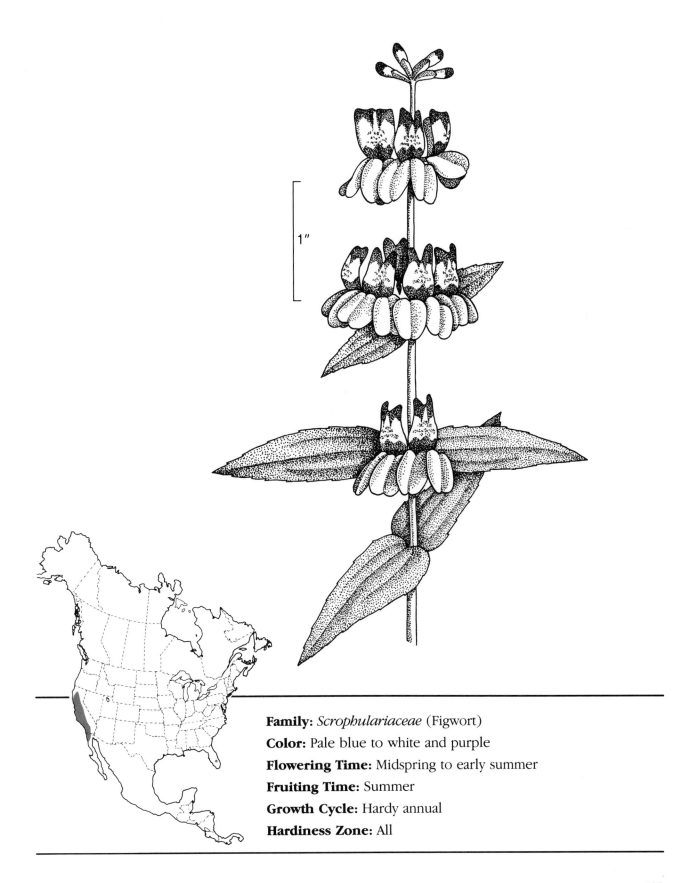

Family: *Scrophulariaceae* (Figwort)

Color: Pale blue to white and purple

Flowering Time: Midspring to early summer

Fruiting Time: Summer

Growth Cycle: Hardy annual

Hardiness Zone: All

CHINESE HOUSES *(Collinsia heterophylla)*

Lance-leaved coreopsis
(Sand coreopsis, tickseed)

Coreopsis lanceolata

The lance-leaved coreopsis is probably the most common coreopsis of the North American prairies. It has long been used as a garden plant and has escaped from cultivation throughout much of the eastern U.S. A member of the aster family, this hardy perennial grows 8–24 inches tall. The smooth, infrequently branched stems become leafy near the ground. The leaves, as one would expect from the common name, are lance-shaped and sometimes have two additional deep, thin lobes at their bases. Blooming begins in late spring as days near their maximum length. The 2-inch, daisylike, yellow flowers are borne on long, smooth, slender stems which make this species an excellent cut flower. The 8 ray flowers are a rich yellow with 4 rounded lobes at their tips, while the disc flowers are a slightly darker yellow. The ⅛-inch-long lance-leaved coreopsis seeds are flat with narrow wings projecting to the side and two short spines extending from the tip. The seed's resemblance to a tick has given this plant one of its common names, tickseed.

CULTURE

Lance-leaved coreopsis requires full sunlight but will grow on moist or dry soils and can tolerate fairly droughty conditions. It is also tolerant of a wide range of soil acidities. Under cultivation it requires little care.

PROPAGATION

This plant is easy to propagate by either seed or root division. The seeds, which do not require a chilling treatment, can be planted ⅛–¼ inch deep in the spring or fall. Germination usually takes place after 2–3 weeks of warm weather in the spring (7–10 days at 70°F). As seedlings are becoming established, they should be thinned to 8–12 inches apart. A few plants may flower the first year, but most will flower the second. Mature plants can be divided easily in the early spring or fall. Divide the roots so that each piece has at least one bud, and plant the sections with the buds 1 inch below the soil surface, spaced a foot apart.

COMPANIONS

Butterfly weed, showy tick trefoil, silky aster, New England aster, rattlesnake master, leadplant.

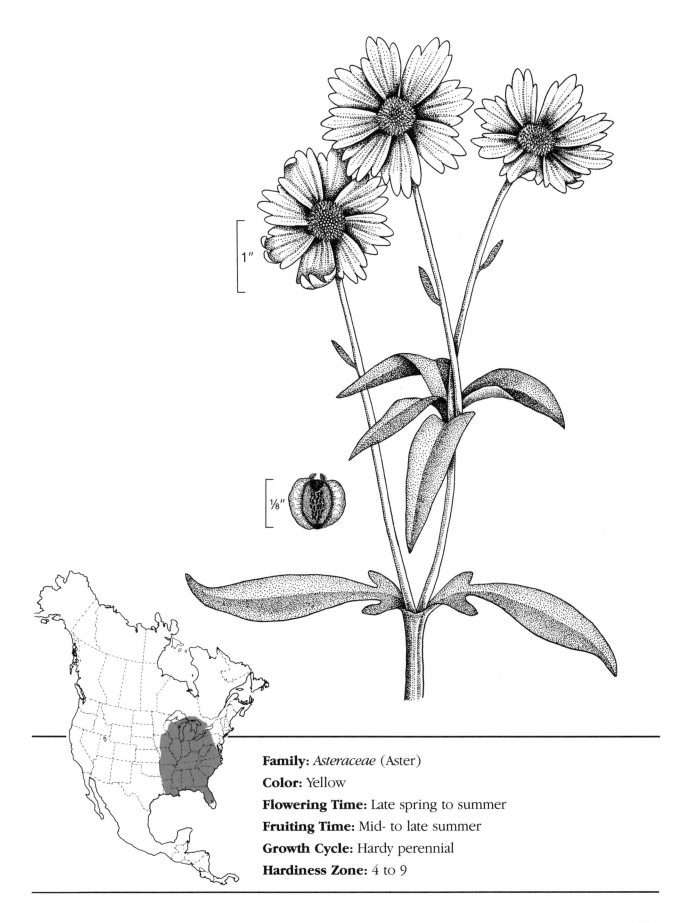

1″

⅛″

Family: *Asteraceae* (Aster)

Color: Yellow

Flowering Time: Late spring to summer

Fruiting Time: Mid- to late summer

Growth Cycle: Hardy perennial

Hardiness Zone: 4 to 9

LANCE-LEAVED COREOPSIS *(Coreopsis lanceolata)*

Bunchberry
(Dwarf cornell)

Cornus canadensis

This relative of the flowering dogwood tree attains a height of only 4–8 inches. Bunchberry spreads by means of slender, forking, woody rhizomes which creep along just under the ground litter and give rise to attractive colonies, forming dense carpets with time. Whorls of 3–9 but usually 4 thick, lustrous, 1–3-inch-long leaves are overtopped by a cluster of small, greenish white flowers. What appear to be 4 creamy white petals are actually bracts that fall away as the fruits develop. The bright red, ¼-inch, berrylike fruits, each with a 2-seeded, light brown stone, are clustered in spectacular bunches. The fruits, often persisting into winter, are edible but unrewarding.

CULTURE Bunchberry grows best in cool, damp locations in regions that do not have excessively hot summers. It is an ideal ground cover where there is partial shade and the soils are acid (pH 4–5) with ample conifer mulch and organic matter. In the sun the plant will do well, but its leaves tend to be much smaller, thicker, and not as deep green.

PROPAGATION Bunchberry may be propagated by seed or division of the rhizomes. Harvest mature fruit in the fall, remove the stones from the pulp, and plant ½ inch deep in a mixture of peat moss and sand. Keep the soil moist. Seeds require cold, moist stratification to germinate, and if planted in flats, they should be left outdoors for the winter. Some of the seeds will germinate 1–3 months into the spring, and the seedlings can be transplanted to permanent locations in the fall. You might want to add new seeds to the flats at this time and leave them out a second winter, because many seeds planted the first year may not have germinated. Flowering usually occurs in the 3rd year. You can divide the rhizomes in the early spring or late fall. Cut 6-inch segments of the rhizome, each with at least one bud. Set the divisions ¼ inch deep, mulch with conifer needles, and keep moist.

COMPANIONS Yellow clintonia, pink lady's slipper, elephantheads.

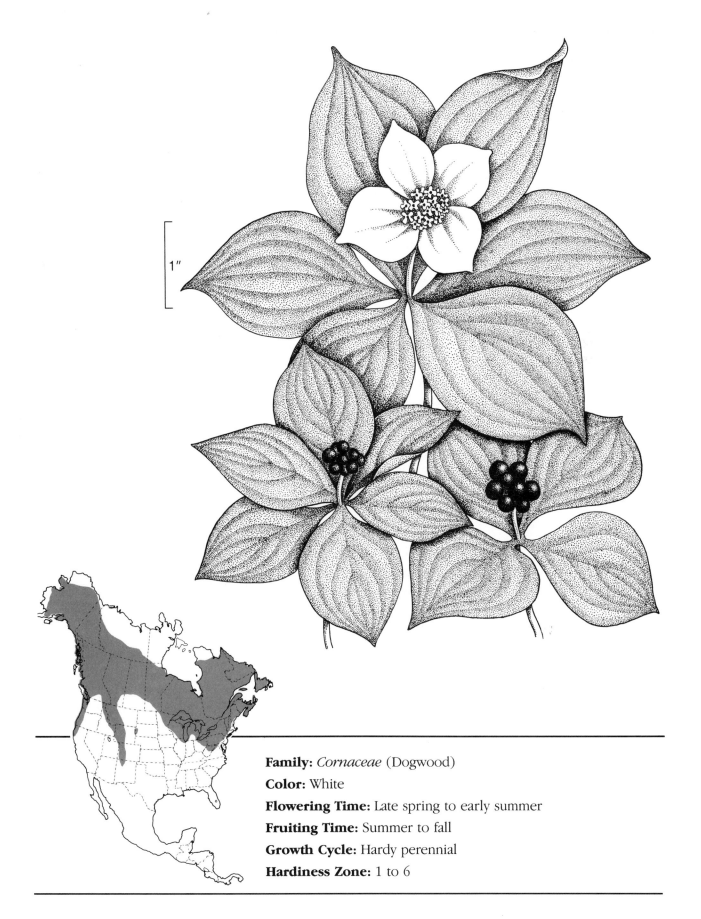

Family: *Cornaceae* (Dogwood)

Color: White

Flowering Time: Late spring to early summer

Fruiting Time: Summer to fall

Growth Cycle: Hardy perennial

Hardiness Zone: 1 to 6

BUNCHBERRY *(Cornus canadensis)*

Cosmos

Cosmos bipinnatus

This annual is a native of Mexico that has found its way farther north and into many seed catalogs. While cosmos may reach 10 feet, stems are more usually 3–5 feet tall. The twice-cut, linear leaves are scattered along the smooth stem. The flower heads are borne atop long stems, a feature that makes cosmos an excellent cut flower. The native varieties have red, pink or white 1–2-inch flowers, but horticultural varieties have flowers up to 6 inches in diameter ranging from the traditional colors to orange and yellow. The ray flowers have a broad petal with 5-toothed tips, while the disc flowers are small and yellow. Each of the narrow, seedlike, ½-inch-long fruits has a beak with three small barbs.

CULTURE Cosmos is one of the easiest wildflowers to cultivate and thrives when neglected, if given a sunny location and dry soil. Not choosy about soils, it even does well where there is little organic matter or native fertility. The best flowers are from plants that have not been fertilized, so lay off the compost or nutrient amendments unless you desire tall plants with a lot of foliage. If you want short, bushy plants, pinch off the leader when the plants are a foot or so high.

PROPAGATION Seed collected in the late summer or fall should be planted in the spring when the soil is warm and danger of frost is past. Plant the seeds ¼ inch deep where you wish the plants to grow, or, where the growing season is short, start the plants indoors in flats or peat pots a month before the usual date of the last frost. Germination takes 1–2 weeks at 65°F, and plants can be transplanted when they are sturdy and there is no danger of frost. Transplant or thin to about 18 inches apart. It takes about 10 weeks from germination to flowering, and though flowering is enhanced by the long nights and short days of late summer, cosmos will bloom even if the days are long.

COMPANIONS Blanketflower, standing cypress, compass plant, lance-leaved coreopsis.

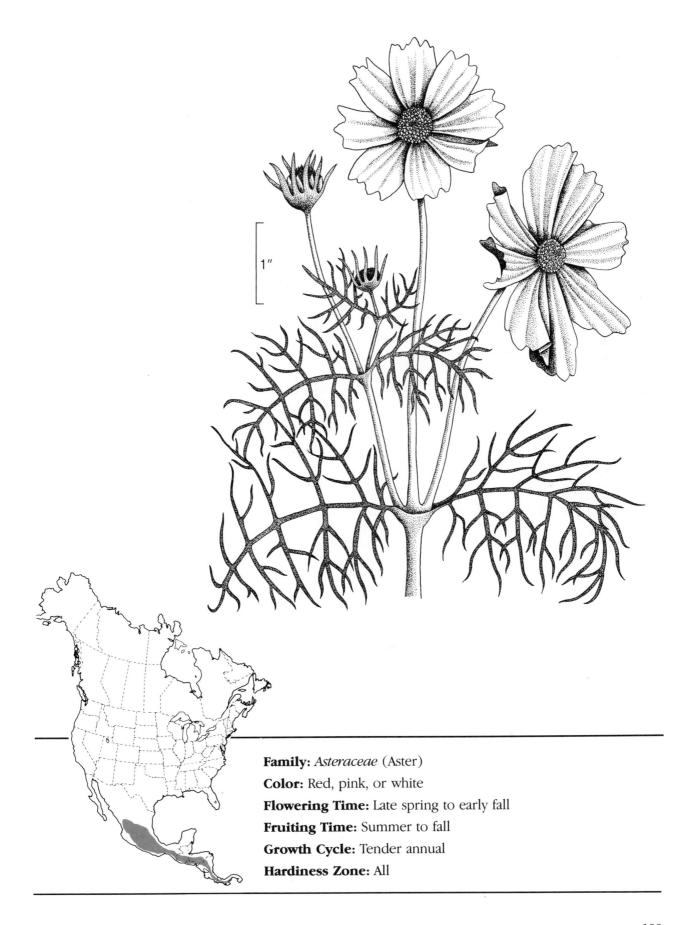

Family: *Asteraceae* (Aster)

Color: Red, pink, or white

Flowering Time: Late spring to early fall

Fruiting Time: Summer to fall

Growth Cycle: Tender annual

Hardiness Zone: All

COSMOS *(Cosmos bipinnatus)*

Pink lady's slipper
(Stemless lady's slipper, moccasin flower, Venus's slipper)

Cypripedium acaule

The pink lady's slipper, although somewhat difficult to grow, is certainly worth the effort. One of the most beautiful of the native orchids, the leafless flowering stalk arises from a pair of 4–15-inch-long basal leaves which are attached to an underground stem. The single, spectacular, 1–2-inch pink flower is reminiscent of a puffy slipper. As the flower swells in the spring it becomes twisted, and the lower petals resemble an inflated sack with a groove down the center. This groove guides bees, flies, and other large insects into the sack to deposit pollen on the stigma. As the insect hunts for the exit from the sack, it picks up a new load of sticky pollen from the anthers and carries it to another flower. The blooms are quite long-lasting, but best not picked. The fruits, which mature during the summer, are filled with small, light, elongate seeds. The root system is fibrous and fragile, and may extend a foot or so beyond the basal leaves.

CULTURE
Pink lady's slippers grow only in soils that are quite acidic (pH 4–4.5 is optimum), but tolerate a variety of moisture conditions from relatively dry to boggy. If your soil is not acid enough, work conifer needles into the soil in spring and mulch again with needles in the fall. Pink lady's slippers are hardy perennials, which grow well in shade, partial shade, and even sunny locations.

PROPAGATION
This is a protected plant in several regions and should never be dug up from the wild. The best approach to growing pink lady's slippers is to purchase plants from reputable commercial growers. In the fall, set the rootstock with the top of the bud just below the soil surface, and mulch well with conifer needles. It is extremely difficult to grow this orchid from seeds, although you may want to try collecting mature seeds in the summer and sprinkling them directly on moistened pine litter where you wish the plants to grow. In early fall the root systems of mature plants can be divided, but use great care because the roots are fragile. Set divided rootstocks about 1 inch deep with the bud ½ inch below the soil surface. Mulch with peat moss or pine needles and keep moist until plants are established.

COMPANIONS
Yellow clintonia, bunchberry.

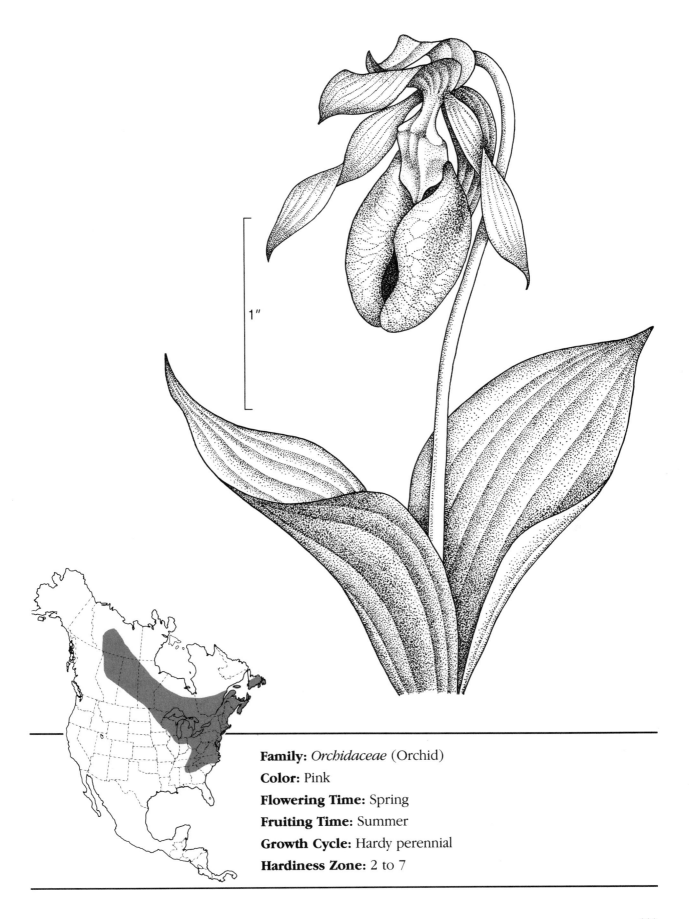

1″

Family: *Orchidaceae* (Orchid)

Color: Pink

Flowering Time: Spring

Fruiting Time: Summer

Growth Cycle: Hardy perennial

Hardiness Zone: 2 to 7

PINK LADY'S SLIPPER *(Cypripedium acaule)*

Showy tick trefoil

Desmodium canadense

This is an aptly named plant of open woods and grasslands of the East and Midwest. Its clusters of flowers are among the showiest of the pea family, its seed segments are reminiscent of small ticks, and its leaves are divided into 3 leaflets, called a trefoil. Showy tick trefoil is a robust hardy perennial with branched stems reaching 4–6 feet in height. Velvety hairs cover the stem and thick, 3-inch-long leaflets, especially toward the top of the plant, and dense clusters of several hundred flowers nod at the top of the stems, the spikes looking flat-topped from a distance. Each pealike, ½-inch-long flower turns from rose-purple to blue with age. At maturity, the thin-walled, velvety, 1–3-inch pod breaks between each of the 3–5 seeds. The pod is covered with minutely hooked bristles so that when the individual segments of the fruit break off, they cling to your clothing or to a passing animal. The root system is a slender, brown, sometimes branched taproot with smaller secondary roots.

CULTURE   Showy tick trefoil grows well in any soil of moderate moisture, in full sun to light shade, and is generally indifferent to soil acidity conditions. Since it is a legume, its root nodules will fix nitrogen from the air and add it to the soil. If you encounter difficulty establishing showy tick trefoil, add an inoculant such as Nitragin-type EL rhizobium. Although the showy tick trefoil may as a young seedling be sensitive to competition from dense grasses, with age it may become large and aggressive, so plant it where there is growing room.

PROPAGATION   Grow showy tick trefoil from seed. The seed does not require any chilling to germinate, but, like many of the legumes, it has a hard seed coat that often slows the germination process by making it difficult for water to enter the seed. The best way to alleviate this problem is to scarify the seeds using sandpaper or to nick the seed coat carefully with a razor or sharp knife. Plant scarified seeds ½–¾ inch deep in the spring. Seeds usually germinate in 2–4 weeks and make rapid growth. If planted in a garden, rather than in grassy locations, the seedlings should be thinned to an 18-inch spacing. Once established, showy tick trefoil will vigorously resprout from the roots if the top is cut, but it is not easy to propagate this plant from root division. Some plants from seed may flower the first year, and most will flower the second.

COMPANIONS   Silky aster, leadplant, lance-leaved coreopsis, butterfly weed, Culver's root.

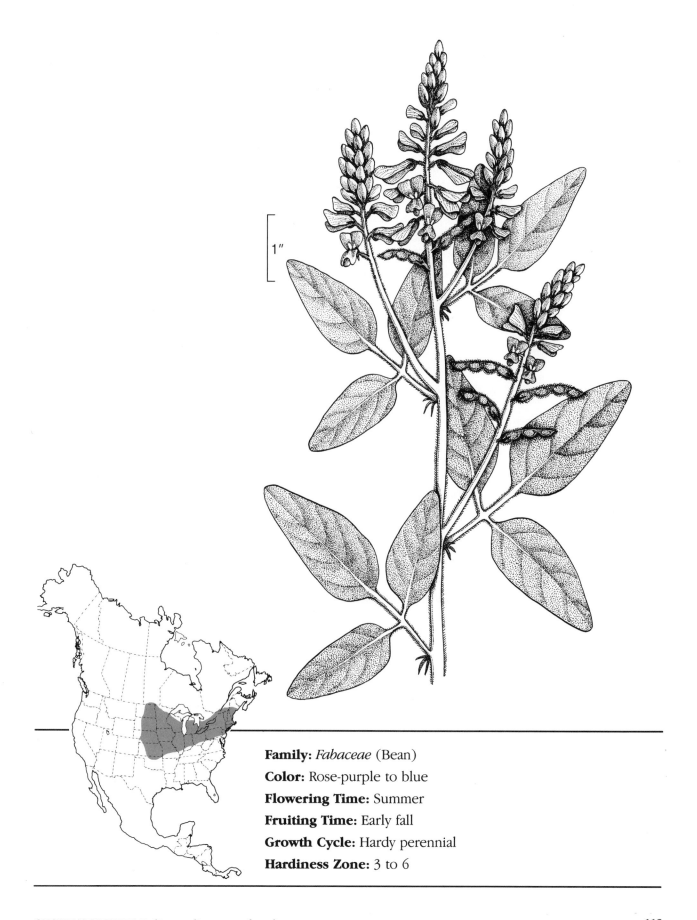

Family: *Fabaceae* (Bean)

Color: Rose-purple to blue

Flowering Time: Summer

Fruiting Time: Early fall

Growth Cycle: Hardy perennial

Hardiness Zone: 3 to 6

SHOWY TICK TREFOIL *(Desmodium canadense)*

Dutchman's breeches

Dicentra cucullaria

The creamy white flowers of this plant, attached to a foot-tall stalk, look like clusters of miniature pantaloons hung upside down to dry. The fleshy flower stalk bears from 4 to 10 fragrant blooms, each with a yellow-cream opening and 2 white spur petals pointing into the air. The flowers last a week or two and are pollinated by queen bumblebees which emerge from hibernation just as the pollen is ripe. Some bumblebees don't bother to enter the flower to obtain the sweet nectar but instead chew holes in the tips of the spur petals. The flower stalks, about 1 foot tall, are surrounded by highly divided gray-green foliage. This foliage dies back in late spring or early summer, and its nutrients and carbohydrates are stored in the white, grainlike tubers that cluster together in a scaly "bulb." The high sugar content in the tubers of this perennial gives it frost-hardiness. The fruit is an oval-shaped capsule containing many tiny, black, glossy seeds, which are usually carried off by ants.

CULTURE While Dutchman's breeches are generally found growing wild in forests and woodlands, they do well under cultivation, especially in soil that is humus-rich and slightly acidic to slightly alkaline (pH 6–8). Plant in shade to partial shade, preferably under maples or other deciduous trees whose leaves form humus rapidly. Moisture should be available, especially in the spring flowering season, but the soil should not be waterlogged. This plant requires 2–3 months with minimum temperature below 40°F in order to emerge in the spring.

PROPAGATION The easiest way to propagate this plant is by division of the scaly bulbs in the early summer to fall. Plant large bulbs about 1 inch deep and smaller bulblets or individual scales of the large bulbs ½ inch deep, mulching with deciduous tree leaves over the winter. It may take several years for the new plants to flower. Propagation from seeds is also possible and requires 2–3 months of moist chilling for germination. As soon as seeds are ripe in the summer, plant them outdoors at a depth of ¼ inch, mulch lightly, and let them overwinter. Since it may take more than a year for the seeds to germinate, if flats are used, let them go for 2 years before you throw out the soil. Expect to wait 3–4 years before seedlings reach maturity.

COMPANIONS Wild ginger, spring beauty, columbine, bloodroot, sharp-lobed hepatica.

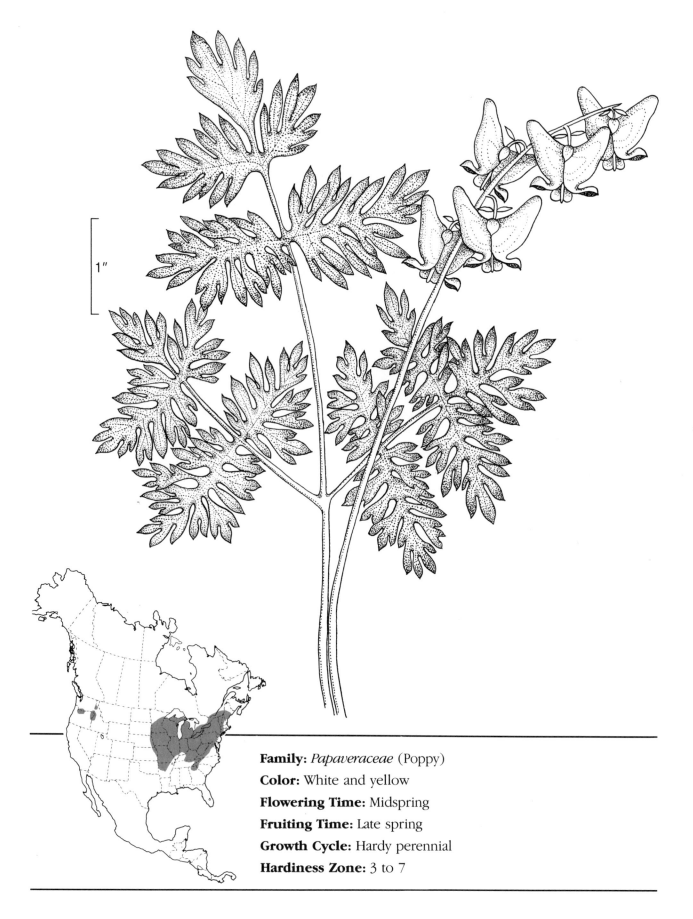

Family: *Papaveraceae* (Poppy)

Color: White and yellow

Flowering Time: Midspring

Fruiting Time: Late spring

Growth Cycle: Hardy perennial

Hardiness Zone: 3 to 7

DUTCHMAN'S BREECHES *(Dicentra cucullaria)*

Western shooting star
(Padres shooting star)

Dodecatheon clevelandii

Resembling miniature cyclamen with pointed centers, the Western shooting stars burst forth in the early spring in the meadows and open woodlands of California's coastal ranges. The smooth or slightly hairy, thick, pale-green, 1½–3-inch-long leaves form a rosette on the ground, out of which rises a 1–1½-foot-high scape bearing 2–16 fragrant flowers with 5 swept-back petals. The flowers range from nearly white through pink to deep rose, but pink is most frequently seen. The bases of the petals have white and yellow bands, and the 5 dark maroon anthers are fused into a tube surrounding the style. As the ½-inch capsular fruit matures and its many small (1/16-inch) seeds ripen, the leaves start to wither and by midsummer no trace of this lovely plant is left above ground. During its dormant period the plant recedes into its fibrous root system underground.

CULTURE Although the Western shooting star grows well under a wide range of light conditions, from full sun to shade, it prefers light shade. In the spring it needs moisture while its leaves and flowers are apparent, but when dormant, this perennial is quite drought resistant and requires very little water. Well-drained but not excessively sandy soils, slightly acid to slightly alkaline (pH 6–7.5), are ideal. Western shooting star is a slow grower, but a nice plant for the rock garden.

PROPAGATION Western shooting star can be propagated by seed or root division. Plant the seeds 1/8–1/4 inch deep in flats, nursery beds, or permanent locations in the fall or spring. Germination does not require stratification, but does need moisture. If in flats or nursery beds, keep the seedlings there until the end of the second year and then transplant them to the desired location. Since the above-ground foliage disappears during the summer, mark the locations of any mature plants you wish to divide, while they are still visible. Divide the rootstocks in the fall, making sure that each piece has at least one bud, and plant the divisions 12–15 inches apart and ½ inch deep. The new divisions should be mulched if planted in cold regions, but remove the mulch in the spring. Plants from divisions take several years to mature and flower, while plants from seed may take 4 or more years.

COMPANIONS Coralbells, chocolate lily, Chinese houses, California poppy.

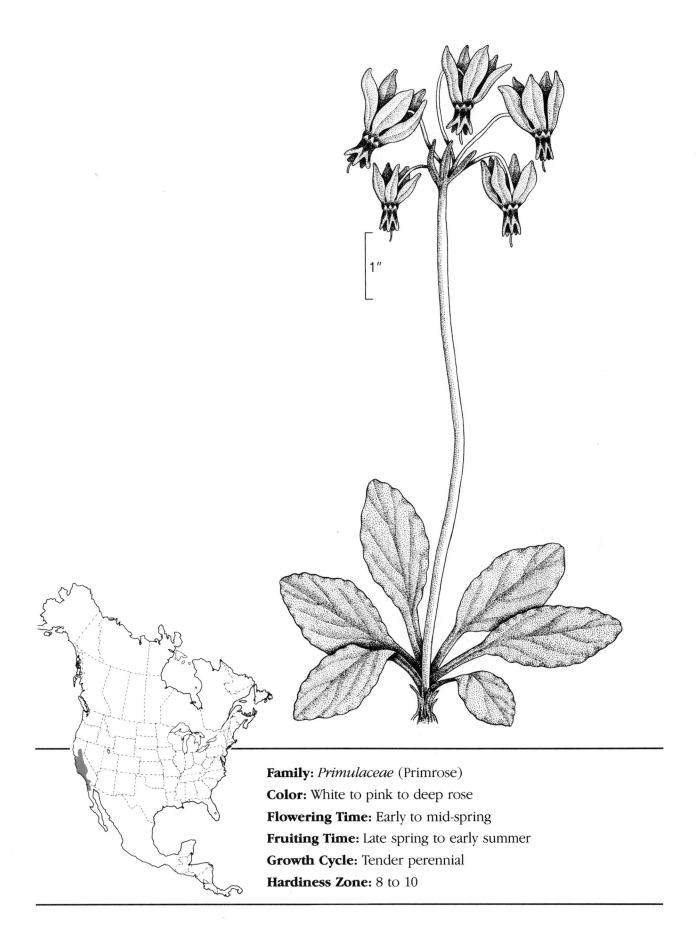

Family: *Primulaceae* (Primrose)

Color: White to pink to deep rose

Flowering Time: Early to mid-spring

Fruiting Time: Late spring to early summer

Growth Cycle: Tender perennial

Hardiness Zone: 8 to 10

1″

WESTERN SHOOTING STAR *(Dodecatheon clevelandii)*

Eastern shooting star
(Midland shooting star)

Dodecatheon media

The shooting stars are among the most intriguing of wildflowers, and the Eastern shooting star is one of the easiest to cultivate. The 3–6-inch-long leaves, which wither by late summer, are entirely basal and have red "petioles" or stems. The 6–24-inch-high flower scape rises out of this rosette of leaves, and clusters of from 4 to more than 100 flowers dangle from the top of the leafless stalk. The 5 pale pink to lilac petals of the ½–1-inch-long flowers are bent backwards like miniature cyclamen, another member of the primrose family. The 5 anthers are fused together in the center of the flower to form a slender, beaklike cone with a dark base and yellow tip, beyond which projects the stigma. The fruit of the Eastern shooting star is a ½-inch capsule, which points upward as it matures. The roots of this hardy perennial consist of a stout rootstock with an extensive network of fibrous roots.

CULTURE

The Eastern shooting star will grow well in light shade to full sun. It is found in open woods and prairies under natural conditions. This plant has a wide tolerance for soil acidity conditions, and can be grown in moist, well-drained soils that are moderately acidic to slightly alkaline (pH 4.5–7.5). They must have sufficient moisture in the spring, but can withstand droughty conditions in the late summer when they are dormant. In regions colder than hardiness zone 6, mulch lightly in late summer and remove the following spring.

PROPAGATION

Eastern shooting star can be propagated by seeds or root divisions. Collect the ripe fruit capsules in the summer and remove the seeds. Plant the seeds thickly in the desired location by scratching them lightly into the surface of the soil, moisten, and leave out over winter. Seeds germinate after moist, cool stratification (2 months at 40°F) and 2 weeks of warm spring weather, producing a fragile seedling with only a few basal leaves the first year. If seedlings are grown in flats left out over the winter, wait until the following summer dormancy period before transplanting to permanent locations. In subsequent years the leaves will increase in number and size, and by the third and fourth year the plant will start to flower. Propagation by root division should be done in late summer or early fall after the leaves have disappeared. During the summer, mark the locations of mature plants you wish to use as propagation stock, since the leaves will be withered by the time you dig the roots. Make cuttings of the rootstock, being sure each piece has at least one bud. Plant the sections with the buds about ½ inch below the soil surface and mulch well, removing most of the mulch in the spring. This method will produce flowering plants in about 2 years.

COMPANIONS

Purple prairie clover, spiderwort, false Solomon's seal, bluets, columbines.

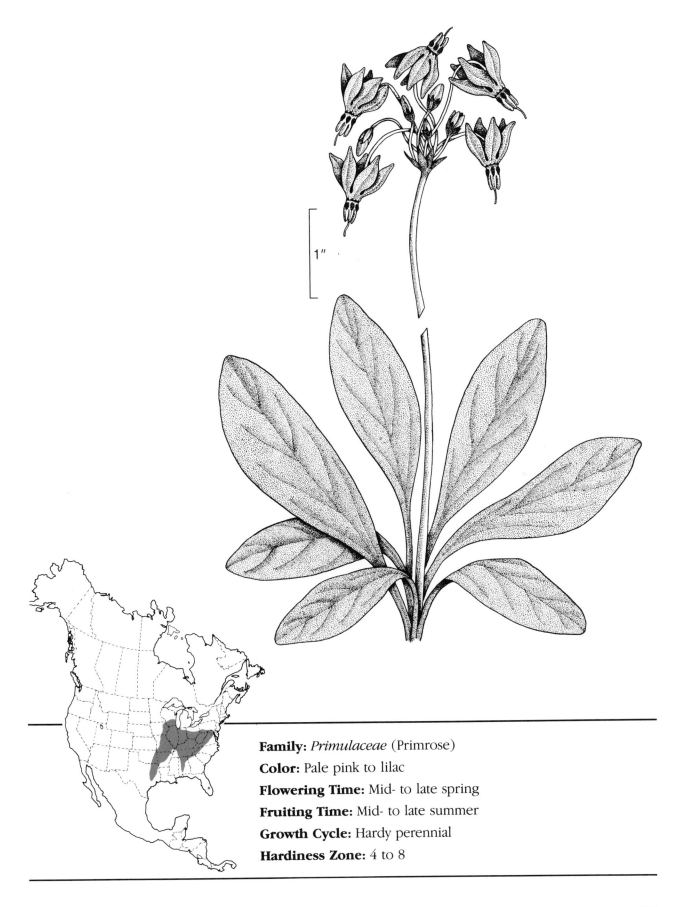

Family: *Primulaceae* (Primrose)

Color: Pale pink to lilac

Flowering Time: Mid- to late spring

Fruiting Time: Mid- to late summer

Growth Cycle: Hardy perennial

Hardiness Zone: 4 to 8

EASTERN SHOOTING STAR *(Dodecatheon media)*

Purple coneflower

Echinacea purpurea

Although purple coneflower is frequently included in flower seed catalogs around the world, it is native to the prairies of the Midwest and the dry open woods of the southeastern U.S. The smooth 2–5-foot-high stems have scattered, rough, 3–8-inch, toothed leaves which become smaller and narrower toward the top of the plant. Purple coneflower is an excellent cut flower, since the single flower heads are borne on long stems and are long lasting. The 2–4-inch flower heads have 12–20 dull purple to crimson ray flowers with drooping petals. The ½–1-inch domed disc is covered with spiny, golden-purple flowers, giving this plant its scientific name *Echinacea* from the Greek word for sea-urchin. The 4-sided, ⅛-inch seeds, shaped like small pyramids, remain attached to the disc, forming a "seed head" after the ray flowers have withered. This hardy perennial has thick, black, edible roots which reportedly increase the body's resistance to infection. Tinctures of the root have been used in folk medicine as a remedy for corns.

CULTURE   Grow purple coneflower in full sun or very light shade. It is not particularly choosy about soil conditions and will even tolerate dry soils, although it does best when the soil is moderately moist but well drained, and rich in humus.

PROPAGATION   This plant can be propagated by seed or root division. Collect the mature discs in the fall and break them open to extract the seeds. Sow seeds ¼ inch deep in permanent locations or in flats that should be left out over winter. After moist stratification, germination occurs in about 2 weeks at 70–75°F. If flats are used, seedlings should be transplanted after the first growing season. Generally the plants start to flower the second year, but if started early, they sometimes flower the first year. Make root divisions in early spring, and plant divided root sections with buds just barely under the soil surface.

COMPANIONS   Black-eyed Susan, lance-leaved coreopsis, butterfly weed, leadplant.

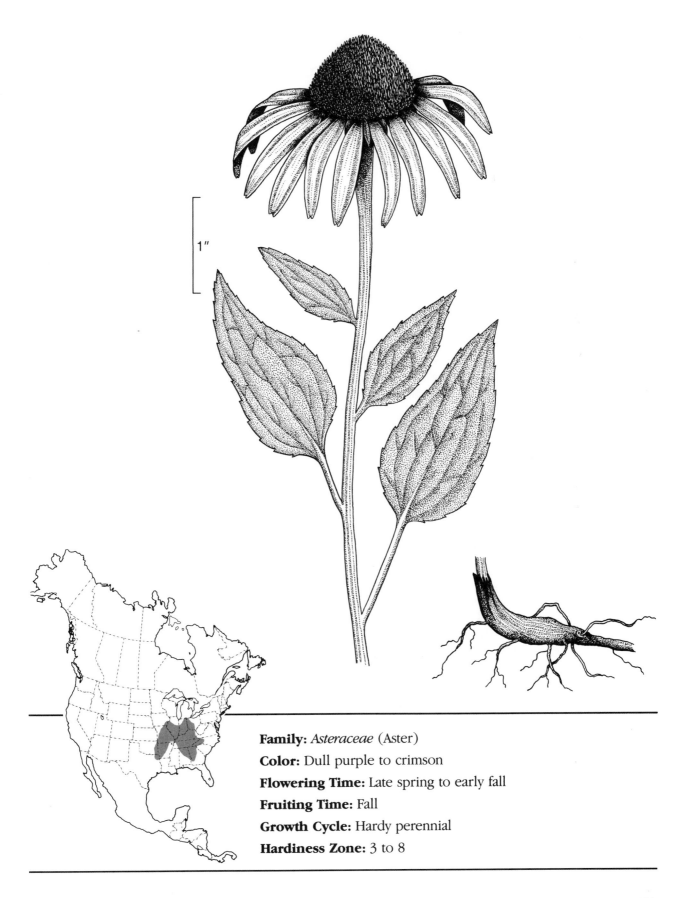

1"

Family: *Asteraceae* (Aster)

Color: Dull purple to crimson

Flowering Time: Late spring to early fall

Fruiting Time: Fall

Growth Cycle: Hardy perennial

Hardiness Zone: 3 to 8

PURPLE CONEFLOWER *(Echinacea purpurea)*

Golden yarrow
Eriophyllum conferiflorum

(Long-stemmed eriophyllum, yellow yarrow)

The English translation of the scientific name *Eriophyllum* is "woolly leaf." The woolly fuzz that densely covers the leaves and stems of this Southwestern California perennial was collected by Native Americans and used as a cure for rheumatism. Its several, 1–2-foot-high, erect, herbaceous stems arise from a woody base. The gray-green, 1–1½-inch-long, erectly clasping leaves are dissected somewhat like the leaf of the garden tansy, and have edges that curl toward their woolly undersides. The leaves are more numerous toward the base of the stem. At the top of the stem are flat-topped clusters of bright golden-yellow yarrow-like flower heads, each head being only ½ inch across. Golden yarrow is not really a yarrow but another member of the aster family. The 4–6 ray flowers have ¼-inch-long round-tipped petals and surround the several disc flowers in the center of the head. Golden yarrow's ⅛-inch seedlike fruit has 4 distinct sides.

CULTURE Golden yarrow should be planted in well-drained, dry soils in sunny locations. The most important aspect of successfully growing this perennial is not over-irrigating when temperatures are cool. Golden yarrow withstands the summer heat and droughty conditions of its native habitat very well; in humid regions, however, the soil may require the addition of coarse sand or gravel. This tender perennial can be grown in hardiness zones 9 and 10, but in zone 8 a heavy winter mulch, to be removed in the spring, is needed. In colder regions, even with a heavy mulch, growing this plant is chancy, unless you want to grow it in a large pot and bring it indoors over the winter.

PROPAGATION Even though golden yarrow is a perennial, its woody stem base and root crown make propagation by division difficult. It is easily propagated by seeds, however, which require no chilling treatment. Plant the seeds in the fall ¼ inch deep and provide moisture until the seedlings become established. Seeds should be planted where the plants are desired since golden yarrow is fairly difficult to transplant.

COMPANIONS Showy penstemon, golden stars, blue dicks, Indian pink.

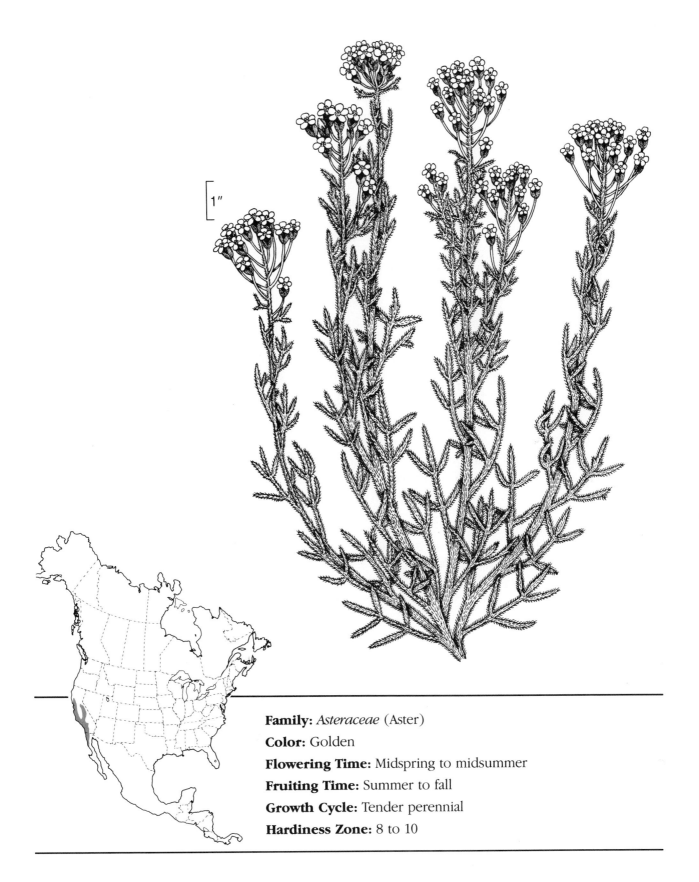

Family: *Asteraceae* (Aster)

Color: Golden

Flowering Time: Midspring to midsummer

Fruiting Time: Summer to fall

Growth Cycle: Tender perennial

Hardiness Zone: 8 to 10

GOLDEN YARROW *(Eriophyllum conferiflorum)*

Rattlesnake master
(Button snakeroot)

Eryngium yuccifolium

Don't be fooled by the name of this unlikely member of the parsley family — it has no proven medicinal value in treating snakebites and has little relation to rattlesnakes at all. Scattered along and clasping the stiff, unbranched, 1–6-foot stem are tough, linear, yuccalike leaves with spiny edges. These may reach 3 feet in length but become considerably shorter toward the flowers. Native Americans used fibers from the leaves to make rope. The individual flowers are quite small but cluster into globular heads ¾–1 inch in diameter, borne on irregularly branching stems near the top of the plant. The 5 greenish white petals are easily overlooked without magnification. After the petals fade and the seed head turns brown, the small fruits remain attached to the flower head, and the ¼-inch seeds retain their sharp scales.

CULTURE Rattlesnake master is a hardy perennial of the prairies and the open woods of the eastern U.S. and should be planted where there is ample sunlight. It grows best in moist, well-drained soils, but, once established, it will tolerate a range of moisture conditions from dry to periodically wet. Not too particular about soil acidity conditions, it requires little care.

PROPAGATION Usually rattlesnake master is propagated by seed, although mature plants divided in either early spring or late fall will flower the first year. Collect the seed in the fall and plant directly where desired or ¼ inch deep in flats containing moist, well-drained soil. Since the seeds need damp stratification (2 months at 40°F) in order to germinate, leave the flats outdoors over winter. Allow the seedlings to grow for one season in the flats or transplant them carefully to a nursery bed for one year before moving them to permanent locations. Some of the plants grown from seed will flower the first year, but most will flower the second. Once established, they will hold their own and self-seed abundantly.

COMPANIONS Leadplant, gayfeather, Culver's root, butterfly weed, black-eyed Susan, silky aster, purple coneflower, lance-leaved coreopsis, and many other plants of open woods and prairies.

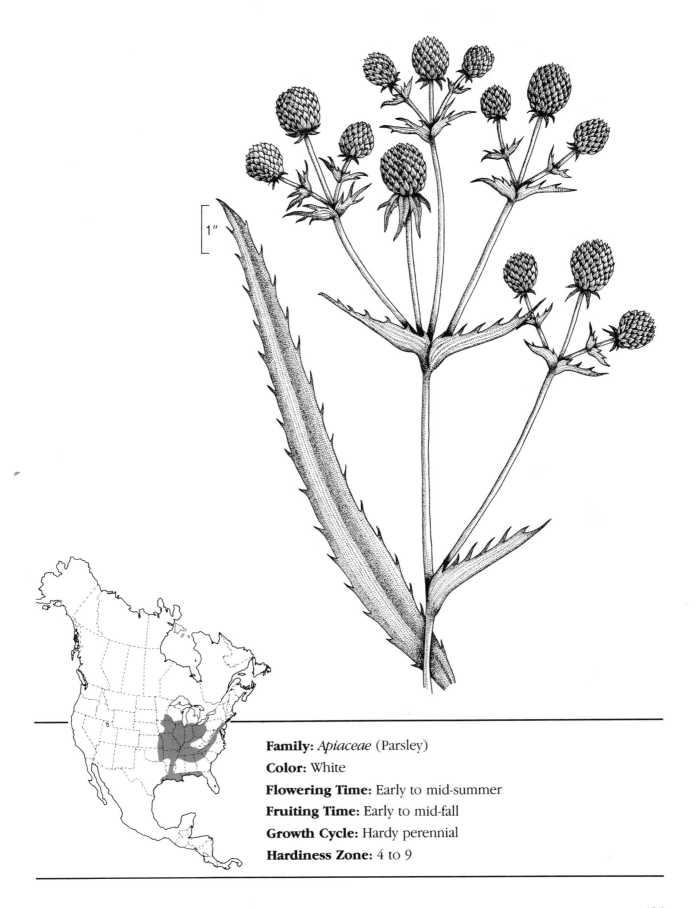

Family: *Apiaceae* (Parsley)

Color: White

Flowering Time: Early to mid-summer

Fruiting Time: Early to mid-fall

Growth Cycle: Hardy perennial

Hardiness Zone: 4 to 9

RATTLESNAKE MASTER *(Eryngium yuccifolium)*

Douglas's wallflower
(Coast wallflower, western wallflower)

Erysimum capitatum

The light burnt-orange color of the Douglas's wallflower makes it one of the loveliest plants in this collection, and even its rarer yellow, brick red, or maroon forms are most appealing. The erect 1–3-foot-high stems bear 1–5-inch-long, slender, lance-shaped leaves with small teeth on their edges. Both the leaves, which are largest and densest near the ground, and the stems are covered with gray hairs. At the top of the stem an oval cluster of fragrant, 4-petaled, ¾–1-inch-wide flowers forms a round-lobed cross tightly surrounding the light-colored stamens and pistil in the center. Douglas's wallflower's fruit resembles a 2–4-inch-long, extremely narrow, 4-sided bean pod, containing a single column of ¹⁄₁₆-inch light brown seeds.

CULTURE
Douglas's wallflower, a biennial, will produce flowers the first year. It is an excellent choice for sunny borders where long-flowering plants are desired. Not choosy about soils as long as they are well drained, it can tolerate dry soils once it becomes established. If given enough water in its native range, Douglas's wallflower can sometimes be grown as a perennial.

PROPAGATION
Propagate this plant by seed. Douglas's wallflower is easy to grow — no stratification treatment is needed and seeds will germinate readily. Plant seed ¼ inch deep, and thin seedlings to 6–8 inches apart. Provide moisture in the spring, when the seedlings are growing most rapidly. In hardiness zones 9 and 10, plant the seeds in late summer or early fall, and in colder regions, start them in pots or flats indoors in the winter and transplant them when danger of frost has passed. Blooming begins in late spring and continues through the summer.

COMPANIONS
California poppy, purple annual lupine, purple heliotrope, blue dicks, golden stars, sky lupine.

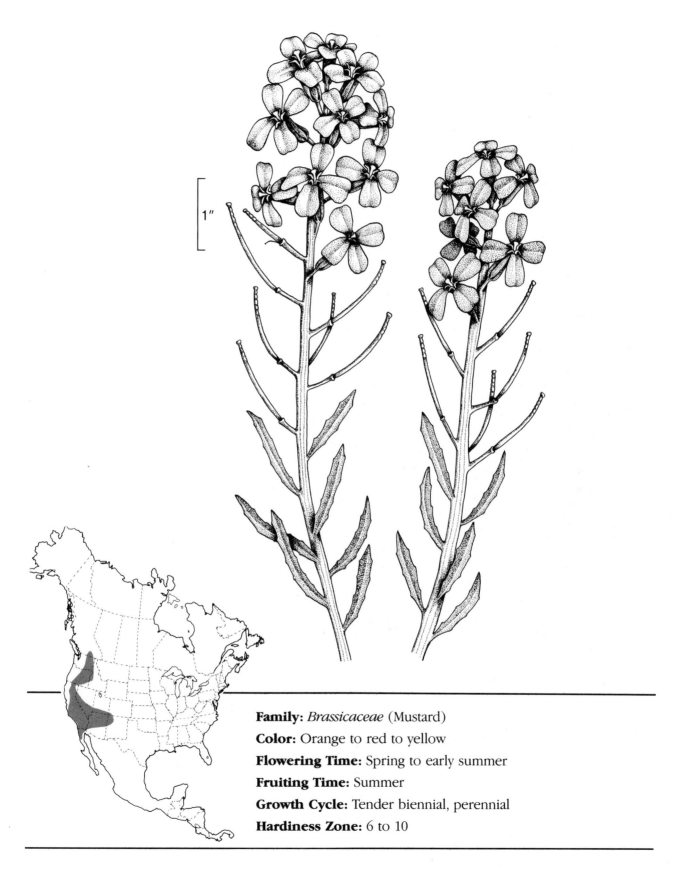

Family: *Brassicaceae* (Mustard)

Color: Orange to red to yellow

Flowering Time: Spring to early summer

Fruiting Time: Summer

Growth Cycle: Tender biennial, perennial

Hardiness Zone: 6 to 10

DOUGLAS'S WALLFLOWER *(Erysimum capitatum)*

Eastern trout lily

Erythronium americanum

(Dogtooth violet, yellow adder's tongue, fawn lily)

One of the early spring wildflowers of the East, trout lilies are only visible for about one month of the year. In the fall the shoot emerges from the ¾-inch corm, which may be as much as a foot deep, and grows toward the soil surface. Sometimes the rolled leaves can be seen above the ground as the snow melts in the spring. Young plants send up a single, fleshy, light green leaf, mottled with tan spots, while mature plants have 2 leaves 3–6 inches long. The 3–8-inch flower stalk bears a single, nodding, 1–1½-inch flower with 3 petals and 3 petal-like sepals, all of which are a rich chrome yellow and bend backwards to fully expose the 6 brown stamens. The fruit, an oblong capsule containing ⅛-inch kidney-shaped seeds, ripens in the late spring or early summer. At about the same time, plants too young to flower sometimes produce white runners that emerge above-ground and reenter the soil several inches away from where the corm originated.

CULTURE

In order to germinate and to flower this hardy perennial requires cold treatment, and its bulb needs about 4 months of night temperatures below freezing or 5 months below 40°F to resume growth in the spring. Trout lilies do all their growing for the year in the spring, and start to go into dormancy just as the deciduous trees overhead fully expand their leaves, so plant them where they will get ample sun at least in the early spring. Since the bulbs are sensitive to dehydration, they should be planted where the soils are moist at depth throughout the year. Trout lilies thrive in a variety of rich soils that are moderately to slightly acidic (pH 5–7).

PROPAGATION

The easiest way to propagate this plant is to purchase mature bulbs from a commercial grower. If planted in late summer or fall at least 5 inches deep, they will eventually seek their own level. Once established, trout lilies spread by seeding and by root offsets. Mark plant locations in spring and dig offsets in late summer, and then set the small bulbs at least 3 inches deep, mulching well. Propagation from seed takes considerable time and patience. Collect seed as it ripens in the late spring or early summer, and immediately plant where wanted, or ¼ inch deep in flats filled with a mixture of sandy loam and compost, keeping seeds moist. Although some seeds may germinate by fall, others wait until the second year. The first year a single small, narrow leaf emerges from a small corm, and both leaf and corm in successive years increase in size. When trout lilies are ready to flower, after 4–7 years, they will finally produce a pair of leaves. Commercially purchased mature bulbs planted in the fall may flower the following spring.

COMPANIONS

Hepatica, trillium, spring beauty, Dutchman's breeches.

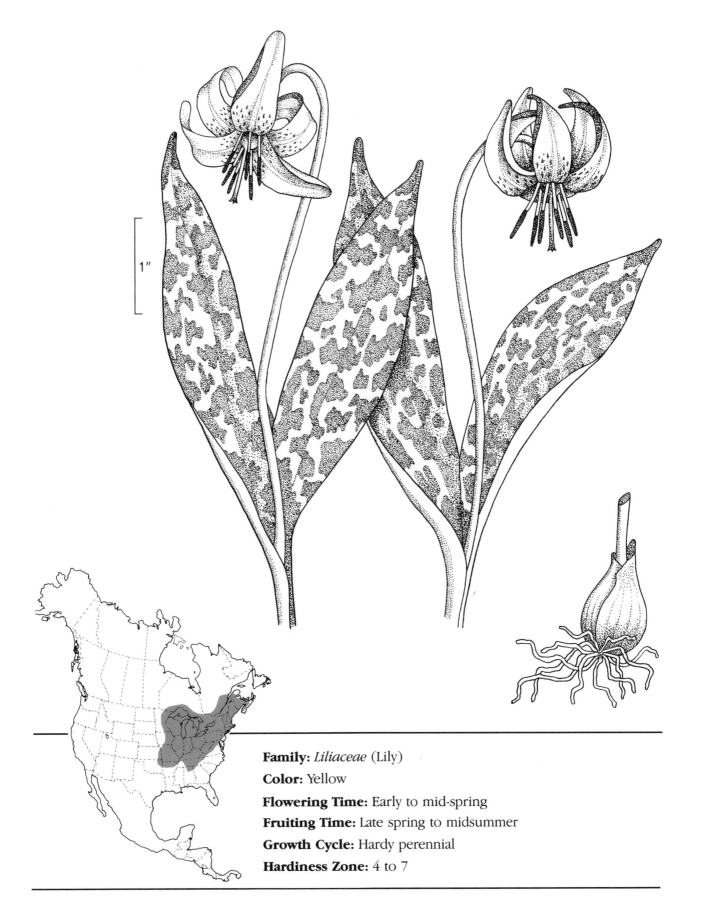

Family: *Liliaceae* (Lily)

Color: Yellow

Flowering Time: Early to mid-spring

Fruiting Time: Late spring to midsummer

Growth Cycle: Hardy perennial

Hardiness Zone: 4 to 7

EASTERN TROUT LILY *(Erythronium americanum)*

Yellow fawn lily

Erythronium grandiflorum

(Glacier lily, snow lily, lamb's tongue, fawn lily)

This hardy perennial blooms as the snows recede in the Rockies, flowering early thanks to winter bud development on the underground shoots. The yellow fawn lily, larger and more robust than its eastern relative, the trout lily, has a pair of fleshy green basal leaves 4–8 inches long. A 1–2-foot-high scape rises from between the leaves, bearing 1–5 very bright yellow, nodding, 2-inch flowers. The sepals and petals look alike and bend back to expose fully the 3-lobed stigma and the long stamens with their brown anthers. The fruit is an oval, 3-sided capsule up to 1 inch long, and the root system is a slender corm about 2 inches long at maturity, growing at a depth of 3–6 inches. As with the trout lily, the immature plants have a single leaf.

CULTURE

It is very difficult to maintain this species in soils that become thoroughly dry during the summer. Moist but well-drained soils and partial shade to full sun are ideal. This hardy perennial grows best in soils that are slightly acid (pH 5–6.5) and rich in organic matter, with additions of compost and over-wintering mulch left in place during the spring.

PROPAGATION

Yellow fawn lily should be propagated from seed or from purchased corms. Plants from seed mature more quickly than those of the trout lily, and you will only have to wait 3 to 5 years rather than 5 to 6. Plant ripe seed ¼ inch deep in a flat filled with a mixture of compost and sand. Keep the soil moist and leave the flats out over the winter so the seeds can be properly chilled. Germination will occur in the spring, when a single leaf will be visible. Light shade and ample moisture should be provided while seedlings become established. Keep the developing plants in the flats or nursery beds for the first year and then transplant the corms 3 inches deep in permanent locations in the fall. If corms are purchased, they should be planted 4–6 inches apart and 3–5 inches deep. Yellow fawn lilies will self-seed in moist, humus-rich soil.

COMPANIONS

Trout lily, Colorado and Eastern columbines, Western and Eastern shooting stars, wild leek, wild ginger.

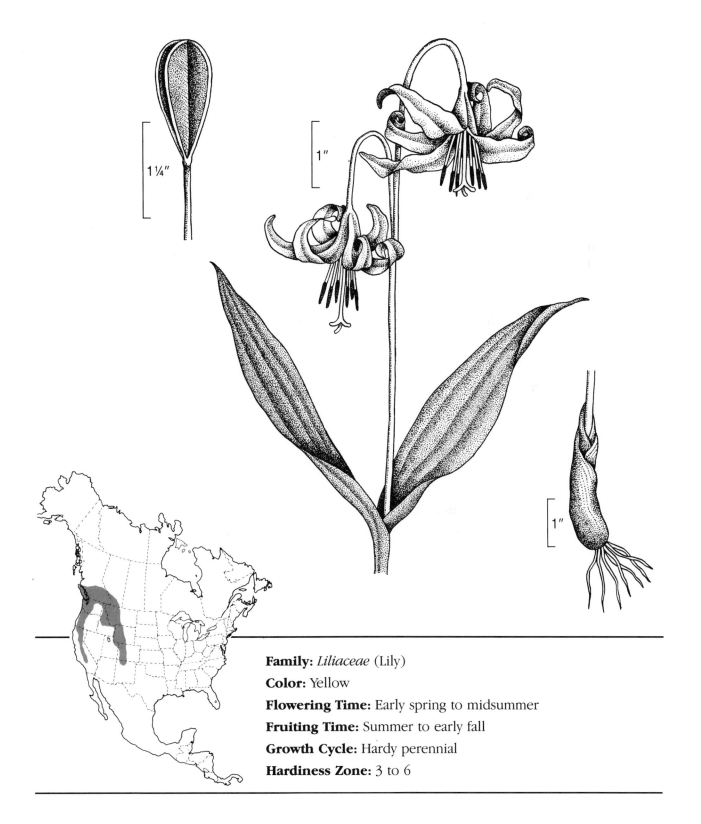

Family: *Liliaceae* (Lily)

Color: Yellow

Flowering Time: Early spring to midsummer

Fruiting Time: Summer to early fall

Growth Cycle: Hardy perennial

Hardiness Zone: 3 to 6

YELLOW FAWN LILY *(Erythronium grandiflorum)*

California poppy
(Copa de oro)

Eschscholzia californica

California should be known as the "Golden State" as much for its state flower, called *copa de oro* or "cup of gold" in Spanish, as for the Gold Rush of 1849. The California poppy has feathery, highly dissected, ¾–2¼-inch-long, blue-green leaves, which clasp the 1–2-foot-high stems supporting single, 1–3-inch-wide, 4-petaled flowers. The lustrous, golden orange or yellow petals open in the sunshine and close at night and on cloudy days. Flowers produced early in the spring tend to be larger than those produced later in the season. The bud is covered by a green, fused, caplike calyx or "calyptra," which is thrust off as the petals expand. The spicy, fragrant flowers have a double-flanged disc below the petals, and at their centers are many stamens with linear anthers and a distinctive 4-part stigma. California poppy has a 2–3-inch-long, 10-nerved, capsular fruit containing many ¹⁄₁₆-inch, gray-brown, roughened seeds. Long before this plant was introduced into European gardens in the 1830s, Native Americans ate the foliage cooked, and used the watery juice of the roots as a pain killer.

CULTURE California poppy is adaptable to almost any garden conditions as long as it has well-drained soil and plenty of sun. In its native California it starts to bloom in late winter and continues through late spring, often flowering again in fall, but as a garden plant elsewhere it blooms all summer long. In hardiness zones 10 to 8 California poppy can be grown as a short-lived perennial, and in zones 7 to 3, as a hardy annual.

PROPAGATION In western regions of hardiness zones 8 to 10 plant the seeds in the fall, and in other regions wait until early spring. It is best to plant the seeds ⅛–¼ inch deep directly where poppies are desired, since they do not transplant well. The seeds will germinate in 2 weeks without chilling treatment, and seedlings grow rapidly. Once established, California poppy will freely self-seed, and in parts of its native range it may even become weedy.

COMPANIONS Blue dicks, tidy tips, sky lupine, golden stars, blue-eyed grass, baby blue-eyes.

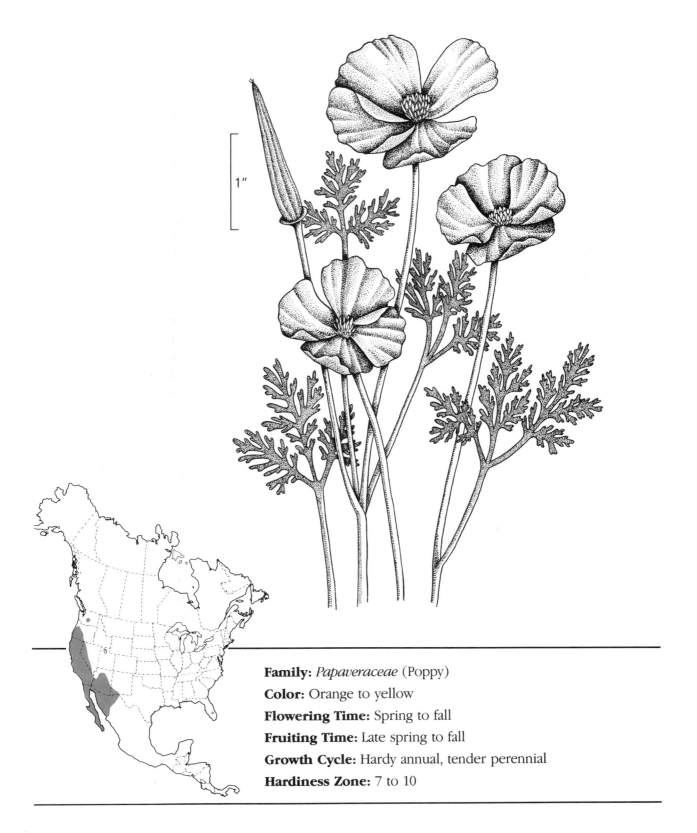

1"

Family: *Papaveraceae* (Poppy)

Color: Orange to yellow

Flowering Time: Spring to fall

Fruiting Time: Late spring to fall

Growth Cycle: Hardy annual, tender perennial

Hardiness Zone: 7 to 10

CALIFORNIA POPPY *(Eschscholzia californica)*

133

Snow-on-the-mountain

Euphorbia marginata

This plant's name probably refers to the white flowers at the top of its 1–3-foot stems, or perhaps to its white-margined leaves, but it is definitely not a reference to the native habitat of this annual of the Great Plains. It is grown as much for its attractive foliage as for its flowers. The 1–3-inch-long leaves clasp the stem and may be light green, variegated, or entirely white. Obviously the entire plant cannot be white or it would be unable to photosynthesize. The erect, many-branched, 1–3-foot-high stems are softly fuzzy and frequently reddish toward the base. Both stem and leaves exude a white, milky sap containing euphorbon, which is an emetic and purgative if taken internally and causes dermatitis if gotten on the skin. This plant also accumulates selenium, a substance toxic to livestock if present in the soil. Therefore, snow-on-the-mountain is best planted where its foliage won't be eaten by livestock or disturbed by children running after baseballs. Do not use it as a cut flower. The small flowers, each with 5 petallike bracts, are borne in showy clusters at the top of the stem. The hairy, green, ¼-inch fruit has 3 lobes and contains several ⅛-inch, rough-surfaced seeds.

CULTURE   This hardy annual is easy to cultivate and can be grown in nearly any garden soil, moist or dry, as long as it is in a sunny spot.

PROPAGATION   Plant seeds in spring or fall in the desired location, ⅛–¼ inch deep.

COMPANIONS   Purple coneflower, blanketflower, Mexican hat, cosmos.

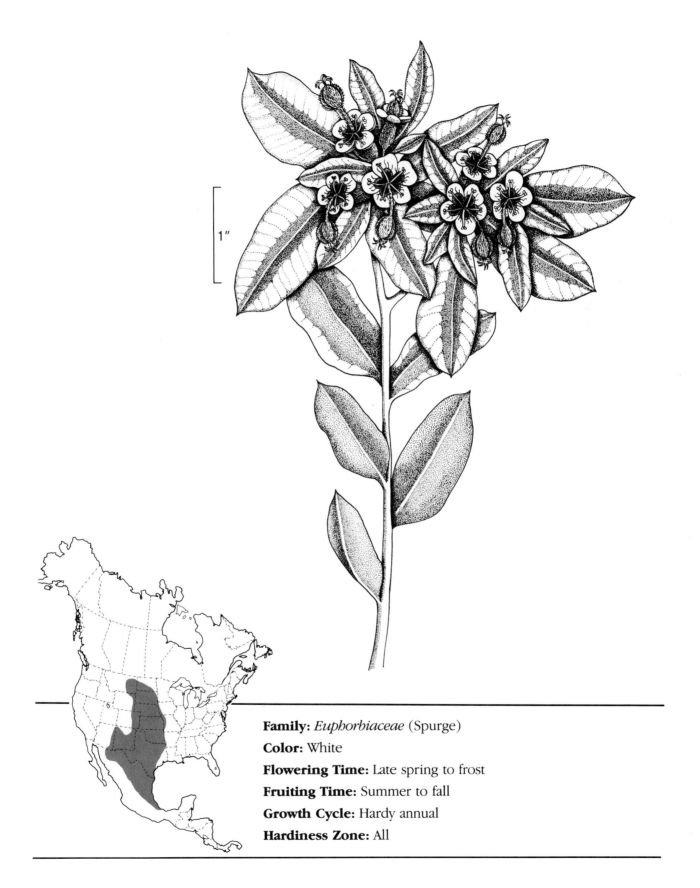

1″

Family: *Euphorbiaceae* (Spurge)

Color: White

Flowering Time: Late spring to frost

Fruiting Time: Summer to fall

Growth Cycle: Hardy annual

Hardiness Zone: All

SNOW-ON-THE-MOUNTAIN *(Euphorbia marginata)*

Chocolate lily
(Mission bells, black lily)

Fritillaria biflora

In heavy, clayey soils of the California Coastal Ranges, this graceful brown-flowered member of the lily family emerges in the spring and disappears by summer. Two to 7 basal leaves 3–5 inches long rise from a deeply seated, fleshy-scaled corm. One to several nodding, bell-shaped flowers resembling inverted tulips are borne on a 6–12-inch-high scape. Each of the 1–2-inch-wide flowers has 3 petals and 3 nearly identical petallike sepals surrounding the 6 stamens and a single pistil with a clefted 3-part stigma. The fruit of the chocolate lily is an inch-long, 6-sided capsule with many flat, brown seeds.

CULTURE   Chocolate lily should be planted in a location that receives sun most of the day, but is at least lightly shaded around noon. While it grows naturally in heavy, coarse, clay soils, it will grow easily with prolonged flowering in normal, well-drained garden soils. In fact, if planted in regions with wet, humid summers, the corm will rot unless it has a very well-drained soil. In these regions, the corms should be allowed to dry out during the summer, so either cover the surface of the soil with plastic sheeting or dig up the corms and store them dry until fall. Outside its native range (hardiness zones 9 and 10) the corms should be heavily mulched for the winter, and in regions colder than hardiness zone 7 dig up the bulbs in the summer and replant them in the early spring. The chocolate lily is an excellent plant for rock gardens. In the humid East it can be grown in deep pots and moved seasonally to the proper environment.

PROPAGATION   It is easier to propagate chocolate lily from division of the scaly corm, but seeds can also be used. Divide the corm scales in the late summer or early fall, planting them in permanent locations 3 inches deep and 4 inches apart. They can also be planted in deep flats or holding beds and left there for several years until the corms increase to ¼–½ inch in diameter, when they should be transplanted to permanent locations. Plant the seeds, which require no chilling treatment, in fall in the West and in spring in the East, placing them ¼–⅓ inch deep in pots, flats, or permanent locations. Keep the seedlings moist until summer begins, and then allow them to remain dry during dormancy. Transplant the dormant corms during the second year. It takes 4 to 6 years to produce flowering plants from seed, 3 to 4 years from divisions.

COMPANIONS   Bitterroot, blue dicks, golden stars, Missouri evening primrose, California poppy.

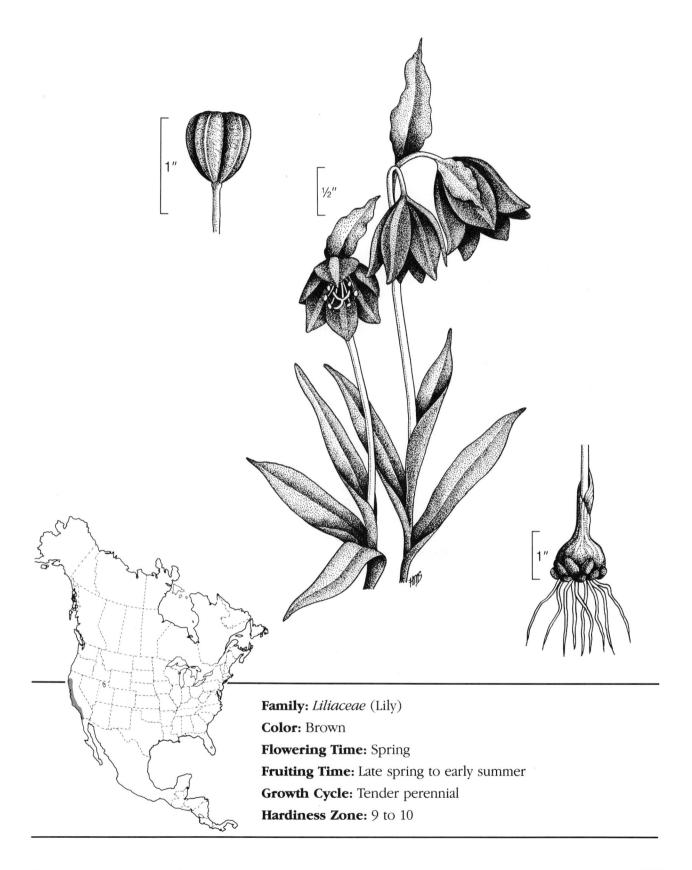

Family: *Liliaceae* (Lily)

Color: Brown

Flowering Time: Spring

Fruiting Time: Late spring to early summer

Growth Cycle: Tender perennial

Hardiness Zone: 9 to 10

CHOCOLATE LILY *(Fritillaria biflora)*

Blanketflower
(Indian blanket, gaillardia)

Gaillardia aristata

This half-hardy perennial blankets much of the Great Plains with yellow and red daisylike flowers all summer long. Blanketflower has long been cultivated as a cut flower and was introduced into Europe as a garden plant in the early 1800s. The thick, hairy, dandelionlike leaves clasp the slender, hairy stems of this erect, 2–4-foot-high plant. The inch-long ray flowers have yellow, 3-toothed tips and dark red to purple bases. While in the bud, the disc flowers are frequently red-orange, but as the fuzzy, 5-lobed flowers open they are generally the same color as the bases of the ray flowers. The ⅛-inch-long, conical, seedlike fruits have tufts of hairs at their bases.

CULTURE Blanketflower is adaptable to most sunny locations and is not particular about soils except that they should be well drained. Don't bother adding compost or other soil amendments to areas contemplated for blanketflower; it does best in infertile soils. Although it is hardy when grown in the Great Plains (zone 3), it is only half-hardy in the humid regions of the East and should be mulched heavily for the winter. Once established, blanketflower is quite drought resistant.

PROPAGATION Blanketflower can easily be propagated by seed or root division, and softwood stem cuttings are also possible. No chilling treatment of the seed is needed, but simply plant in the fall or spring ⅛–¼ inch deep in a sunny location on well-drained soil. The seeds may also be started indoors in the early spring and transplanted to permanent locations after all danger of frost has passed. Germination takes only a week or two and often plants from seeds will flower by the end of the first summer. Root divisions can be made in the early spring. Even though the blanketflower has a taproot, it can be divided vertically. Be sure to divide the root so that each section has at least one bud and as many of the smaller lateral roots as possible. Plant sections 10–12 inches apart with the buds just at the soil surface. Since blanketflower is not a long-lived perennial, it may be necessary to divide the clumps every 2 or 3 years to keep it growing vigorously. Softwood cuttings can be made from the stems in the late spring, but seed and root division propagation are easier.

COMPANIONS Butterfly weed, wood lily, lance-leaved coreopsis, wild bergamot, prickly poppy.

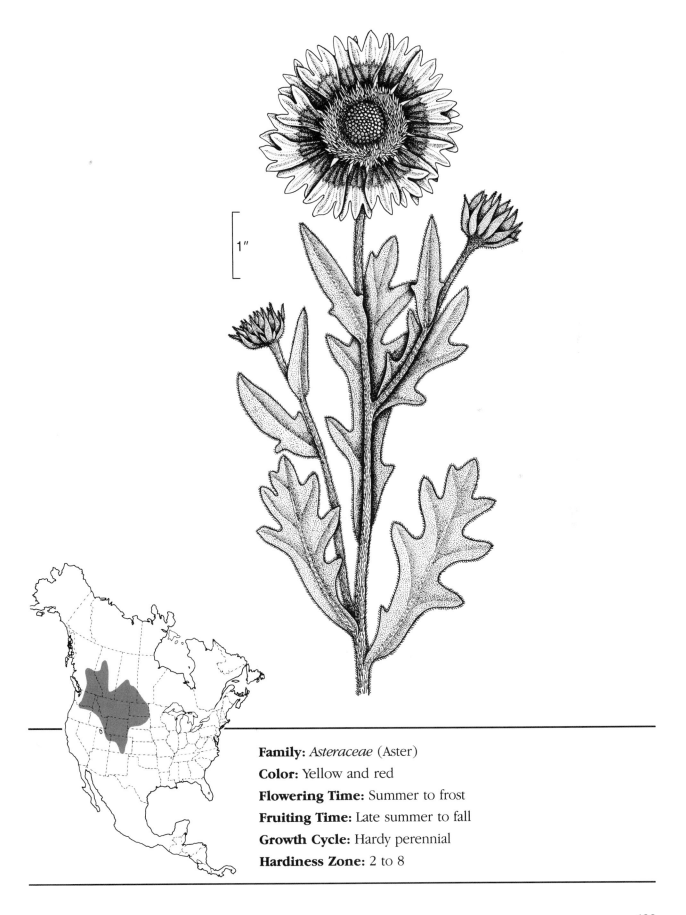

1"

Family: *Asteraceae* (Aster)

Color: Yellow and red

Flowering Time: Summer to frost

Fruiting Time: Late summer to fall

Growth Cycle: Hardy perennial

Hardiness Zone: 2 to 8

BLANKETFLOWER *(Gaillardia aristata)*

Wintergreen
(Teaberry, checkerberry)

Gaultheria procumbens

Wintergreen is as desirable to grow for its foliage as for its red berries and white flowers. Both the fruits and the leathery evergreen leaves contain the aromatic wintergreen oil. Although the leaves and fruits of wintergreen, or teaberry, are frequently used in herb teas, oil of wintergreen is toxic if consumed internally in a concentrated form. The young leaves, not as leathery as the old ones, are a light shade of green. Wintergreen spreads from creeping stolons just below the surface of the soil. Tiny, slender, semi-woody stems rise to a height of 2–4 inches and in late spring may bear 1 or 2 nodding white flowers less than ½ inch long. The urn-shaped, 5-lobed flowers dangle below the ¾-inch leaves. The fruits are red, pulpy berries with many small brown seeds. The flesh of the berry becomes mealy and pink with age, and often the fruits will remain attached to the plant until the next spring. Chipmunks, grouse, mice, and birds eat the fruits, and deer eat the leaves during the winter.

CULTURE   Wintergreen is quite tolerant of shade, but it grows and flowers best in sunny openings with light shade during midday. It is not choosy about soil conditions as long as the soil is acid (pH 4–6.5) with abundant organic matter. It can grow on soils ranging from dry sands to wet peats, and is found growing naturally both in piney woods and in bogs.

PROPAGATION   Wintergreen is a relatively easy plant to grow even though it may only spread 4–6 inches a year. Make cuttings of the stems and runners in early summer before they become woody, and plant in a flat with a moist mixture of sand and peat moss. Transplant the following spring to an appropriate location. The seed of wintergreen requires moist chilling (40°F) for 1–2 months in order to germinate. Collect fruits in the fall and sow seeds thickly on a mixture of sand and fine-milled peat moss, then cover with a thin layer of peat moss. Germination may be slow, so don't give up for at least two springs. It is wise to protect the flats in winter with hardware cloth or screen to prevent rodents from eating the seeds. Remove the screen in the spring and provide light shading. Transplant to permanent locations in the fall or the following spring.

COMPANIONS   Partridgeberry, bunchberry, yellow clintonia, shinleaf.

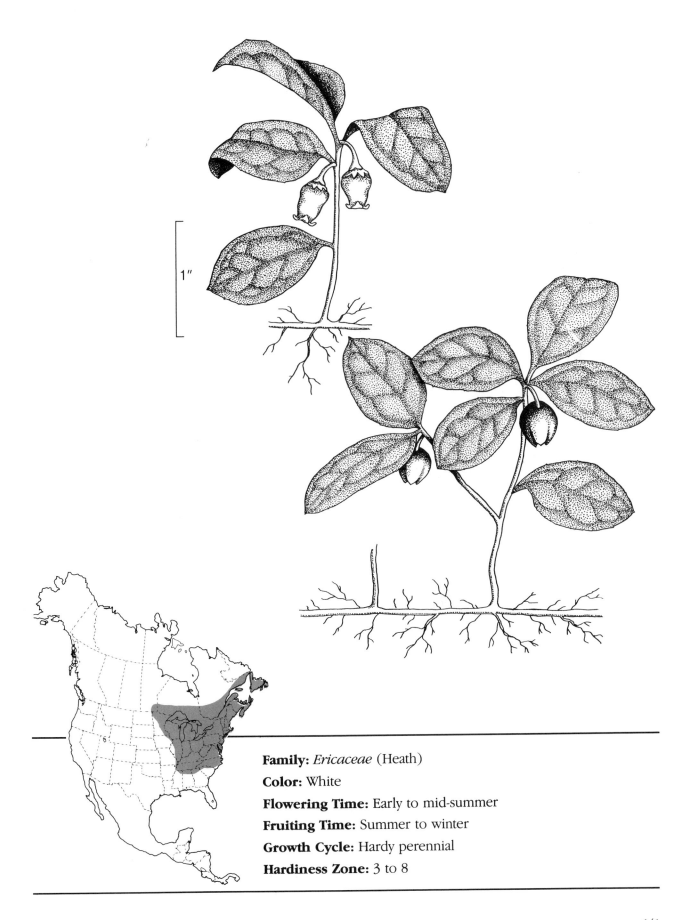

1"

Family: *Ericaceae* (Heath)

Color: White

Flowering Time: Early to mid-summer

Fruiting Time: Summer to winter

Growth Cycle: Hardy perennial

Hardiness Zone: 3 to 8

WINTERGREEN *(Gaultheria procumbens)*

Closed gentian
(Bottle gentian, blind gentian)

Gentiana andrewsii

Not only is the closed gentian one of the easiest of the gentians to cultivate, but it has unusual and interesting flowers as well. The clusters of 2–5 flowers are borne in the notches of the upper leaves of this 1–2-foot hardy perennial. The 1½-inch flowers have 5 petals, ranging in color from navy blue to blue-violet and even white, attached to one another by petallike pleats that form a tube. Although this tube appears to lack an opening, inspiring the plant's common names of closed, bottle, and blind gentian, pollinating insects, especially bees, force their way into the flower without much difficulty. Surrounded by the petals and unseen from outside the flower are the 5 stamens, their anthers fused together. The reddish stems are clasped by the pairs of 2–4-inch leaves, whose size increases toward the top of the stem. The fruit of the closed gentian is a capsule containing ⅛-inch, light tan, winged seeds, and the root system is a root crown with many white, fibrous roots.

CULTURE
An excellent garden plant, closed gentian is adaptable to a wide variety of conditions, from full sun to light shade, from dryish soils to damp soils, and from neutral to slightly acidic soil (pH 5–7.5). It grows best in a sandy loam, rich in humus and moist throughout the growing season.

PROPAGATION
Closed gentians can be propagated either by seed or by divisions of the root crown. Root-crown division should be done in fall or early spring. Divide crowns into pieces, each with at least one bud, and plant 1 foot apart with the buds at the top of the crown about 1 inch below the soil surface. Germination requires stratification (3 months at 40°F) and is enhanced by exposure to the light, so lightly scatter the seeds just on the surface of a flat containing a mixture of loam and compost. Do not scratch the seeds into the soil, but moisten and give a light covering of mulch. Leave the flats out for the winter so the seeds can be chilled, or artificially refrigerate moistened seeds and then plant in flats indoors in early spring. Remove mulch in the spring so that seeds can be exposed to the light, but keep the soil surface moist. The seeds will germinate 1–4 weeks after spring temperatures top 65°F, but the process may be slow. The first year the seedlings will form only a rosette of leaves and should be provided with light shade and moisture. Leave seedlings in the flat for the first growing season, transplant them to a holding bed for the second year, and then move them to a permanent location the following year. Plants from seed will usually flower in the third or fourth year.

COMPANIONS
Cardinal flower, New England aster, turtlehead, larger blue flag, nodding wild onion.

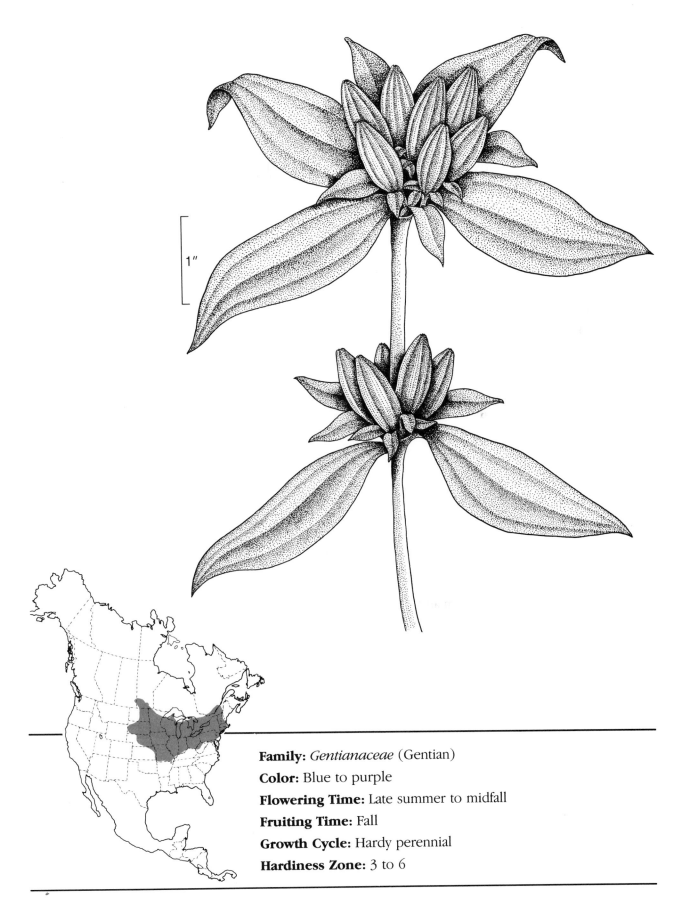

Family: *Gentianaceae* (Gentian)

Color: Blue to purple

Flowering Time: Late summer to midfall

Fruiting Time: Fall

Growth Cycle: Hardy perennial

Hardiness Zone: 3 to 6

CLOSED GENTIAN *(Gentiana andrewsii)*

Sharp-lobed hepatica
(Sharp-lobed liverwort, sharp-lobed liverleaf)

Hepatica acutiloba

The hepaticas are about the earliest of the spring wildflowers in the eastern United States. The common names of this hardy perennial refer to the 3-lobed, somewhat leathery leaves which look to some like a piece of liver. About 2 inches long and 4 inches broad, the leaves remain a dark brownish green over the winter, and then wither as new leaves emerge in the spring. Both the 3–4-inch leaf stalks and flower stalks are covered with silky hairs pointing downward. The flowers have 3 small, unlobed leaves at their bases, and 5–18 petal-like sepals, ranging in color from blue to pink to white. Numerous pistils and stamens in the centers of the flowers are visited by bees and flies. The flowers open with the morning sun but close and droop in the evening, in cloudy weather, and on cold days. The seedlike fruits of hepaticas are about ⅛ inch long, green-brown, and fuzzy.

CULTURE

Hepaticas are found growing in woods with calcium-rich soils. In the garden they should be provided with ample amounts of compost and planted in lightly shaded areas where the soil remains moist, but not wet, throughout the summer. Hepaticas prefer slightly acidic to slightly alkaline soils, so be sure to adjust the soil pH to between 6 and 7.5 by the addition of ground limestone if necessary. They also benefit from a light overwinter mulch of calcium-rich leaves such as maple, ash, birch, or basswood. Hepaticas require cold for renewal of their growth and for optimum germination of their seeds, and therefore they are successfully grown only north of hardiness zone 9.

PROPAGATION

Hepaticas can be propagated either from root divisions or from seed. Divide rootstocks in the fall, being careful not to break the attached leaves, which contain nutrient and energy reserves for next spring's flowers. Plant the divisions with the buds at the soil surface and the leaves above the soil. Mulch lightly for the winter. Seeds may be sown as soon as ripe in the spring or in the fall but should be kept moist. Sow seeds ¼ inch deep in well-composted loam of the appropriate pH, and mulch lightly to conserve moisture. If flats are used, place them in shady locations and keep them out over the winter. Some germination may occur by fall in spring-sown seeds, but most seeds require overwintering. It is a good idea to remove some of the mulch from the seedbed in the spring. Plants from seed generally blossom the second year.

COMPANIONS

Bloodroot, Jack-in-the-pulpit, columbines, wild ginger.

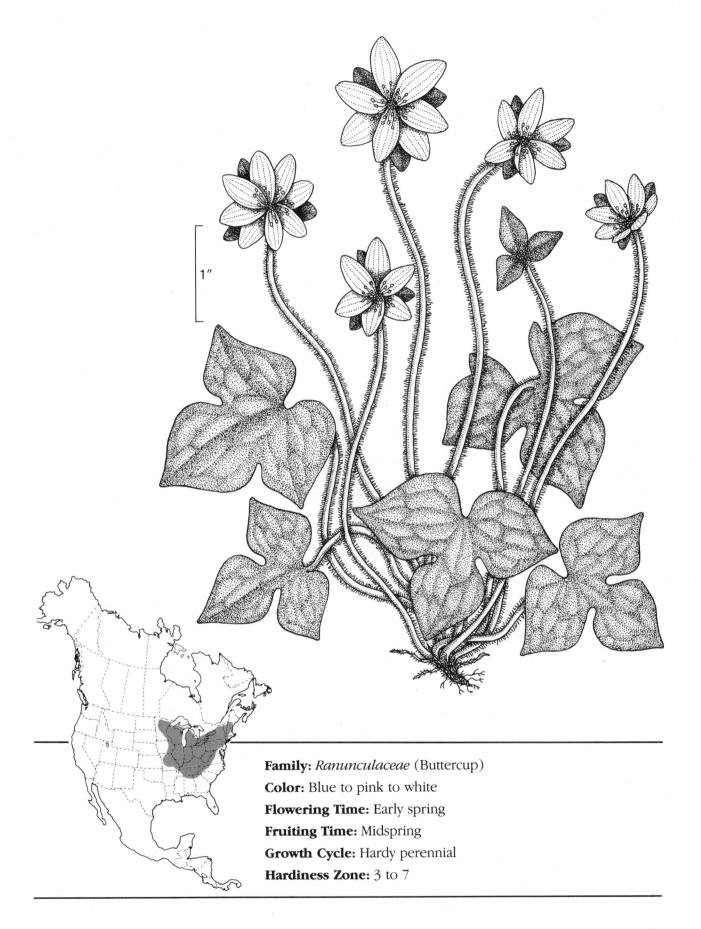

Family: *Ranunculaceae* (Buttercup)

Color: Blue to pink to white

Flowering Time: Early spring

Fruiting Time: Midspring

Growth Cycle: Hardy perennial

Hardiness Zone: 3 to 7

SHARP-LOBED HEPATICA *(Hepatica acutiloba)*

Coralbells

Heuchera sanguinea

This lovely, hardy perennial, a favorite in European and North American gardens, is a native of moist, shady areas in the mountains of the Southwest. Coralbells, like other members of the saxifrage family, have a mound of heart-shaped, geranium-like leaves. In the long days of late spring a 1–2-foot, velvety scape, bearing loose clusters of pink to bright red bell-like flowers, rises from the mound of leaves. Each of the ¼–½-inch-long flowers has 5 red sepals and 5 small, lobed, red petals. The long scape, low foliage, and long-lasting blooms make coralbells an excellent plant for shady borders, rock gardens, or cut flowers.

CULTURE Coralbells can be planted in full sun to partial shade. The plant grows best in soils that are only slightly acid (pH 6–7) and moist throughout the summer, although it is not terriby choosy.

PROPAGATION Coralbells are easily propagated by seed, division, or leaf cuttings. Light stimulates seed germination, so the seeds should be planted only ⅛ inch deep, at most. Plant ripe seeds in flats in the summer, or plant commercially available seeds in the spring or fall. Germination takes about 2 weeks in the spring, once temperatures reach 70°F, and the plants will flower the second year. To propagate vegetatively, divide roots in the late fall or early spring, allowing each section several buds. Plant the divisions 10–15 inches apart with the buds just at the soil surface. If leaves are cut in the late summer or fall, set in moist sand, and provided with light shade, they will root easily and can be transplanted when roots are fully developed.

COMPANIONS Colorado columbine, closed gentian, Eastern and Western shooting star, nodding wild onion, false dragonhead.

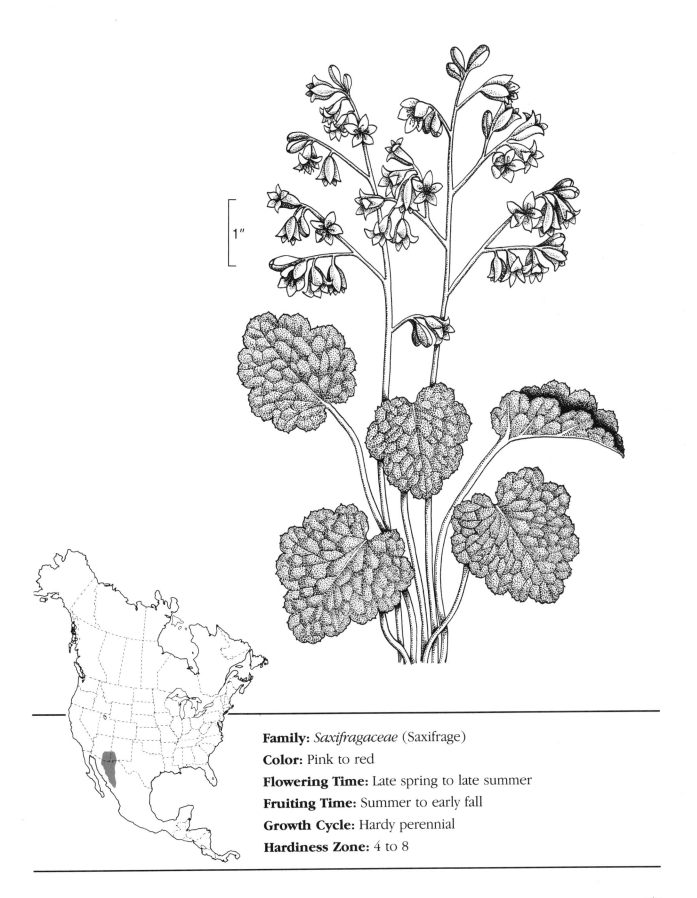

Family: *Saxifragaceae* (Saxifrage)

Color: Pink to red

Flowering Time: Late spring to late summer

Fruiting Time: Summer to early fall

Growth Cycle: Hardy perennial

Hardiness Zone: 4 to 8

CORALBELLS *(Heuchera sanguinea)*

Bluets
(Quaker ladies, innocence)

Houstonia caerulea

These small, delicate plants, found in grassy fields and thickets in the eastern United States, are hardy perennials or "winter annuals," with seed germinating in fall and flowering in the spring. The tiny (¼–½-inch) trumpet-shaped flowers have yellow centers in pleasant contrast to the 4 blue to lilac lobes, which form a cross. The thin stems are short, only 2–8 inches high, with a pair of narrow, tiny leaves, while the leaves at the base of the flower stem are broader and more numerous. The fruit is a small capsule with many minute seeds. Bluets tend to grow in clumps, spreading from seed or from short rhizomes which send up clusters of shoots.

CULTURE Bluets thrive in open sunny locations, in woodland openings, on the margins of brooks, and in very light shade. They do well when grown among the grasses of lawns and fields, but care should be taken not to mow them too early in the spring before they have had an opportunity to set seed. Bluets require a soil that is both acidic (pH 5–7) and somewhat moist.

PROPAGATION Bluets are easy to propagate both from divisions and from seed. Dig the plants in the spring, before or after flowering, or in the fall. Carefully divide the plants and replant with the basal leaves just above the surface of the soil. Bluets are most conspicuous when in flower, so mark their location when you can easily spot them in the grass. Since the seed germinates best after cold-damp stratification, refrigerate seeds collected in the summer until you plan to plant them the following spring. The seeds can be sown at a shallow depth or lightly scratched into the soil in either spring or fall. Fall-sown seed will generally flower the next spring. Once established, bluets self-seed with ease.

COMPANIONS Trout lily, wood lily, columbines, meadow beauty.

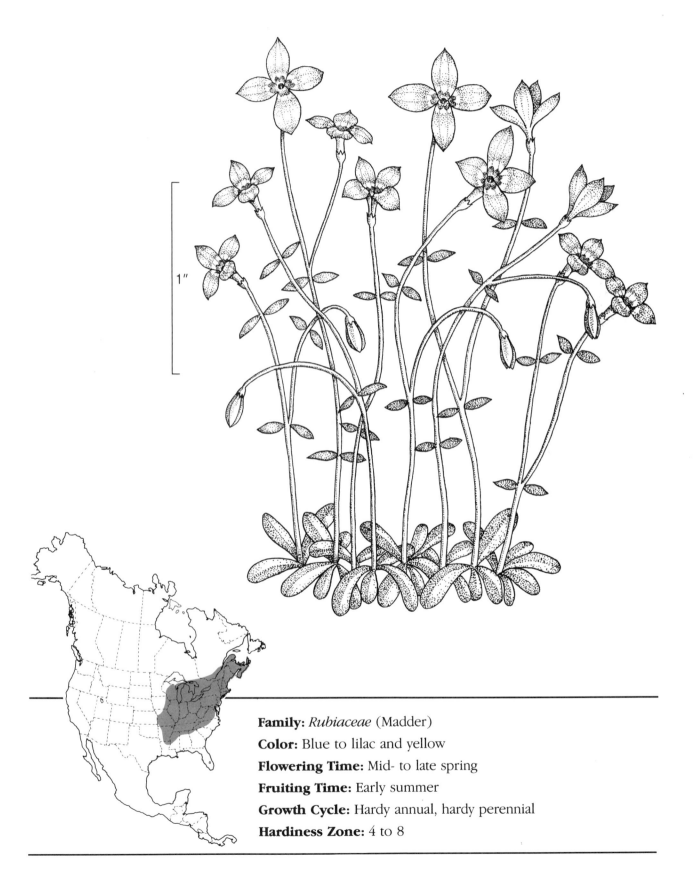

1"

Family: *Rubiaceae* (Madder)

Color: Blue to lilac and yellow

Flowering Time: Mid- to late spring

Fruiting Time: Early summer

Growth Cycle: Hardy annual, hardy perennial

Hardiness Zone: 4 to 8

BLUETS *(Houstonia caerulea)*

149

Old-man-of-the-mountain
(Alpine sunflower, sun god)

Hymenoxys grandiflora

This very hardy perennial grows above the timberline high in the Rockies. Out of a low mat of feathery, 3–4-inch-long leaves, covered with cottony white hairs, rise 3–4-inch sunflowerlike flower heads on stems usually less than a foot long. Often the stems are so short that the large flowers appear embedded in the foliage. The flower heads usually face eastward, toward the rising sun. The 30 or so inch-long ray flowers have broad, overlapping, bright yellow petals with 3 teeth at the tip, and surround the broad, domed disc of small, densely packed, tubular flowers. Numerous woolly, leafy bracts surround each flower head. The 5-sided, conical, seedlike fruits are hairy with narrow scales at the top.

CULTURE

Old-man-of-the-mountain is a plant of the alpine tundra and high meadows. It requires full sunlight and well-drained soils that are moist during the growing season. It grows best in gravelly, limestone-rich soils. This hardy perennial is ideal for rock gardens in hardiness zone 4 and colder.

PROPAGATION

Old-man-of-the-mountain is best propagated by seed. Collect the seeds in the late summer when fruits are ripe. Plant ¼ inch deep in a permanent location or in flats filled with sand or coarse soil, and leave outdoors for the winter. It is likely that old-man-of-the-mountain, like most other alpine plants, has seeds whose springtime germination is enhanced by stratification. Transplant seedlings as soon as they are sturdy and several inches high, so as not to interfere with the developing taproot.

COMPANIONS

Yellow clintonia, bunchberry, bitterroot.

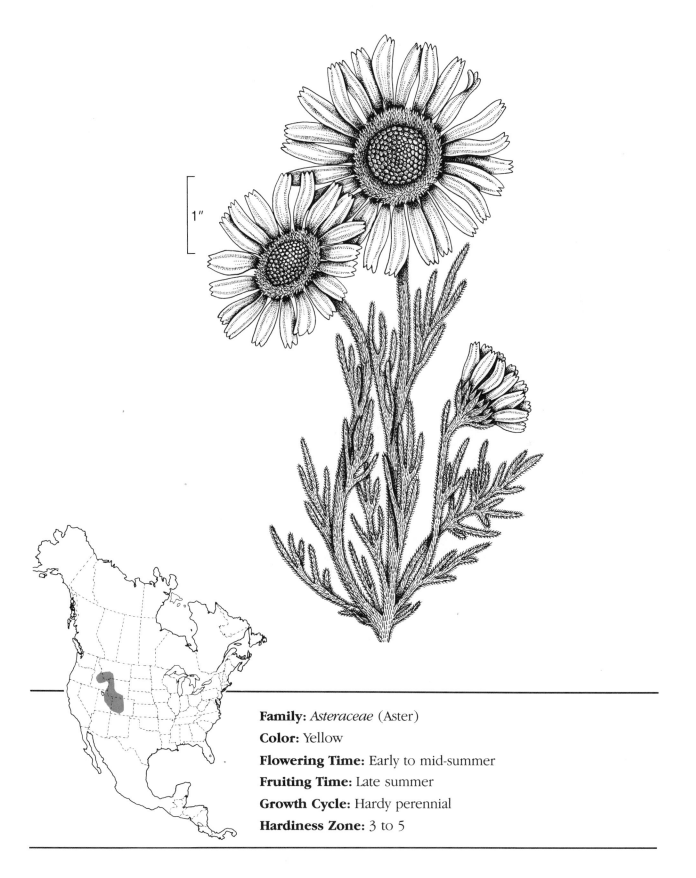

Family: *Asteraceae* (Aster)

Color: Yellow

Flowering Time: Early to mid-summer

Fruiting Time: Late summer

Growth Cycle: Hardy perennial

Hardiness Zone: 3 to 5

OLD-MAN-OF-THE-MOUNTAIN *(Hymenoxys grandiflora)*

Standing cypress
(Texas plume, Spanish larkspur, scarlet gilia)

Ipomopsis rubra
(Gilia coronopifolia, Gilia rubra)

This native of the Southeast and Mexico used to be frequently cultivated in northern gardens, and it deserves a return to popularity. Bright scarlet tubular flowers, whose openings exactly fit the heads of its main pollinators, ruby-throated hummingbirds, are scattered near the tops of the 2–5-foot-high stem. Each erect, unbranched stem may bear up to 100 inch-long, 5-lobed flowers, red on the outside and streaked with yellow or spotted with red on the inside. Five stamens are attached to the inside of the floral tube just above the abundant nectar, the hummingbirds' reward, which is produced at the base of the flower. Each flower opens for only 2 to 5 days, but the overall flowering season is quite long as blooming progresses downward from the top of the stem. The narrow, highly divided leaves, somewhat reminiscent of cypress needles, are usually less than an inch long. The fruit is a ¼-inch-long capsule.

CULTURE

Although sometimes found growing along riverbanks, standing cypress is fairly drought tolerant and grows well on light, well-drained, sandy soils as well. It can be cultivated in areas of full sun to partial shade and is an especially effective background plant because of its height and spectacular flowers.

PROPAGATION

Standing cypress seeds should be planted ¼ inch deep in the desired location. Germination, which is enhanced by darkness, will occur in a week or two of temperatures of 65–70°F. The first year the seedling resembles a small cypress tree. Since it is a biennial, the plant will flower during the second growing season. Plant the seeds 2 years in succession to ensure an abundance of flowers each year. Although standing cypress is classified as a hardy biennial, it sometimes grows as a perennial and freely self-seeds when established.

COMPANIONS

Cosmos, blanketflower, American bellflower, lance-leaved coreopsis, cardinal flower.

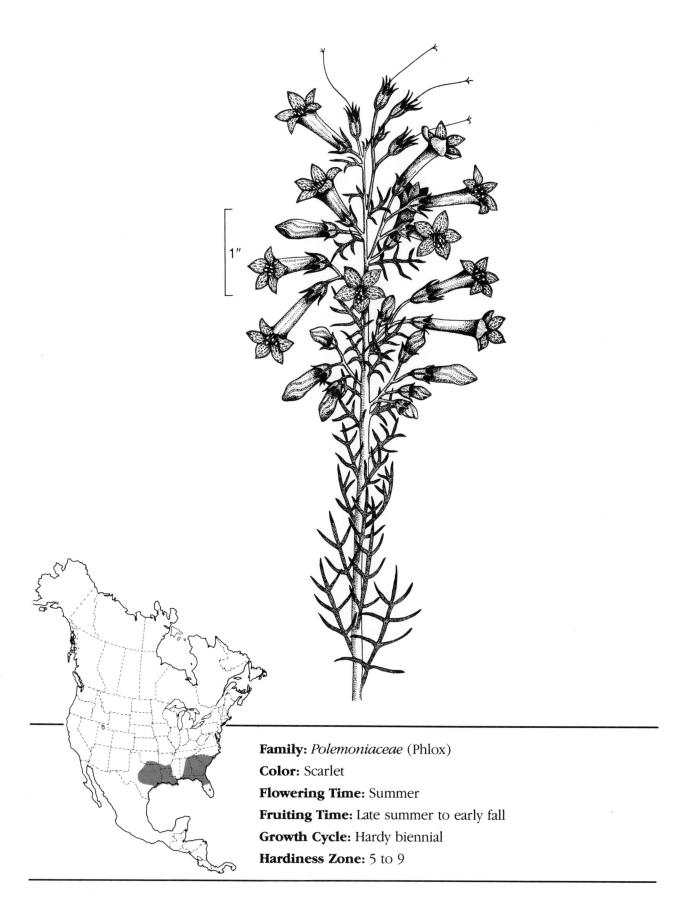

1"

Family: *Polemoniaceae* (Phlox)

Color: Scarlet

Flowering Time: Summer

Fruiting Time: Late summer to early fall

Growth Cycle: Hardy biennial

Hardiness Zone: 5 to 9

STANDING CYPRESS *(Ipomopsis rubra)*

Douglas's iris
(Mountain iris)

Iris douglasiana

While the flowers of this West Coast native, popular with rock gardeners, are usually blue, the colors can range from buff to red-purple. The tufts of 6 or so 1–2-foot, sword-shaped leaves arise from a short, stout, creeping rhizome. Frequently these tough yet flexible leaves have reddish bases. Several showy, 3–4-inch flowers, each with 3 downward-curving, petallike, 2-inch sepals, emerge from leafy bracts atop the 1–2-foot scape. The 3 petallike, 1½-inch style branches with crested stigmas rest against the sepals and encircle the stamens. Each of the 3 narrow 2½-inch petals stands erect. Botanists have noted that a small proportion of the flowers have sterile stamens, and these tend to flower and set fruit earlier in the season. Copious amounts of nectar are produced by Douglas's iris, an ample reward for the bees and bumblebees that pollinate the plant. The ovary, tipped with nipple-like projections, develops into a 2-inch-long 3-sided capsule filled with rounded seeds.

CULTURE

In its native coastal habitat Douglas's iris starts to bloom in midwinter, and flowering progresses inland through the spring. While it can be grown in full sun, it prefers light shade and well-drained but moist soils rich in organic matter. Douglas's iris is a tender species and difficult to grow as a perennial in regions colder than hardiness zone 8, but the rhizomes can be dug up and brought indoors for the winter.

PROPAGATION

Propagate this species either by rhizome divisions or by seed. Divide rhizomes after flowering by cutting the leaves back to about 5 inches and then cutting between the tufted clumps. Set the segments 6–12 inches apart with the leaf bases barely below the soil surface. The seeds of Douglas's iris require moist stratification (3 months at 40°F) and subsequent leaching by ground water to remove germination inhibitors. Plant the seeds ¼–⅓ inch deep in permanent locations, nursery beds, or flats that are left out over the winter. Leave seedlings in the holding beds or flats for the first season before transplanting them to permanent locations. It generally takes several years for seed-propagated plants to flower.

COMPANIONS

Cardinal flower, Western shooting star, blue-eyed grass, coralbells.

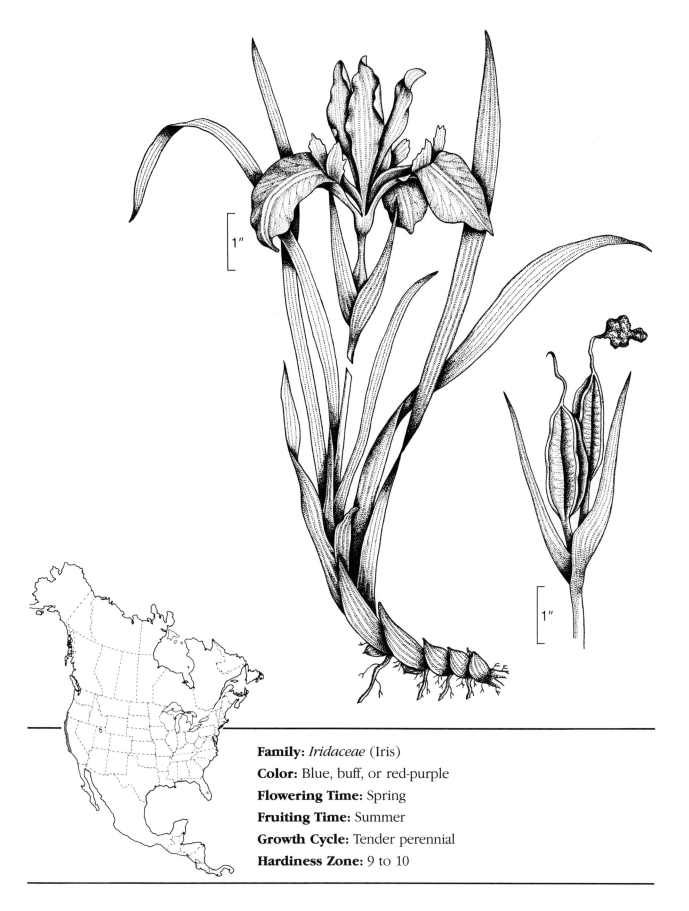

1"

1"

Family: *Iridaceae* (Iris)

Color: Blue, buff, or red-purple

Flowering Time: Spring

Fruiting Time: Summer

Growth Cycle: Tender perennial

Hardiness Zone: 9 to 10

Larger blue flag
(Wild iris)

Iris versicolor

The larger blue flag strongly resembles its domesticated relatives. The firm, sword-shaped leaves, sometimes purplish at the base, are 8–36 inches long and generally overtopped by a flower stalk or scape. Both leaves and flower stalks arise from stout, light-colored, creeping rhizomes, which are poisonous. Each stalk bears 1 or 2 blue flowers which look like slightly scaled-down versions of the garden irises. As with other irises, the flowers emerge from a papery spathe and have a distinctive 3-part arrangement. The 3 true petals point skyward, while the 3 petallike sepals, sometimes called "falls," droop down and flutter in the breeze, giving the plant the common name blue flag. Between the petals and the sepals are 3 arching, blue, petallike styles ending in thin stigma lips. Hidden beneath the styles are the stamens. This unusual arrangement of floral parts ensures cross pollination. When a bee lands on the flower, it is guided to the nectar by the dark purple lines on the sepals, a route that takes it first past the stigma, which is dusted by pollen from the bee's back, and then past the stamens, where the insect inadvertently picks up another load. The flowers last 3–6 days and shrivel as the oval 3-part fruit capsule starts to develop. The seeds are glossy, brown, and disc-shaped.

CULTURE
The larger blue flag is a plant of wet meadows, stream banks and marshes. Even though it can tolerate complete submergence, it is not necessary to have the soil constantly wet, and the plant can be easily grown in slightly moist gardens. Full sun or very light shade and a soil that has a pH anywhere between 5 and 7 are the only other requirements. This is not a demanding plant.

PROPAGATION
Propagation of blue flag is similar to division of most garden iris. Since some people may develop a skin rash upon touching iris roots, it is wise to wear gloves or wash your hands immediately after handling the rhizomes. Once flowering is over in summer, cut the leaves back to about 6 inches and divide the rhizomes with a sharp knife. Plant each piece of rhizome with its attached clump of leaves so that the root system spreads horizontally just below the soil surface. Many of the divisions will flower the next year. To propagate from seed, plant when ripe ⅓ inch deep in the desired location or in flats containing a mixture of peat moss and loam. Keep seeds moist and cool over the winter for rapid, successful germination the following spring. Seedlings can be carefully transplanted from the flats in the spring. It takes about 3 years for plants from seeds to mature and flower.

COMPANIONS
Cardinal flower, Jack-in-the pulpit, turtlehead, false Solomon's seal, spiderwort.

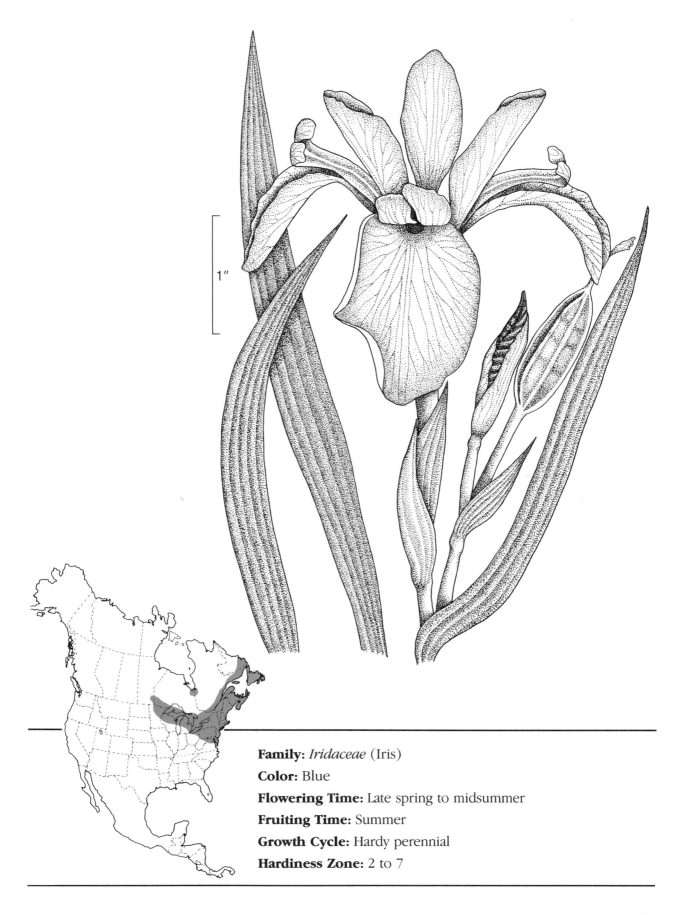

1"

Family: *Iridaceae* (Iris)

Color: Blue

Flowering Time: Late spring to midsummer

Fruiting Time: Summer

Growth Cycle: Hardy perennial

Hardiness Zone: 2 to 7

LARGER BLUE FLAG *(Iris versicolor)*

Goldfields
(Sunshine, baeria, coast goldfields)

Lasthenia californica
(L. chrysostoma, Baeria chrysostoma)

The prospectors in the Gold Rush didn't have to look very hard to find this small annual, for each spring it fills vast stretches of California grasslands with brilliant yellow. The ½–1-inch-wide, yellow, daisylike flower heads top 6-inch-high, sometimes branching stems. Each flower head has between 10 and 14 ¼–⅓-inch-long ray flowers encircling the numerous, slightly darker disc flowers. In its native California, goldfields is pollinated by flies. Pairs of inch-long, grasslike, clasping leaves are scattered along the reddish stems, which, like the leaves, are sparsely covered with sharp, stiff hairs. The small, seedlike fruits of goldfields have 4 sides. Frequently goldfields is listed in seed catalogs by its old generic name, *Baeria,* honoring the Russian zoologist Karl Ernst von Baer.

CULTURE
Goldfields is an annual of meadows and open woods, and grows best in full sun to light shade. In dry, clayey soils goldfields is short and relatively unbranched, but in moister, richer soils it may reach nearly a foot in height and branches freely.

PROPAGATION
Goldfields is propagated as an annual only from seed. Plant the seeds ¼ inch deep where desired in late fall in hardiness zones 9 and 10, and in early spring in colder regions. In the West, goldfields germinates over the winter and quickly flowers in the warmth of spring. In other regions it should be grown as a spring annual planted as soon as the soil can be worked. Goldfields self-seeds freely in its native range, once established, but elsewhere it is advisable to collect the seed as it matures and save it for planting the following spring.

COMPANIONS
Tidy tips, California poppy, baby blue-eyes, wind poppy, owl's clover.

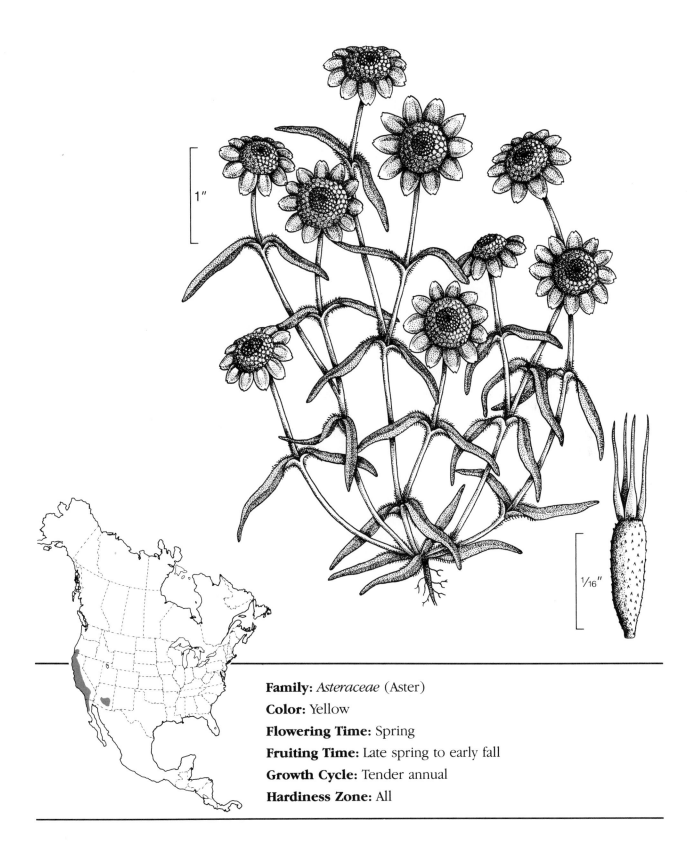

1"

1/16"

Family: *Asteraceae* (Aster)

Color: Yellow

Flowering Time: Spring

Fruiting Time: Late spring to early fall

Growth Cycle: Tender annual

Hardiness Zone: All

GOLDFIELDS *(Lasthenia californica)*

Tidy tips
(Coastal tidy tips)

Layia platyglossa

The tips of this member of the aster family are not actually tidier than those of other composite species, but the plant does have ray flowers with white, 3-toothed petal tips, contrasting with deep yellow petal bases. Tidy tips stands 4–12 inches high with fragrant, 1–1½-inch-wide flower heads atop sprawling, branched stems. While most of the ray flowers have both white and yellow petals, some individuals are all white or all yellow. The disc flowers in the center of the flower heads are yellow with long black anthers, which project beyond the tubular petals and provide an interesting contrast to the ray flowers. Tufted, ⅛-inch-long, dandelion-like seeds are produced by both ray and disc flowers and are released by the summer breezes. Both the stems and the scattered, ½-inch-long leaves are densely hairy.

CULTURE Grow tidy tips in the full sun. Although it is quite adaptable to a variety of garden soils, it does best in sandy loams. The soils should be slightly moist in the early spring, when the seedlings of this annual are growing rapidly, but thereafter the soil can be on the dry side.

PROPAGATION Sow seeds in the fall in the plant's native range, the California grasslands, and in early spring elsewhere. No chilling treatment is needed, and in cold regions tidy tips can be easily started indoors in late winter. Plant seeds ⅛–¼ inch deep in sandy soil and keep moist until germination takes place 1–2 weeks later. Seedlings will grow rapidly and produce flowers in about 60 days. Tidy tips will self-seed in many areas.

COMPANIONS Goldfields, baby blue-eyes, farewell-to-spring, owl's clover, sky lupine, and many other West Coast annuals.

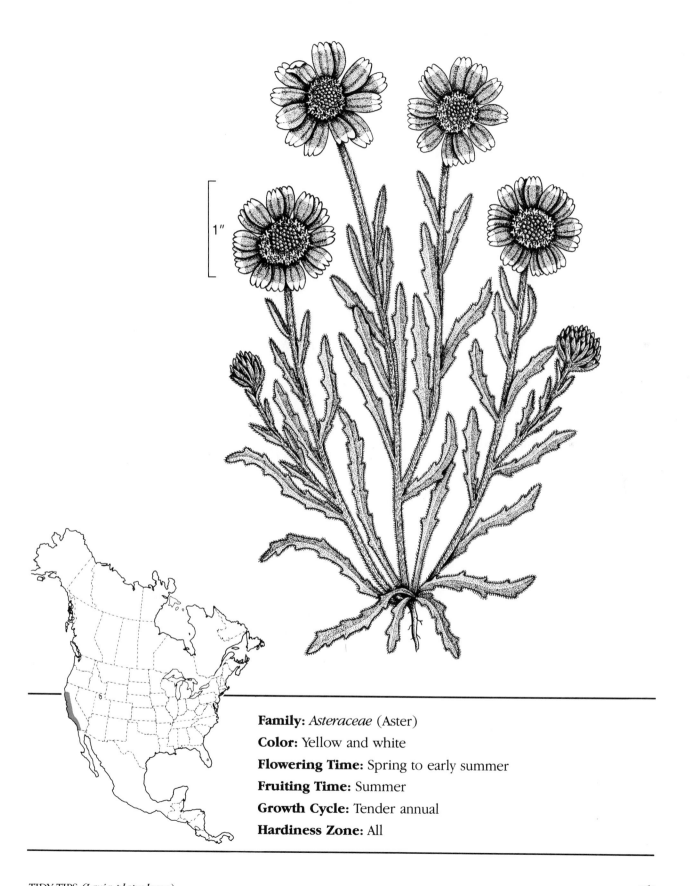

1"

Family: *Asteraceae* (Aster)

Color: Yellow and white

Flowering Time: Spring to early summer

Fruiting Time: Summer

Growth Cycle: Tender annual

Hardiness Zone: All

TIDY TIPS *(Layia platyglossa)*

Bitterroot

Lewisia rediviva

Captain Meriwether Lewis collected a specimen of this plant on July 1, 1806 near the present site of Missoula, Montana, while on his exploration of the Louisiana Purchase. Several years later, a Mr. M'Mahon of Philadelphia took that dried specimen, planted it, and reported that the plant returned to life. The scientific name is thus both a tribute to Captain Lewis and the Latin translation of "restored to life." Despite the common name "bitterroot," the fleshy taproots of the young plants were eaten both raw and cooked by Native Americans. During midsummer, bitterroot is dormant and hidden below the ground. In late summer the root comes to life, and many succulent, 1–3-inch-long leaves appear in clumps at the soil surface, remaining green over the winter and disappearing in the spring. As the spring snows recede, a single spectacular flower appears on each short (4–6-inch) stem in the center of a rosette of leaves, the 4–9 flat, petallike sepals and 12–18 petals ranging in color from deep rose to pink-streaked to white. In the center of the 2-inch-wide flower are numerous stamens and a single ovary with a many-branched style. Individual flowers remain open for several days, but wither once they are pollinated. The bitterroot fruit is a ¼-inch capsule with many tiny, black, shiny seeds. By the time the fruit has ripened in late spring, little of the plant remains above the ground.

CULTURE
Bitterroot is an ideal plant for any rock garden. While it is an extremely hardy perennial, it does not require cold temperatures and can be grown even in hardiness zone 10. Plant bitterroot in well-drained soil in full sun. It needs moisture while flowering and when leaves are visible, but should not be watered during its summer dormancy. In the humid eastern regions of the U.S., note the location of the plant while it is blooming. When the flower withers, cover it with an upside-down flower pot or plastic sheet to reduce the amount of rainwater penetrating the soil. Remember to remove the covering in the late summer.

PROPAGATION
Bitterroot is best propagated by seed, although the root can tolerate division and rough handling. Stratification at 33°F for three months, though not necessary, greatly enhances germination. In the fall, lightly sprinkle seeds in the desired location or in deep flats filled with coarse, gravelly sand. If you leave the flats out over winter, some of the seeds will probably have germinated by spring. The seedlings have 2 fleshy cotyledons, and will develop a few more small leaves and a 3–4-inch pale orange taproot the first growing season. When the leaves wither, the root can be transplanted to a permanent location with the buds barely above the soil surface. By the third growing season the root system will be well developed and the plants may start to flower.

COMPANIONS
Old-man-of-the-mountain, Missouri evening primrose, coralbells, pasque-flower.

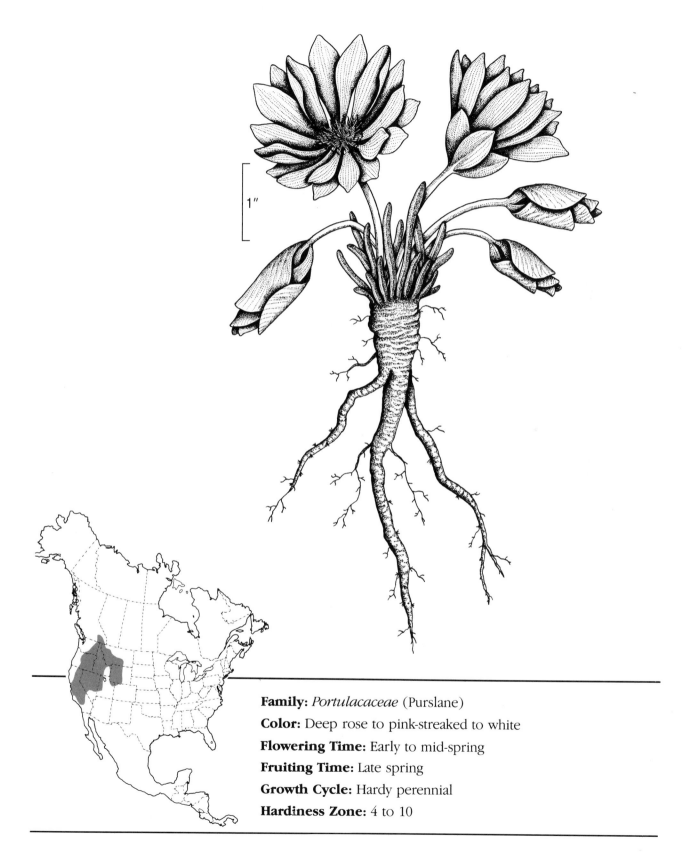

1″

Family: *Portulacaceae* (Purslane)

Color: Deep rose to pink-streaked to white

Flowering Time: Early to mid-spring

Fruiting Time: Late spring

Growth Cycle: Hardy perennial

Hardiness Zone: 4 to 10

BITTERROOT *(Lewisia rediviva)*

Gayfeather

Liatris pycnostachya

(Prairie blazing star, tall blazing star, thick-spike gayfeather, button snakeroot)

The graceful lavender spikes of gayfeather sway in the summer winds of the prairies of the U.S. heartland. It has other common names, such as blazing star (although it is no relation to blazing star on p. 178) and button snakeroot, which refer to the showy display of flower heads densely crowded into a 6–12-inch spike atop an unbranched, 1–5-foot stem. The flower heads have 5–7 individual flowers, each with 5 long, slender, pointed petals, and bloom first at the top of the stem and then progress toward the bottom. The hairy stems are densely covered with 4-inch, fuzzy, grasslike leaves, usually drooping at the tips. The seeds are ⅙ inch long with tufts of hairs at their tips. The root system consists of an inch-long bulbous corm from which fibrous roots extend. Gayfeather and its close relatives have long been cultivated in European gardens as bedding plants and for cut flowers.

CULTURE   While this long-blooming hardy perennial is drought resistant, it grows best in soils that are moist, well drained, and slightly acid to neutral (pH 5.5–7). Gayfeather can be planted in full sun or in areas with sun most of the day. Provide a thick winter mulch in regions colder than hardiness zone 5, removing most in early spring. Gayfeather sometimes require staking, and so are ideal for the backs of borders, or for prairies and meadows with medium to tall grass species to help support the spikes.

PROPAGATION   Gayfeather can be propagated by seed or by division of the corm. Seed propagation tends to be preferable, but the seeds require moist stratification (3 months at 40°F) in order to germinate. Nick the seeds with a sharp knife and plant in the fall about ¼ inch deep in flats filled with a mixture of sandy loam and compost. Leave outdoors for the winter, and the seeds will germinate after 2–3 weeks of warm temperatures in the spring. The seedlings should be left in the flat for the first growing season since the newly forming roots are quite fragile. Transplant the small corms that form by the first fall to a nursery bed or a permanent location. Many will produce flowering plants the next summer, and all should flower the third year. Spring is the best time to divide the corms in regions colder than hardiness zone 6 since they are sensitive to frost-heaving. Divide the corm vertically into pieces, each with at least one bud. Plant the divisions vertically, spaced 1–2 feet apart, with the buds 2 inches below the soil surface.

COMPANIONS   Culver's root, Eastern shooting star, spiderwort, rattlesnake master, and many other prairie plants.

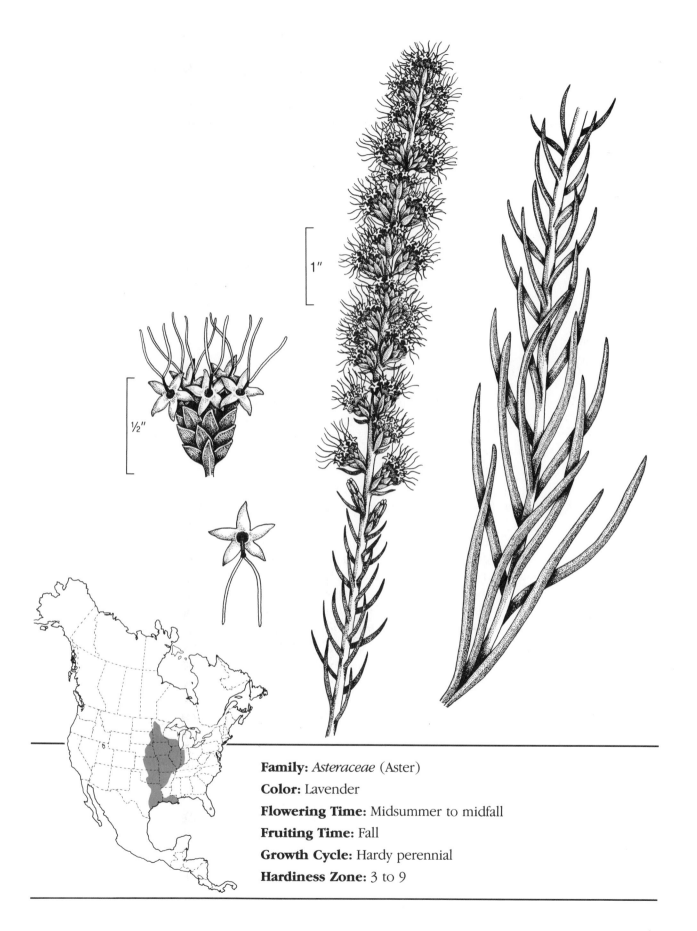

Family: *Asteraceae* (Aster)

Color: Lavender

Flowering Time: Midsummer to midfall

Fruiting Time: Fall

Growth Cycle: Hardy perennial

Hardiness Zone: 3 to 9

1"

½"

GAYFEATHER *(Liatris pycnostachya)*

Wood lily
(Wild red lily, flame lily)

Lilium philadelphicum
(Lilium umbellatum)

This attractive lily grows both in open eastern woodlands and in western grasslands. One of the few lily species with flowers that point upward, wood lilies have gaps between the bases of the petals and the sepals, which allow rainwater to drain out. The flowers range from bright red, in parts of the plant's western range, to orange, but all have purple spots on the petals and petallike sepals. Flowers occur singly or in clusters atop an 8–36-inch stem. In the eastern variety the leaves are arranged in whorls around the stem, while in the western variety they are scattered along the stem. The roots of this hardy perennial arise from a deep-seated, white, scaly bulb an inch or so in diameter. New bulbs are formed at the sides of the mature bulb each year. The fruit of the wood lily is a 1–2-inch capsule densely packed with flat, ¼-inch seeds with papery wings.

CULTURE

While one variety of wood lily will grow in swamps, others grow in relatively dry prairies. One of the most drought-tolerant lily species, it generally grows best in well-drained soils. Although wood lilies do grow in the light shade of open woodlands, they should be planted where they can get full sun for at least part of the day. They do best in soils that are rich in humus and moderately acidic (pH 4–6).

PROPAGATION

Propagation is easiest from divisions of the scaly bulb, which can be dug as soon as the lily goes into dormancy and the seed is ripe in the late summer. Be careful, when digging the bulbs, not to damage the roots of the mature plant. The small offset bulbs can be planted about 3 inches deep and mulched with pine needles and oak leaves, or individual bulb scales of the mature bulb can be planted ½ inch deep in flats filled with light sandy soil mixed with peat moss and left out to overwinter. Replant the old bulb about 5 inches deep. When seedlings become dormant the next year, transplant the small bulbs 3 inches deep in the desired location. It will take several years for the plants to reach maturity and flower. Propagation from seed is slower, but generally successful. Plant seeds in outdoor flats as in bulb scale propagation, keeping the seedbed moist but not wet. The seeds will generally germinate in the fall, overwinter as tiny bulbs, and resume growth the following spring. Transplant the small bulbs when they are dormant the following summer. Seedlings from seeds will generally produce a single leaf the first year and take 3–5 years to reach maturity and flower.

COMPANIONS

A large number of companions, ranging from prairie plants like gayfeather, butterfly weed, and asters, to plants of open woodlands like bluets, Solomon's seal, and mayapple.

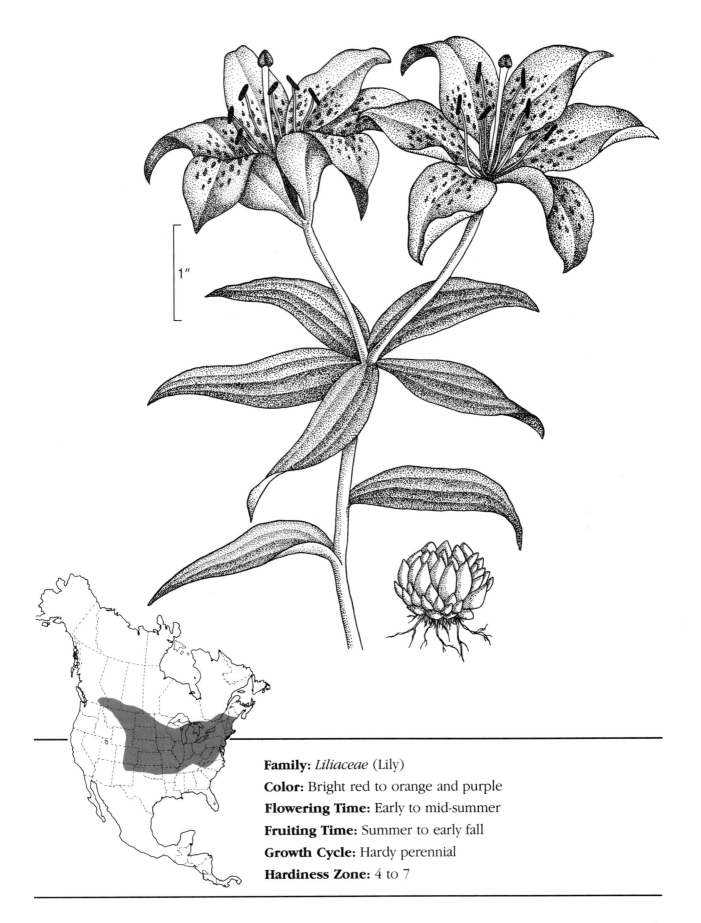

1"

Family: *Liliaceae* (Lily)

Color: Bright red to orange and purple

Flowering Time: Early to mid-summer

Fruiting Time: Summer to early fall

Growth Cycle: Hardy perennial

Hardiness Zone: 4 to 7

WOOD LILY *(Lilium philadelphicum)*

167

Linanthus

Linanthus grandiflorus

(Mountain phlox, California phlox, large-flowered linanthus)

Linanthus is a strikingly beautiful spring annual of the Coastal Ranges in California. The 4–20-inch-high stems are encircled by whorls of dark green leaves, deeply cleft into inch-long, linear, tinelike segments. Dense clusters of silky white, inch-long, trumpet-shaped flowers tinged with pink or lavender are borne at the tops of the stems. The hairy calyx surrounds the flower tube, which opens into 5 broad petals. Inside the throat of the flower 5 golden stamens are visible above the stigmas and the ring of tufted hairs. Linanthus has a capsular fruit with 1/16-inch irregularly angled, light brown, membrane-coated seeds.

CULTURE
In its native California, linanthus forms dense colonies in the spring and then usually dies out during the summer dry season, but the long flowering period can be further prolonged by periodic watering. Plant this annual in full sun on light, sandy soils. The soils should be moist but not wet while the seedlings are growing rapidly in the spring, and then irrigated only if the soil becomes overly dry.

PROPAGATION
Sow the seeds 1/8–1/4 inch deep in their desired locations. The seeds require no chilling treatment and should be planted in the fall in their native range and in the midspring elsewhere.

COMPANIONS
California poppy, wind poppy, tidy tips, baby blue-eyes and other West Coast annuals.

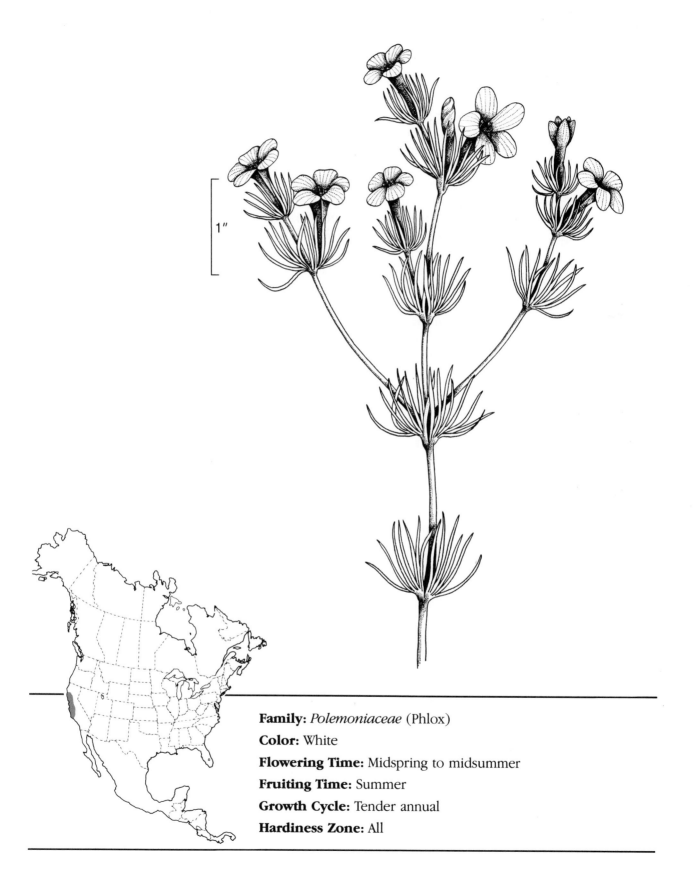

1"

Family: *Polemoniaceae* (Phlox)

Color: White

Flowering Time: Midspring to midsummer

Fruiting Time: Summer

Growth Cycle: Tender annual

Hardiness Zone: All

LINANTHUS *(Linanthus grandiflorus)*

Blue flax
(Prairie flax)

Linum lewisii

This widely distributed perennial of the western two-thirds of North America is a close relative of the European species from which linen is made. Blue flax stands 1–3 feet high with clusters of 1½-inch sky blue flowers arching to one side atop slender stems. Flowering begins with the long days of spring and continues through the summer. The 5-petaled flowers usually last only a day before withering in the hot sun, but new blooms appear in the cluster every day. At the center of the flower are 5 light-colored stamens and 5 stigmas. The fruit is a ¼-inch capsule containing 10 shiny, dark, flattened ⅛-inch seeds. The several stems, which arise in a clump, are densely covered by narrow, 1-inch leaves.

CULTURE   Blue flax is a plant of open habitats and thus requires full sun. It will grow robustly on soils ranging from alkaline to acidic (pH 5–7.5) as long as the soil is well drained and dry. It grows well in gardens, but should not be watered excessively. A very hardy perennial, blue flax can be grown in virtually all hardiness zones.

PROPAGATION   Blue flax is usually propagated by seed. Root division is generally not as successful since the plant is difficult to transplant. In the fall or spring, plant the seeds ⅛ inch deep where you wish them to grow. Germination, which is stimulated by light, is generally rapid as temperatures reach 70°F in the spring. Blue flax will generally flower the first year, and will self-seed once established.

COMPANIONS   Blanketflower, butterfly weed, lance-leaved coreopsis, Mexican hat.

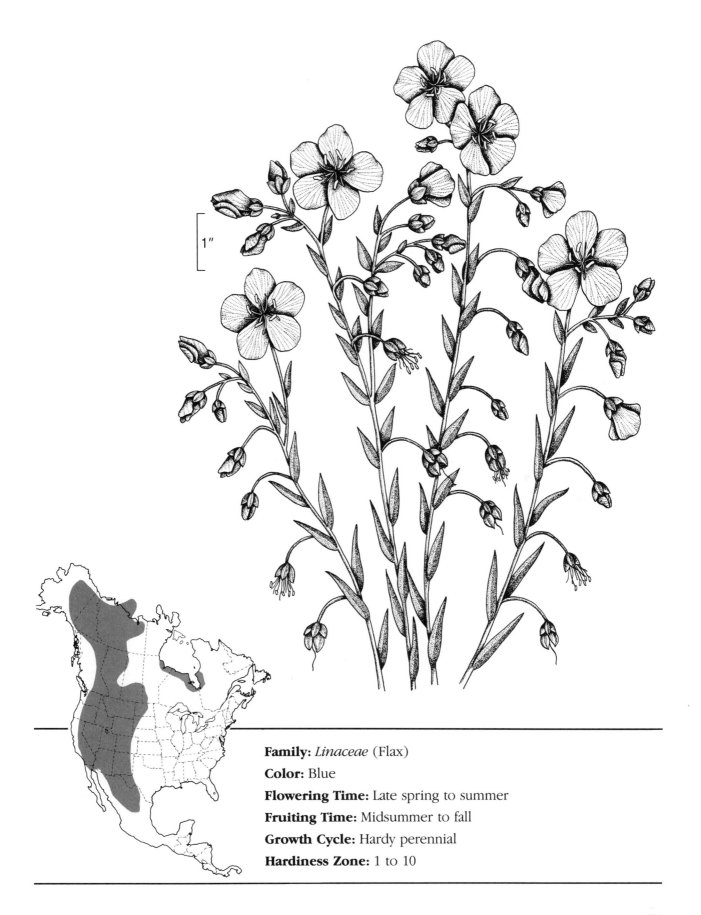

Family: *Linaceae* (Flax)

Color: Blue

Flowering Time: Late spring to summer

Fruiting Time: Midsummer to fall

Growth Cycle: Hardy perennial

Hardiness Zone: 1 to 10

BLUE FLAX *(Linum lewisii)*

Cardinal flower

Lobelia cardinalis

The cardinal flower is one of the least subtle wildflowers and a beautiful addition to any sunny, moist location. Usually 1–3 feet high, the plants may reach 5 feet under optimum conditions. The scarlet to deep red, inch-long flowers, borne in open clusters at the top of the stem, are tubular with 2 erect lobes on the upper lip and 3 pointed lobes on the lower lip. The fused stamens and style protrude from between the lobes of the upper lip and have a hairy white "beard." Pollen is shed from the anthers before the flower's stigma is mature, and dusts the heads of hummingbirds, the main pollinators, as they drink the sweet nectar. Actually, not all cardinal flowers produce nectar, but those that do sometimes have holes chewed through the base of their tubes by bumblebees taking a shortcut in. The fruit is a 2-part capsule containing many small (1/20-inch), elliptical, shiny brown seeds with fluted projections. The fibrous white roots form an extensive network as they grow quickly in damp soils. The cardinal flower has a wide-ranging distribution, although some botanists claim the eastern and western plants are different species.

CULTURE   Cardinal flower is a plant of moist, wet, or even submerged soils, which are partially exposed to the sun, but it is quite adaptable to normal garden conditions. It grows well in slightly acidic to neutral soils (pH 5.5–7) but soil pH is not as important as maintenance of soil moisture. This perennial is hardy to zone 4.

PROPAGATION   Cardinal flower is easily propagated by seed, division, or layering. Germination is enhanced by moist stratification and requires exposure of the seed to light. In the fall, sprinkle the seeds on top of humusy soil in flats, moisten, and provide as thin a layer of mulch as possible. Leave the flats outdoors over winter, keeping the soil moist at all times. To let light in without drying the soil, cover the top of the flat with a sheet of transparent plastic film. Germination should occur after about 3 weeks of warm weather in the spring. Allow the seedlings to grow the first summer in the flat, and then transplant them to their permanent locations in the fall or following spring. Plants from seed will usually flower the second year. Make root divisions in the late fall or early spring. Set rootstocks 6–12 inches apart with buds just at soil surface, and mulch for the winter. To propagate by "layering," in midsummer, carefully bend the stem over so it is resting on the ground, and stake the tip. Cover the stem with 1/4 inch of soil and keep moist. Along the buried stem, new roots will form and new shoots will emerge. In the fall the stem segments between the new shoots can be cut and the new plants can be transplanted.

COMPANIONS   Larger blue flag, American bellflower, New England aster, nodding wild onion, closed gentian, turtlehead.

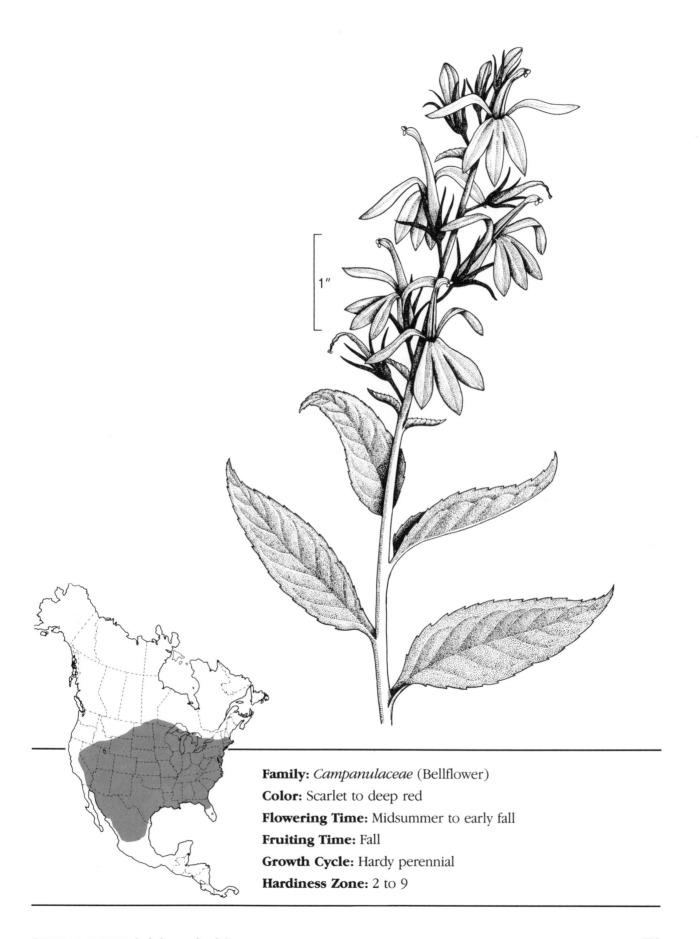

Family: *Campanulaceae* (Bellflower)

Color: Scarlet to deep red

Flowering Time: Midsummer to early fall

Fruiting Time: Fall

Growth Cycle: Hardy perennial

Hardiness Zone: 2 to 9

CARDINAL FLOWER *(Lobelia cardinalis)*

Sky lupine
(Field lupine, Douglas's lupine)

Lupinus nanus

The flowers of this petite annual lupine mirror the coastal California skies in springtime, with whorls of blue and white pealike flowers atop 4–20-inch stems. Each of the ½-inch-long flowers has a rich blue top petal, known as a banner. At its base is a white or yellow spot flecked with dark blue. The lateral petals, or wings, and the 2 lower petals fused into the "keel" are clear blue. A short fuzzy beanlike pod contains 4–8 gray-brown, mottled, ⅛-inch seeds, which are ejected from the pods as the fruits ripen. The leaves of sky lupine are palmately compound with 5–7 narrow, inch-long leaflets, covered with long hairs.

CULTURE

Grow this annual in full sun on soils that are on the dry side, like sandy loams and dryish clayey loams. The seedlings need moisture in early spring while they become established, but little water once flowering starts. Overwatering can lead to mildew problems in humid regions. If inoculation is necessary to establish sky lupine in your soil, use *Lupinus* rhizobia (Nitragin-type Lupinus Special #2).

PROPAGATION

As with other annuals, sky lupine is propagated only by seed. To collect the seeds in the wild, gather the pods when they turn brown and place them in a paper bag. Fold the top of the bag closed so the seeds aren't shot out while you have your back turned. The seeds do not require chilling, but do require scarification in order to germinate. Rub the seeds briskly between two sheets of medium grit sandpaper to scratch the seed coat and allow moisture to enter. Letting the seeds soak in warm (180°F) water and then cool overnight will also enhance germination. Plant the seeds ¼ inch deep in the desired location. Germination takes 2–3 weeks at 68°F, and seedlings should be thinned to 2–3 inches apart after a month or so. In their native range, sky lupines generally self-seed.

COMPANIONS

California poppy, tidy tips, Douglas's wallflower, golden yarrow, goldfields, farewell-to-spring.

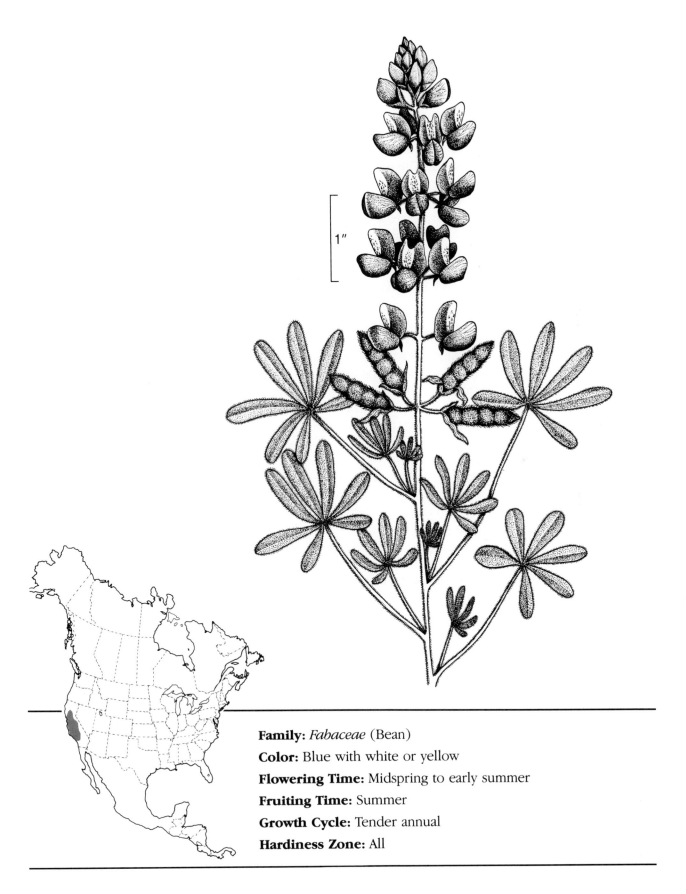

Family: *Fabaceae* (Bean)

Color: Blue with white or yellow

Flowering Time: Midspring to early summer

Fruiting Time: Summer

Growth Cycle: Tender annual

Hardiness Zone: All

SKY LUPINE *(Lupinus nanus)*

Purple annual lupine
(Arroyo lupine, succulent lupine)

Lupinus succulentus

With the growing disturbance of the Southern California landscape, this lovely annual has increasingly become a weedy roadside plant. Purple annual lupine is also abundant immediately following fires in the coastal sage scrub of its native range. The succulent, fleshy, 8–24-inch stems have 7–9 dark green, smooth, round-tipped, 2–3-inch leaflets making up the palmately compound leaves, which track the sun from east to west during the daylight hours. Clusters of deep purple to dark blue to rusty red blooms are borne at the tops of the stems. Each of the ½-inch-long flowers is a solid color except for the uppermost banner petal, which has a yellow center. Honeybees are the major pollinator of the purple annual lupine. The 2-inch-long pod-fruits have 8–10 brown, mottled, ¼-inch-long seeds.

CULTURE   Purple annual lupine is quite adaptable to garden conditions. It should be grown in full sun on dry, well-drained soils. Keep the soil moist as the seeds are germinating and the seedlings become established, but don't overwater in humid regions, or mildew diseases of the leaves may result. If you need to inoculate purple annual lupine to establish it in your soil, use *Lupinus* rhizobia (Nitragin-type Lupinus special #5).

PROPAGATION   Like many other legume seeds, purple annual lupine germinates best following scarification, or nicking of the seed coat. Rub the seeds between two sheets of medium grit sandpaper and allow the seeds to soak overnight in warm water before planting at a depth of ⅛–¼ inch. Plant seeds in the fall in their native range, and in the early spring elsewhere. If you start the seeds indoors in the early spring, transplant the seedlings to desired locations before they get too large, or establishment may be difficult. Thin seedlings to 6 inches apart.

COMPANIONS   Sky lupine, wind poppy, golden yarrow, Douglas's wallflower, blazing star, and other West Coast annuals.

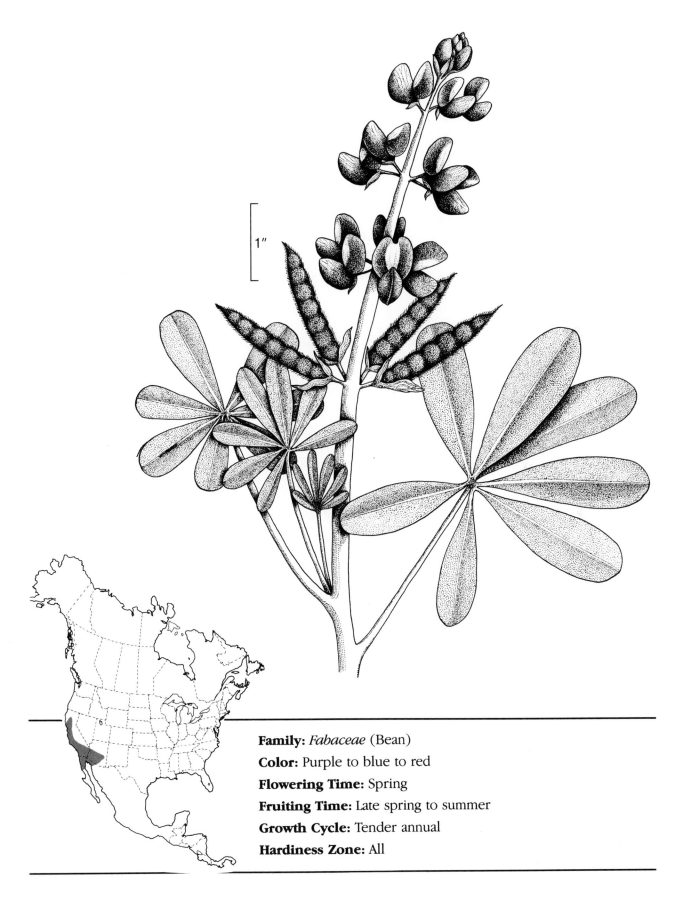

1"

Family: *Fabaceae* (Bean)

Color: Purple to blue to red

Flowering Time: Spring

Fruiting Time: Late spring to summer

Growth Cycle: Tender annual

Hardiness Zone: All

PURPLE ANNUAL LUPINE *(Lupinus succulentus)*

Blazing star
(Evening star)

Mentzelia lindleyi
(Bartonia aurea)

Not only does this 5-petaled star come out in the evening, but it also has a meteor shower of golden stamens at its center. This 1–4-foot-high annual has 2–3-inch-long, clasping, coarsely toothed, hairy, dandelion-like leaves scattered along its hairy stems. Groups of 2–3 fragrant, 2–3-inch, golden yellow flowers open in the evening at the tops of the plant, and close by noon the next day. The individual flowers have 5 broad, rounded petals with pointed tips, frequently with splotches of red-orange at their bases. Many long stamens with yellow anthers rest against the petals as the flower opens, but rise in a cluster at the center of the flower by the following morning. The 1–1½-inch-long, hairy, capsular fruit is filled with many small (1/16-inch) angular seeds.

CULTURE Blazing star should be grown on moist to dry soils in the full sun. Well-drained soils are essential for successfully maintaining this plant, which is otherwise adaptable to sandy or clayey soils of just about any fertility. Soils should be kept moist until flowering starts and then should be allowed to dry out.

PROPAGATION This annual is propagated by seed which should be sown in the fall in hardiness zones 9 and 10, and in the spring in other regions. The seed does not require chilling treatment for germination. Plant the seeds 1/8 inch deep in well-drained soil where desired, or in flats for a prolonged flowering season in the East. Transplant or thin the seedlings to 6 inches apart. In its native range, once established, blazing star freely self-seeds.

COMPANIONS Golden poppy, lupines, penstemons, purple heliotrope.

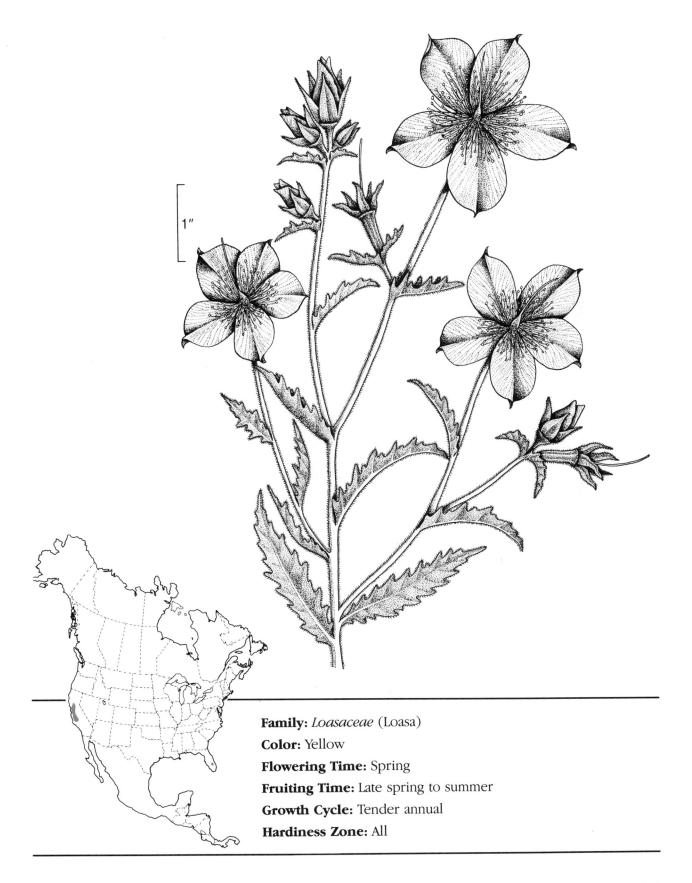

Family: *Loasaceae* (Loasa)

Color: Yellow

Flowering Time: Spring

Fruiting Time: Late spring to summer

Growth Cycle: Tender annual

Hardiness Zone: All

BLAZING STAR *(Mentzelia lindleyi)*

Virginia bluebells
(Virginia cowslip)

Mertensia virginica

Virginia bluebells have a long tradition of success in the gardens of both North America and Europe, where they are called mertensias. This handsome plant has clusters of pale blue flowers on a stem that is coiled at the tip, a trait common with other members of the forget-me-not family. The trumpet-shaped, inch-long flowers are woolly inside and have 5 somewhat puckered lobes. The flowers are pink as they emerge from the bud but quickly turn sky-blue or lavender-blue. The smooth, succulent, 8–24-inch-high stems have 3-inch pale gray-green leaves scattered below the flowers. The fruits of the Virginia bluebells are ⅛-inch nutlets, fleshy at first, and then dry and wrinkled with white ridges. The entire top of the plant starts to go into dormancy in early summer just as the fruits become fully mature. The leaves and stem wither and disappear entirely by mid-summer as the plant retreats back to its black, tuberous root system.

CULTURE Virginia bluebells adapt well to the garden, their only consistent requirement being moist soils. They can be planted successfully in full sun to partial shade, and they tolerate soils that are moderately acid to slightly alkaline (pH 5.5–8).

PROPAGATION This plant can be propagated from either seeds or root divisions. Seeds can be planted in the summer or fall and germinate best in spring if chilled during the winter. Seeds should be planted about ¼ inch deep and kept moist. It takes about 3 years for seedlings to mature and flower. Divide roots just after the top of the plant withers. It is a good idea to mark the location of vigorous, mature plants to use as propagation stock before their tops disappear in the early summer. Set root segments, each with at least one bud, 1 inch deep and give a light mulch of deciduous leaves. Once established, Virginia bluebells self-seed readily.

COMPANIONS White baneberry, Jack-in-the-pulpit, spring beauty, wild ginger, Eastern shooting star.

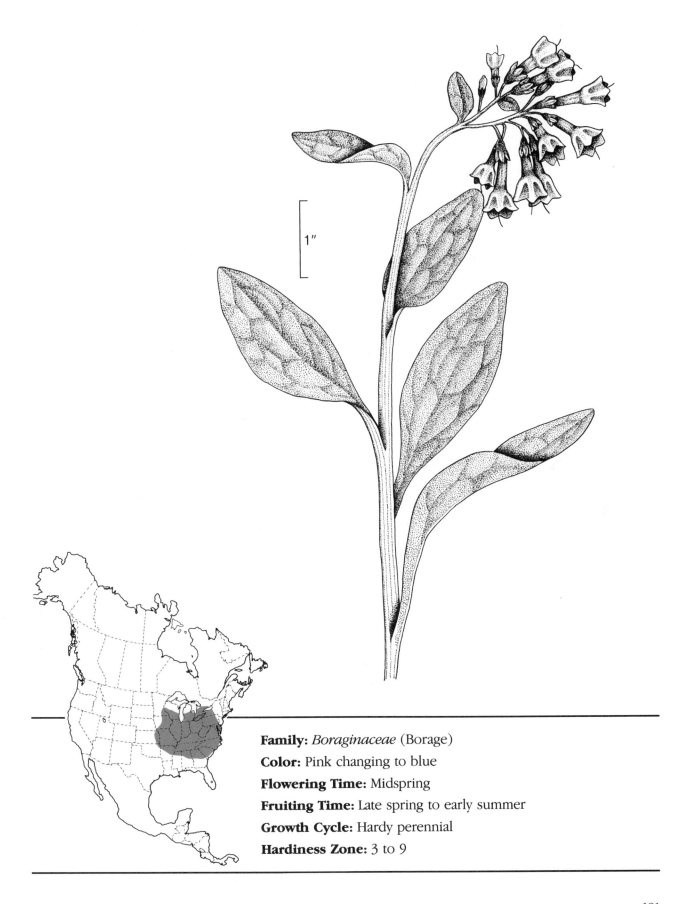

Family: *Boraginaceae* (Borage)

Color: Pink changing to blue

Flowering Time: Midspring

Fruiting Time: Late spring to early summer

Growth Cycle: Hardy perennial

Hardiness Zone: 3 to 9

VIRGINIA BLUEBELLS *(Mertensia virginica)*

Partridgeberry
(Twinberry, checkerberry, running box)

Mitchella repens

A favorite for indoor terraria, partridgeberry is even more effective as ground cover in cool, shady locations outdoors. The stems of this hardy perennial trail over the ground, barely reaching an inch in height. Its pairs of small, round, dark green, glossy leaves are evergreen and frequently variegated with white. The flowers, like the leaves, come in pairs, and are usually white or very light pink, fragrant, and shaped like small trumpets with 4 pointed lobes. From the pair of flowers a single red, berrylike, edible fruit is produced by the fusion of the two ovaries. The fruits, which have a peppermint taste, contain 4–8 bony gray nutlets, and persist through the winter, or until grouse, quail, or other ground-foraging birds find them.

CULTURE   Partridgeberry grows best in cool, moist, shaded, and, especially, humus-rich soils. It has its maximum growth when temperatures are below 60°F in the spring, before the deciduous trees have leafed out. It can be grown on dry to moist soils, but prefers the latter. Partridgeberry will also tolerate a range of soil acidity from pH 4–6. A light mulching with pine or hemlock needles can supply the proper organic matter and acidity conditions.

PROPAGATION   The easiest way to propagate partridgeberry is from divisions or cuttings of the running stems. One method is to cut a 6–12-inch piece from the leading tip of the plant in spring, carefully uprooting the section to avoid breaking off the small roots. Plant the section in well-drained soil into which you have worked compost and peat moss. Keep the cuttings moist and they will root with ease and generally bear flowers the second year. Propagation from seed is usually much slower. The seeds require moisture and cold stratification for proper germination. Gather the fruits in the fall and remove the nutlets from the pulp. Plant the seeds ¼ inch deep in flats containing a mixture of sand, compost, and peat moss. Cover the flats with a ¼-inch layer of pine needles and leave out for the winter. Germination in the spring generally takes 2–3 weeks, once the temperature has risen above 60°F. Transplant the seedlings to permanent locations in the fall. Since partridgeberry can be grown south of its natural range, if provided with a shady, acid, moist environment, seeds planted in those areas should be artificially stratified in moist peat moss at 40°F for at least 6 weeks.

COMPANIONS   Wintergreen, pink lady's slipper, trilliums, yellow clintonia, bunchberry.

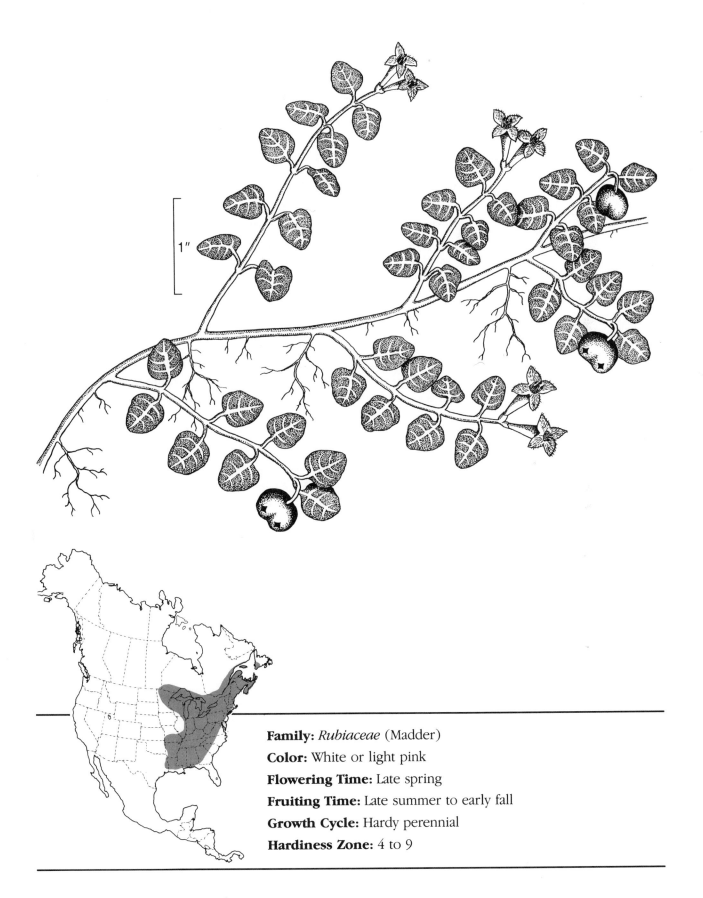

Family: *Rubiaceae* (Madder)

Color: White or light pink

Flowering Time: Late spring

Fruiting Time: Late summer to early fall

Growth Cycle: Hardy perennial

Hardiness Zone: 4 to 9

PARTRIDGEBERRY *(Mitchella repens)*

Wild bergamot

Monarda fistulosa

Wild bergamot's membership in the mint family is indicated by the familiar square stems. The name wild bergamot refers to the similarity between the pungent aromas of this plant's foliage and the fruit of the bergamot orange tree of Europe, and indeed the leaves can be used as an herb tea. Wild bergamot also makes a good cut flower. The 2–4-foot-high, fuzzy stems bear pairs of firm, 3-inch-long, hairy, gray-green leaves and a 2-inch whorl of lilac to pink flowers in clusters at the top of the plant. The 2-lobed upper lip of the tubular, 1-inch flower bears a tuft of hairs and arches over the 3-lobed lower lip. The long stamens protrude from the throat of the flower and arch slightly upward. The seeds are $\frac{1}{16}$-inch elliptical nutlets.

CULTURE Wild bergamot is a widely distributed hardy perennial which grows well in full sun to light shade. While typically found growing in dry, open meadows, grasslands, and woods, it responds well to moisture if the soil is well drained, but may develop mildew on its leaves if grown in too humid a location. Soil acidity conditions (pH 5–7.5) are not as important as situating the plants where they are exposed to the full sun at least part of each day.

PROPAGATION The easiest way to propagate wild bergamot is from seeds. In the fall, plant the seeds $\frac{1}{4}$ inch deep in flats or in the desired location. They can also be planted indoors in the early spring. The seeds don't require stratification, although germination may be faster if they are given a chilling treatment. Stratified seeds germinate quickly in the spring (1–2 weeks) and grow rapidly, sometimes producing flowers in the first year. Most of the plants grown from seed will flower the second year. By the end of the first season wild bergamot will start to produce multiple shoots, and over time the plants may become bunchy, even crowding out other plants in their immediate vicinity. Clumps can be divided in the spring and the pieces of rhizome with buds set 1 inch deep and 1–2 feet apart. Avoid fall divisions, since wild bergamot is susceptible to winter-kill.

COMPANIONS Black-eyed Susan, gayfeather, Culver's root, New England aster, butterfly weed.

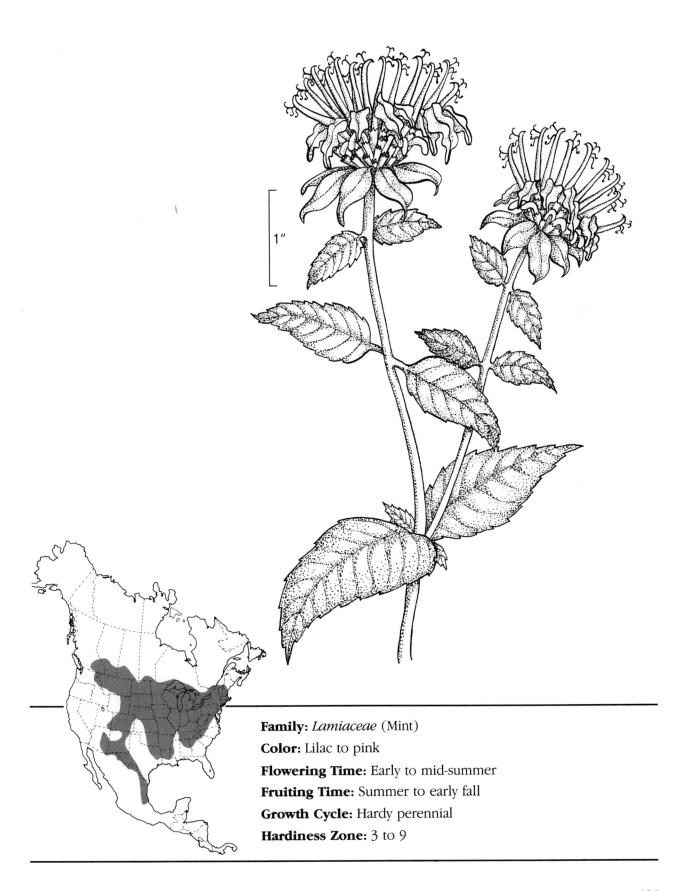

1"

Family: *Lamiaceae* (Mint)

Color: Lilac to pink

Flowering Time: Early to mid-summer

Fruiting Time: Summer to early fall

Growth Cycle: Hardy perennial

Hardiness Zone: 3 to 9

WILD BERGAMOT *(Monarda fistulosa)*

Baby blue-eyes
(Marianas, California bluebells)

Nemophila menziesii

Some botanists divide this annual into three separate species. However, as Europeans have known for over a century, any of the forms are easily grown and make attractive additions to the garden. Baby blue-eyes has spreading, straggling, branched stems with pairs of 1–2-inch-long, somewhat hairy leaves resembling those of the dandelion except that they have small rounded lobes. Atop the 10–20-inch stems are 1–1½-inch-wide flowers with 5 broad petals, 5 stamens with dark anthers, and a pistil with a branched style. Most often the petals are blue at the rounded tip and white with blue flecks or radiating streaks at the base, but in some forms the petals are all blue, or sky blue with dark blue dots at their bases. Bees visit the flowers in search of nectar and remove the pollen several days prior to the stigma becoming fully exposed, a timing pattern that enhances cross pollination, though individual flowers are self-fertile. Baby blue-eyes' flowers open and close in response to air temperature, the petals folding inward at night or in the cold. Extremely hot weather, however, shortens its flowering season. The fruit is a ¼–½-inch round, hairy capsule containing 10–20, dark, ⅛-inch seeds.

CULTURE

This hardy annual grows best in full sun to partial shade, on well-drained soils that are moist but not wet. The flowering season can be prolonged if the soils are kept moist while the plants are in flower. Baby blue-eyes is adaptable to the usual range of soil nutrient and pH conditions found in most gardens and is easy to cultivate.

PROPAGATION

In hardiness zones 9 and 10 the seeds should be planted in the fall, and elsewhere in the early spring. With fall planting, seeds will germinate in the fall and the seedlings will remain as a rosette of leaves until flowering the following spring. The seeds, which require no chilling treatment for germination, should be planted ⅛ inch deep in the desired location. Germination is most rapid (1–2 weeks) when the seeds are kept moist and are planted when the day length is relatively short and the soil temperature is below 80°F. In many regions baby blue-eyes will self-seed.

COMPANIONS

California poppy, tidy tips, Chinese houses, Western shooting star, linanthus, farewell-to-spring.

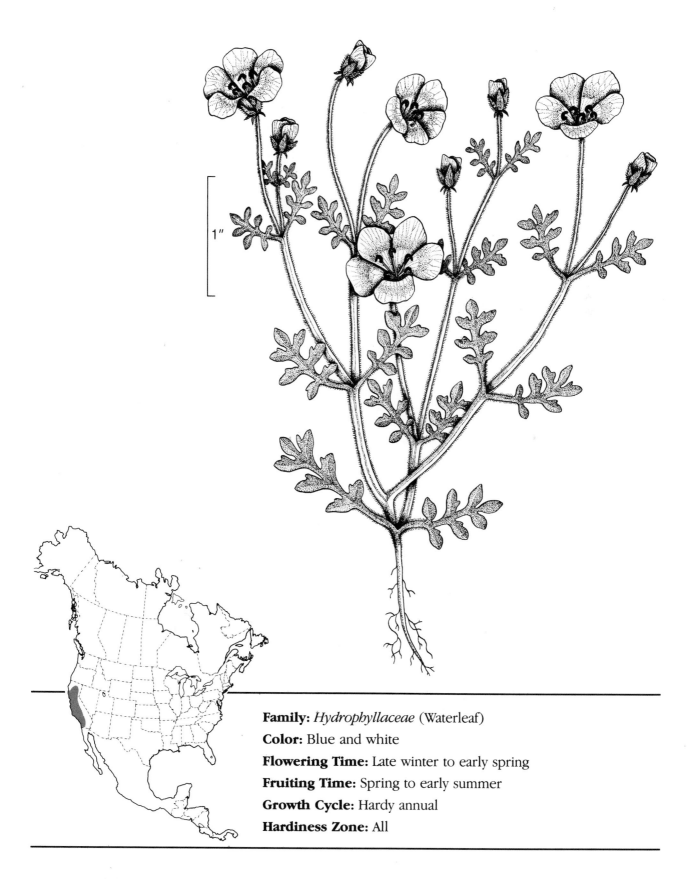

1"

Family: *Hydrophyllaceae* (Waterleaf)

Color: Blue and white

Flowering Time: Late winter to early spring

Fruiting Time: Spring to early summer

Growth Cycle: Hardy annual

Hardiness Zone: All

BABY BLUE-EYES *(Nemophila menziesii)*

187

Giant evening primrose
(Hooker's evening primrose)

Oenothera hookeri

This is one of the largest and showiest of the evening primroses. There are several naturally occurring subspecies of this plant with differing heights and varying flower sizes. The giant evening primrose is usually 3–5 feet tall, although there are reports of plants ranging from 1 foot to 9 feet in height. Regardless of the eventual height of the stem, this biennial spends its first year as a low rosette of leaves, clumped at the ground surface. The second year the stem bolts, and numerous 5–10-inch-long leaves appear scattered along the reddish stem. The leaves, stems, and bases of the flower clusters are frequently covered with soft hairs. Clusters of bright yellow, saucer-shaped flowers are borne at the tops of the stems. To the human eye, the petals appear a uniform rich yellow, but to the bees that pollinate this species and can see ultraviolet light, the flowers display yellow and purple petals. Each of the 2½–3½-inch flowers has 4 broad petals which unfurl in the evening and wither in the noonday sun, turning orange with age. The fruit is a slender, 1–2-inch-long, woody capsule containing many tiny seeds.

CULTURE
Giant evening primrose should be planted in full sun and given ample room. It is not fussy about soil acidity conditions, and while it grows best in moist soils, it is also tolerant of moderately dry soils. This biennial can be grown in hardiness zones 4 to 10.

PROPAGATION
The easiest way to propagate giant evening primrose is from seed. Seed planted in spring or fall should be scratched into the surface of the soil in the desired location and kept moist. No stratification of the seed is needed. Thin the seedlings to 12–18 inches apart or more. Seedlings will form a rosette the first season and flower the second season. As with other biennials, it is a good idea to plant the seeds two successive years to establish a continuously flowering population.

COMPANIONS
Cardinal flower, Rocky Mountain penstemon, meadow beauty, bear grass.

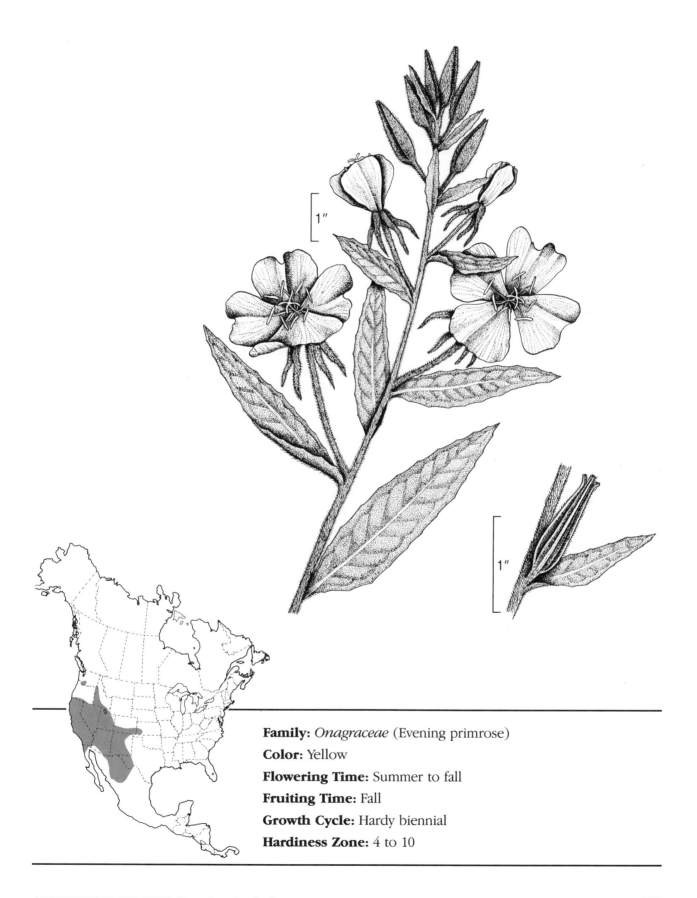

Family: *Onagraceae* (Evening primrose)

Color: Yellow

Flowering Time: Summer to fall

Fruiting Time: Fall

Growth Cycle: Hardy biennial

Hardiness Zone: 4 to 10

GIANT EVENING PRIMROSE *(Oenothera hookeri)*

189

Missouri evening primrose   *Oenothera missouriensis*
(Ozark sundrops, glade lily, Missouri primrose)

A relative of the garden sundrop *(Oenothera fruticosa)*, Missouri evening primrose is considerably shorter (8–10 inches high) and has larger (3–6-inch), showier flowers. The short, hairy stems are densely covered with 5-inch-long, thick, narrow, lance-shaped leaves, and the erect flower buds are spotted with red. Brilliant yellow, 4-petaled flowers droop somewhat as they open in the evening, and fade the next day. As with other members of the evening primrose family, this species has 8 stamens and a 4-part, cross-shaped stigma. The slender style is surrounded by the green calyx tube, which is so long (2–5 inches) it might be mistaken for the flower stalk. The fruit is a large (2–3-inch), ovaloid, 4-winged pod with many small seeds. Missouri evening primroses have deep taproots.

CULTURE

Missouri evening primrose requires full sun and little water. This, combined with its low stature and showy flowers, makes it an excellent rock garden plant. It grows in rocky, gravelly, and sandy soils with good to excessive drainage and can be grown in the slightly acidic to slightly alkaline soils typical of gardens. The Missouri evening primrose is a perennial hardy to zone 4.

PROPAGATION

This plant can easily be propagated from seed or stem cuttings, though the taproot makes root divisions tricky. Since Missouri evening primrose is difficult to transplant, it is best to scratch the seeds gently into the surface of the soil where plants are desired. The seeds don't require stratification in order to germinate and can be planted in either spring or fall. They will germinate in 2–3 weeks at temperatures of 70–75°F, and will generally flower in 2 years. An alternative method of propagation is to make stem cuttings in the early summer. Place the cut segment in moist sand and keep the soil damp, but not wet. Carefully transplant to a permanent location when the plant enters dormancy in the fall.

COMPANIONS

Bitterroot, purple coneflower, pasqueflower, purple prairie clover.

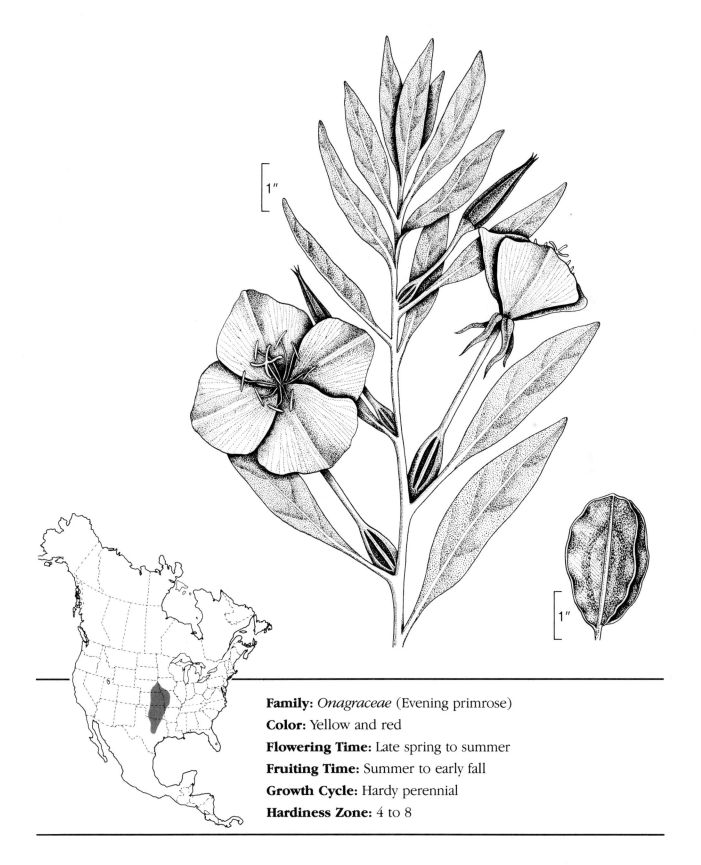

Family: *Onagraceae* (Evening primrose)

Color: Yellow and red

Flowering Time: Late spring to summer

Fruiting Time: Summer to early fall

Growth Cycle: Hardy perennial

Hardiness Zone: 4 to 8

MISSOURI EVENING PRIMROSE *(Oenothera missouriensis)*

Owl's clover
(Escobita, pink paint brush)

Orthocarpus purpurascens

The small flowers of this sometimes parasitic relative of the snapdragon resemble the heads of owls, hence its common name. The Spanish common name *escobita* translates to "little broom," describing the upright tufts of flowers and bracts that cover the top of the stem. The stem is 4–16 inches high and densely covered with ascending, ½–2-inch, threadlike leaves and masses of ½–¾-inch rose and yellow or rose and white flowers. A desert variety of this species has more deeply pigmented flowers. The upper lip of the flower is formed by the fusion of 2 petals into a velvety, rose-purple beak and projects over the swollen, lighter-hued, 3-lobed lower lip, dotted with yellow or purple. While each flower has stamens and a pistil with a large stigma, insects must bring pollen from different plants in order for it to produce seeds. Below each of the flowers is a 5- to 7-lobed, bright crimson or purple bract. The fruit is a ½-inch-long capsule filled with very small seeds. A plant of southwestern grasslands, owl's clover is frequently parasitic on the roots of grasses, from which it obtains some of its nourishment.

CULTURE

Although owl's clover is usually a parasitic plant in its native range, it can easily be cultivated in garden habitats without host grass plants. Even in the wild owl's clover does not require the presence of host plants in order to germinate and establish itself. Grow owl's clover in full sun on well-drained soils. Sandy soils that are moist in the spring are ideal for this species. Once flowering has started, the soils can be allowed to become drier.

PROPAGATION

Propagation of owl's clover is by seed, which requires no chilling treatment. Scratch the seeds into the soil in the desired location, and keep moist while they germinate and establish seedlings. Seeds should be planted in the fall in the plant's native Southwest and in the spring elsewhere. It can be started indoors in the winter and transplanted outdoors in the spring. Plant the seeds in pots or flats filled with a mixture of sand and peat moss, and keep moist, but not overly wet.

COMPANIONS

Goldfields, tidy tips, sky lupine, wind poppy, annual purple lupine, California poppy.

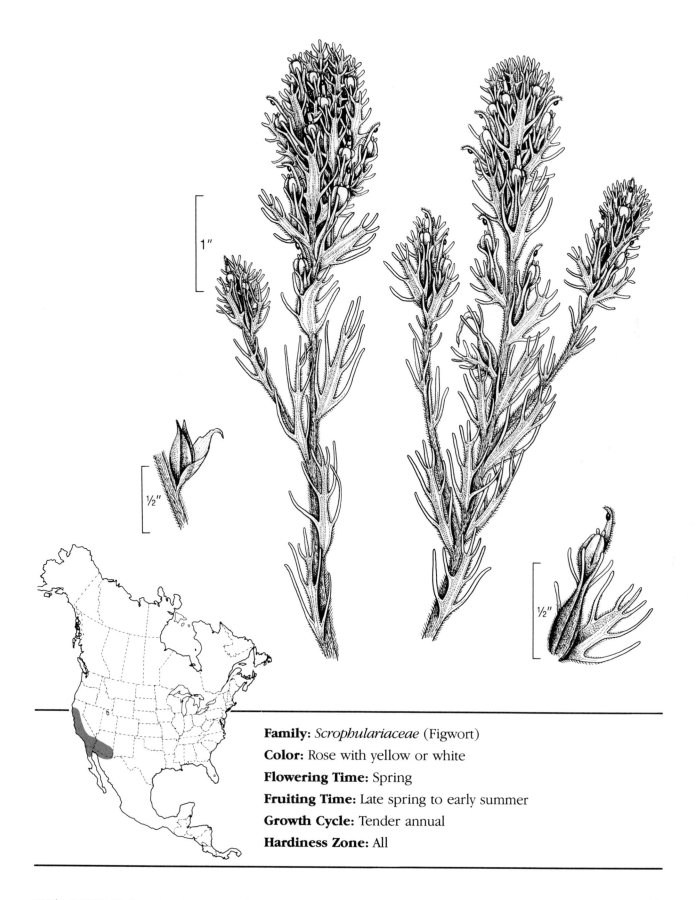

Family: *Scrophulariaceae* (Figwort)

Color: Rose with yellow or white

Flowering Time: Spring

Fruiting Time: Late spring to early summer

Growth Cycle: Tender annual

Hardiness Zone: All

OWL'S CLOVER *(Orthocarpus purpurascens)*

Elephantheads
(Little pink elephants, elephantella)

Pedicularis groenlandica

This hardy perennial of wet alpine meadows and boreal regions sports what might be the most fantastic flowers of any plant in North America. Each of the many flowers clustered on the 6–24-inch-high scape resembles the head of a miniature pink elephant. The elephant's dark trunk and lighter forehead are actually formed by the flower's upper lips, while the ears and the rest of the head are formed by the lower 3 lips. The flowers bloom just as worker bumblebees emerge in the spring. By rapidly beating their wings, the insects can dislodge and collect clouds of pollen. Elephantheads are pollinated only by bumblebees and won't produce seeds otherwise, but since the flowers do not produce any nectar, the pollen is the bumblebees' only reward. The fruit is a ¼-inch capsule containing ⅛-inch seeds. The smooth, fernlike leaves are 2–10 inches long, sharply lobed, and most abundant near the base of the scape.

CULTURE

Elephantheads is a plant of cold, wet meadows. It should be planted where the summer temperatures are not excessive and soil moisture is abundant. You don't need an alpine meadow to grow this plant, but it requires moisture and full sun.

PROPAGATION

Elephantheads seed requires damp stratification (40°F for 2–3 months) to ensure germination. In the fall, plant the seeds ⅛–¼ inch deep in flats containing a mixture of compost, loam, and peat moss. Leave the flats out over the winter, and germination will start in the spring. Leave the seedlings in the flats for the first growing season, and then transplant them to permanent locations when dormant in the fall.

COMPANIONS

Bunchberry, yellow clintonia.

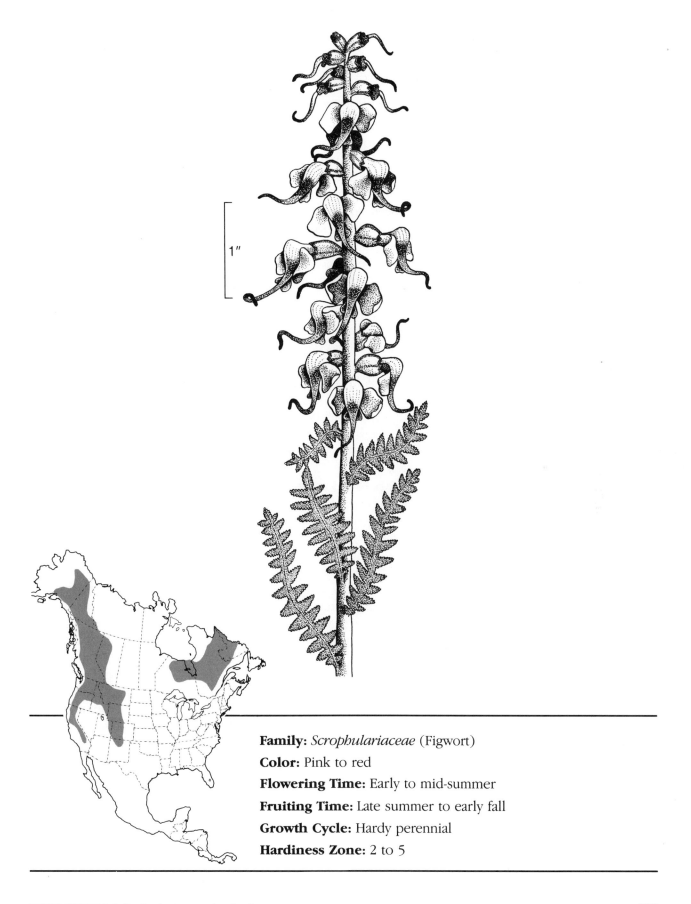

Family: *Scrophulariaceae* (Figwort)

Color: Pink to red

Flowering Time: Early to mid-summer

Fruiting Time: Late summer to early fall

Growth Cycle: Hardy perennial

Hardiness Zone: 2 to 5

1"

ELEPHANTHEADS *(Pedicularis groenlandica)*

Platte River penstemon
(Wasatch penstemon, beardtongue)

Penstemon cyananthus

The Platte River in Wyoming and the Wasatch Mountains in Utah have both given their names to this lovely blue-violet penstemon. The name penstemon is derived from the 5 stamens belonging to plants in this genus, although only 4 of the stamens are fertile. The fifth stamen, golden in this species, is typically quite hairy and gives the penstemon another common name, "beardtongue." The Platte River penstemon has erect, smooth, 1–2-foot-high stems with pairs of clasping, lance-shaped, 1–4-inch leaves. Densely clustered rings of bright blue to blue-violet flowers are borne at the top of the stem. Each of the inch-long, smooth, tubular flowers has a 2-lobed upper lip and a 3-lobed lower lip. The capsular fruit splits open when it is ripe to reveal many small, irregularly angled seeds.

CULTURE

Penstemons should be grown in sunny, open locations with soils that are moist to dry, but very well drained. Sandy loam soils are ideal, and heavy soils should be lightened by the addition of sand. Once established, this hardy perennial is relatively drought resistant and should not be overwatered because of possible root rot and mildew problems. Platte River penstemon can be grown in hardiness zones 3 to 6.

PROPAGATION

While Platte River penstemon can be propagated by stem cuttings and root divisions, propagation by seed is the preferred method. The seeds do not require chilling to germinate, so they can be planted in the spring as soon as the soils are warm. The seeds may germinate better, however, when exposed to light, so barely scratch them into the surface of the soil and keep moist until the seedlings become established. Alternatively, they can be started indoors in the early spring in flats or peat pots and transplanted outdoors when danger of frost is past. These plants may actually bloom by the end of the first year, although flowering in the second year is more common. Root divisions in the late fall are another means of propagating this species. Divide the rootstock, making sure that each division has at least one shoot bud, and plant the segments with the bud just at the soil surface. Softwood cuttings made in the summer from non-flowering shoots is a third way of propagating Platte River penstemon. A 6–7-inch cutting should be planted 3 inches deep in sharp sand and kept moist, but not wet, until the roots develop. Plant the dormant rootstock in the late fall with the newly formed buds just at the ground surface.

COMPANIONS

Showy penstemon, Rocky Mountain penstemon, standing cypress, purple coneflower, blue flax.

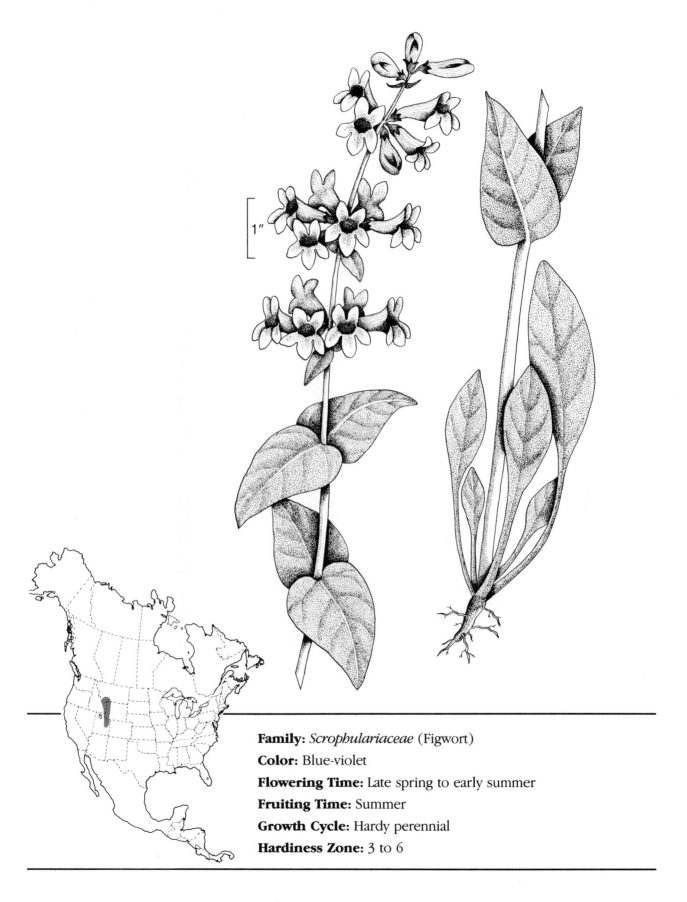

Family: *Scrophulariaceae* (Figwort)

Color: Blue-violet

Flowering Time: Late spring to early summer

Fruiting Time: Summer

Growth Cycle: Hardy perennial

Hardiness Zone: 3 to 6

PLATTE RIVER PENSTEMON *(Penstemon cyananthus)*

197

Showy penstemon
(Royal penstemon)

Penstemon spectabilis

Showy penstemon is a relatively tall plant (2–4 feet high) with a spectacular display of up to 100 flowers on the upper half of its stem. The inflated, tubular, 1–1½-inch-long flowers may range in color from blue to violet to rose to pink. The 2 rounded lobes of the upper lip of the flower and the 3 of the lower lip are usually blue, while the inside of the flower is white. The ½-inch-long capsular fruits contain many tiny angular seeds. Showy penstemon has interesting foliage as well, with pairs of coarsely toothed, 1–4-inch-long, bright green leaves clasping the stem. The upper leaves frequently have their bases fused together, so that it appears that the stem is growing through them.

CULTURE

Showy penstemons need sunny locations with dry or very well-drained soils. They will tolerate light shade but not wet soils. Do not overwater showy penstemon since they are susceptible to root rot, especially when the plants are dormant. The ideal soil acidity conditions are around neutral (pH 6–8).

PROPAGATION

Showy penstemon can be propagated from stem cuttings and root divisions, but propagation by seed is the best method. Plant the seeds in the spring as soon as the soils are warm. The seeds do not require chilling, but may germinate better when exposed to light. Plant by barely scratching them into the surface of the soil and keep moist until the seedlings become established. Alternatively, they can be started indoors in the early spring and transplanted outdoors when danger of frost is past. These plants will bloom during the first year, so they can be grown as annuals outside their native range. Root divisions in the late fall are another means of propagating this species. Divide rootstock, being sure that each division has at least one shoot bud, and plant the segments with the bud just at the soil surface. You can also propagate showy penstemon by making softwood cuttings from non-flowering shoots in the summer. A 6–7-inch cutting should be planted 3 inches deep in sharp sand and kept moist, but not wet, until the roots develop. Plant the dormant rootstock in the late fall with the newly formed buds just at the ground surface.

COMPANIONS

Rocky Mountain penstemon, Platte River penstemon, standing cypress, purple coneflower, blue flax.

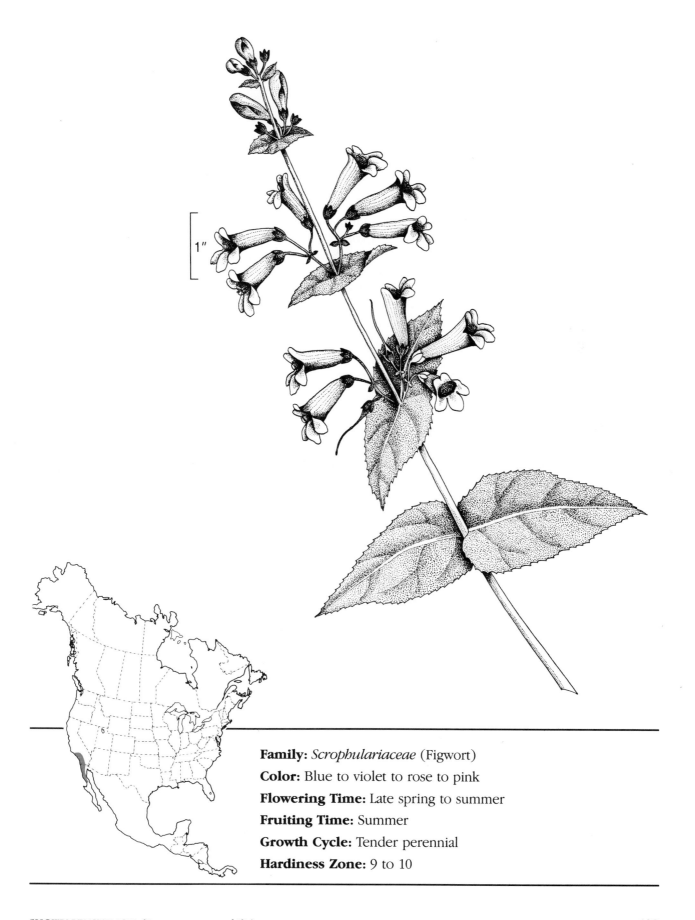

Family: *Scrophulariaceae* (Figwort)

Color: Blue to violet to rose to pink

Flowering Time: Late spring to summer

Fruiting Time: Summer

Growth Cycle: Tender perennial

Hardiness Zone: 9 to 10

1″

SHOWY PENSTEMON *(Penstemon spectabilis)*

Rocky Mountain Penstemon
(Porch penstemon)

Penstemon strictus

True to its name, this medium-sized penstemon is a plant of the western side of the Continental Divide. Rocky Mountain penstemon stands 1–2½ feet high, with royal blue to purple flowers to one side of the upper half of the stem. Flowers of this species vary in size from ¾–1¾ inches long. The considerable variation in flower size and shape is due to the evolutionary interplay between populations of Rocky Mountain penstemon and the different-sized local pollinating insects. The upper lip of the tubular flower has 2 lobes which project forward like a visor over the lower lip's 3 deeply cleft, downwardly bent lobes. The resemblance of the upper lip to a roof and the lower lip to steps is the origin of the common name "porch penstemon." The 4 fertile stamens, their anthers covered by long, tangled hairs, give a fuzzy appearance to the inside of the flower's throat. The fifth, sterile stamen is usually heavily bearded, but sometimes lacks hair entirely. Not only are the flowers variable, but the pairs of leaves range from narrow and grasslike to rather broad and lance-shaped. The leaves are a deeper green than the stem, which is covered with a whitish, waxy coating.

CULTURE

This hardy perennial should be planted in full sun to light shade on well-drained, sandy, gravelly, or stony soils. While moisture is essential for the seedlings to become established, the mature plants are quite drought tolerant and do better in dryer soils. In regions with hot summer temperatures, they do better in locations that are lightly shaded from the noontime sun.

PROPAGATION

Propagation by either root divisions or seed is successful, but seeds are usually used. Plant the seeds in the fall after the fruits are fully mature. Seed germination is enhanced by a moist chilling treatment (2–3 months at 40°F). The seeds may also germinate better when exposed to light, so plant them by barely scratching them into the surface of the soil and keep them moist until the seedlings become established. Generally seeds will germinate in 1–2 weeks of temperatures above 60°F. Some plants from seed may bloom during the first year, and most will the second. Rocky Mountain penstemon can also be propagated by root divisions in the late fall or early spring. Divide rootstock, being sure that each division has at least one bud. Plant the segments 1–2 feet apart with the bud just at the ground surface. With time, several stems will emerge from the rootstock, and the clumps can be divided again.

COMPANIONS

Showy penstemon, Platte River penstemon, standing cypress, purple coneflower, blue flax.

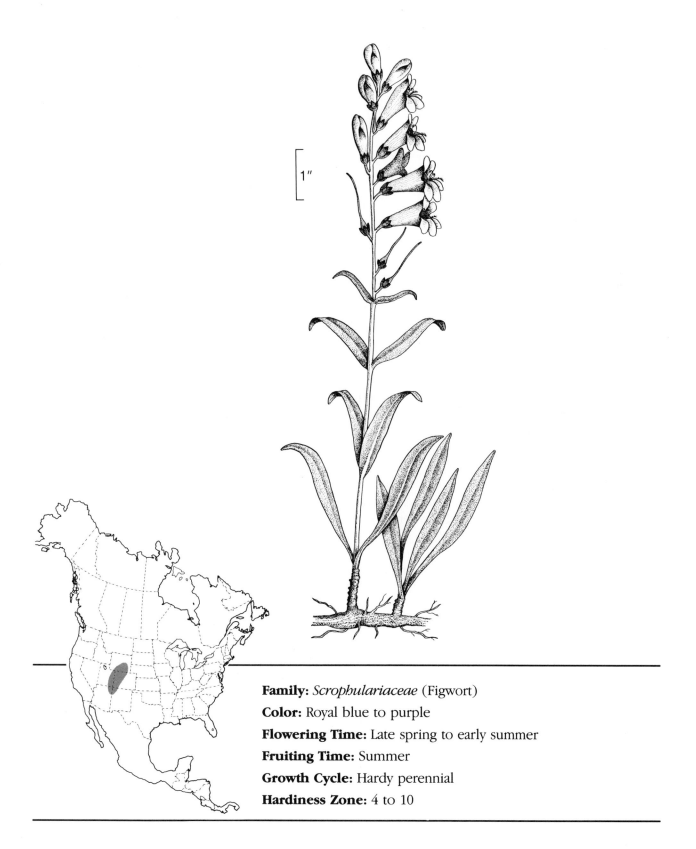

Family: *Scrophulariaceae* (Figwort)

Color: Royal blue to purple

Flowering Time: Late spring to early summer

Fruiting Time: Summer

Growth Cycle: Hardy perennial

Hardiness Zone: 4 to 10

ROCKY MOUNTAIN PENSTEMON *(Penstemon strictus)*

Purple prairie clover

Petalostemum purpureum

A plant of prairies and dry hills, this member of the pea family has cylindrical, densely packed, ½–2-inch flower heads perched atop a 1–3-foot upright stem. Each individual ¼-inch flower has a single small rose-purple to crimson petal with 5 stamens projecting beyond it. The flowers in bloom appear as a ring around the flower head, starting at the bottom and progressing to the top. The fruits are tiny, thin pods containing 1 or 2 small seeds. Most of the leaves, with their 3–5 narrow, inch-long leaflets, are at the bottom of the stem. The short vertical rootstock has fibrous roots with nodules that are inhabited by nitrogen-fixing microorganisms. With time, the roots may become deep and extensive.

CULTURE   Purple prairie clover should be planted in areas with full sun. It does best on well-drained, warm soils that are slightly acidic (pH 5.5–6.5), and, once established, is quite drought resistant. Since this plant is susceptible to attack from damping-off fungus, plant it where the soil is not overly wet, and irrigate it sparingly. If inoculation is necessary in order to establish seeds in your soil, use Saintfoin-type rhizobia (Nitragin-type F).

PROPAGATION   Seeds are the best means of propagating this legume, since the root system is difficult to divide. Collect the seeds when the flower heads are dry and gray, and scarify to hasten germination by rubbing them gently between sanding blocks. Seeds can be planted ¼–½ inch deep in flats or in nursery beds during the fall or early spring. They will germinate readily with warm spring weather if their seed coats have been abraded. Seedlings should be thinned to 6 inches apart. Transplant the yearling plants in the fall to permanent locations. Plants from seed will flower the second year.

COMPANIONS   Gayfeather, rattlesnake master, silky aster, wild bergamot.

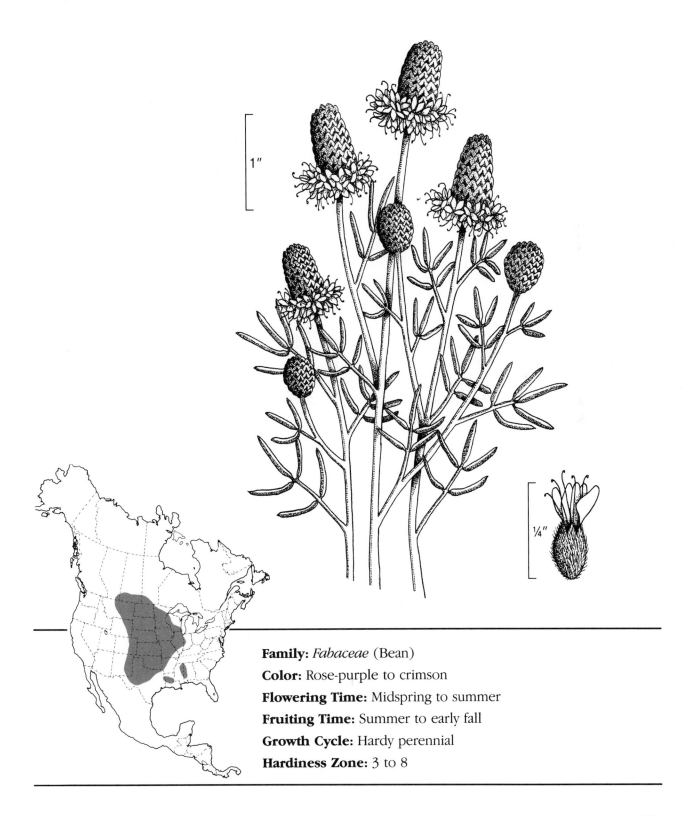

1"

¼"

Family: *Fabaceae* (Bean)

Color: Rose-purple to crimson

Flowering Time: Midspring to summer

Fruiting Time: Summer to early fall

Growth Cycle: Hardy perennial

Hardiness Zone: 3 to 8

PURPLE PRAIRIE CLOVER *(Petalostemum purpureum)*

Purple heliotrope
(Bee food, lacy phacelia, tansy phacelia)

Phacelia tanacetifolia

This tall, erect annual has long been a favorite in western gardens. The 1–3-foot-high stems and the divided, feathery, tansy-like, clasping leaves are covered with short, stiff hairs. The ½-inch-wide lavender-blue flowers, in fiddlehead clusters near the tops of the stems, attract numerous honeybees, hence the common name "bee food." Long, filamented stamens and clefted styles extend well beyond the throats of the 5-lobed, bell-shaped flowers. The fruits are round ⅛-inch capsules containing two rounded, gray-brown, ¹⁄₁₆-inch seeds.

CULTURE   Cultivate purple heliotrope in full sun on well-drained soils. Keep the soil moist early in the spring and while the plants are becoming established, after which it can be allowed to dry out.

PROPAGATION   This annual is propagated only from seeds. While no stratification treatment is needed, germination of the seeds is strongly inhibited by the light as long as the seed coat is intact. For proper germination, scarify the seeds by rubbing them between two sheeets of medium grit sandpaper, or by carefully nicking the seeds with a sharp knife. Then soak the seeds overnight in water. Optimum germination temperature is a relatively cool 60°F. In purple heliotrope's natural range, seeds should be planted ⅛ inch deep in the late fall. Elsewhere, plant the seeds in the early spring when the soil temperature nears 60°F.

COMPANIONS   Blazing star, linanthus, Douglas's wallflower, coralbells.

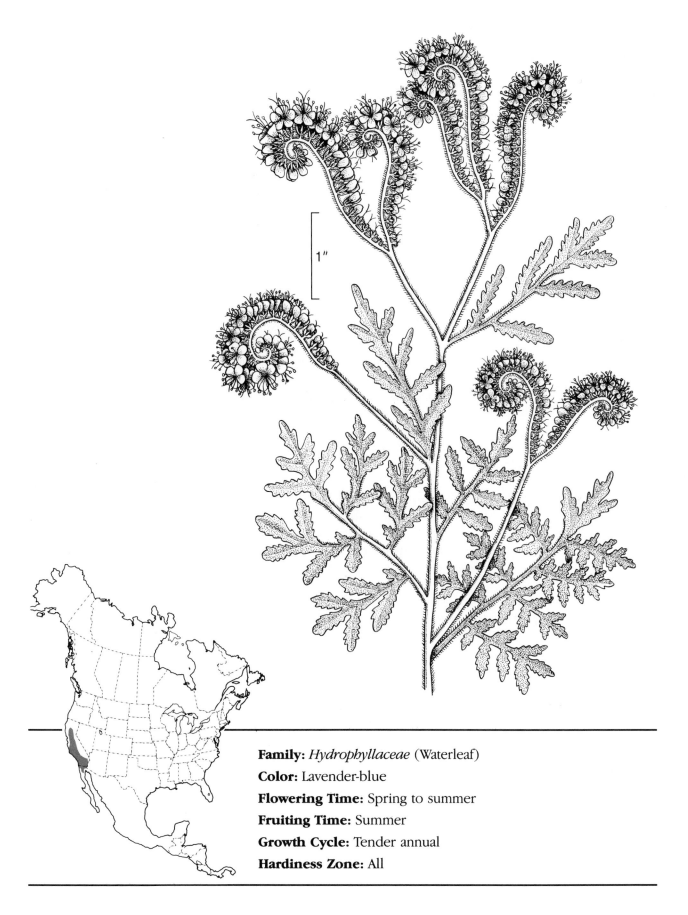

Family: *Hydrophyllaceae* (Waterleaf)

Color: Lavender-blue

Flowering Time: Spring to summer

Fruiting Time: Summer

Growth Cycle: Tender annual

Hardiness Zone: All

PURPLE HELIOTROPE *(Phacelia tanacetifolia)*

Annual phlox
(Drummond's phlox)

Phlox drummondii

The common annual phlox listed in many seed catalogs is native to East Texas, where groups of tens of thousands of plants add brilliant pink, red, and purple hues to the spring landscape. This "winter annual" blooms in the early spring and produces seeds that are dormant until the Texan autumn rains stimulate germination. The young plant overwinters as a rosette of leaves hugging the ground. In late winter or early spring, as the days are getting longer, the plant bolts and produces a 6–18-inch-high stem with flat-topped clusters of brightly colored flowers. Each of the ½–¾-inch flowers has 5 broad petals, the native varieties having light centers contrasting with the shades of the rounded petal tips. Flowers remain open for up to 8 days, during which they are pollinated by a variety of butterflies. Fruits mature in about a month and then the capsules explosively eject their ⅛-inch seeds, some as far as 13 feet from the parent plant, though 3–4 feet is more typical. The stems of annual phlox are covered with short, sticky hairs and have single, clasping leaves scattered along them, rather than the pairs of leaves that characterize other species of phlox. The shiny yellow-green leaves are not as hairy as the stems. One familiar name for the plant, "Drummond's phlox," is in honor of Thomas Drummond, a 19th century Scottish botanist who sent seeds of the plant to England in 1835 after his botanical exploration of Texas.

CULTURE

Annual phlox is one of the easiest native plants to grow in the garden. It requires full sun but is not at all fussy about other soil conditions, as long as the soil is well drained. In its native Texas, the length of the flowering season depends on how long the spring rains last, but with irrigation, and removal of the withering flowers before they set seed, flowers can be prolonged until frost.

PROPAGATION

Propagate annual phlox by seed. Sow seeds ¼ inch deep outdoors in the early spring or late fall. Germination, which is most rapid in the dark, takes 2–3 weeks at 70°F, and the plants will start to flower about 2 months later. In regions with short growing seasons, or if a longer flowering season is desired, start annual phlox in small pots or peat pots indoors in the late winter, and transplant to the garden in the spring.

COMPANIONS

California poppy, baby blue-eyes, lance-leaved coreopsis, Missouri evening primrose, tidy tips, Platte River penstemon, and many others.

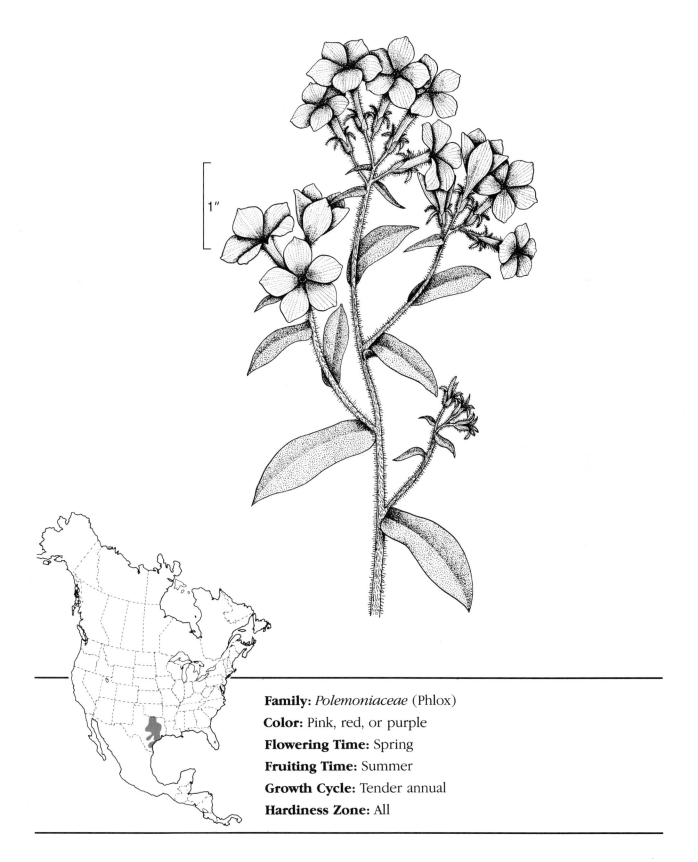

Family: *Polemoniaceae* (Phlox)

Color: Pink, red, or purple

Flowering Time: Spring

Fruiting Time: Summer

Growth Cycle: Tender annual

Hardiness Zone: All

ANNUAL PHLOX *(Phlox drummondii)*

False dragonhead
(Obedient plant)

Physostegia virginiana

The smooth, wandlike stems of false dragonhead are frequently seen growing in clumps in wet prairies, meadows, and moist, open woods in the eastern U.S. and Canada. This member of the mint family spreads by underground stolons, from which arise 2–4-foot-high stems with pairs of 3–5-inch-long, lance-shaped, sharp-toothed leaves and a terminal spike of lavender to pink flowers. The inch-long flowers have 5 triangular lobes, 2 forming an inflated upper lip and 3 forming a lower lip. False dragonhead is also called obedient plant because if its individual flowers are moved laterally, they stay put rather than springing back. The long-lasting blooms make this an excellent cut flower. The fruits are ⅛-inch dull brown nutlets. Each fall the above-ground stem dies back after flowering, but the extensive system of stolons and white fibrous roots sends up new shoots the following spring.

CULTURE
This is an easy perennial to cultivate since it is relatively indifferent to soil acidity conditions (pH 5–7), and tolerates a variety of light conditions from full sun to half-shade. The most important factor in cultivating false dragonhead is to maintain ample soil moisture. A moist, well-drained soil, rich in humus, is ideal, although once established the plant will grow to a lesser height in dry soils. Hardy to zone 3, false dragonhead should be given a thick layer of mulch over the winter in zone 4 and colder regions.

PROPAGATION
False dragonhead can easily be propagated by seed and stolon division. Plant the seeds, as soon as they are ripe in the fall, ¼ inch deep in flats containing a mixture of loam and humus. The flats should be left out over the winter since germination of the seeds is enhanced by damp stratification (3 months at 40°F). Germination takes place in the spring several weeks after temperatures rise into the 70°F range, and seedlings can be transplanted to permanent locations in the fall. Plants from seed will produce flowers the second year, and will increase in number in subsequent years as they spread by means of stolons. The clumps that form can be divided in the early spring or late fall. Cut the stolon connections with a sharp spade, and replant the rootstocks 1 foot apart with the top of the crown just at the soil surface. If divided in the fall, the plants should be mulched.

COMPANIONS
Cardinal flower, turtlehead, closed gentian, New England aster.

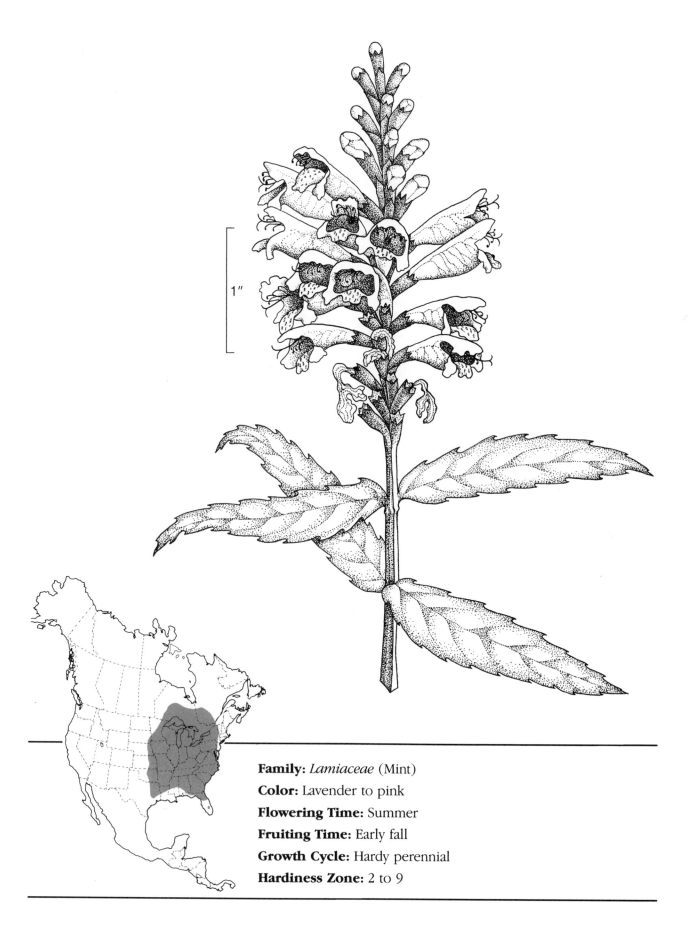

Family: *Lamiaceae* (Mint)

Color: Lavender to pink

Flowering Time: Summer

Fruiting Time: Early fall

Growth Cycle: Hardy perennial

Hardiness Zone: 2 to 9

1"

FALSE DRAGONHEAD *(Physostegia virginiana)*

Mayapple
(Mandrake)

Podophyllum peltatum

Mayapple, a natural ground cover, carpets eastern woodlands with colonies of up to a thousand plants growing together. The 12–18-inch-high shoots are of two kinds — the non-flowering stem, bearing a single broad leaf with 5–9 deeply cleft lobes, and the flowering stem, bearing a pair of leaves. As the shoots emerge in spring the leaves expand, looking like parasols rising from the ground. The buds emerge 2–3 weeks later, from between the pairs of leaves, covered by 3 green bracts, which will fall off as the flowers open. The nodding, fragrant, 2-inch blooms, with 6–9 waxy white petals encircling the yellow stamens and pistil, last about a week, and depend on bumblebees for pollination. In late spring or early summer the sweet, lemon-shaped, 1–2-inch fruit ripens, turning from green to yellow. Then in midsummer the foliage withers back to its creeping, branched rhizomes and fibrous roots. The Eastern box turtle eats mayapples and disperses their seeds to new locations, enhancing germination of the ¼-inch, light brown, elliptical seeds by passage through its digestive system. To humans, however, all parts of the mayapple except the flesh of fully ripe fruits are poisonous, due to the presence of the bitter resin podophyllin.

CULTURE

Mayapple makes its best growth in spring just before the leaves of deciduous trees are fully expanded. Although it blooms most vigorously where it is sunny in the early spring, mayapple can tolerate fairly dense shade during the summer. In the garden, the plant does well both in full sun and in shady borders. Since mayapple is a hardy perennial which appears to require cool winter temperatures for resumption of growth and flowering in the spring, it may be difficult to grow in locations warmer than hardiness zone 8. It is not choosy about soils, as long as they are relatively moist and have moderately acidic to neutral conditions (pH 4–7).

PROPAGATION

The easiest way to propagate mayapple is from divisions of the rhizomes, wearing gloves or washing your hands immediately after handling, since people with sensitive skin may develop a rash after touching the roots. The non-flowering shoots produce buds on the rhizome before withering in the late summer. Divide the rhizomes in the fall, with at least one bud on each piece. Plant the divisions 1 inch deep with the buds pointing up. Mulch with an inch or so of deciduous leaves. Mayapple is easy to establish, and given ample moisture and sunlight it may even have to be contained to keep it from crowding out other plants. Seed germination, on the other hand, is enhanced by moist stratification for 2–3 months. Remove the seeds from the fruit as soon as they are ripe in the fall, and plant thickly, ½ inch deep in flats that are left out for the winter. They will germinate in the spring and the seedlings will have a single, unlobed leaf the first year. It will take several years for mayapples grown from seed to flower.

COMPANIONS

Solomon's seal, false Solomon's seal.

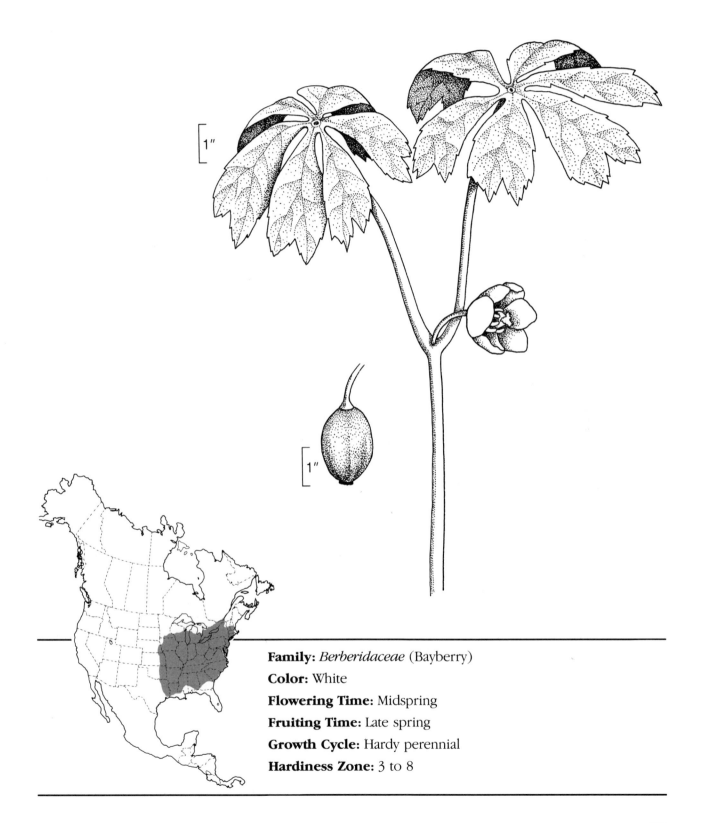

1"

1"

Family: *Berberidaceae* (Bayberry)

Color: White

Flowering Time: Midspring

Fruiting Time: Late spring

Growth Cycle: Hardy perennial

Hardiness Zone: 3 to 8

MAYAPPLE *(Podophyllum peltatum)*

Solomon's seal

Polygonatum biflorum

There are a variety of theories concerning how this hardy perennial got its common name. Some suggest that the circular scars caused by the shedding of the previous year's shoots from the gnarled, fleshy, underground rhizome are reminiscent of King Solomon's governmental seals. Others think that the reference to Solomon is related to the 6-pointed star pattern, evident when the rhizome is cut in cross-section. Regardless of which interpretation is correct, Solomon's seal is an attractive addition to a garden of wildflowers. The arching stems are 1–3 feet high with 2 rows of flat 3–5-inch lance-shaped leaves clasping the stem. The yellow-green flowers, usually in pairs, hang down from the axils of the leaves. The ½–1-inch-long tubular flowers have 6 short, rounded lobes, and the pairs of round, blue-black berries about ¼ inch in diameter have 3–6 elliptical seeds.

CULTURE   Solomon's seal can be grown in a wide variety of environments. It can be planted in open sun even though it is naturally found flourishing in shady habitats. While it grows best where soils are moist and the pH is 4.5 to 5.5, it is tolerant of variable moisture conditions and soil acidities from pH 4 to 7. Solomon's seal appears to need cool temperatures to break its winter dormancy and may be difficult to maintain in regions warmer than hardiness zone 8.

PROPAGATION   Solomon's seal can be propagated by rhizome divisions or by seed. Divide the rhizomes in the spring or fall when the plants are dormant. Cut pieces of the rhizome with at least one bud on each and set them horizontally with the buds pointing up, 18 inches apart and 1 inch deep. Seeds should be collected after the fruits are mature and have turned black, but before they dry out. Remove the seeds from the fruit and plant them ½ inch deep in outdoor beds or flats to be left out over winter. Keep the seedbed moist. It is essential that the seeds be given a moist, cold treatment (2 months at 40°F) for germination to occur. Solomon's seal seeds also germinate better in the dark than in the light, so a top dressing of compost and a thin layer of leaf mulch may further enhance their germination in the spring. Be patient — it often takes 2 years for Solomon's seal seeds to germinate, and 2–4 more years for seedlings to reach flowering size.

COMPANIONS   Trilliums, false Solomon's seal, Virginia bluebell, wood lily.

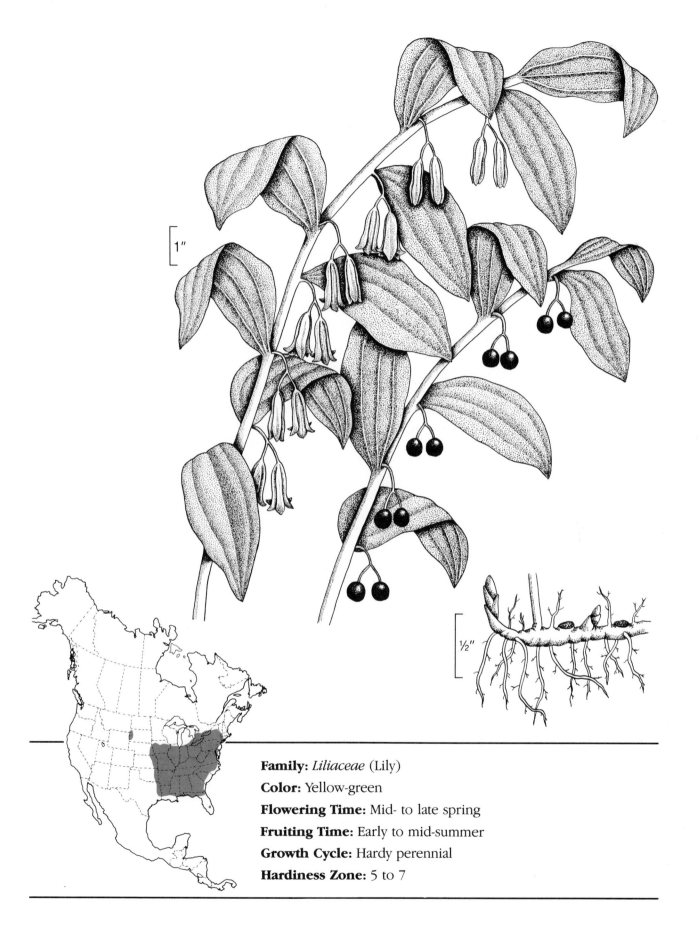

Family: *Liliaceae* (Lily)

Color: Yellow-green

Flowering Time: Mid- to late spring

Fruiting Time: Early to mid-summer

Growth Cycle: Hardy perennial

Hardiness Zone: 5 to 7

SOLOMON'S SEAL *(Polygonatum biflorum)*

Shinleaf

Pyrola elliptica

Shinleaf is not particularly easy to bring into the garden, but it is one of the few eastern woodland plants to flower in midsummer in deep shade. Therefore, it is worth the effort if you desire a prolonged succession of flowering hardy perennials. The evergreen leaves of shinleaf are about 3 inches long, elliptical, as the scientific name indicates, dull green, and clustered in a rosette arrangement at the ground surface. The flower scape is 4–12 inches high and bears 3–21 nodding white flowers, frequently tinged with pink or veined with green. Each of the 5-petaled flowers is about ⅓ inch across and has a long, pendant pistil, and the fruit is a small capsule with many minute, elongated seeds. Shinleaf has a creeping underground root and stem system, and frequently colonies of the plants can be found growing together.

CULTURE   Shinleaf is a plant of deep shade. It can be grown in either moist or relatively dry soils, but has a definite preference for acidic soil conditions (pH 4.5–5.5). It also grows best where there is ample organic matter in the soil. Liberal additions of compost, adjusted to the appropriate acidity by the addition of peat moss and conifer needles, aids in the establishment and maintenance of the species.

PROPAGATION   Shinleaf is difficult to propagate from seed because it is slow to germinate. The seeds should be planted where they can overwinter and receive cold temperature treatment. Prepare a seedbed or flat with a mixture of sandy loam, compost, and peat moss, sprinkle the seeds on top, and cover with a thin layer (¼ inch) of finely milled peat moss. Keep moist and be patient. An alternative is to propagate shinleaf by dividing the runners in the early spring or midfall, replanting the divisions about 18 inches apart with the buds just at the surface of the soil.

COMPANIONS   Partridgeberry, wintergreen, bunchberry, yellow clintonia, pink lady's slipper.

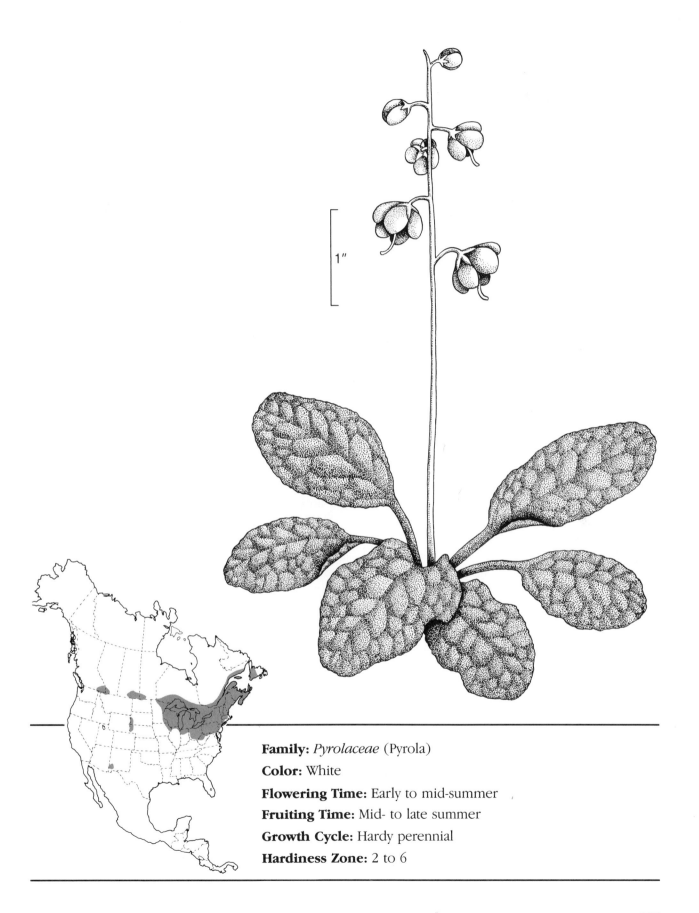

Family: *Pyrolaceae* (Pyrola)

Color: White

Flowering Time: Early to mid-summer

Fruiting Time: Mid- to late summer

Growth Cycle: Hardy perennial

Hardiness Zone: 2 to 6

SHINLEAF *(Pyrola elliptica)*

Mexican hat
(Coneflower, red Mexican hat, upright coneflower, prairie coneflower)

Ratibida columnifera
(R. columnaris, Lepachys columnaris)

The central brown discs of this member of the aster family protrude ½–2½ inches beyond the drooping ray flowers, giving the 1–3-inch flower heads the appearance of sombreros. When the dark purple, tubular flowers start blooming from the base of the discs the hats even appear to have hatbands. This hardy perennial has branched, 1½–3-foot-high shoots with deeply cleft, feathery leaves on the lower portion of the stem, frequently with short stiff bristles. Flowering begins in the long days of late spring and continues until fall. The 3–7 flowers are borne on leafless stems, making the Mexican hat an excellent cut flower. Ray flowers may be entirely yellow or yellow with red bases, the latter form frequently being called red Mexican hat. The seedlike ⅛-inch-long fruit has a fringe on one edge and 2 teeth projecting from one end. The root system is a diffuse taproot. Although the many common names associated with the two different color forms of Mexican hat and the frequent listing of the plant as *Ratibida columnaris* or *Lepachys columnaris* in seed catalogs can cause confusion, they are all one species.

CULTURE   Mexican hat should be grown in the full sun on well-drained soils. It grows particularly well in soils that are slightly acidic to alkaline (pH 6–8), but is adaptable to normal garden soils. Once established it requires little water, being relatively drought tolerant, and can withstand competition from other wildflowers and grasses.

PROPAGATION   Mexican hat is one of the easiest wildflowers to propagate from seed. Seeds may be either planted directly or planted in flats for future transplantation. In the fall or spring plant ¼ inch deep in sandy loam or sandy soil. Unstratified seeds will germinate, but the best results are obtained if seeds are chilled at 40°F for 9 weeks, and then germinated at 80°F. Germination is rapid, once temperatures are warm. Mexican hat can be grown as an annual if the growing season is long enough. If you live in a cold climate, you may want to start it indoors in late winter and transplant 8–12 inches apart in permanent locations when the seedlings are sturdy. Even plants from seed that are planted outdoors in the spring will bloom the second year. In hardiness zone 5 and colder regions, it is prudent to give Mexican hat a good winter mulch, and remove it in the spring.

COMPANIONS   Lance-leaved coreopsis, butterfly weed, black-eyed Susan, rattlesnake master, purple coneflower, prickly poppy, penstemons.

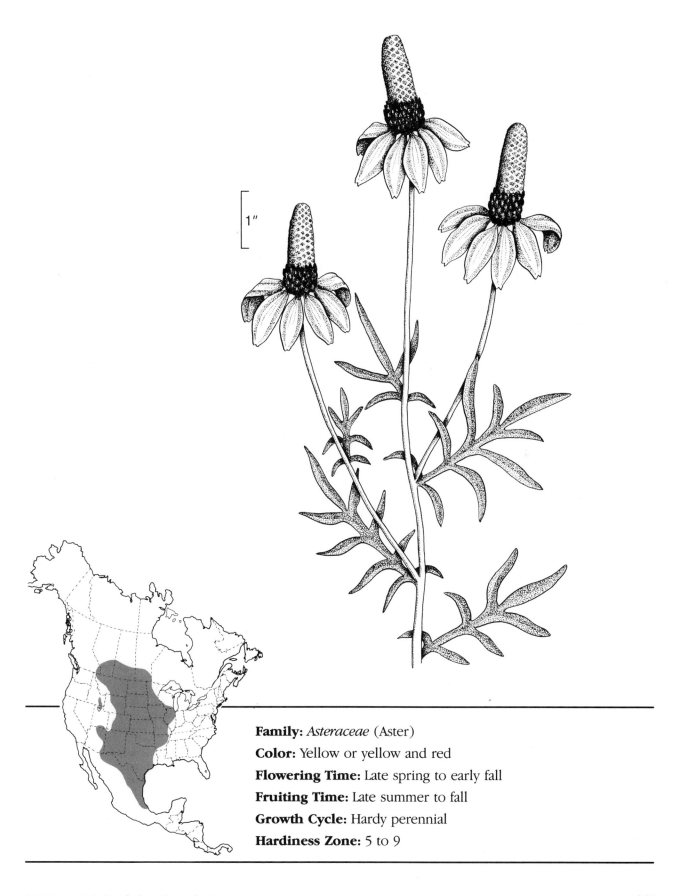

Family: *Asteraceae* (Aster)

Color: Yellow or yellow and red

Flowering Time: Late spring to early fall

Fruiting Time: Late summer to fall

Growth Cycle: Hardy perennial

Hardiness Zone: 5 to 9

MEXICAN HAT *(Ratibida columnifera)*

Meadow beauty
(Deergrass)

Rhexia virginica

An aptly named plant, for it is one of the most beautiful flowers growing in wet meadows and prairies in the East. The stems have 4 ridges and vary greatly in height from 4 inches to 2½ feet. Its pairs of 2-inch-long light green leaves are bristly, especially on the upper surface. The exquisite 1–1½-inch flowers cluster at the top of the stem, with 4 rounded, rose-crimson petals surrounding the yellow pistil and the ring of curved golden stamens in the center of the flower. The petals frequently fall off by early afternoon. The fruit is a 4-part capsule resembling a small copper urn or pitcher, and contains numerous tiny, coiled, snail-shaped seeds. Meadow beauty has a tuberous root system from which finer roots extend. The shoots of the plant are a favorite food of deer in the southeastern U.S., giving this species the common name deergrass.

CULTURE

Meadow beauty thrives in wet, acid soils. The soil should have a pH between 4 and 5 and be moist or damp through most of the growing season. Soils that are more alkaline should be adjusted to the proper pH by the addition of peat moss. Plant meadow beauty in the full sun to partial shade. This hardy perennial can withstand the cold, acid conditions of boggy areas, where it grows in its native northeastern U.S., but can adapt to garden conditions if proper acidity and moisture are maintained.

PROPAGATION

Meadow beauty is easily propagated by seed or tuber division. Plant seeds as soon as they are ripe in late summer or early fall. Sprinkle seeds on the surface of a flat filled with a mixture of peat moss and sand, moisten, and cover with a thin layer of peat moss. Germination in spring is enhanced by moist stratification (2–3 months at 40°F), so leave the flats outdoors for the winter. Be sure to keep the seedlings well watered. The newly formed tubers can be planted 1 inch deep in permanent locations in the fall. Plants from seed mature in about 2 years. Divide tubers of mature plants in the early spring or late fall, making sure that each division has at least one bud. Plant the segments 12 inches apart and with the buds 1–1½ inches below the soil surface. Cuttings can also be made from newly growing stems in the early summer. Place 6-inch cuttings 3 inches deep in moist sand and provide shade. Plant the newly formed tubers in the fall after the plant has become dormant.

COMPANIONS

Culver's root, turtlehead, New England aster, gayfeather.

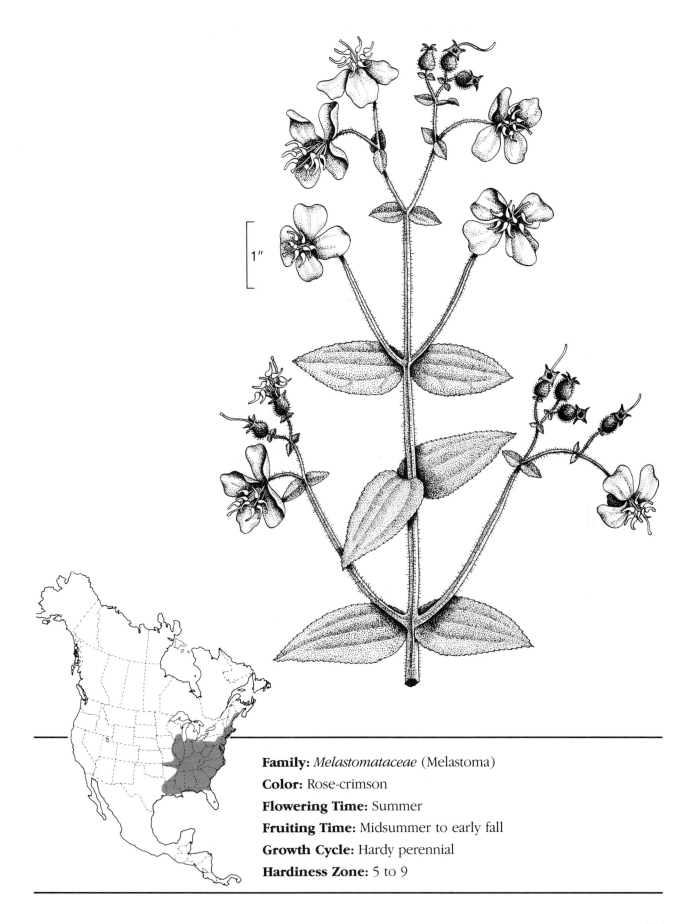

Family: *Melastomataceae* (Melastoma)

Color: Rose-crimson

Flowering Time: Summer

Fruiting Time: Midsummer to early fall

Growth Cycle: Hardy perennial

Hardiness Zone: 5 to 9

MEADOW BEAUTY *(Rhexia virginica)*

Pasture rose
(Prairie rose, Carolina rose)

Rosa carolina

There is a simple elegance to this relative of fancy garden roses. A low (1–3-foot-high) shrub with single, upright, sparsely prickly stems arising from spreading underground stolons, pasture rose is a fine addition to borders of the garden. The 2-inch flowers have 5 pale pink petals encircling a ring of numerous, bright yellow stamens. The fruit, a ⅓-inch hip, turns from dark green to bright red as it matures. The hip contains several bony, tan, ⅛-inch seeds, and remains on the plant during the winter or until it is eaten by birds. The seeds that survive the passage through a bird's digestive system have an excellent germination rate.

CULTURE

While pasture roses are among the most shade-tolerant of roses, they grow best in open, sunny locations. They prefer moderately acid soils (pH 4.5–6), which are moist but well drained. Once established, pasture roses can tolerate fairly dry soils. This perennial requires relatively little care and is hardy to zone 4.

PROPAGATION

Pasture rose can be propagated by seed, cuttings, or stolon division. The stems arising from the underground stolons can be separated and transplanted in the late fall or early spring. Divide the stolons, using a sharp spade to cut them. Replant the separated plants with the root crown just at the soil surface. Green-wood or softwood cuttings can be made in the early spring after vigorous shoot growth has just started. Cut 6–7-inch pieces and plant 3 inches deep in moist sand, keeping moist but not too wet, and providing shade. Replant in a permanent location, after the stem loses its leaves in the fall. Collect seeds as soon as the hips have turned red in the late summer or early fall. The seeds should not be allowed to dry out, or germination may be difficult. Extract the seeds from the pulpy hip and plant them thickly ¼ inch deep in a flat containing a mixture of sand and peat moss. Seeds require stratification (3 months at 40°F) and may benefit from scarification. Leave the flats outside for the winter. Even under the best of conditions seed germination may be slow, so leave the flat out for a second winter as well, before you become discouraged and throw out the soil. Transplant the seedlings when they become several inches high and have a well-developed root system. Some plants from seed may bloom the second year, but usually it takes 3–4 years to reach the flowering stage. Once established, pasture rose will spread by extension of its stolons.

COMPANIONS

Gayfeather, butterfly weed, black-eyed Susan, silky aster, New England aster, wood lily.

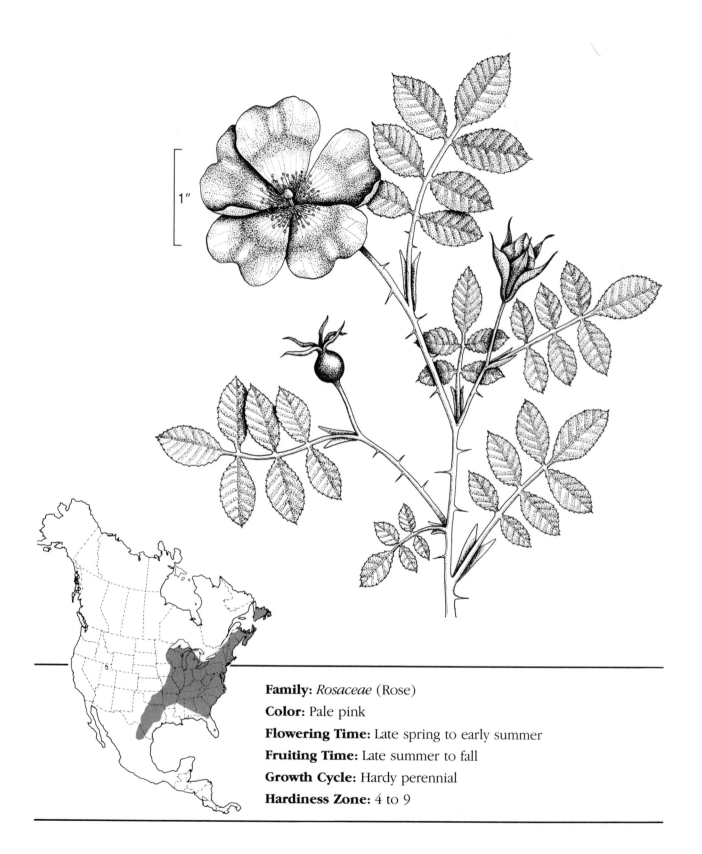

1″

Family: *Rosaceae* (Rose)

Color: Pale pink

Flowering Time: Late spring to early summer

Fruiting Time: Late summer to fall

Growth Cycle: Hardy perennial

Hardiness Zone: 4 to 9

PASTURE ROSE *(Rosa carolina)*

Black-eyed Susan
(Brown-eyed Susan)

Rudbeckia hirta
(R. serotina)

Black-eyed Susan is a hardy perennial that can be grown as an annual in most locations. In the eastern third of the United States its first flowering signifies that summer has arrived, and its last flowering, that summer has gone. Originally native only to the Midwest, black-eyed Susan expanded its range after its seeds were accidentally shipped to the East with clover seeds and planted in farm fields. The 1–3-foot-high stems and scattered 4-inch-long leaves are covered with short, bristly hairs. The 2–3-inch flower heads are borne on a relatively long stalk, making the black-eyed Susan an attractive cut flower. The individual flowers clustered together in the flower head, like other members of the aster family, are of two sorts. The center, a hemispherical disc of tiny, chocolate-brown flowers, is surrounded by 10–20 petallike, orange-yellow, 1-inch-long ray flowers. Sometimes the ray petals are a darker red-orange at the base. The total effect is of a yellow daisy with a domed brown center. The ridged ⅛-inch seeds mature several weeks after the ray flowers wither. The root system tends to be fibrous and may be extensive in old, established plants.

CULTURE
Black-eyed Susan is a plant of sunny habitats, but can tolerate light shading. It is quite indifferent to soil conditions and will do well in dry, infertile soils if there is sufficient moisture for it to become established. It grows exceptionally well under cultivation and may even become somewhat aggressive if given abundant sun, moisture and nutrients. If started early, black-eyed Susan can be grown as an annual just about anywhere.

PROPAGATION
Propagate black-eyed Susan from seed, since it is nearly impossible to divide the root system successfully. Sow the ⅕-inch-long, black seeds about ⅓ inch deep in loamy soil as soon as they are ripe in the summer or early fall. Germination takes place in the spring after about 2 weeks of daytime temperatures between 65 and 75°F. Many of the plants will flower the first year and nearly all will flower the second year. Since black-eyed Susans sometimes grow as biennials, you may want to plant seeds two years in a row to ensure a healthy population of flowering plants. Seeds can also be sown in flats, left out over the winter, and transplanted the following spring when the seedlings have become sturdy. Once established, they self-seed well. Black-eyed Susan seed requires cold treatment for germination (3 months at 40°F), and without it the seeds remain dormant. To grow this species in hardiness zones warmer than zone 8, refrigerate the seeds for 3 months before planting them, and then treat the plant as an annual.

COMPANIONS
Purple coneflower, New England aster, butterfly weed, wild bergamot, Culver's root, false dragonhead, and many others.

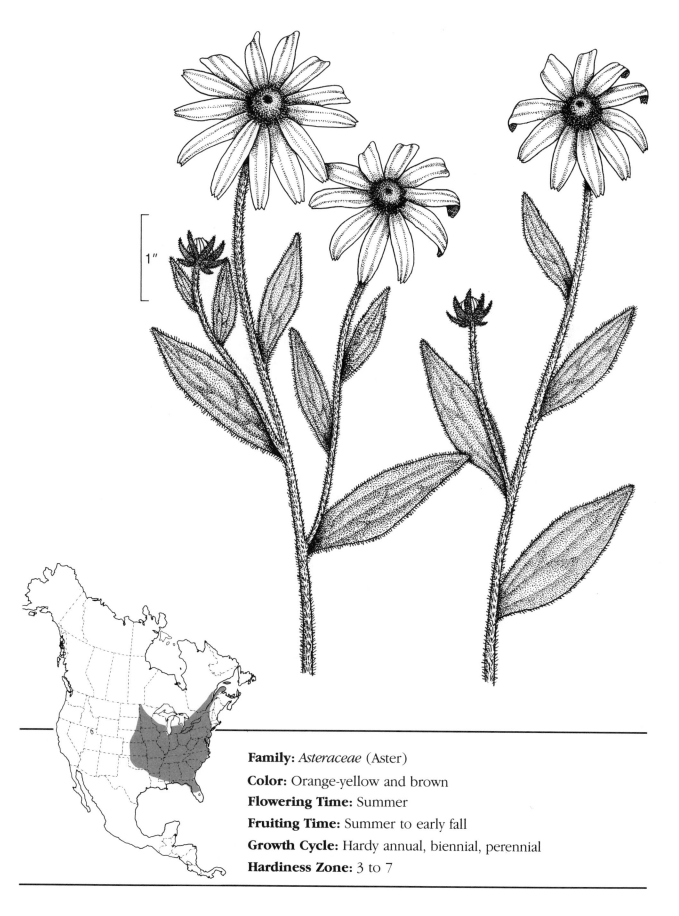

Family: *Asteraceae* (Aster)

Color: Orange-yellow and brown

Flowering Time: Summer

Fruiting Time: Summer to early fall

Growth Cycle: Hardy annual, biennial, perennial

Hardiness Zone: 3 to 7

BLACK-EYED SUSAN *(Rudbeckia hirta)*

Scarlet sage

Salvia coccinea

This native of the Southeast should not be confused with the commonly cultivated scarlet sage *Salvia splendens,* which is a native of Brazil. The North American native has all of the color of its South American relative, but lacks its harshness. Soft hairs cover the square, dark green stems and the pairs of 1–2-inch, heart-shaped, scalloped leaves, particularly their undersides. On the top half of the 1–2-foot-high stems are tiered whorls of 6–10 bright scarlet flowers, each with a tubular, often purple calyx surrounding the inch-long, smooth, tubular corolla. The corolla has an upper lip with 2 lobes and a larger lower lip with 3 lobes, the middle one being notched. Scarlet sage fruits are small (⅛-inch) nutlets.

CULTURE

Scarlet sage is a tender perennial that can be grown as an annual. It should be planted in full sun on well-drained soils. Hot sandy soils are ideal since scarlet sage requires little watering once it is established. In northern areas (hardiness zone 7 and colder) a heavy mulch is needed over the winter and should be removed in the spring. In its native range, scarlet sage grows as a perennial and self-seeds easily.

PROPAGATION

In hardiness zone 7 and colder, you can grow scarlet sage as an annual, starting the seedlings indoors and transplanting them outdoors, spacing the plants 6–12 inches apart, when all danger of frost has passed. Or they can be grown outdoors from seed, heavily mulched over the winter, and will bloom the following year. In the Southeast, their native range, they can be planted in the spring or fall in permanent locations. Germination requires no chilling treatment, but is inhibited by light. Plant the seeds ¼–⅜ inch deep in sandy, well-drained soil. Keep the soil moist but not overly wet. Stem cuttings can also be made in the spring. Plant 7-inch sections 3 inches deep in sharp sand, provide with moderate shade, and keep moist until roots form and the plant becomes established.

COMPANIONS

Mexican hat, butterfly weed, black-eyed Susan, blanketflower, prickly poppy.

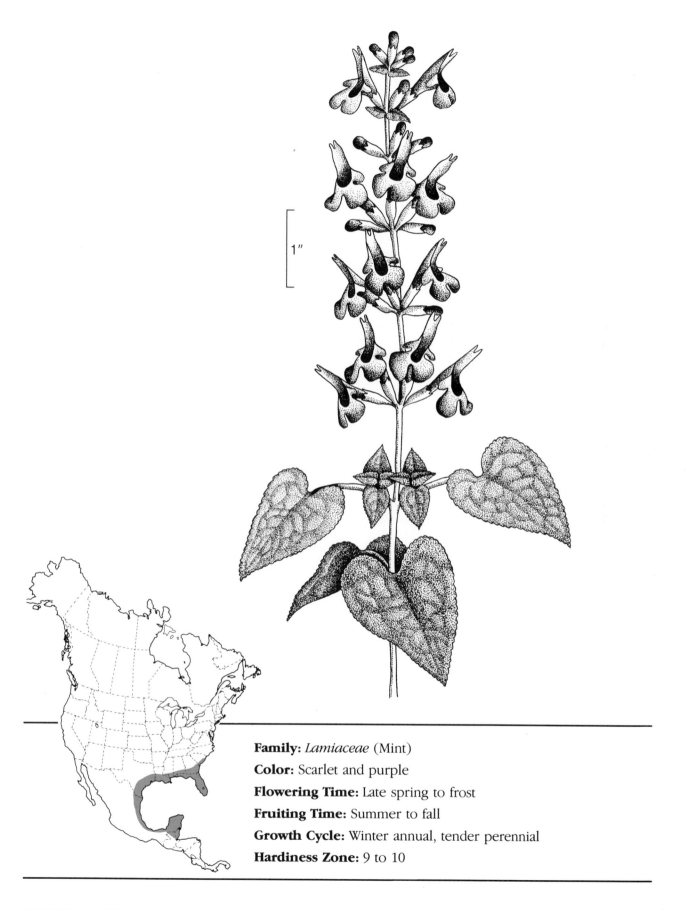

1"

Family: *Lamiaceae* (Mint)

Color: Scarlet and purple

Flowering Time: Late spring to frost

Fruiting Time: Summer to fall

Growth Cycle: Winter annual, tender perennial

Hardiness Zone: 9 to 10

SCARLET SAGE *(Salvia coccinea)*

Bloodroot   *Sanguinaria canadensis*

Both the common and scientific names of this plant refer to the carmine-colored juice in its rhizomes and roots. This fluid contains an acrid, toxic alkaloid, *sanguinarine,* which causes nausea, irritation of mucus membranes and even nerve poisoning, if taken internally. However, the sap has long been used in combination with oak bark to make a natural red dye. The leaves and flowering stem arise from the rhizome in early spring. At first the leaves are wrapped around the flower bud, and then the daisylike flower expands above the unfurling leaves. The rounded leaves are pale green and 4–8 inches broad, with shallow, wavy lobes. While the leaves remain green for most of the growing season, the delicate flowers last only a few days and the entire flowering season lasts a week or two. The 8–16-inch flowering stems bear a single flower 1–2 inches in diameter, which usually has 8 (but sometimes 6–12) white, daisylike petals surrounding the many yellow central stamens. The flowers close at sunset and are too fragile to be picked. The fruit is a cigar-shaped capsule containing glossy brown ⅛-inch seeds with prominent crests called "caruncles." Ants are the primary dispersal agents of bloodroot seeds, carrying them off by the caruncle, which they later chew off, and burying them. Many of the seeds then germinate the following spring.

CULTURE   Bloodroots can be grown in locations from full sun to full shade as long as they have sun in the early spring when they emerge from the ground, flower, and do most of their growing. If grown in full sun to light shade bloodroots may spread rapidly and make an excellent ground cover. Although bloodroots grow best when the pH is 5–7, ample humus and moisture are more important. The soil should have good but not excessive drainage. Mulch the plants with a thin layer of deciduous leaves during the winter in hardiness zones 3 and 4.

PROPAGATION   Bloodroots propagate easily from both rhizome divisions and seed. Dig the rhizomes in the late summer when the leaves have just finished yellowing. Wear gloves, and wash your hands after handling the roots of this plant. Plant horizontally ¾ inch deep with the buds near the soil surface, and mulch with a thin layer of leaves. Plants from rhizome divisions may flower the following spring. Propagation from seeds is easiest when freshly ripe seeds are collected from the fruits as they split open in the mid- to late spring. The seeds will germinate best if kept moist and given a cold treatment for 2–3 months over winter. Place the seeds directly where you want the plants to grow, or on the surface of flats filled with loam, and keep moist. Give the seeds a ½-inch top dressing of compost mixed with peat moss. Since bloodroot seeds are eaten by mice, it is prudent to cover the flats with hardware cloth or screening for the winter. Seedlings can be transplanted the following summer and take about 3 years to flower.

COMPANIONS   Trillium, wild ginger, white baneberry, columbines, Dutchman's breeches, sharp-lobed hepatica.

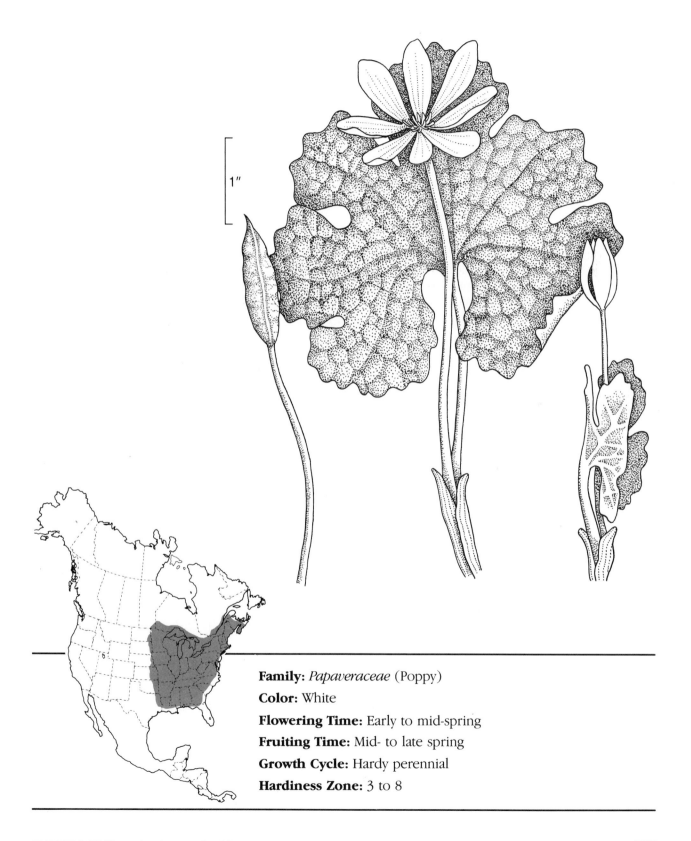

1"

Family: *Papaveraceae* (Poppy)
Color: White
Flowering Time: Early to mid-spring
Fruiting Time: Mid- to late spring
Growth Cycle: Hardy perennial
Hardiness Zone: 3 to 8

BLOODROOT *(Sanguinaria canadensis)*

Indian pink

Silene californica

This pink is bright red — atop its several 6–18-inch branched stems are showy scarlet flowers 1–1½ inches across. The flowers have 5 broad petals, each with 4 round-tipped lobes, a narrow outer pair and a wide inner pair. The 3 styles and 10 stamens protrude from the center of the flower. A 1-inch tubular calyx with 5 teeth surrounds the base of the flower, and later covers the 1-inch elongated capsular fruit until it ruptures open to reveal numerous red-brown seeds. The pairs of 1½–3-inch-long dark green leaves, like the stems they clasp, are covered with minute, sticky, soft, hairs. As the fruits ripen in the summer, the foliage dries out and withers. Indian pink's taproot may be 4 inches long.

CULTURE Indian pink will grow well in light shade to partial sun. Although it needs moderate moisture during the start of the flowering season, it should dry out as it enters dormancy in the last half of the summer. While the soil should be well drained, Indian pink is relatively indifferent to soil acidity conditions. This perennial is not hardy enough to be grown in regions colder than hardiness zone 8, and Indian pinks may be a challenge to grow in the humid eastern part of the country. They are worth the effort, however, even if one has to use deep flower pots and move them seasonally to match the plant's environmental preferences.

PROPAGATION Indian pink should be propagated by seed, since it is difficult to divide the deep taproot. In its native range, plant the seeds ⅛ inch deep in the fall in the desired locations. Elsewhere, plant Indian pink in the spring where desired or in deep pots. The seeds do not require stratification treatment, but germination may be slow and erratic. The first year the seedling will produce few leaves but an extensive taproot. If pots are used, leave the seedlings in the pot until the fall. Then carefully transplant the dormant roots, disturbing them as little as possible, 8–12 inches apart with the root crown just below the soil surface. Indian pink grown from seed will flower the second year.

COMPANIONS Blue dicks, Chinese houses, Douglas's wallflower, purple annual lupine, blazing star.

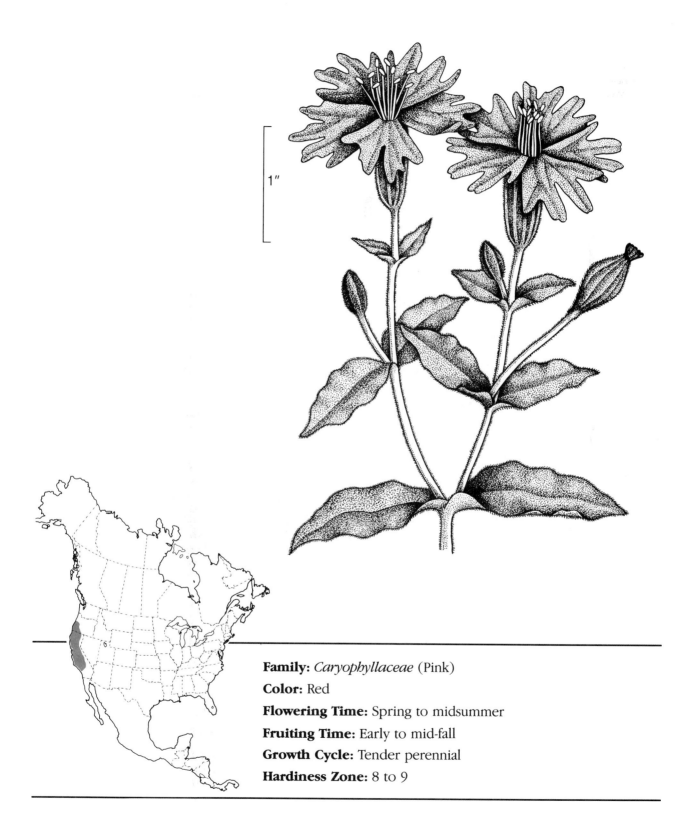

1"

Family: *Caryophyllaceae* (Pink)

Color: Red

Flowering Time: Spring to midsummer

Fruiting Time: Early to mid-fall

Growth Cycle: Tender perennial

Hardiness Zone: 8 to 9

INDIAN PINK *(Silene californica)*

Compass plant
(Rosin weed)

Silphium laciniatum

The handsome yellow sunflowerlike flowers of this magnificent 3–12-foot-high plant of prairies and grasslands are rivaled only by its unusual foliage. These deeply cut, angularly lobed, clasping, hairy leaves are oriented vertically rather than horizontally, and the lower ones may approach 2 feet in length. The leaf blades point north and south, thereby avoiding the heat of the noonday sun and earning the plant its common name. Scattered along the top half of the bristly, resinous stem are 2–5-inch flower heads, with 20 to 30 long yellow ray flowers surrounding the 1-inch yellow discs. The blooming season may last up to 2 months. The relatively large (½-inch-long) seeds are covered with tough seed coats. Compass plant has a large, woody taproot which may reach down 15 feet.

CULTURE

Compass plant requires a lot of space to grow and with time may form clumps. The only specific requirement of this easily cultivated hardy perennial is that it should be planted in full sun. It is adaptable to a wide variety of soil and moisture conditions, once it is established.

PROPAGATION

The easiest way to propagate compass plant is by seed. Germination requires damp stratification (2 months at 40°F), and is enhanced by scarification. To scarify the seed, nick the seed coat with a sharp knife prior to planting. In the fall, plant the seeds ⅓–½ inch deep in a deep flat and leave outdoors over the winter. Germination is rapid (2 weeks) when temperatures near 70°F in the spring. Transplant the seedlings when they are several inches tall. Alternatively, the seeds can be planted in permanent locations in the fall, but it is advisable to clear away the roots of competing grasses to give the seedlings a chance to become established. The first year the seedling will have but a single leaf, and it will take 2–3 years for the plants to mature and produce flowers.

COMPANIONS

Rattlesnake master, purple prairie clover, showy tick trefoil, silky aster.

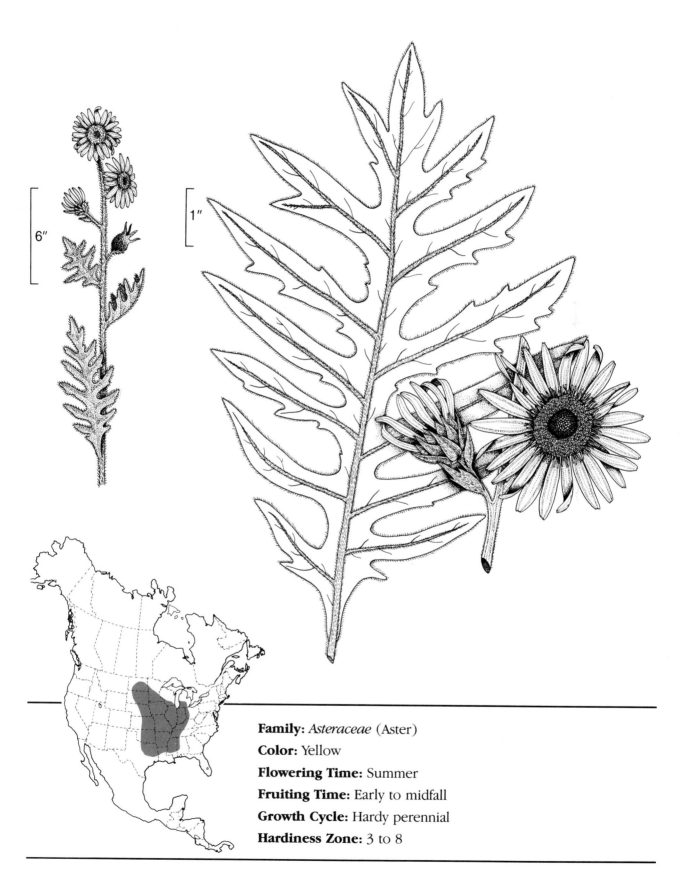

Family: *Asteraceae* (Aster)

Color: Yellow

Flowering Time: Summer

Fruiting Time: Early to midfall

Growth Cycle: Hardy perennial

Hardiness Zone: 3 to 8

COMPASS PLANT *(Silphium laciniatum)*

Blue-eyed grass

(Western blue-eyed grass, California blue-eyed grass, azulea)

Sisyrinchium bellum

The translation of the scientific name of this West Coast perennial is "beautiful *Sisyrinchium*," and beautiful it is. It is a member of the iris family, although its flowers don't look much like those of Douglas's iris (page 155) or larger blue flag (page 157). Blue-eyed grass has small, saucer-shaped, purple-blue to lilac flowers with 3 petals and 3 identical petallike sepals enclosed by a pair of bracts. The petals, which open with the sun and close at night and in cloudy weather, have blunt tips with a projecting point. At the golden center of the flower are 3 stamens and a stigma that becomes 3-clefted after fertilization. Each of the inch-wide flowers is relatively short-lived, but since they are in clusters of 4 to 7, the spring flowering season is fairly long. A round capsule develops in the early summer and contains a few ⅛-inch, black seeds. The foliage of blue-eyed grass looks like 4–16-inch-high clumps of grass, and without flowers present, one might easily mistake this plant for grass. In addition, the branched stems, which are slightly taller than the leaves, are flattened, resembling the stems of the plant's namesake. Fibrous roots of blue-eyed grass spread vigorously with time, and the species may form dense colonies.

CULTURE

Blue-eyed grass grows naturally around pools that hold water in late winter and spring but dry up by early summer. While it is flowering, this species benefits from temporarily wet soils, but the soils should be allowed to dry out during the summer. As long as blue-eyed grass is grown in the full sun and the soils are dry in summer, it can be grown on any kind of soil ranging from sands to loams to clays. There are a number of subspecies and varieties of blue-eyed grass, and some can be grown as annuals to hardiness zone 6. The plants can be success-fully grown in pots that are left out in the spring, given little water during the summer, and brought indoors over winter. In winter, they should be kept moist. Blue-eyed grass is also an attractive addition to a rock garden.

PROPAGATION

Blue-eyed grass can be propagated by root divisions or by seed. Divide the clumps early in the spring, just as the grasslike foliage is emerging. Set the bases of the shoots ¼–½ inch deep and tamp the soil to ensure good root con-tact. On the West Coast, the plant's native range, plant the seeds ¼ inch deep in the desired locations in late summer or early fall. The seeds do not require strat-ification or other treatment. Germination will take place by the early spring, and plants from seed will usually flower the second year. No thinning is needed. In areas outside its native range, plant the seeds in the early spring.

COMPANIONS

Blue dicks, California poppy, golden stars, blazing star, owl's clover, bitterroot, Missouri evening primrose.

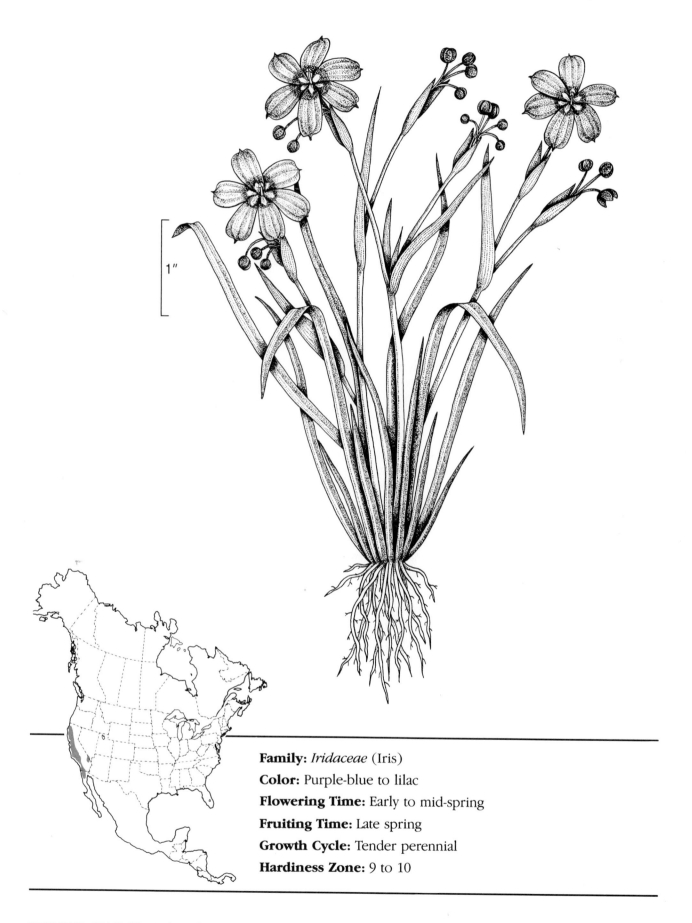

Family: *Iridaceae* (Iris)

Color: Purple-blue to lilac

Flowering Time: Early to mid-spring

Fruiting Time: Late spring

Growth Cycle: Tender perennial

Hardiness Zone: 9 to 10

BLUE-EYED GRASS *(Sisyrinchium bellum)*

False Solomon's seal

Smilacina racemosa

Like the Solomon's seal, the false Solomon's seal has a knotted, thick rhizome, and 5–12 leaves in two rows along the stem. While the arching stems of both plants are 1–3 feet long, the stem of the false Solomon's seal has a zig-zag to it. The flowers are quite different as well. The numerous creamy white flowers of false Solomon's seal are clustered in a 6–12-inch-long cluster at the end of the stem. Each of the ¼-inch flowers has 6 petallike parts. The fruits, ⅛-inch berries, contain 1–2 round seeds and turn from green to a translucent ruby red as they ripen. The fruits are sweet smelling and edible, but you have to race the birds and small mammals to find them.

CULTURE

The best situation for this hardy perennial is partial to full shade in soils that are moist and rich in humus. Although they will grow in full sun or in drier environments, they tend to be somewhat stunted. False Solomon's seal does best in moderately acidic soils with pH 5–6.5.

PROPAGATION

False Solomon's seal can be propagated by either rhizome division or seed. The plant naturally spreads by extension of its rhizomes and is easy to establish. Divide the rhizomes when the plant is dormant in the fall. Space rhizome divisions, each with at least one bud, at least a foot apart, and set them horizontally at a depth of 1½ inches. A thin layer of mulch will help to retain moisture. Plants from rhizome divisions will generally flower the second year. For optimal germination, seeds should be gathered as soon as the fruits ripen in the summer and should not be allowed to dry out. Germination is greatly enhanced by cold, moist stratification (40°F for 3–4 months) and by darkness, since light inhibits the process. To ensure that the seed is in darkness, leave on an inch-thick mulch of deciduous leaves through the spring. Even under the best of conditions the seeds are slow to germinate, frequently taking 2 years, so be patient. If you plant them ¼ inch deep in flats that are left out over the winter, let them go through a second spring before discarding the soil. Have patience also as you wait for false Solomon's seal to flower after the seeds have germinated — it may take 5 years.

COMPANIONS

Solomon's seal, columbines, bloodroot, white baneberry.

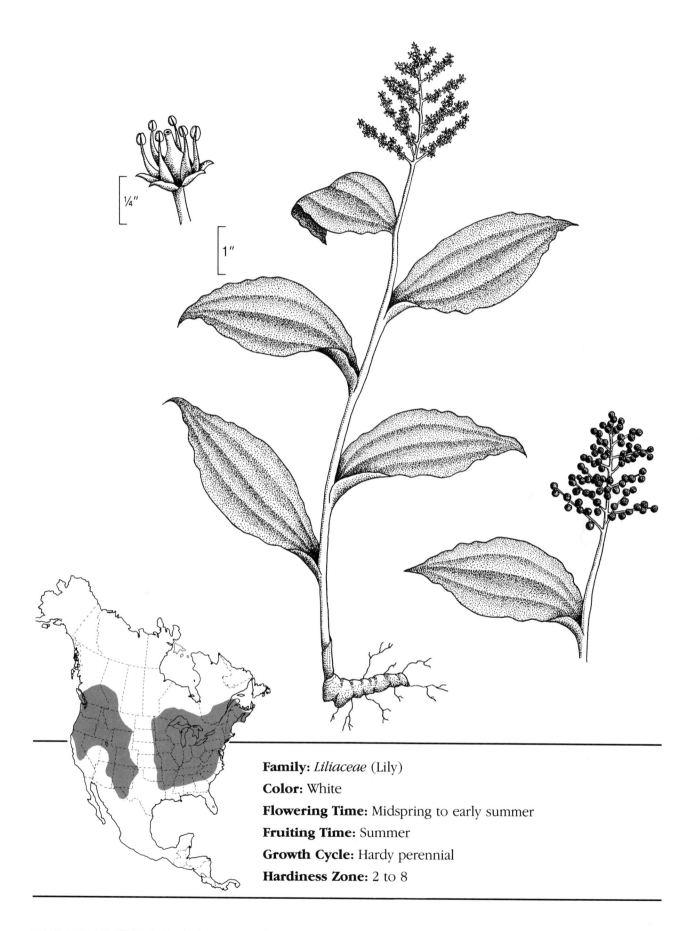

Family: *Liliaceae* (Lily)

Color: White

Flowering Time: Midspring to early summer

Fruiting Time: Summer

Growth Cycle: Hardy perennial

Hardiness Zone: 2 to 8

FALSE SOLOMON'S SEAL *(Smilacina racemosa)*

Desert mallow
(Desert hollyhock)

Sphaeralcea ambigua

With its flowers resembling miniature vermilion hollyhocks, the desert mallow adds a splash of springtime orange to the cold deserts of the Southwest. This somewhat shrubby perennial grows 1½–3 feet high with both its stems and its leaves densely covered with gray hairs. Although not a poppy at all, this plant is locally known as "sore-eye poppy" because the hairs are irritating to the eyes. The maplelike 1–2½-inch leaves have 3 rounded lobes and scalloped edges. Numerous ½–1½-inch-wide red-orange flowers are scattered about near the tips of the branched stems. Each of the flowers has 5 petals and many stamens which clasp the elongated style. The fruits are in a hemispherical arrangement with 12–16 segments attached at their bases in the center of the flower, each ¼-inch segment having a notch on the inside and containing two seeds. The main root system is somewhat woody.

CULTURE

This hardy perennial can endure both freezing winter temperatures and the desert heat of summer. It should be grown in full sun on well-drained, sandy soils. Although it is a plant of arid environments, it benefits from late fall and winter moisture.

PROPAGATION

Desert mallow should be propagated by seed. While the seeds require no stratification, they respond to late fall and winter rains. Plant the seeds ¼ inch deep in the fall in the desired locations. Usually they will germinate over winter and grow rapidly in the spring. Some flowers may appear the first year, and abundant blooms will appear the second.

COMPANIONS

Douglas's wallflower, desert marigold, golden yarrow, purple heliotrope.

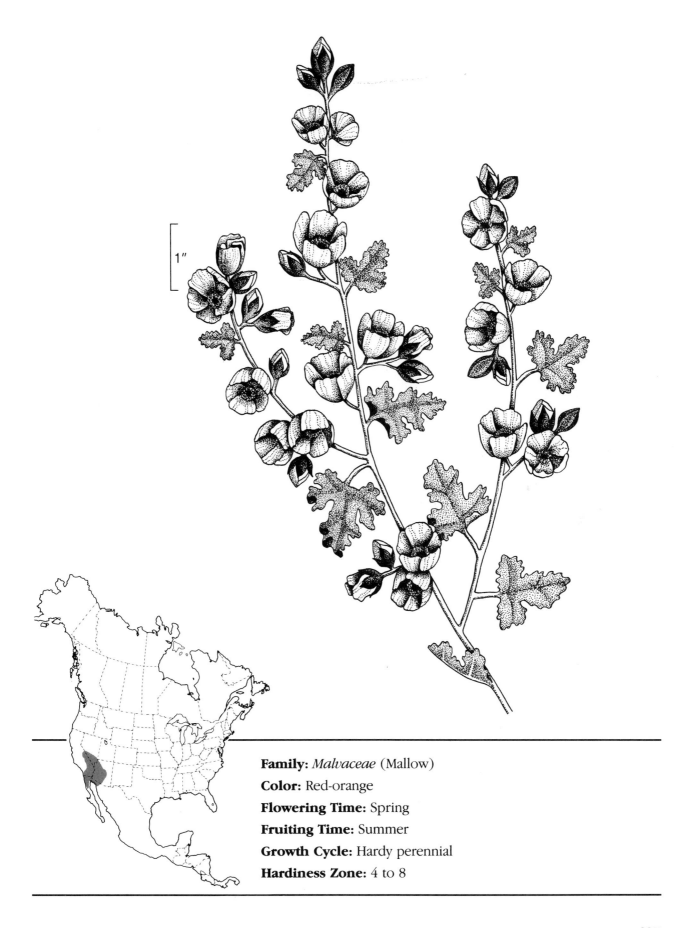

Family: *Malvaceae* (Mallow)
Color: Red-orange
Flowering Time: Spring
Fruiting Time: Summer
Growth Cycle: Hardy perennial
Hardiness Zone: 4 to 8

DESERT MALLOW *(Sphaeralcea ambigua)*

Wind poppy
(Flaming poppy, blood drop)

Stylomecon heterophylla

The flaming red-orange flowers of the wind poppy are borne on 1–2-foot-high stems that sway in the spring breezes of western California. The 1–2-inch-wide flowers have 4 broad, silky, vermilion petals with dark purple spots at their bases. Farther south wind poppies are usually smaller than those from central California. In the center of the flower are many purple filaments, each with a bright yellow anther. The stamens encircle an elongated style and a round, 4–8-lobed, yellow, caplike stigma. The 1–6-inch-long, deeply cleft, round-lobed leaves, like the stem, have a yellow sap. Leaves are densest near the ground, and the long flowering stem with its single nodding bud rises from a rosette of leaves. As the flower bud opens, it becomes erect, and the 2 sepals that covered the tightly compacted petals open and fall off. The blooms are quite fragile, and therefore don't make particularly good cut flowers. The ½-inch-long capsule fruit of the wind poppy has an unusual shape, like a ribbed toy top, with 8 pores at the top through which the small seeds are dispersed.

CULTURE
Wind poppies can be grown in a range of light conditions from full sun to shade, but do best in locations that are sunny part of the day and shady for at least several hours. The soils should be moderately moist, and good drainage is a more important factor than whether the soil is light or heavy. This annual does very well under normal garden conditions, especially in shady borders and on the edges of woodlands.

PROPAGATION
The only way to propagate wind poppy is by seed. Scratch the seeds lightly into the surface of the soil, and then keep moist but not wet until the flowering period has passed. Seeds should be planted in the fall in wind poppy's native range, and in the spring elsewhere. Or you can start the seedlings in peat pots indoors in late winter and transplant the entire pot, after removing the bottom, to the desired location. In its natural range wind poppy will self-seed, forming spectacular clumps of plants in the garden.

COMPANIONS
Chinese houses, coralbells, purple annual lupine, baby blue-eyes, Douglas's iris, California poppy, Douglas's wallflower.

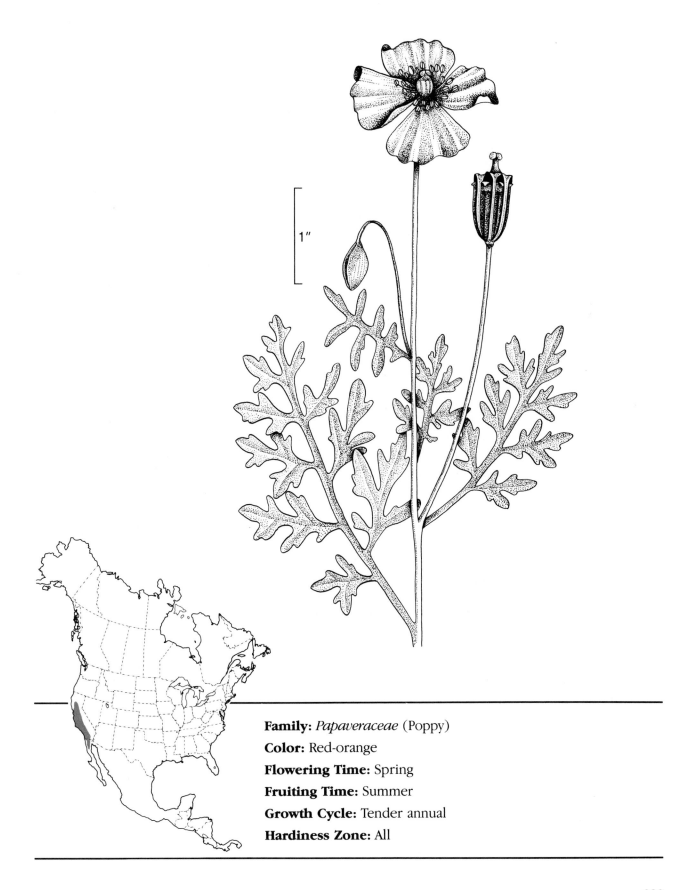

1"

Family: *Papaveraceae* (Poppy)

Color: Red-orange

Flowering Time: Spring

Fruiting Time: Summer

Growth Cycle: Tender annual

Hardiness Zone: All

WIND POPPY *(Stylomecon heterophylla)*

Spiderwort

Tradescantia virginiana

Spiderwort is an old garden favorite that sometimes escapes back into its native habitat, the woods and meadows of the eastern United States. The stems grow 2–12 inches high and are partially covered by clasping, linear, 4–8-inch-long leaves, both leaves and stems being smooth and dull green. The sepals, which cover the flower buds at the top of the stem, are hairy and look inflated. The 3-petaled, 1-inch-wide flowers range from light blue to lavender to rose, colors that contrast nicely with the golden-yellow stamens at the center of the flower. The blossoms cluster above 3 long leafy bracts. Spiderwort is a member of the dayflower family, but individual flowers may scarcely last 8 hours, opening in the morning and withering by midafternoon. Since the flowers are in clusters with only two or so in bloom at a time, the plant may flower for extended periods. The fruit is a ¼-inch capsule with several ⅛-inch, oval seeds. The roots of spiderwort are fibrous and the stolons of this plant will often spread to form colonies.

CULTURE

Spiderwort is an easy plant to grow in gardens, because it tolerates a wide variety of conditions. It can be grown in full sun or shade, and in relatively dry or even damp soils. This hardy perennial is also indifferent to soil acidity conditions, although it grows best where the soil pH is 5.5–7. When given abundant sun, moisture and nutrients, spiderworts may want to crowd out other plants in the garden. If this should happen, contain the colony of spiderwort with plastic or metal strips sunk in the ground.

PROPAGATION

While spiderwort may spread easily from its tangle of fibrous roots, the easiest way to propagate the plant is from stem cuttings made in the summer. Set cuttings an inch or so deep in sand and keep moist while the new roots are forming at the cut end. Transplant the rooted cuttings in the fall. Seeds may be collected and sown in either late summer or early fall. Place them ⅓ inch deep in loamy soil, and keep moist. Seeds usually germinate after 2–3 weeks of temperatures of 70–75°F. Another means of propagating spiderwort is by cutting plugs or sods of the tangle of roots in the early spring or late fall, when the plants are dormant, and then transplanting them.

COMPANIONS

Plant spiderwort by itself or with other aggressive plants such as black-eyed Susan, or other established plants such as New England aster, butterfly weed, and Solomon's seal.

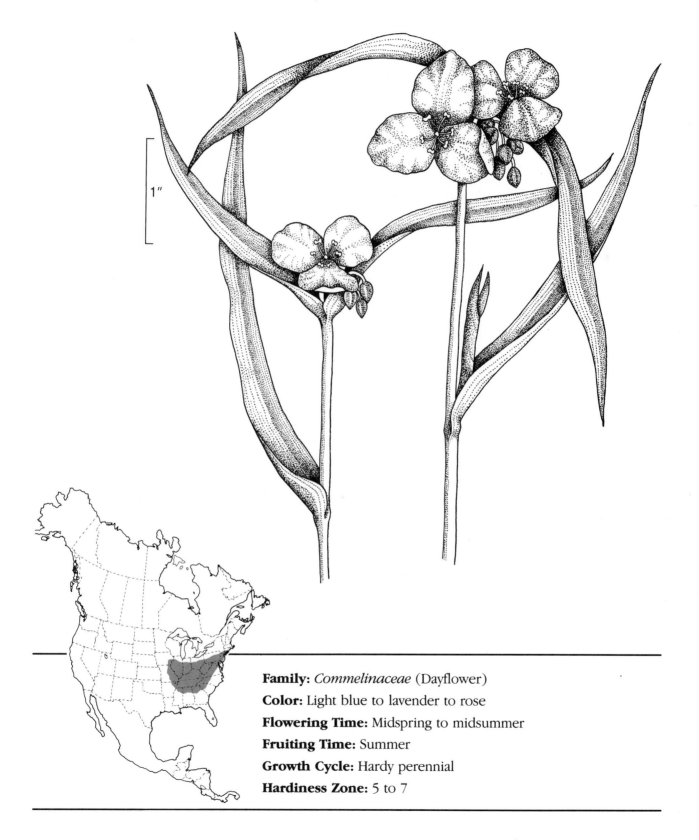

1"

Family: *Commelinaceae* (Dayflower)
Color: Light blue to lavender to rose
Flowering Time: Midspring to midsummer
Fruiting Time: Summer
Growth Cycle: Hardy perennial
Hardiness Zone: 5 to 7

SPIDERWORT *(Tradescantia virginiana)*

Purple trillium

(Wakerobin, stinking Benjamin, red trillium)

Trillium erectum

The purple trillium is one of the commonest yet most striking trilliums in the eastern United States. This hardy perennial has a single whorl of 3 diamond-shaped leaves which clasp its 6–18-inch-high stem. Perched above the leaves is a single nodding flower on a 1–4-inch stem. One of purple trillium's other familiar names is stinking Benjamin; indeed some, but not all, of its flowers smell like rancid meat, which attracts its major pollinator, the big green fleshfly. The 3-petaled flowers are usually crimson to maroon although there are yellow to white forms as well. The petals arch slightly backward and alternate with the 3 green sepals. In the center of the 1–2-inch flower are 6 stamens with yellow anthers. The petals of the purple trillium wither after 2–3 weeks, as the fleshy, oval, berrylike fruit develops. When the fruit is fully ripe it is ½-1 inch long, dark red, and contains many small (1/10-inch) brown seeds. The root system of purple trillium is a stout, brown, bulbous rhizome with many stringy roots, which may be very deep beneath the soil surface.

CULTURE

Purple trillium is a plant of rich woods and thrives in deep leaf mold. Plant it in areas that are sunny in the early spring and receive light to heavy shade once trees have leafed out. Work plenty of compost into the top 6–12 inches of the soil and mulch the plants over the winter with deciduous tree leaves. The soils should be moist, but not excessively so. Purple trillium will grow in a variety of soil conditions between pH 4.5 and 6.5. However, it does require winter cold during its dormant period, for continued growth the next spring, and therefore it may be difficult to maintain this species in areas warmer than hardiness zone 7.

PROPAGATION

Purple trillium is easy to propagate by seeds or root division. Collect the seeds as soon as the fruit is ripe and dark red, but do not let the seeds dry out. Separate the seeds from the fruit and plant them ¼ inch deep in humus-rich loam. Keep the seeds moist and give them a thin mulch of deciduous tree leaves. Alternatively, the seeds may be planted in flats containing a mixture of loam and compost, and left outdoors for the winter. If seeds don't germinate in spring, leave the flats out for a second winter and spring. Stratification is necessary for proper germination, and even then germination may be slow. Seedlings will have only a single leaf the first year and may be transplanted to permanent locations late the following summer. It will take several years for the plants from seed to reach maturity and flower. Propagation by rhizome division should be done during the midsummer when the small, new rhizome extensions can be carefully cut from the parent and planted about 2 inches deep in the desired location. This method may be only slightly quicker than from seed.

COMPANIONS

White trillium, wild leek, Jack-in-the-pulpit, trout lily, bloodroot.

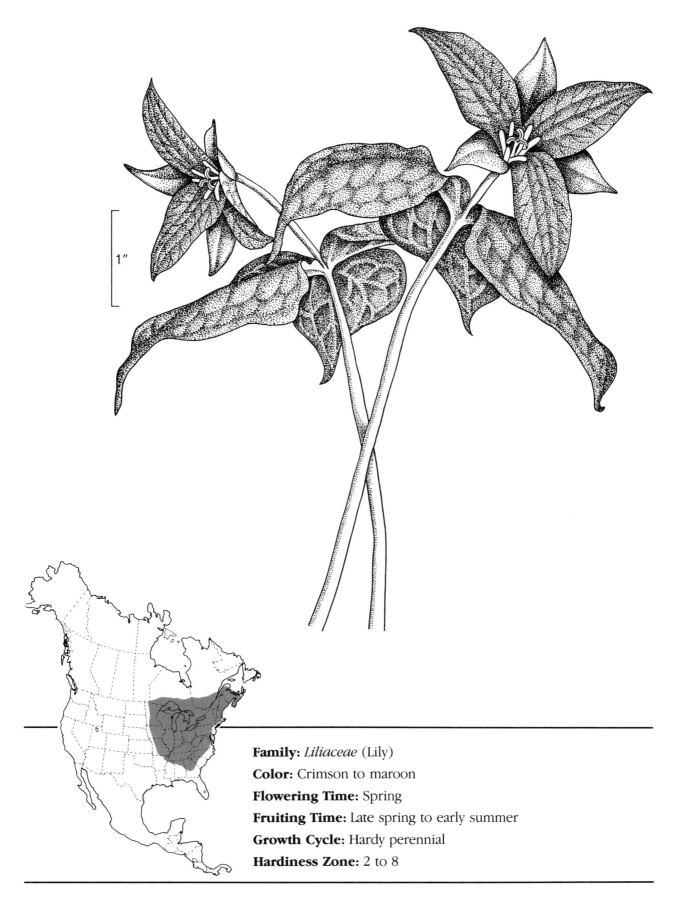

1"

Family: *Liliaceae* (Lily)

Color: Crimson to maroon

Flowering Time: Spring

Fruiting Time: Late spring to early summer

Growth Cycle: Hardy perennial

Hardiness Zone: 2 to 8

PURPLE TRILLIUM *(Trillium erectum)*

White trillium
(Large-flowered trillium)

Trillium grandiflorum

The white trillium is probably the handsomest of the trilliums, and no stranger to gardens. Once established it may grow to form large colonies of 6–18-inch high plants with showy 2–3-inch flowers. The stems emerge in the spring from a large rhizome. The 3 leaves, though somewhat narrower than those of the purple trillium, are attached to the stem in a similar whorled fashion. The 3 petals have wavy margins and are usually white although there are forms of the plant with green or green and white striped flowers. The flowers last about a month, then fade to pale pink with age, and then wither. The ovoid, 6-angled fruit is filled with many ⅛-inch, brown seeds. The seeds of the white trillium are produced parthenogenetically, that is, without the benefit of fertilization.

CULTURE This is the easiest trillium to cultivate and naturalizes well where there are the necessary year-round moisture and low winter temperatures. White trillium grows best in moist yet well-drained soils that are rich in organic matter. Sandy loams with thick humus layers are ideal for planting this species — as is any well-drained garden soil with large quantities of compost worked 8 inches in. Best growth is attained where it is sunny in the spring and lightly shaded after the trees overhead have leafed out. A soil pH of 6–7 is ideal but not essential for successfully raising this plant. Since cold winter temperatures are required by white trillium in order to complete its life cycle, it may be difficult to maintain it naturally in regions warmer than hardiness zone 7.

PROPAGATION White trillium is propagated by seed and by rhizome division. Collect the seeds from ripe fruits and separate them from the pulp, keeping them from drying out or germination will be more difficult. Plant them ¼ inch deep in humus-rich loam. Keep the seeds moist and give them a thin top dressing of compost and a mulch of deciduous tree leaves. The seeds may also be planted in flats containing a mixture of sand, loam, and compost, and should be left outdoors for the winter. As with purple trillium, stratification is necessary for proper germination. Depending on environmental conditions, it may take as little as 3 years, or as many as 10, to produce mature plants from seed. Rhizome divisions are best done in the late summer, and sections should be planted 12–18 inches apart and 3–5 inches deep. The roots will spread, and colonies increase in number, with age. Plants propagated by rhizome division will flower several years sooner than those from seed.

COMPANIONS Solomon's seal, hepatica, bloodroot, purple trillium, Jack-in-the-pulpit, and other woodland plants.

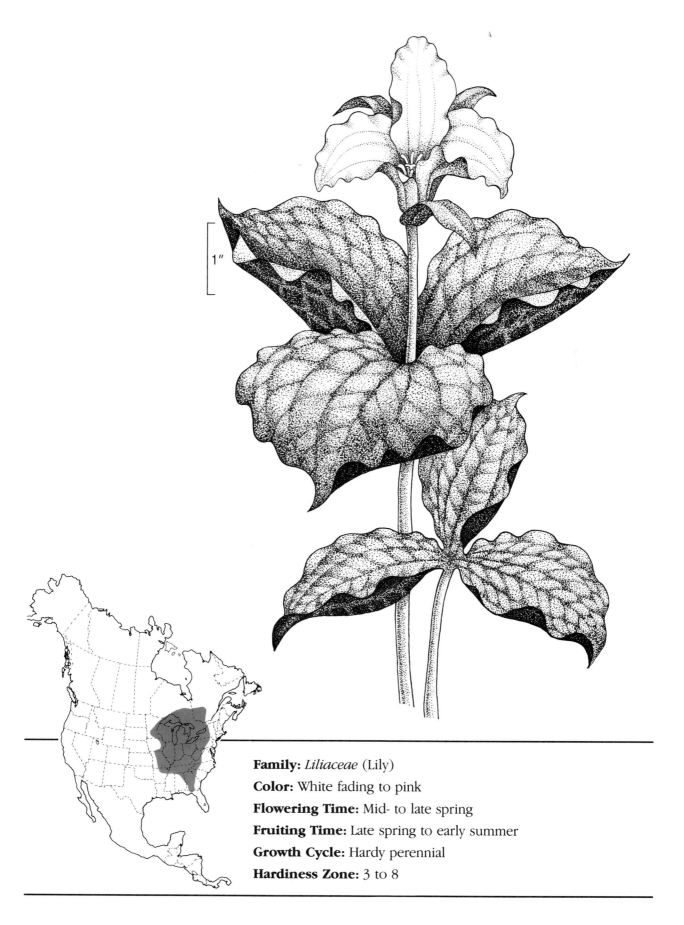

Family: *Liliaceae* (Lily)

Color: White fading to pink

Flowering Time: Mid- to late spring

Fruiting Time: Late spring to early summer

Growth Cycle: Hardy perennial

Hardiness Zone: 3 to 8

WHITE TRILLIUM *(Trillium grandiflorum)*

Southwestern verbena

(Gooding's verbena, Southwestern vervain)

Verbena gooddingii

This low verbena grows on sandy soils and in the mountains from the Mojave Desert in California to Texas. Both the stems and the deeply divided, 3-lobed leaves are quite hairy. Broad, rounded clusters of about a dozen lavender flowers are borne atop the several 6–8-inch scapes. Individual tubular flowers are ¾–1 inch wide with 5 petals, the one in the lower middle sometimes being larger than the others and more conspicuously notched. Each of the flowers produces 4 narrow ⅛-inch-long nutlets.

CULTURE
The flowering season of Southwestern verbena is dependent upon moisture and temperature. In California it is in blossom from April to June, while in other regions it may flower as early as February or as late as October. Southwestern verbena is quite drought tolerant and requires little water to maintain itself. Moderate watering, however, will prolong the flowering season in those regions prone to summer aridity. It can tolerate moist soils well if the drainage is sufficient, but should be planted in the full sun.

PROPAGATION
Propagate Southwestern verbena from seed. The seeds require no chilling treatment; simply plant them ¼ inch deep in the desired location in the spring, and thin plants to 8–12 inches apart. In cold regions this half-hardy perennial can be grown as an annual, started indoors in the late winter and transplanted to a permanent location when all danger of frost has passed. If grown as a perennial, apply a substantial layer of mulch in the fall, and remove it the following spring. In its native range, Southwestern verbena will reseed itself once established.

COMPANIONS
Coralbells, bitterroot, Missouri evening primrose, pasqueflower, annual phlox.

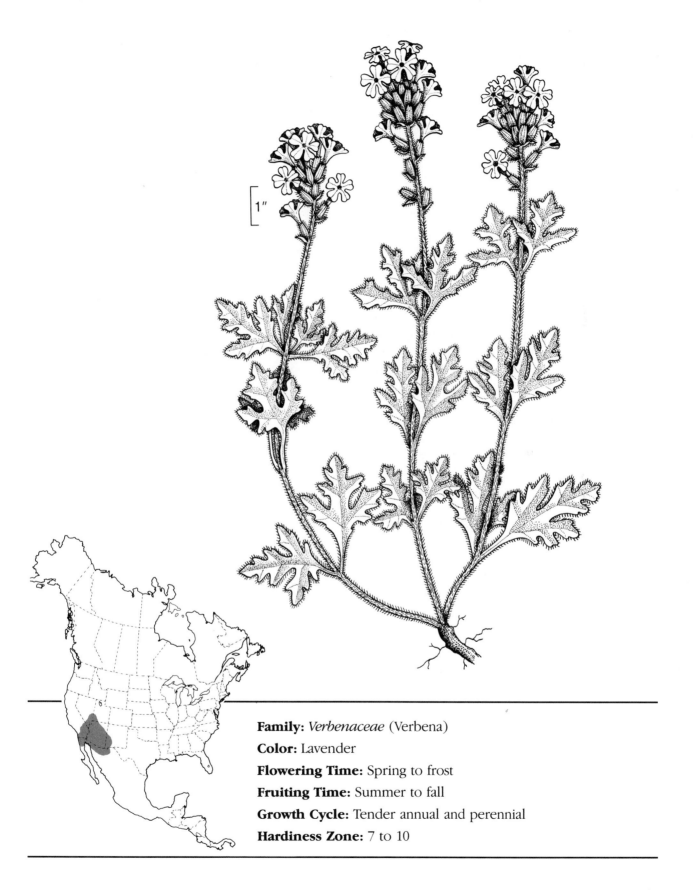

Family: *Verbenaceae* (Verbena)

Color: Lavender

Flowering Time: Spring to frost

Fruiting Time: Summer to fall

Growth Cycle: Tender annual and perennial

Hardiness Zone: 7 to 10

SOUTHWESTERN VERBENA *(Verbena gooddingii)*

Culver's root
(Culver's physic)

Veronicastrum virginicum

The common names of this plant refer to the medicinal use of the roots which allegedly were prescribed by a Doctor Culver. The roots contain *leptandrin,* a potent cathartic and emetic, and Native Americans used this plant as a remedy for several ailments. The unbranched stems grow 2–6 feet tall and are topped by several spikes of densely clustered white or purplish flowers. Each of the tiny, trumpet-shaped flowers has 4 lobes beyond which extend 2 stamens. The total effect is of a candelabra of tapering bottle brushes. The flowering season is quite long, and Culver's root makes an excellent cut flower. The fruits are small capsules containing many minute seeds. The dark green leaves are sharply toothed and arranged in whorls around the stem. The fibrous, extensive roots are yellow.

CULTURE

Culver's root is an ideal hardy perennial for cultivation in gardens since it is so adaptable. It grows well in full sun or in locations with moderate shade. Any soil with average to damp moisture will do, and Culver's root is also quite indifferent to soil acidity conditions (pH 4.5–7). It does grow best where there is ample organic matter in the soil, so annual additions of compost may be beneficial. With age, Culver's root tends to form clumps, but it is not overly aggressive.

PROPAGATION

While Culver's root can be propagated by seed and stem cuttings, it is most effectively propagated by root division. Divide roots in the late fall or early spring while the plants are dormant. Cut the rootstock into segments, each of which should have a bud. Set the pieces about a foot apart with the bud just at the soil surface, and mulch for the winter. Stem cuttings should be made in the early summer. Plant 6-inch stem sections 3 inches deep in sand, keeping the cuttings moist and providing shade for the first growing season. Transplant them to permanent locations in the fall. It typically takes 3 years for cuttings to mature and flower. Seeds can also be scratched into the surface of the soil in the desired location or in flats to be left outdoors over the winter. As with cuttings, propagation by seed is slower than by root division.

COMPANIONS

False dragonhead, gayfeather, New England aster, American bellflower, turtlehead.

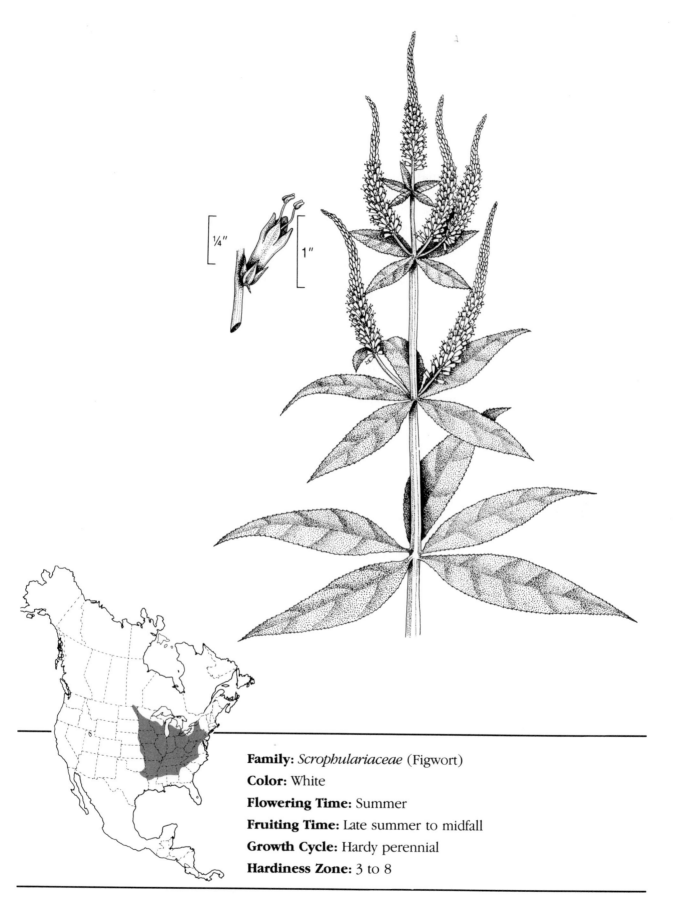

Family: *Scrophulariaceae* (Figwort)

Color: White

Flowering Time: Summer

Fruiting Time: Late summer to midfall

Growth Cycle: Hardy perennial

Hardiness Zone: 3 to 8

CULVER'S ROOT *(Veronicastrum virginicum)*

Mule's ears

(Mule's-ear wyethia, dwarf sunflower)

Wyethia amplexicaulis

The long leaves of this southwestern montane composite resemble the ears of a mule, but rather than being hairy, they are covered with a resinous varnish. From amid clumps of 8–24-inch, dark green, aromatic leaves rise 1–2-foot-high stems, bearing clasping leaves and a cluster of several 3–5-inch-wide, sunflower-like blossoms. The flower head in the center of the cluster tends to be the largest. The 13 to 21, 1–1½-inch ray flowers are bright lemon yellow, and the numerous disc flowers, a deeper yellow. The seedlike fruit of mule's ears is 4-sided with a low crown of scales at one end. Thick taproots and fibrous roots extend from the underground rhizome. It is obvious why this plant is sometimes called dwarf sunflower; the other name, wyethia, is in honor of Captain Nathaniel J. Wyeth, who led the botanical expedition that discovered this genus in the 1830s.

CULTURE Mule's ears, while a plant of open terrain, should be given ample moisture during the flowering season. Moist but well-drained sandy loams are ideal soils for this perennial, which is hardy to zone 4.

PROPAGATION The easiest way to propagate mule's ears is by seed. Seed should be planted ¼ inch deep in the fall in permanent locations or in deep flats that are left out during the winter. The seed should receive a moist stratification treatment (3 months at 40°F) for proper germination to occur in the spring. If flats or pots are used, transplant the dormant plants to permanent locations during the next fall. Mule's ears can also be propagated by rhizome division. In the fall or early spring, divide the rhizome, each piece having at least one bud. Plant the divisions 8–12 inches apart, with the bud just below the soil surface.

COMPANIONS Coralbells, Douglas's iris, larger blue flag, false dragonhead, Eastern shooting star, Western shooting star.

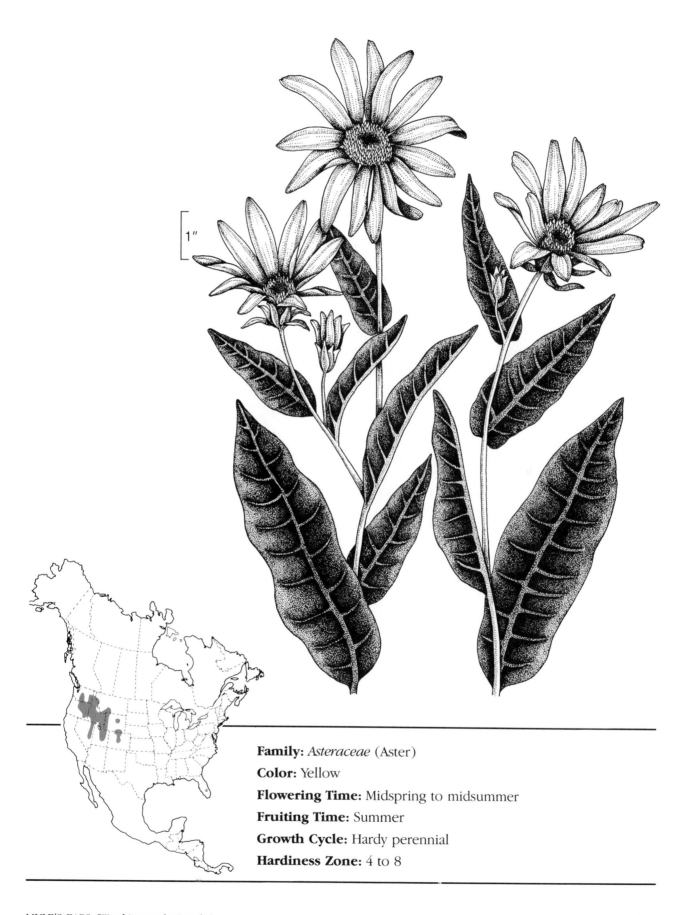

1″

Family: *Asteraceae* (Aster)

Color: Yellow

Flowering Time: Midspring to midsummer

Fruiting Time: Summer

Growth Cycle: Hardy perennial

Hardiness Zone: 4 to 8

MULE'S EARS *(Wyethia amplexicaulis)*

Bear grass

(Squaw grass, elk grass, Indian basket grass)

Xerophyllum tenax

The stiff, narrow, rough-edged, 1–2-foot-long basal leaves of this member of the lily family were used by Native Americans to make baskets and garments. This handsome plant of the mountains of the Pacific Northwest stands 2–5 feet high, the leaves diminishing in size toward the top of the stem. A dense, conical cluster of creamy white, ½-inch-wide flowers fills the upper third of the stout scape. The small (⅜-inch-long), flat flowers have stamens as long as the 3 white petals and 3 petallike sepals. Bear grass's fruit is a 3-grooved capsule containing several ⅛-inch-long seeds. After bear grass flowers, the shoot and old basal leaves die, and small offsets previously produced at the base of the plant start to grow rapidly. The root system is a short, thick, woody rhizome, which gives rise to many fibrous roots.

CULTURE

Bear grass can be grown in the full sun or partial shade, light, filtered shade being best. It is naturally found on dryish soils, but can be grown in the garden if the soil is well drained. This hardy perennial is quite drought resistant, once established, and requires little attention. The soils should be slightly acidic to nearly neutral (pH 5.5–7.5).

PROPAGATION

Bear grass can be propagated by either seed or root and offset division. Seed propagation is the slowest method, since it takes several years for plants to mature and produce flowers. The seeds require no chilling treatment for germination—simply plant them ¼ inch deep in the fall in flats, nursery beds, or permanent locations. Root divisions can be made in the early spring or late fall. Divide the rhizome so that each section has at least one bud, and plant the sections 2–3 feet apart and 1 inch deep in well-drained soil. The buds should be pointing toward the soil surface. Small offsets that form before flowering can also be used for propagation. In the early spring or late fall, cut off the offset with its associated roots and plant 2–3 feet apart with the crown just at the soil surface.

COMPANIONS

Wood lily, cosmos, showy tick trefoil, compass plant, standing cypress.

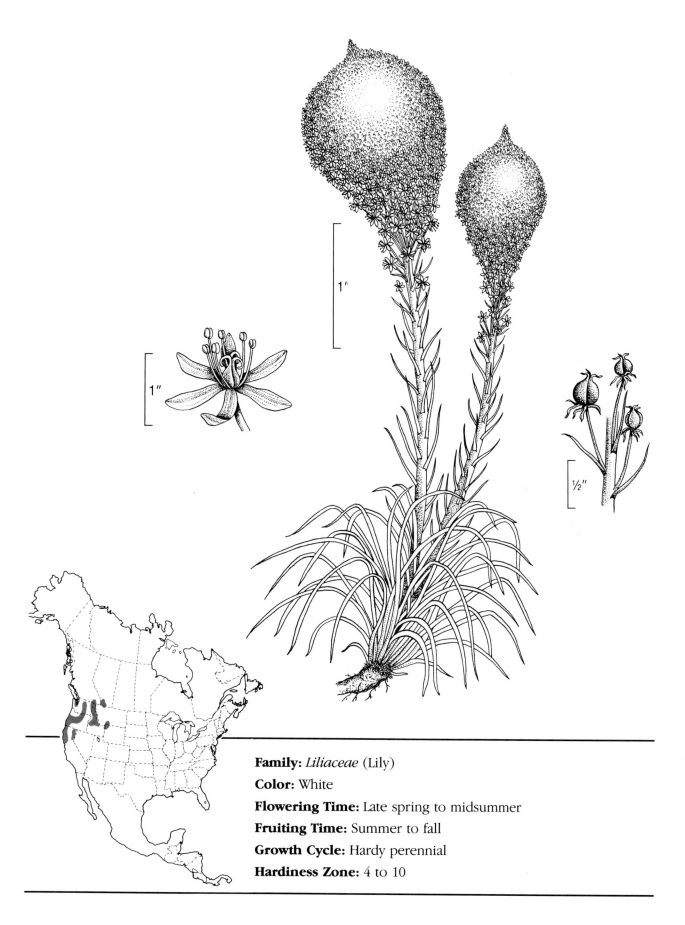

Family: *Liliaceae* (Lily)

Color: White

Flowering Time: Late spring to midsummer

Fruiting Time: Summer to fall

Growth Cycle: Hardy perennial

Hardiness Zone: 4 to 10

BEAR GRASS *(Xerophyllum tenax)*

Our Lord's candle
(Spanish bayonet, Quixote plant, chaparral yucca)

Yucca whipplei

Two of the most common names for this plant, "Our Lord's candle" and "Spanish bayonet," seem at odds with each other. The first name, given by early Padres in California, refers to the spectacular candelabra of fragrant white flowers. The other name, which could have been given by anyone backing into the plant, refers to the unforgiving, spine-tipped, swordlike leaves. The tough, stiff, gray-green leaves of mature plants are 1–3 feet long, rough-edged, and arranged like a hemispherical pin cushion. The leaves increase in size with age, sometimes growing for many years before spectacularly flowering. Then, a 4–20-foot-tall scape erupts and bears up to thousands of creamy white, nodding flowers in a 2–4-foot-long cluster. Sometimes the flowers are tinged with lavender or green. Each flower opens in the evening and lasts for several days, but the flowering period takes 2–7 weeks to progress from the bottom to the top of the inflorescence. Each of the 1–1½-inch bell-like flowers has 3 petallike sepals and 3 identical petals. In the center of the flower are 3 stamens with white filaments and golden anthers, and a 3-angled style with a light green, stalked stigma. The fruits of the plant are 1–2-inch-long 6-segmented pods which open when mature and scatter the numerous flat, black seeds. Several months after fruiting, the entire plant usually dies, although subspecies from the northern part of the range usually produce new shoots at the base of the dead clump of leaves.

CULTURE

This perennial of the chaparral grows in dry, stony, well-drained soils in open, sunny locations. It takes up a lot of space since it may grow to be 6 feet in diameter. Its natural environment is one of wet winters and dry summers, so allow the plant to dry out over the summer. Our Lord's candle is not particularly hardy and is sensitive to prolonged temperatures below freezing, so it is difficult to maintain this species to the flowering stage in hardiness zones colder than 10. However, in cold climates it can be grown successfully as a pot or container plant the way agaves generally are. If grown in a medium-sized pot, it will grow slowly and remain a manageable, but non-flowering, size for many years.

PROPAGATION

Our Lord's candle is propagated by seed, which require no chilling treatment, and should be planted in the fall, ¼–½ inch deep in the desired location. Germination is sometimes enhanced by soaking the seeds in water for 2 days prior to planting them. Thin the seedlings to 2–5 feet apart. Seeds can also be planted in flats and the seedlings carefully transplanted 2–5 feet apart at the end of the first summer. In regions other than its native range, our Lord's candle will not produce seeds from the flowers because its only pollinator, the yucca moth, is absent (see page 4). You can either attempt to pollinate the flowers by hand or simply buy more seeds from a commercial source. Since the plants die after fruiting, be sure to plant the seeds several years in succession.

COMPANIONS

Golden yarrow, blazing star, golden stars, desert marigold, purple heliotrope.

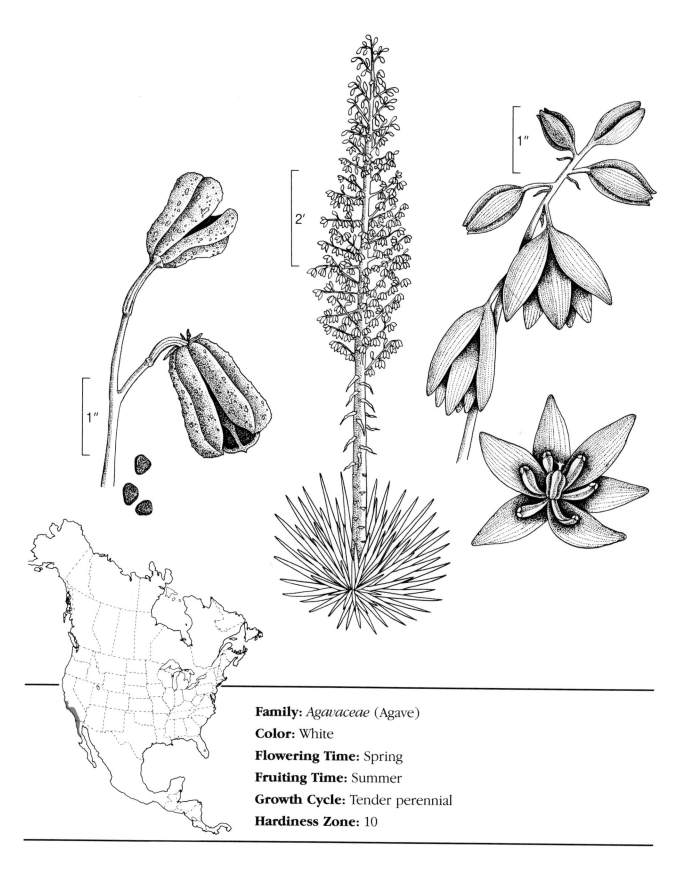

Family: *Agavaceae* (Agave)

Color: White

Flowering Time: Spring

Fruiting Time: Summer

Growth Cycle: Tender perennial

Hardiness Zone: 10

OUR LORD'S CANDLE *(Yucca whipplei)*

APPENDICES

Suppliers

Send payment in the appropriate currency, i.e., U.S. dollars to U.S. businesses and Canadian dollars to Canadian businesses.

Arizona

Hubbs Brothers Seed Company
1522 N. 35th Street
Phoenix, AZ 85008
602-267-8132
Sells seeds retail and wholesale, by mail order and phone order. Free catalog. Native seeds from Sonoran & Mojave Deserts.

Southwestern Native Seeds
P.O. Box 50503
Tucson, AZ 85703
Sells seeds retail by mail order. Catalog: $1.00. Southwestern desert & mountain wildflowers & shrubs.

Wild Seed
P.O. Box 27751
Tempe, AZ 85282
602-968-9751
Sells seeds wholesale by mail order and phone order. Free catalog. Southwestern desert & mountain wildflowers, mixes.

British Columbia

Alpenglow Gardens
13328 King George Highway
Surrey, BC V3T 2T6 CANADA
Sells live plants retail by mail order. Catalog: $1.00. Specializing in alpine & rock garden plants.

California

Blue Oak Nursery
2731 Mountain Oak Lane
Rescue, CA 95672
916-677-2111
Sells live plants retail and wholesale, by mail order and phone order. Free catalog. Specializing in western state natives.

Carter Seeds
475 Mar Vista Drive
Vista, CA 92083
800-872-7711 (in CA 800-624-5700)
Sells seeds wholesale by mail order and phone order. Free catalog.

Common Ground Garden Supply
2225 El Camino Real
Palo Alto, CA 94306
415-328-6752
Sells seeds retail. Wildflower seed mixes for different habitats, and special orders.

Fowler Nurseries
525 Fowler Road
Newcastle, CA 95658
916-645-8191
Sells seeds and live plants, retail and wholesale, by mail order and phone order. Catalog: $2.00.

J.L. Hudson, Seedsman
P.O. Box 1058
Redwood City, CA 94064
Sells seeds retail and wholesale, by mail order. Catalog: $1.00. Wildflowers & rare plants from around the world.

Larner Seeds
P.O. Box 60143
Palo Alto, CA 94306
415-941-9710
Sells seeds and live plants, retail and wholesale, by mail order and phone order. Catalog: $.50. Native species from California & New England.

Pacific Tree Farms
4301 Lynnwood Drive
Chula Vista, CA 92010
619-422-2400
Sells seeds and live plants, retail and wholesale, by mail order and phone order. Catalog: $1.50. Natives for mild climates.

The Theodore Payne Foundation
10459 Tuxford Street
Sun Valley, CA 91352

818-768-1802
Sells seeds and live plants, retail, by mail order (seeds only) and phone order. Free catalog. California native wildflowers & mixes.

Pecoff Brothers Nursery & Seed
Route 5, Box 215 R
Escondido, CA 92025
619-744-3120
Sells seeds and live plants, retail and wholesale, by mail order and phone order. Free catalog. Specializing in drought-tolerant wildflowers.

Redwood City Seed Company
P.O. Box 361
Redwood City, CA 94064
415-325-7333
Sells seeds and live plants, retail and wholesale, by mail order and phone order. Southwestern seeds collected on demand.

Clyde Robin Seed
P.O. Box 2366
Castro Valley, CA 94546
415-581-3468
Sells seeds retail and wholesale, by mail order and phone order. Catalog: $2.00. Full range of wildflower seeds.

S & S Seeds
P.O. Box 1275
Carpinteria, CA 93013
805-684-0436
Sells seeds wholesale by mail order and phone order. Free catalog. Southwestern natives for reclamation & revegetation.

Stover Seed Company
1415 E. 6th Street/P.O. Box 21488
Los Angeles, CA 90021
213-626-9668
Sells seeds wholesale by phone order. Free catalog.

Wapumne Native Plant Nursery Company
8305 Cedar Crest Way
Sacramento, CA 94826

916-383-5754
Sells seeds and live plants, retail and wholesale, by mail order and phone order. California perennials, shrubs, & trees.

Colorado

Anderson Seed Company
717 6th Street
Greeley, CO 80631
303-356-7400
Sells seeds wholesale by phone order. Wildflower seeds by the pound.

Applewood Seed Company
5380 Vivian Street
Arvada, CO 80002
303-431-6283
Sells seeds wholesale by mail order and phone order. Free catalog.

Arkansas Valley Seeds, Inc.
P.O. Box 270
Rocky Ford, CO 81067
303-254-7460
Sells seeds retail and wholesale by mail order and phone order. Free list. Field seeds of grasses, shrubs & wildflowers.

Carhart Feed & Seed
P.O. Box 55, Third & Guyman
Dove Creek, CO 81324
Sells seeds retail and wholesale. Native plant seeds for land reclamation.

Helix Seeds
4880 Pearl Street
Boulder, CO 80301
Sells seeds wholesale. Seeds available through garden & hardware stores.

Connecticut

Comstock, Ferre & Company
263 Main Street, P.O. Box 125
Wethersfield, CT 06109
Sells seeds and live plants, retail, by mail order (seeds only). Free catalog.

Florida

Gann's Tropical Greenery & Natives
  Nursery
22140 SW 152nd Avenue
Goulds, FL 33170
305-248-5529

Sells live plants retail and wholesale, by mail order and phone order. Free catalog. Plants native to Florida.

Georgia

H.G. Hastings
P.O. Box 4274
Atlanta, GA 30302
800-334-1771
Sells seeds retail by mail order and phone order. Free catalog.

Idaho

Idaho Grimm Growers Warehouse
P.O. Box 276
Blackfoot, ID 83221
Sells seeds retail and wholesale, by mail order and phone order. Free list. Field seeds & wildflowers.

Jacklin Seed Company
W. 5300 Jacklin Avenue
Post Falls, ID 83854
800-635-8726
Sells seeds retail and wholesale, by mail order and phone order. Free list. Wildflower mixes for reclamation.

Northplan Seed Producers
P.O. Box 9107
Moscow, ID 83843
208-882-8040
Sells seeds and live plants, retail and wholesale, by mail order and phone order. Catalog: $.50. Western wildflower & grass seed for land reclamation.

Winterfeld Ranch Seed Company
P.O. Box 97
Swan Valley, ID 83449
Sells seeds wholesale. Free list.

Illinois

Lafayette Home Nursery
R.R. Box 1A
Lafayette, IL 61449
309-995-3311
Sells seeds and live plants, retail and wholesale, by mail order (seeds only) and phone order. Send large SASE for catalog. Native prairie grass and wildflower mixes.

Midwest Wildflowers
P.O. Box 64
Rockton, IL 61072
Sells seeds retail by mail order. Catalog: $.50. Midwestern wildflowers.

The Natural Garden
38 W. 443 Highway 64
St. Charles, IL 60174
312-584-0150
Sells seeds and live plants, retail and wholesale, by mail order (seeds only) and phone order. Catalog: $2.00. Illinois native wildflowers and grasses.

R.H. Shumway
P.O. Box 777
Rockford, IL 61105
Sells seeds retail and wholesale, by mail order and phone order. Catalog: $1.00.

Sunshine Seed Company
R.R. #II, Box 176
Wyoming, IL 61491
309-286-7356
Sells seeds retail and wholesale, by mail order and phone order. Catalog: $1.00, refundable. Native seeds of Illinois, California and the Southwest.

Windrift Prairie Nursery
Dot & Doug Wade
Route 2
Oregon, IL 61061
815-732-6890
Sells seeds and live plants, retail, by mail order and phone order. Send 2 first-class stamps for catalog. Native Midwest prairie species.

Iowa

Henry Field Seed & Nursery Company
407 Sycamore
Shenandoah, IA 51602
712-246-2110
Sells seeds retail by mail order and phone order. Free catalog.

Kansas

Sharp Brothers Seed Company
P.O. Box 140
Healy, KA 67850
316-398-2231

Sells seeds retail and wholesale, by mail order and phone order. Free catalog. Great Plains wildflower and grass seed.

Louisiana

Jack P. Price Nursery
Route 9, Box 657
Shreveport, LA 71107
318-929-3984
Sells live plants retail and wholesale, by phone order.

Maine

Daystar
Route 2, Box 250
Litchfield, ME 04350
Sells live plants retail and wholesale, by mail order. Catalog: $1.00. New England rock garden plants.

Maryland

Native Seeds, Inc.
14590 Triadelphia Mill Road
Dayton, MD 21036
301-596-9818
Sells seeds and live plants, retail and wholesale, by mail order and phone order. Free catalog.

Massachusetts

Garden in the Woods
Hemenway Road
Framington, MA 01701
617-877-6574
Sells seeds and live plants, retail, by mail order. Free catalog. Sales are seasonal.

Weston Nurseries, Inc.
P.O. Box 186, Route 135
Hopkinton, MA 01748
617-435-3414
Sells seeds and live plants, retail and wholesale, by phone order. Free catalog. Landscaping perennials including native plants.

Michigan

Dutch Mountain Nursery
7984 N. 48th Street, R-1
Augusta, MI 49012
616-731-5232

Sells seeds and live plants, retail, by mail order and phone order. Catalog: $.50. Mostly native shrubs, but some wildflowers as well.

Minnesota

Prairie Moon Nursery
Route 3, Box 163
Winona, MN 55987
507-452-5231
Sells seeds and live plants, retail and wholesale, by mail order and phone order. Send 2 first-class stamps for catalog. Northern midwestern natives.

Prairie Restorations, Inc.
P.O. Box 327
Princeton, MN 55371
612-389-4342
Sells seed and live plants, retail and wholesale, by mail order. Free catalog. Sales limited to within 200 miles of Princeton, MN.

S & R Seed Company
Box 86
Cass Lake, MN 56633
218-335-2363
Sells seeds retail by mail order and phone order.

Missouri

Manglesdorf Seed Company
P.O. Box 327
St. Louis, MO 63166
314-535-6700
Sells seeds and live plants wholesale by mail order and phone order. Free list. Wildflower and range grasses.

Nebraska

Bluebird Nursery, Inc.
Route 1, Box 298
Clarkson, NE 68629
402-892-3457
Sells seeds and live plants, retail and wholesale, by mail order and phone order. Free catalog.

Flatland Impressions
1219 16th Street
Aurora, NE 68818
402-694-5535

Sells live plants retail and wholesale, by mail order. Custom grower of native plants.

Horizon Seeds
P.O. Box 81823
1600 Corn Husker Highway
Lincoln, NE 68501
Sells seeds retail and wholesale, by mail order.

Stock Seed Farms
Route 1, Box 112
Murdock, NE 68407
402-867-3771
Sells seeds retail and wholesale, by mail order and phone order. Free catalog. Prairie wildflowers & grasses.

New Jersey

Thompson & Morgan
P.O. Box 1308
Jackson, NJ 08527
800-367-7333
Sells seeds and live plants, retail and wholesale, by mail order and phone order. Free catalog.

New Mexico

Bernardo Beach Native Plant Farm
Star Route 7, Box 145
Veguita, NM 87062
Sells seeds and live plants, retail and wholesale, by mail order. Send 4 first-class stamps for catalog. Drought-tolerant natives of Midwest and Southwest.

Curtis & Curtis
Star Route Box 8A
Clovis, NM 88101
505-762-4759

Sells seeds retail and wholesale, by mail order and phone order. Free list.

C H & E Diebold, Ltd.
Box 330, RFD 3
Los Lunas, NM 87031
Sells seeds wholesale.

Plants of the Southwest
1812 Second Street
Santa Fe, NM 87501
505-983-1548

Sells seeds retail and wholesale, by mail order and phone order. Catalog: $1.00. Drought-tolerant natives.

New York

Botanic Garden Seed Company, Inc.
9 Wyckoff Street
Brooklyn, NY 11237
718-624-8839
Sells seeds retail and wholesale, by mail order and phone order. Catalog available, write for price.

Harris Moran Seed Company
3670 Buffalo Road
Rochester, NY 14624
716-594-9411
Sells seeds retail and wholesale, by mail order and phone order. Free catalog.

Wildginger Woodlands
P.O. Box 1091
Webster, NY 14580
716-872-4033
Sells seeds and live plants retail by mail order. Catalog: $1.00 (refundable).

North Carolina

Holbrook Farm & Nursery
Route 2, Box 223B
Fletcher, NC 28732
704-891-7790
Sells live plants retail by mail order and phone order. Catalog: $2.00 (refundable with order).

Passiflora
P.O. Box 393
Germanton, NC 27019
919-591-5816
Sells seeds and live plants retail by mail order and phone order. Catalog: $1.00 (refundable with order).

We-Du Nurseries
Route 5, Box 724
Marion, NC 28752
704-738-8300
Sells live plants retail and wholesale, by mail order and phone order. Catalog: $.50. Southeastern natives.

Ontario

C.A. Cruickshank, Inc.
1015 Mt. Pleasant Road
Toronto, ONT M4P 2M1 CANADA
416-488-8292
Sells seeds and live plants retail by mail order and phone order. Catalog: $2.00 for 2-year subscription. Woodland and bulb species.

Oregon

Russel Graham
4030 Eagle Crest Road N.W.
Salem, OR 97304
503-362-1135
Sells live plants retail and wholesale, by mail order and phone order. Catalog: $2.00.

Great Western Seed Company
P.O. Box 387
Albany, OR 97321
Sells seeds wholesale. Free catalog.

Nature's Garden
Route 1, Box 488
Beaverton, OR 97007
503-649-6772
Sells seeds and live plants, retail and wholesale, by mail order. Catalog: $1.00 (refundable with purchase).

Northwest Biological Enterprises
23351 S.W. Bosky Dell Lane
West Linn, OR 97068
503-638-6029
Sells seeds and live plants, retail and wholesale, by mail order. Catalog: $1.00. Pacific Northwest natives.

Siskiyou Rare Plant Nursery
2825 Cummings Road
Medford, OR 97501
503-772-6846
Sells live plants retail by mail order. Catalog: $1.50. Rock garden and woodland plants of the Northwest.

Pennsylvania

Appalachian Wildflower Nursery
Route 1, Box 275A
Reedsville, PA 17084
717-667-6998

Sells seeds and live plants, retail and wholesale, by mail order and phone order. Send 1 first-class stamp for list.

Beachley-Hardy Seed Company
P.O. Box 336
Camp Hill, PA 17011
717-737-4529
Sells seeds wholesale by phone order.

W. Atlee Burpee Company
300 Park Avenue
Warminster, PA 18974
215-674-4900
Sells seeds retail and wholesale, by mail order and phone order. Free catalog.

Painted Meadow Seeds
P.O. Box 1865
Kingston, PA 18704
717-283-2911
Sells seeds retail and wholesale, by mail order. Free catalog.

South Carolina

George W. Park Seed Company
P.O. Box 31
Greenwood, SC 29647
803-374-3341
Sells seeds and live plants, retail and wholesale, by mail order and phone order. Free catalog.

R.H. Shumway
P.O. Box 1
Graniteville, SC 29829
Sells seeds retail and wholesale, by mail order and phone order. Catalog: $1.00.

Woodlanders, Inc.
1128 Colleton Avenue
Aiken, SC 29801
803-648-7522
Sells live plants retail by mail order. Catalog: $1.50. Herbaceous and woody perennials.

Tennessee

Native Gardens
Route 1, Box 494
Greenback, TN 37742
615-856-3350

Sells seeds and live plants, retail and wholesale, by mail order and phone order. Catalog: $.50. Propagated wildflowers.

Natural Gardens
113 Jasper Lane
Oak Ridge, TN 37830
Sells seeds and live plants retail by mail order. Catalog: $.50.

Sunlight Gardens, Inc.
Route 3, Box 286 B
Loudon, TN 37774
615-986-6071
Sells live plants retail and wholesale, by mail order. Free catalog.

Texas

Greenhills Center
7575 Wheatland Road
Dallas, TX 75249
214-296-1955
Sells seeds and live plants, retail and wholesale, by mail order and phone order. Free catalog. Native plants of the Dallas region.

Horizon Seeds
Box 886
Hereford, TX 79045
806-258-7288
Sells seeds retail and wholesale, by phone order.

Douglass W. King Company
P.O. Box 20320
San Antonio, TX 78286
512-661-4191
Sells seeds retail and wholesale, by mail order and phone order. Texas grasses and wildflowers.

Lone Star Growers
Route 9, Box 220
San Antonio, TX 78227
512-677-8020
Sells live plants wholesale. Free list.

The Lowrey Nursery
2323 Sleepy Hollow Road
Conroe, TX 77385
713-367-4076
Sells seeds and live plants, retail. Mail order limited.

Native Son Nursery
8600 Webberville Road
Austin, TX 78724
512-926-6301
Sells seeds retail and wholesale, by mail order and phone order. Free catalog. Species native to Central Texas.

Sharp Brothers Seed Company
4378 Canyon Drive
Amarillo, TX 79109
316-398-2231
Sells seeds retail and wholesale, by mail order and phone order. Free catalog.

Utah

NPI
417 Wakara Way
Salt Lake City, UT 84108
801-582-0144/801-768-4422
Sells seeds and live plants wholesale, by mail order and phone order. Free catalog. Wildflowers, native mixes, and shrubs.

Vermont

Putney Nursery, Inc.
Putney, VT 05346
802-387-5577
Sells seeds and live plants retail, by mail order and phone order. Free catalog.

Washington

Wild Westerners — McLaughlin's Seeds
P.O. Box 550
Mead, WA 99021-0550
509-466-0230
Sells seeds retail and wholesale, by mail order and phone order. Catalog: $1.00. Hardy wildflower seeds, especially perennials.

Wisconsin

Boehlke's Woodland Gardens
County Aire Road W140 N10829
Germantown, WI 53022
Sells live plants retail by mail order. Catalog: $.50. Midwestern woodland and prairie species.

Cliffords Perennial & Vine
Route 2, Box 320
East Troy, WI 53120

Sells live plants retail and wholesale, by mail order. Free catalog.

Great Lakes Wild Flowers
Box 1923
Milwaukee, WI 53201
Sells live plants retail and wholesale, by mail order. Free list. Great Lakes natives.

Little Valley Farm
R.R. 1, Box 287
Richland Center, WI 53581
603-538-3180
Sells seeds and live plants, retail and wholesale, by mail order and phone order. Catalog: $.25. Woodland, wetland, and prairie species.

Natural Habitat Nursery
4818 Terminal Road
McFarland, WI 53558
608-838-3376
Sells seeds retail and wholesale, by mail order and phone order. Free catalog. Prairie seed.

Prairie Nursery
Route 1, Box 365
Westfield, WI 53964
Sells seeds and live plants, retail and wholesale, by mail order. Free catalog. Prairie wildflowers and grasses.

Prairie Ridge Nursery
9738 Overland Road, R.R. 2
Mt. Horeb, WI 53572
608-437-5245
Sells seeds and live plants, retail and wholesale, by mail order and phone order. Catalog: $.50. Native prairie plants.

Prairie Seed Source
P.O. Box 83
North Lake, WI 53064
Sells seeds retail by mail order. Free catalog. Prairie species.

Sperka's Woodland Acres Nursery
Route 2
Crivitz, WI 54114
Sells live plants retail by mail order. Send 1 first-class stamp for list. Hardy native wildflowers and ferns.

Superior View Farm
Route 1, Box 199
Bayfield, WI 54814
715-779-5404
Sells live plants retail and wholesale, by mail order and phone order. Free catalog.

Wehr Nature Center
9701 W. College Avenue
Franklin, WI 53132
414-425-8550
Sells seeds retail by mail order and phone order. Free list. Native prairie wildflower mixes.

Wildlife Nurseries
P.O. Box 2724
Oshkosh, WI 54903
414-231-3780
Sells seeds retail by mail order and phone order. Catalog: $1.00. Wetland species for attracting wildlife.

Botanical Gardens

The following is a list of botanical gardens, arboreta, and nature centers that have gardens or natural areas dedicated to native plants. Many of these organizations provide additional services and have garden shops where books, seeds, and live plants can be purchased.

Alabama

Birmingham Botanical Garden
2612 Lane Park Road
Birmingham, AL 35223
205-879-1227
Free. Open all year, daylight hours. Sells seeds and live plants. Tours of wildflower garden.

Arizona

Arizona-Sonora Desert Museum
Route 9, Box 900
Tucson, AZ 85743
602-883-1380
Entrance fee: $5.00. Open all year, 8 am–sunset. Sells seeds and live plants. Emphasis on water-thrifty plants.

Boyce Thompson Southwestern
   Arboretum
P.O. Box AB
Superior, AZ 85273
602-689-2811
Entrance fee: $1.50. Open all year, 8 am–5 pm. Sells seeds and live plants. Drought-tolerant plants.

Desert Botanical Garden
1201 North Galvin Parkway
Phoenix, AZ 85008
602-941-1217
Entrance fee: $2.50. Open all year, 9 am–sunset, 7 am–sunset (July & August). Sells seeds and live plants. Wildflower Network & Richter Memorial Library.

British Columbia

University of British Columbia Botanical
   Garden
6501 NW Marine Drive
Vancouver, BC V6T 1W5 CANADA
604-228-3928
Entrance fee: $2.00. Open all year, daylight hours. Sells seeds and live plants. Special native and alpine gardens.

Van Dusen Gardens
5251 Oak Street
Vancouver, BC V6M 4H1 CANADA
604-266-7194
Entrance fee: $3.00. Open all year, 10 am–8 pm (summer), 10 am–4 pm (winter). Sells seeds and live plants. Additional indoor wildflower exhibits.

California

Descanso Gardens
1418 Descanso Drive
La Canada, CA 91011
Entrance fee: $1.50. Open all year, 9 am–5 pm. Sells live plants.

Huntington Botanical Gardens
1151 Oxford Road
San Marino, CA 91108
818-405-2100
Entrance fee: $2.00 donation. Open all year, except holidays, 1–4 pm Tues.–Sun. Sells live plants.

Joseph McInnes Memorial Botanical
   Gardens
Mills College/Seminary Avenue &
   MacArthur Blvd.
Oakland, CA 94613
415-430-2158
Free. Open all year, 8 am–5 pm Mon.–Fri.

The Living Desert
47-900 S. Portola Avenue
Palm Desert, CA 92260
619-346-5694
Entrance fee: $3.00. Open Sept. 1–June 15, 9 am–5 pm. Sells seeds and live plants. Eight different desert regions represented.

Los Angeles State and County Arboretum
301 N. Baldwin Avenue
Arcadia, CA 91006-2697
818-446-8251
Entrance fee: $1.50. Open all year, 9 am–5 pm. Sells seeds.

Rancho Santa Ana Botanical Garden
1500 N. College Avenue
Claremont, CA 91711
714-626-3922
Free. Open all year, except holidays, 8 am–5 pm. Sells live plants. Several different native plant gardens.

Regional Parks Botanic Garden
Tilden Regional Park
Berkeley, CA 94708-1199
415-841-8732
Free. Open all year, except holidays, 8:30 am–5 pm, 8:30 am–6 pm in summer. Sells seeds and live plants.

Santa Barbara Botanic Garden
1212 Mission Canyon Road
Santa Barbara, CA 93105
805-682-4726
Free. Open all year, 8 am–sunset. Sells seeds and live plants. Several different native gardens.

South Coast Botanic Garden
26300 Crenshaw Boulevard
Palos Verdes Peninsula, CA 91011
818-790-5571
Entrance fee: $1.50. Open all year, 9 am–5 pm. Sells seeds and live plants.

Strybing Arboretum & Botanical Gardens
Golden Gate Park (9th Ave. & Lincoln
   Way)
San Francisco, CA 94122
415-558-3622

Free. Open all year, 8 am–4:30 pm Mon.–Fri., 10 am–5 pm weekends & holidays. Sells seeds and live plants.

University Arboretum
University of California — Davis
Davis, CA 95616
916-752-2498
Free. Open all year, daylight hours. Sells seeds and live plants.

University of California Botanical Garden
Centennial Drive
Berkeley, CA 94720
415-642-3343
Free. Open all year, except Christmas, 9 am–4:45 pm. Sells seeds and live plants. Large collection of California natives.

U.C.–Santa Cruz Arboretum
University of California
Santa Cruz, CA 95064
408-429-2657
Free. Open all year, daylight hours. Sells live plants. A growing collection of native California wildflowers.

Colorado

Aspen Center for Environmental Studies
Box 8777
Aspen, CO 81611
303-925-5756
Entrance fee: contribution. Open all year, daylight hours. Sells live plants.

Denver Botanic Gardens
1005 York Street
Denver, CO 80206
303-575-2547
Entrance fee: $3.00. Open all year, except Christmas and New Year's Day, 9 am–4:45 pm. Sells seeds and live plants. Also administers Walter S. Reed and Mount Goliath nature preserves.

Connecticut

Bartlett Arboretum of the University
   of Connecticut
151 Brookdale Road
Stamford, CT 06903
203-322-6971
Free. Open all year, 8:30–sunset.

The Connecticut Arboretum at
   Connecticut College
Williams Avenue
New London, CT 06320
203-447-1911
Free. Open all year, daylight hours. Emphasis on native woody perennials.

Connecticut Audubon Society's Larsen
   Sanctuary
2325 Burr Street
Fairfield, CT 06430
203-259-6305
Entrance fee: $1.00. Open all year, daylight hours. Sells seeds and live plants.

White Memorial Foundation
Route 202, P.O. Box 368
Litchfield, CT 06759
203-567-0857; Museum 203-567-0015
Free. Open all year, daylight hours. Museum open 9 am–5 pm Tues.–Sat., 11 am–5 pm Sun.

District of Columbia

Kenilworth Aquatic Gardens
Douglas Street NE
Washington, DC 20019
202-426-6905
Free. Open all year, 7 am–5 pm. Native aquatic and wetland gardens.

United States Botanic Garden
Maryland Avenue & 1st Street, S.W.
Washington, D.C. 20024
202-225-8333
Free. Open all year, 9 am–5 pm (winter), 9 am–9 pm (summer).

U.S. National Arboretum
3501 New York Avenue, N.E.
Washington, DC 20002
202-475-4815
Free. Open all year, 8 am–5 pm weekdays, 10 am–5 pm weekends. Workshops and symposia on native plants.

Florida

Mounts Horticultural Learning Center
531 N. Military Trail
West Palm Beach, FL 33406
305-683-1777

Free. Open all year, except holidays, 8:30 am–5 pm Mon.–Sat., 1–5 pm Sun. Free information. Part of Florida Cooperative Extension Service.

Sanibel-Captiva Conservation Foundation
P.O. Drawer S, 3333 Sanibel-Captiva Road
Sanibel, FL 33957
813-472-2329
Entrance fee: $1.00. Open all year, 9:30 am–4:30 pm Mon.–Sat. (winter); 9:30 am–3:30 pm Mon.–Fri. (summer). Sells live plants. Native plant landscape counseling available.

Georgia

Atlanta Botanical Garden
Piedmont Park at The Prado
P.O. Box 77246
Atlanta, GA 30357
404-876-5858
Entrance fee: $2.00. Open all year, 9 am–5 pm. Sells seeds and live plants.

Atlanta Historical Society
3101 Andrews Drive, NW
Atlanta, GA 30305
404-261-1837
Entrance fee: $4.50. Open all year, except holidays, 9–5:30 Mon.–Sat., 12–5 pm Sun. Sells seeds.

Callaway Gardens
Pine Mountain, GA 31822
404-663-2281, ext. 154
Entrance fee: $3.75 Open all year, 7 am–5 pm. Sells seeds.

The State Botanical Garden of Georgia
University of Georgia
2450 S. Milledge Avenue
Athens, GA 30605
404-542-1244 Office; 404-542-6329
   Visitor Center
Free. Open all year, 9 am–4:30 pm Mon.–Sat., 11:30 am–4:30 pm Sun. Sells seeds and live plants. Seminars and workshops on native plant gardening.

Hawaii

Waimea Arboretum
59-864 Kamehameha Highway
Haleiwa, HI 96712

808-638-8511

Entrance fee: $6.95. Open all year, 10 am–5:30 pm. Sells seeds and live plants.

Illinois

Chicago Botanic Garden
Lake-Cook Road, P.O. Box 400
Glencoe, IL 60022
312-835-5440

Entrance fee: $1.00 parking. Open all year, except Christmas, 8 am–sunset. Sells seeds.

Chicago Wildflower Works
Daley Bicentennial Plaza
Grant Park between Monroe & Randolph
    Streets
Chicago, IL

Free. Open all year, all day. This extensive native and exotic wildflower garden, covering the roof of the Monroe Street Parking Garage in downtown Chicago, was designed by artist Chapman Kelley and is maintained by the Chicago Park District.

Edward L. Ryerson Conservation Area
21950 N. Riverwoods Road
Deerfield, IL 60015
312-948-7750

Free. Open all year, 8:30 am–5 pm. Wide range of programs and native plant displays.

James Woodworth Prairie Preserve
9831 Milwaukee Avenue (½ mile north of
    Golf Rd.)
Niles–Glenview, IL
312-965-3488

Free. Open June through Sept., except major holidays, 10 am–3 pm. A 5-acre virgin tallgrass prairie with interpretative center and demonstration gardens surrounded by suburbia. The University of Illinois acts as custodian.

Lincoln Memorial Garden
2301 East Lake Drive
Springfield, IL 62707
217-529-1111

Free. Open all year, daylight hours. Sells seeds and live plants.

Morton Arboretum
Lisle, IL 60532
312-968-0074

Entrance fee: $3.00 per car. Open all year, 9 am–7 pm (summer), 9 am–5 pm (winter). Prairie restorations.

Severson Dells Environmental Education
    Center
8786 Montague Road
Rockford, IL 61102
815-335-2915

Free. Open all year, 8 am–4 pm Tues.–Sat., 1–5 pm Sun. Sells seeds.

Indiana

Hayes Regional Arboretum
801 Elks Road
Richmond, IN 47374
317-962-3745

Free. Open all year, 8 am–5 pm Tues.–Sat., 1–5 pm Sun. Sells Seeds.

Iowa

Bickelhaupt Arboretum
340 S. 14th Street
Clinton, IA 52732
319-242-4771

Free. Open all year, daylight hours.

Des Moines Botanical Center
909 East River Drive
Des Moines, IA 50316
515-283-4148

Entrance free: $.50. Open all year, 10 am–6 pm Mon.–Thurs., 10 am–9 pm Fri., 10 am–5 pm weekends. Sells seeds. Several workshops each year, prairie restoration.

Kansas

Cimarron National Grassland
Elkhart, KS 67950
316-697-4621

Free. Open all year, daylight hours.

Soil Conservation Service
Plant Materials Center
Route 2, Box 314
Manhattan, KS 66502

913-539-8761

Free. Open all year, 8 am–4 pm weekdays. Plant materials for conservation use.

Kentucky

Bernheim Forest Arboretum & Nature
    Center
Route 245
Clermont, KY 40110

Free. Open Mar. 15–Nov. 15, 9 am–1 hour before sunset. Sells seeds and live plants.

Land Between the Lakes
Tennessee Valley Authority
Golden Pond, KY 42231
502-924-5602, Administration;
    502-924-5509, Nature Center

Free. Open all year, daylight hours. Woodlands Nature Center.

Maine

Wild Gardens of Acadia
Acadia National Park
Sieur de Monts Spring
Bar Harbor, ME 04609

Free. Open all year, daylight hours. Project of the Bar Harbor Garden Club.

Maryland

Cylburn Arboretum Association
4915 Greenspring Avenue
Baltimore, MD 21209
301-367-2217

Free. Open all year, 6 am–9 pm. Sells live plants.

London Town Publik House & Gardens
839 Londontown Road
Edgewater, MD 21037-2197
301-956-4900

Entrance fee: $2.00. Open all year, 10 am–4 pm Tues.–Sat., 12–4 pm Sun. Sells seeds and live plants.

Massachusetts

Arnold Arboretum
The Arborway
Jamaica Plain, MA 02130
617-524-1717

Free. Open all year, daylight hours. Part of Harvard University.

Berkshire Garden Center
State Routes 183 & 102
Stockbridge, MA 01262
413-298-3926
Entrance fee: $2.00 May–October. Open all year, 10 am–5 pm. Sells seeds and live plants. Wildflower displays.

Garden in the Woods
Hemenway Road
Framingham, MA 01701
617-877-6574
Entrance fee: $3.50. Open April 16–Oct. 31, 9 am–4 pm. Sells seeds and live plants. Home of the New England Wild Flower Society.

Michigan

Hidden Lake Gardens
Route 50
Tipton, MI 49287
517-431-2060
Entrance fee: $1.00. Open all year, 8 am–sunset (summer), 8 am–4:30 pm (winter). Part of Michigan State University.

Matthaei Botanical Gardens
The University of Michigan
1800 North Dixboro Road
Ann Arbor, MI 48105
313-763-7060
Free. Open all year, 8 am–sunset (grounds), 10 am–4:30 pm (conservatory). Sells live plants. A variety of different native gardens, prairie restoration.

Whitehouse Nature Center
Albion College
Albion, MI 49224
517-629-2030
Free. Grounds open all year, daylight hours. Building open 9 am–5 pm Mon.– Fri., Interpretive Center open 1–5 pm weekends. Wildflower garden, woodland garden, restored prairie, and arboretum of native Michigan woody plants.

Minnesota

Como Park Conservatory
Midway Parkway & Kaufman Drive
Saint Paul, MN 55103
612-489-0868
Free. Open all year, daylight hours.

Eloise Butler Wildflower and Bird
  Sanctuary
Theodore Wirth Park
½ mile north of Highway 12
Minneapolis, MN 55409
612-348-5702
Free. Open April 1–Oct. 31, 7:30 am–sunset. Operated by Minneapolis Park and Recreation Board.

Minnesota Landscape Arboretum
3675 Arboretum Drive, P.O. Box 39
Chaska, MN 55317
612-443-2460
Entrance fee: $2.00. Open all year, 8 am–9 pm (summer), 8 am–6 pm (winter).

Mississippi

Mynelle Gardens
4736 Clinton Boulevard
Jackson, MS 39209
601-960-1894
Entrance fee: $2.00. Open all year, 9 am–6 pm (March–Oct.), 8 am–5 pm (Nov.–Feb.). Sells seeds. Occasional lectures on native plants.

Missouri

Missouri Botanical Garden
4344 Shaw Boulevard
St. Louis, MO 63110
314-577-5100
Entrance fee: $1.00. Open all year, 9 am–8 pm (May–Sept.), 9 am–5 pm (Sept.– May). Sells seeds and live plants. Large variety of programs and gardens.

Missouri Prairie Foundation
P.O. Box 200
Columbia, MO 65205
Free. Open all year, daylight hours. Maintains 9 prairie areas — contact office for locations.

Shaw Arboretum of the Missouri
  Botanical Garden
I-44 & Rt. 100, P.O. Box 38
Gray Summit, MO 63039
314-577-5138
Entrance fee: $1.00. Open all year, 7 am–sunset. 10 miles of woodland trails, Ozark wildflowers.

Montana

Arboretum & Gardens
Department of Plant & Soil Science
Montana State University
Bozeman, MT 59717
406-994-4601
Free. Open all year, daylight hours.

Nebraska

Chet Ager Nature Center
Pioneers Park
Lincoln, NE 68502
402-471-7895
Free. Open all year, 8:30 am–8:30 pm (June–Aug.), 8:30 am–5 pm (Sept.–May).

Maxwell Arboretum
University of Nebraska
Lincoln, NE 68583-0823
402-472-2971
Free. Open all year, daylight hours.

New Jersey

Leonard J. Buck Gardens
R.D. 2, Layton Road
Far Hills, NJ 07931
201-234-2677
Entrance fee: $.50 donation. Open all year, 10 am–4 pm Mon.–Sat., 1–6 pm Sun. (summer), 1–5 pm (winter).

Frelinghuysen Arboretum
53 E. Hanover Avenue
Morristown, NJ 07960
201-829-0474
Free. Open all year, except weekends. Dec.–Feb. 9 am–sunset.

Cora Hartshorn Arboretum
324 Forest Drive
Short Hills, NJ 07078
201-376-3587
Free. Open all year, 2:30–4:30 pm Tues.– Thurs., 9:30–11:30 am Sat.; 3–5 pm Sun. in May & Oct.

New Mexico

Living Desert State Park
P.O. Box 100
Carlsbad, NM 88220
505-887-5516

Entrance fee: $1.00. Open all year, 8 am–8 pm (summer), 9 am–5 pm (winter).

Soil Conservation Service Plant Materials
  Center
1036 Miller St., S.W.
Los Lunas, NM 88003
505-821-4555
Free. Open all year, by arrangement. Tests and develops conservation plants.

New York

Bayard Cutting Arboretum
Montauk Highway
Oakdale, NY 11769
516-581-1002
Entrance fee: $1.50, April–Nov. Open all year, 10 am–4 pm Wed.–Sun.

Brooklyn Botanic Garden
1000 Washington Avenue
Brooklyn, NY 11225
718-622-4433
Free. Open April–Oct., 10:30 am–3:30 pm Tues.–Fri.

Brooklyn Botanic Garden Research
  Center
712 Kitchawan Road
Ossining, NY 10562
914-941-8886
Free. Open all year, daylight hours. Workshops.

Clark Garden
I.U. Willets Road
Albertson, NY 11507
516-621-7568
Entrance fee: $1.50. Open all year, 9 am–4:30 pm. Sells seeds and live plants. Affiliated with the Brooklyn Botanic Garden.

Cornell Plantations
One Plantations Road
Ithaca, NY 14850
607-256-3020
Free. Open all year, daylight hours.

Institute of Ecosystem Studies
Mary Flagler Carey Arboretum
Route 44A
Millbrook, NY 12545
914-677-5343

Free. Open all year, 9 am–4 pm Mon.–Sat., 1–4 pm Sun. Sells seeds and live plants.

Knox Headquarters & Jane Colden Native
  Plant Sanctuary
Box 207, Forge Hill Road
Vails Gate, NY 12584
914-561-5498
Free. Open all year, 10 am–5 pm Wed.–Sun., 1–5 pm Sun.

Mohonk Mountain House & Gardens
Mohonk Lake
New Paltz, NY 12561
914-255-1000
Entrance fee: $4.00. Open all year, varying hours. A resort with gardens and trails. Write or call for information.

Museum of the Hudson Highlands
Box 181, The Boulevard
Cornwall-on-Hudson, NY 12520
914-534-7781
Entrance fee: $1 donation. Open all year except major holidays, 11 am–5 pm Mon.–Thurs. and Sat., 1:30–5 pm Sun. (summer), 2–5 pm Mon.–Thurs., 11 am–5 pm Sat., and 1:30–5 pm Sun. (winter). Closed Fridays. A 3-acre tallgrass prairie reconstruction, and 90 acres of woodlands.

New York Botanical Garden
Bronx Park (Southern Boulevard)
Bronx, NY 10458
212-220-8700
Entrance fee: $2.50 parking. Open April–Oct. 8:30–4:30 pm. Sells seeds and live plants. Detailed educational programs.

Queens Botanical Garden
43-50 Main Street
Flushing, NY 11355
718-886-3800
Free. Open all year, 9 am–sunset. Sells seeds and live plants.

Root Glen
Hamilton College
107 College Hill Rd.
Clinton, NY 13323
315-853-4502
Free. Open all year, daylight hours.

Trailside Nature Museum
Ward Pound Ridge Reservation
Cross River, NY 10518
914-763-3993
Free. Open all year, daylight hours.

North Carolina

Herbert Bluethenthal Memorial
  Wildflower Preserve
Department of Biological Sciences
U.N.C.-Wilmington
601 S. College Road
Wilmington, NC 28403-3297
919-395-3481
Free. Open all year, daylight hours.

Sarah P. Duke Gardens
Duke University
Durham, NC 27706
919-684-3698
Free. Open all year, 8 am–sunset.

North Carolina Botanical Garden
U.N.C.-Chapel Hill, Totten Center 457-A
Chapel Hill, NC 27514
919-967-2246
Free. Open all year, except holidays, 8 am–5 pm Mon.–Fri., 10 am–4 pm Sat., 2–5 pm Sun. Sells seeds and live plants.

Reynolda Gardens
Wake Forest University
100 Reynolda Village
Winston-Salem, NC 27109
919-761-5593
Free. Open all year daylight hours.

U.N.C.-Charlotte Botanical Garden
Van Landigham Glen
Biology Department/U.N.C.C.
Charlotte, NC 28223
704-597-4055
Free. Open all year, daylight hours.

North Dakota

Gunlogson Arboretum
Icelandic State Park
Highway 5 – West
Cavalier, ND 58220
701-265-4561
Entrance fee: $1.50 per car. Open all year, daylight hours. 200 acres.

USDA Soil Conservation Service
Plant Materials Center
P.O. Box 1458
Bismark, ND 58502
701-663-1180
Free. Open 8 am–4:30 pm Mon.–Fri.

Ohio

Aullwood Audubon Center and Farm
1000 Aullwood Road
Dayton, OH 45414
513-890-7360
Entrance fee: $1.50; National Audubon Society members free. Open all year 9 am–5 pm Mon.–Sat., 1–5 pm Sun. Closed major holidays. Marshes, woodlands, fen, wildflower trail, and native Ohio restored tallgrass prairie. Seed collection program.

Aullwood Garden
900 Aullwood Road
Dayton, OH 45414
513-278-8231
Free. Open all year, Tues.–Sun., daylight hours. Operated by Park District of Dayton–Montgomery County.

Cedar Bog State Memorial
980 Woodburn Road
Urbana, OH 43078
513-484-3744
Entrance fee: $1.50. Open all year, by appointment only. 428 acres, operated by the Ohio Historical Society.

Cincinnati Nature Center
4949 Tealtown Road
Milford, OH 45150
513-831-1711
Entrance fee: $1.00 parking. Open all year, 7:30 am–8:30 pm Mon.–Fri. (summer); 8:30 am–7:30 pm Mon.–Fri. (winter).

Civic Garden Center of Greater
 Cincinnati
2715 Reading Road
Cincinnati, OH 45206
513-221-0981
Free. Open Jan. 16–Dec. 21, 9 am–4 pm Tues.–Fri, 9 am–3 pm Sat. Sells seeds and live plants. Periodic classes on native plant gardening.

Cleveland Museum of Natural History
Wade Oval, University Circle
Cleveland, OH 44106
216-231-4600
Entrance fee: $2.75. Open all year, 10 am–5 pm Mon.–Sat., 1 pm–5:30 pm Sun. Sells seeds and live plants.

Crosby Gardens
5403 Elmer Drive
Toledo, OH 43615
419-536-8365
Free. Open all year, daylight hours.

The Garden Center of Greater Cleveland
11030 East Boulevard
Cleveland, OH 44106
216-721-1600
Free. Open all year, daylight hours.

Glen Helen
Antioch University
405 Corry Street
Yellow Springs, OH 45387
513-767-7375
Free. Open all year, daylight hours. Trailside museum open 10–12 am and 1–5:30 pm Tues.–Fri., noon–5:30 pm weekends. 1000-acre nature preserve, restored prairie.

Holden Arboretum
9500 Sperry Road
Mentor, OH 44060
216-946-4400
Entrance fee: $2.50. Open all year, 10 am–5 pm Tues.–Sun. Sells live plants.

Inniswood Botanical Garden & Nature
 Preserve
940 Hempstead Road
Westerville, OH 43081
614-895-6216
Free. Open all year, 8 am–4:30 pm Tues.–Sat., 12–5 pm Sun. Operated by the Metropolitan Park District of Columbus & Franklin Counties.

Kingwood Center
900 Park Avenue West
Mansfield, OH 43358
419-522-0211
Free. Open all year, 8 am–sunset. Sells live plants. Library.

Oklahoma

Oxley Nature Center
Mohawk Park
(mailing address: 200 Civic Center)
Tulsa, OK 74103
918-832-8112
Entrance fee: $1.00 parking, weekends. Open all year, 8 am–5 pm. Varied programs on native plants.

Tulsa Garden Center
2435 S. Peoria Avenue
Tulsa, OK 74114
919-749-6401
Free. Open all year, 9 am–4 pm Mon.–Fri. Sells seeds and live plants. Library, seminars & workshops.

Oregon

The Berry Botanic Garden
11505 SW Summerville Avenue
Portland, OR 97219
503-636-4112
Entrance fee: $15 annual membership. Open all year, by appointment, Mon.–Fri. Sells live plants. Programs on native plants for members.

Castle Crest Wildflower Gardens
Crater Lake National Park
Crater Lake, OR 97604
Entrance fee: $2.00 admission to C.L.N.P. Open July–Sept., daylight hours.

Darlington Wayside
84505 Highway 101
Florence, OR 97439
503-997-3851
Free. Open all year, daylight hours.

Hoyt Arboretum
4000 SW Fairview Boulevard
Portland, OR 97221
503-228-8732
Free. Open all year, daylight hours. Sells seeds and live plants.

Pennsylvania

Appleford
770 Mt. Moro Road
Villanova, PA 19085

215-527-4280

Free. Open all year, 9 am–sunset.

Barnes Foundation Arboretum
57 Lapsley Lane
Merion, PA 19066
215-664-8880

*Free. Open all year, 9:30 am–4 pm Mon.–
Sat., 1:30–4:30 pm Sun.*

Bowman's Hill Wildflower Preserve
Washington Crossing Historic Park
Route 22
Washington Crossing, PA 18977
215-862-2924

*Free. Open all year, 9 am–5 pm. Sells seeds
and live plants. Monthly programs on
native plants.*

Delaware Valley College Arboretum
Delaware Valley College
Doylestown, PA 18901
215-345-1500

Free. Open all year, daylight hours.

Henry Foundation for Botanical Research
801 Stony Lane
Gladwyne, PA 19035
215-525-2037

*Free. Open April–Oct., 10 am–4 pm Tues.
& Thurs.*

Longwood Gardens
U.S. Route 1
Kennett Square, PA 19348
215-388-6741

*Entrance fee: $5.00. Open all year, 9
am–6 pm (summer), 9 am–5 pm (winter).
Sells seeds and live plants.*

Morris Arboretum
University of Pennsylvania
Hillcrest Avenue
Chestnut Hill, PA 19118
215-242-3399

*Entrance fee: $2.00. Open all year, except
Christmas & New Year's Day, 10 am–5 pm
(spring–fall), 10 am–4 pm (winter). Sells
live plants. Periodic courses.*

Wildflower Reserve of Raccoon Creek
State Park
RD #1
Hookstown, PA 15050

412-899-3611/412-899-2200

*Free. Open all year, 8 am–sunset. One of
the most impressive stands of wildflowers
in western Pennsylvania.*

South Carolina

Brookgreen Gardens
Murrells Inlet, SC 29576
803-237-4218

*Entrance fee: $3.00. Open all year, 9:30
am–4:45 pm. Sells seeds.*

Clemson University Horticultural
Gardens
Perimeter Road
Clemson, SC 29632
803-656-3403

Free. Open all year, daylight hours.

Columbia Museum
1519 Senate Street
Columbia, SC 29201
803-799-2810

*Entrance fee: $2.00. Open all year, 10
am–5 pm Tues.–Fri., 1–5 pm weekends.
Closed Monday. Wildflower garden maintained by the Palmetto Garden Club.*

Tennessee

Cheekwood Botanical Gardens & Fine
Arts Center, Inc.
Forrest Park Drive
Nashville, TN 37205
615-356-3306

*Entrance fee: $2.50. Open all year 9
am–5 pm Tues.–Sat., 12–5 pm Sun. Library and wildflower nursery. 5 acres.*

Dixon Gallery & Gardens
4339 Park Avenue
Memphis, TN 38117
901-761-5250

*Entrance fee: $1.00. Open all year, except
holidays, 11 am–5 pm Tues.–Sun. Sells
seeds and live plants.*

Memphis Botanic Garden
750 Cherry Road
Memphis, TN 38117
901-685-1566

*Free. Open all year, 8 am–sunset. Sells
seeds and live plants.*

Texas

Fort Worth Botanic Garden
3220 Botanic Garden Drive
Fort Worth, TX 76107
817-870-7686

*Free. Open all year, 8 am–11 pm Mon.–
Sun. Sell seeds and live plants.*

San Antonio Botanical Center
555 Funston Place
San Antonio, TX 78209
512-821-5115

*Entrance fee: $1.25. Open all year, 9
am–6 pm Wed.–Sun. Sells seeds. Drought-
resistant native plant project.*

Utah

State Arboretum of Utah
University of Utah
Salt Lake City, UT 84112
801-581-5322

*Free. Open all year, 8 am–5 pm Mon.–Fri.
Sells live plants.*

Vermont

Park-McCullough House
West & Park Streets
North Bennington, VT 05257
802-442-5441

*Entrance fee: $3.00. Open May–Oct., 10
am–4 pm Sun.–Fri., 10 am–2 pm Sat.*

Vermont Wildflower Farm
Route 7
Charlotte, VT 05445
802-452-3500

*Entrance fee: $2.00. Open May–Oct., 10
am–5 pm. Sells seeds.*

Virginia

Blandy Experimental Farm
Orland E. White Arboretum
University of Virginia
Boyce, VA 22620
703-837-1758

Free. Open all year, daylight hours.

Maymont Park
1700 Hampton Street
Richmond, VA 23220

804-358-7166

Free. Open all year, daylight hours. Sells seeds and live plants.

Wildflower Garden on Mill Mountain
Roanoke, VA 24014

703-343-6757

Free. Open March–Nov., 9 am–sunset. Part of the Garden Club of America.

Washington

The Northwest Native Garden
Point Defiance Park
5402 N. Shirley
Tacoma, WA 98407

206-591-5328

Free. Open all year, dayligth hours. Six botanic zones, maintained by Tacoma Garden Club.

West Virginia

Cathedral State Park
Route 50
Aurora, WV 26705

304-735-3771

Free. Open all year, 6 am–10 pm. Virgin eastern hemlock tract.

Core Arboretum
Department of Biology, P.O. Box 6057
West Virginia University
Morgantown, WV 26505-6057

304-293-5201

Free. Open all year, daylight hours.

Wisconsin

Alfred Boerner Botanical Gardens
Witnall Park, 5879 S. 92nd Street
Milwaukee (Hales Corners), WI 53130

414-425-1131

Free. Open April–Oct., 8 am–sunset. Native plant rock gardens.

Schlitz-Audubon Nature Center
1111 E. Brown Deer Road
Milwaukee, WI 53217

414-352-2880

Entrance fee: $1.00. Open all year, except holidays, 9 am–5 pm Tues.–Sun. Programs on native plant gardens.

University of Wisconsin Arboretum
1207 Seminole Highway
Madison, WI 53711

608-263-7888

Free. Open all year, 7 am–10 pm. Visitor center open 9 am–4 pm, weekdays; 12:30–4 pm, weekends. Extensive areas of restored plant communities.

Native Plant and Horticultural Societies

This is a listing of native plant societies, botanical organizations, and horticultural societies that are interested in native plants.

Alabama

Alabama Wildflower Society
% George Wood
Route 2, Box 115
Northport, AL 35476

Alaska

Alaska Native Plant Society
P.O. Box 141613
Anchorage, AK 99514
Publishes a newsletter.

Arizona

Arizona Native Plant Society
P.O. Box 41206 Sun Station
Tucson, AZ 85717
Publishes The Plant Press. *Six chapters in the state.*

Arkansas

Arkansas Native Plant Society
% Mr. Don Peach
Route 1, Box 282
Mena, AR 71953

British Columbia

Alpine Garden Club of British Columbia
% R.W. Mansfield
P.O. Box 102
Madeira Park, BC V0N 2H0 CANADA
Publishes Monthly Bulletin. *Seed exchanges and plant sales.*

Vancouver Island Rock & Alpine Garden Society
% P.O. Box 6507
Postal Station C
Victoria, BC V8P 5M4 CANADA
Publishes a newsletter.

Vancouver Natural History Society
% U.B.C. Botanical Garden
Vancouver, BC V6T 1W5 CANADA

California

California Native Plant Society
909 12th Street
Sacramento, CA 95814
Publishes Fremontia *and* Bulletin. *Twenty-six chapters.*

Southern California Horticultural Institute
P.O. Box 49798 Barrington Station
Los Angeles, CA 90049
Publishes a newsletter Pacific Horticulture *available to members.*

Colorado

Colorado Native Plant Society
Box 200
Fort Collins, CO 80522
Publishes a newsletter. Regional chapters.

Connecticut

Connecticut Botanical Society
% Donald Swan
1 Livermore Trail
Killingworth, CT 06417
Publishes a newsletter.

Connecticut Horticultural Society
150 Main Street
Wethersfield, CT 06109
Publishes a newsletter.

District of Columbia

Botanical Society of Washington
Department of Botany — NHB/166
Smithsonian Institution
Washington, DC 20560

Florida

Florida Native Plant Society
1203 Orange Avenue
Winter Park, FL 32789
Publishes Palmetto.

Horticulture Study Society of Florida
3280 S. Miami Avenue
Miami, FL 33129
Publishes The Horticulturist. *Associated with Miami Museum of Science and Agricultural Extension Service.*

Pensacola Wildflower Society
% Jim Dyehouse
3911 Dunwoody Drive
Pensacola, FL 32503

Georgia

Georgia Botanical Society
% Dr. Frank McCamey, Treasurer
1676 Andover Court
Doravilla, GA 30360

The Garden Club of Georgia
325 S. Lumpkin Street
Athens, GA 30602

Hawaii

Hawaiian Botanical Society
% Dept. of Botany — U. Hawaii
3190 Maile Way
Honolulu, HI 96822

Idaho

Idaho Native Plant Society (Pahove Chapter)
Box 9451
Boise, ID 83707

Illinois

Chicago Horticultural Society
P.O. Box 400
Glencoe, IL 60022
Parent organization of Chicago Botanic Garden. Garden available to members.

Illinois Native Plant Society
Department of Botany
Southern Illinois University
Carbondale, IL 62901
Publishes The Harbinger *and* Erigenia. *Sells books on native plants.*

Iowa

Iowa State Horticultural Society
State House
Des Moines, IA 50319
Publishes Iowa Horticulturist.

Kansas

Kansas Wildflower Society
Mulvane Art Center — Washburn
  University
17th & Jewell Street
Topeka, KS 66621
Publishes a newsletter.

Louisiana

Louisiana Native Plant Society
% Richard Johnson
Route 1, Box 151
Saline, LA 71070

Maine

Josselyn Botanical Society
% Dr. Charles D. Richards
Deering Hall, University of Maine
Orono, ME 04469

Massachusetts

Massachusetts Horticultural Society
300 Massachusetts Avenue
Boston, MA 02115
Publishes Horticulture *and* The Leaflet.
*Offers courses and lectures on native
plant gardening.*

New England Botanical Club
Botanical Museum
Oxford Street
Cambridge, MA 02138
Publishes Rhodora.

New England Wild Flower Society, Inc.
Garden in the Woods
Hemenway Road
Framingham, MA 01701
Publishes a newsletter.

Michigan

Michigan Botanical Club
Matthaei Botanical Gardens
1800 Dixboro Road
Ann Arbor, MI 48105

Minnesota

Minnesota Native Plant Society
220 BioSci Center — University of
  Minnesota
1445 Gortner Avenue
St. Paul, MN 55108

Minnesota State Horticultural Society
University of Minnesota
St. Paul, MN 55108
Publishes Minnesota Horticulturist.

Mississippi

Mississippi Native Plant Society
% Travis Salley, Secretary
202 N. Andrews Avenue
Cleveland, MS 38732

Missouri

Missouri Native Plant Society
Box 6612
Jefferson City, MO 65102-6612
Publishes Missouriensis. *Meetings open to
the public.*

Nevada

Northern Nevada Native Plant Society
Box 8965
Reno, NV 89507
Publishes Mentzelia *and a newsletter.*

New Jersey

New Jersey Native Plant Society
% Frelinghuysen Arboretum
Box 1295R
Morristown, NJ 07960

New Mexico

Native Plant Society of New Mexico
P.O. Box 5917
Santa Fe, NM 87502

New York

Horticultural Society of New York
128 W. 58th Street
New York, NY 10019
Garden *available to members.*

Torrey Botanical Club
New York Botanical Garden
Bronx Park
Bronx, NY 10458
Publishes Bulletin.

North Carolina

North Carolina Wildflower Preservation
  Society
% North Carolina Botanical Garden
UNC-CH Totten Center, 457-A
Chapel Hill, NC 27514
*Publishes a newsletter. Programs at the
North Carolina Botanical Garden,
Chapel Hill, NC.*

Ohio

Cincinnati Wildflower Preservation
  Society
% Dr. Victor G. Soukup
Department of Biology
University of Cincinnati
Cincinnati, OH 45221

Inniswood Society
Inniswood Botanical Garden
940 Hempstead Road
Westerville, OH 43081

Garden *available to members.*

Native Plant Society of Northeastern Ohio
6 Louise Drive
Chagrin Falls, OH 44022
Publishes On the Fringe. *Monthly lectures
and field trips.*

Oklahoma

Goldenrod Hollow
% Drs. Connie & John Taylor
Route 1, Box 157
Durant, OK 74701

Oregon

Native Plant Society of Oregon
% Dr. Frank A. Lang
Department of Biology
Southern Oregon State College
Ashland, OR 97520
Publishes Bulletin. *Regional chapters.*

Pennsylvania

Pennsylvania Horticultural Society, Inc.
325 Walnut Street
Philadelphia, PA 19106
Publishes News *and* Green Scene. *Field
trips.*

Pennsylvania Native Plant Society
1806 Commonwealth Building
316 Fourth Avenue
Pittsburgh, PA 15222

Philadelphia Botanical Club
Academy of Science
19th and Parkway
Philadelphia, PA 19103

Tennessee

Tennessee Native Plant Society
% Department of Botany
University of Tennessee
Knoxville, TN 37916

Texas

Native Plant Society of Texas
P.O. Box 23836 — TWU Station
Denton, TX 76204

Utah

Utah Native Plant Society
% The State Arboretum of Utah
University of Utah, Building 436
Salt Lake City, UT 84112
Publishes The Sego Lily. *Several chapters.*

Virginia

Virginia Wildflower Preservation Society
Box 844
Annandale, VA 22003
Publishes Bulletin *and newsletters.*
*Several chapters, Wildflower Week events,
and other activities.*

Washington

Washington Native Plant Society
% Dr. Arthur R. Kruckeberg
Department of Botany
University of Washington
Seattle, WA 98195

West Virginia

West Virginia Native Plant Society
Herbarium, Brooks Hall
West Virginia University
Morgantown, WV 26506

Wyoming

Wyoming Native Plant Society
P.O. Box 1471
Cheyenne, WY 82001

National Organizations

American Horticultural Society
P.O. Box 0105
Mt. Vernon, VA 22121
Publishes American Horticulturist.
*Wildflower Rediscovery Project, Gar-
dener's Information Service, and other
programs.*

American Penstemon Society
% Orville M. Steward
Box 281, Penguin Court
Laughlintown, PA 15655
*Newsletter, slide library, seed exchange,
publishes field guides to penstemons.*

American Rock Garden Society
% Buffy Parker, Secretary
15 Fairmead Road
Darien, CT 06820
Publishes Quarterly Bulletin. *Twenty re-
gional chapters.*

National Council of State Garden Clubs
4401 Magnolia Avenue
St. Louis, MO 63110
Publishes The National Gardener *and the*
Directory to Resources on Wildflower
Propagation *($3.00).*

National Wildflower Research Center
2600 FM 973 North
Austin, TX 78725
Publishes Wildflower.

Operation Wildflower
National Council of State Garden Clubs
Mrs. C. Norman Collard, Chairman
Box 860
Pocasset, MA 02559

Soil Conservation Society of America
7515 Northeast Ankeny Road
Ankeny, IA 50021
Publishes Sources of Native Seeds and
Plants *($3.00).*

The Canadian Wildflower Society
35 Bauer Crescent
Unionville, ONT CANADA L3R 4H3
Publishes Wildflower.

References

Abbot, C., 1979. *How to Know and Grow Texas Wildflowers, 2nd edition.* Green Horizons Press, Kerrville, TX.

Gardening with natives of Texas environs.

Aiken, G.D., 1968. *Pioneering with Wildflowers.* Prentice-Hall, Englewood Cliffs, NJ.

A book on northeastern woodland natives written by the late senator from Vermont, a professional horticulturist.

Bailey, L.H., 1935. *The Standard Cyclopedia of Horticulture.* Macmillan, New York, NY. 3639 pp.

A classic gardening encyclopedia containing information on numerous native wildflowers as well as domesticated species.

Batson, W.T., 1984. *Landscape Plants for the Southeast.* U. South Carolina Press, Columbia, SC. 406 pp.

Some herbaceous, but mostly woody perennials for the Southeast, presented in outline form.

Birdseye, C. & E. Birdseye, 1951. *Growing Woodland Plants.* Dover, New York, NY. 223 pp.

A guide to gardening with 200 northeastern native species of woodland habitats.

Bruce, H., 1976. *How to Grow Wildflowers and Wild Shrubs and Trees in Your Own Garden.* Van Nostrand/Reinhold, New York, NY. 294 pp.

East Coast woody and herbaceous perennials, presented in an anecdotal style.

Cook, A.D. ed., 1983. *Low Maintenance Gardening.* Brooklyn Botanic Garden, Brooklyn, NY. *(Plants and Gardens,* Brooklyn Botanic Garden Record, Vol. 40, No. 1.)

Crockett, J.U. & O.E. Allen, 1977. *Wildflower Gardening.* Time-Life Books, Alexandria, VA. 160 pp.

Coast-to-coast examples of natives for the garden, with color illustrations.

Durand, H., 1923. *Wildflowers and Ferns: In Their Homes and In Our Gardens.* Putnams, New York, NY. 394 pp.

An early classic on northeastern wildflowers.

Foster, H.L., 1968. *Rock Gardening: A Guide to Growing Alpines and Other Wildflowers in the American Garden.* Bonanza Books, New York, NY. 466 pp.

A classic with a good deal of information on native plants in rock gardens.

Hartmann, H.T. & D.E. Kester, 1975. *Plant Propagation.* 3rd ed. Prentice-Hall, Englewood Cliffs, NJ. 662 pp.

A standard text about plant propagation.

Hersey, J., 1964. *Wild Flowers to Know and Grow.* Van Nostrand, Princeton, NJ. 235 pp.

Concentrates on northeastern perennials and wildflowers.

Hill, L., 1985. *Secrets of Plant Propagation.* Garden Way Publishing, Pownal, VT. 168 pp.

How to propagate woody and herbaceous plants.

Hull, H.S., ed. 1982. *Handbook on Gardening with Wildflowers.* Brooklyn Botanic Garden, Brooklyn, NY. *(B.B.G. Plants & Gardens 18* (1).) 85 pp.

A variety of articles about native plant gardening.

Kenfield, W.G., 1970. *The Wild Gardener in the Wild Landscape.* Hafner, New York, NY. 232 pp.

An interesting book on naturalistic landscaping in the Northeast.

Kruckeberg, A.R., 1982. *Gardening with Native Plants of the Pacific Northwest.* U. Washington Press, Seattle, WA.

Trees, shrubs and herbaceous perennials of the Pacific Northwest.

Martin, A.C., H.S. Zim, & A.L. Nelson, 1951. *American Wildlife and Plants.* Dover, New York, NY. 500 pp.

While not a book about wildflower gardening, this book is quite helpful in planning gardens to attract various wildlife species.

Montgomery, F.H., 1977. *Seeds and Fruits of Plants of Eastern Canada and Northeastern United States.* U. Toronto Press, Toronto, ONT. 232 pp.

A useful guide to seeds and fruits of native plants.

Phillips, H.R., 1985. *Growing and Propagating Wild Flowers.* U. North Carolina Press, Chapel Hill, NC. 331 pp.

Excellent book on eastern native plants, concentrating on seed collection and propagation methods.

Rock, H.W., 1981. *Prairie Propagation Handbook,* Wehr Nature Center, Whitnall Park, Hales Corners, Milwaukee County, WI. 74 pp.

A tabular guide to prairie wildflowers and grasses, their habitats, harvest dates, and propagation requirements.

Schmidt, M.G., 1980. *Growing California Native Plants.* U. California Press, Berkeley, CA. 366 pp.

A comprehensive treatment of California wildflowers and woody perennials.

Smith, J.R. & B.S. Smith, 1980. *The Prairie Garden.* U. Wisconsin Press, Madison, WI. 219 pp.

70 native wildflowers of midwestern prairies.

Sperka, M., 1973. *Growing Wildflowers.* Scribner's, New York, NY. 277 pp.

An excellent treatment of northeastern wildflowers.

Steffek, E.F., 1983. *The New Wild Flowers and How to Grow Them.* Timber Press, Portland, OR. 186 pp.

A sampling of wildflowers from North America, with useful tables of species from various regions and habitats.

Sullivan, G.A. & R.H. Dailey, 1981. *Resources on Wildflower Propagation.* National Council of State Garden Clubs, Inc., St. Louis, MO. 331 pp.

A bargain at $3.00. Contains a wealth of technical information about plants native to various sections of the U.S.

Tasker, G. & S.T. Moss, *Wild Things — The Return of Native Plants.* Florida Native Plant Society, 1203 Orange Avenue, Winter Park, FL 32789.

Trees, shrubs, and wildflowers native to Florida. ($5.00 plus $1.00 postage).

Taylor, K.S. & S.F. Hamblin, 1976. *Handbook of Wildflower Cultivation.* Collier Books, New York, NY.

Covers a variety of eastern wildflowers.

Wilson, W.H.W., 1984. *Landscaping with Wildflowers and Native Plants.* Ortho Books, San Francisco, CA. 96 pp.

Listings of native plants for various regions and habitats.

Workman, R., 1979. *Growing Native.* Sanibel-Captiva Conservation Foundation, Sanibel, FL 33957.

Native plants for landscaping in coastal South Florida. ($9.95 plus $1.50 postage).

Glossary

Annual. A plant whose life cycle from seed to mature plant, producing flowers, fruits, and seeds, is completed in a single growing season. After seeds are produced, the plant usually dies.

Anther. A pollen-producing sac attached to the filament in the male portion of a flower.

Axil. The point of attachment between stem and leaf.

Basal rosette. An arrangement of leaves radiating from a short stem at the ground surface. Most biennials have a rosette form during their first growing season.

Biennial. A plant whose life cycle extends over two growing seasons. The first year the seed germinates, producing a seedling that usually remains short over the winter. The second growing season the seedling rapidly elongates, flowers, produces seeds, and then dies.

Bolting. The rapid elongation and flowering of biennials during their second growing season.

Bract. A modified leaflike structure, often resembling a petal, surrounding a flower or flower cluster.

Bulb. A fleshy rootstock composed of leaf bases or scaly leaves.

Calyx. The collective term for the sepals of a flower.

Capsule. A dry fruit that splits open to release its seeds.

Complete flowers. Flowers with sepals, petals, stamens, and a pistil all present.

Composite flower. A flower made up of many individual florets clustered into a common head, as is typical in members of the aster family.

Compound leaf. A leaf that is divided into two or more separate leaflets.

Corm. A fleshy rootstock formed by a short, thick, underground stem.

Corolla. The collective term for the petals of a flower.

Crest. A ridge of tissue.

Disc flower (disc floret). One of the small, tubular flowers that form the central disc of flower heads in many members of the aster family.

Dissected. Deeply divided or split into lobes.

Dormancy. The resting or inactive phase of plants or seeds. Dormancy of shoots is usually in response to unfavorable environmental conditions. The breaking of seed dormancy requires moisture and sometimes cold temperatures and abrasion of the seed coat.

Entire. A leaf margin that is smooth and lacking teeth.

Fibrous roots. A root system with many thin or branched root elements.

Filament. The anther-bearing stalk of a stamen.

Floret. One of the small flowers that is clustered together forming the composite flower head in members of the aster family. Florets may be either tubular disc florets or straplike ray florets.

Flowering shoot. A stem that produces flowers.

Flower head. A cluster of florets or small flowers gathered together on a common receptacle, typically found in members of the aster family.

Forcing. Inducing a perennial to flower out of season. Forcing often involves artificial chilling followed by warming the plant.

Germination. The breaking of dormancy in seeds or the sprouting of pollen grains deposited on a stigma.

Habitat. The kind of environment inhabited by a particular species.

Half-hardy. An annual plant that is sown in early spring and flowers in summer.

Hardiness zone. An index relating geographic regions to a plant's ability to withstand minimum winter temperatures. Hardiness zones developed by the U.S. Department of Agriculture range from zone 1, with a minimum temperature of $-50°F$, to zone 10, with minimum temperatures of 30 to 40°F.

Hardy annual. An annual plant whose seeds can withstand subfreezing winter temperatures and whose seedlings can withstand spring frosts.

Hardy perennial. A perennial plant that is not permanently injured or killed by subfreezing temperatures.

Herbaceous. Plants that lack woody tissues and therefore "die back" to the soil surface at the end of the growing season.

Inoculant. A commercially formulated strain of rhizobium added to the soil to aid in the establishment of various members of the bean family.

Inoculation. The addition of rhizobia to the soil.

Keel. The lower, pouchlike lip of flowers of certain members of the bean family. The keel is formed by the fusion of two petals.

Leaflets. The individual segments of a compound leaf.

Legume. A dry, flattened pod fruit that splits open at both edges when mature, as is found in members of the bean family. The term is also applied to the species of the bean family.

Long-day plant. A plant that flowers in response to the short nights of late spring and early summer.

Moist chilling treatment. A means of enhancing the germination of some seeds by storing them under moist conditions at low temperatures prior to planting them.

Nodules. Outgrowths on the roots of plants in the bean family that are inhabited by nitrogen-fixing microorganisms known as rhizobia.

Non-flowering shoot. A stem that does not produce flowers; a vegetative shoot.

Ovary. The swollen base of a pistil, containing ovules. The ripening ovary, which is sometimes fused to the receptacle, becomes the fruit.

Ovules. The female sex cells that become seeds following fertilization.

Palmate. A pattern of compound leaflets or leaf venation, with elements radiating from a central point.

Peduncle. The main flowering stalk of a plant.

Perennial. A plant whose life cycle extends for an indefinite period beyond two growing seasons. These plants generally do not die following flowering.

Perfect flowers. Flowers with both stamens and a pistil, but lacking either sepals and/or petals.

Petal. A modified leaf attached to the receptacle outside the stamens and inside the calyx. Petals are usually showy and serve to attract pollinators to the flower.

Petiole. The stalk that attaches a leaf to a stem.

pH. A measure of the acidity/alkalinity of a substance ranging from 0 (strongly acidic) to 14 (strongly alkaline), with 7 being neutral.

Pistil. The female sexual part of a flower, consisting of the stigma, style, and ovary.

Pollen. The powdery material produced in anthers, containing the male sex cells of flowering plants.

Pollination. The transfer of pollen from an anther to a stigma.

Propagation. Increasing the numbers of plants through seeds, cuttings, or divisions.

Ray flower (ray floret). One of the small flowers with a straplike petal, usually arranged in rings around the margin of flower heads in members of the aster family.

Receptacle. The fleshy tissue at the tip of a flower stalk to which flower parts are attached. Different species may have receptacles that are positioned below the ovary, form a cup around the ovary, or completely enclose the ovary.

Rhizobia. Microorganisms that inhabit nodules on the roots of members of the bean family. These organisms have the ability to take nitrogen from the air and create nitrogen compounds usable by their host plants.

Rhizome. A horizontal, usually branched, underground stem with buds and roots.

Root division. Propagating plants by cutting vertically between root segments.

Root rot. Plant diseases, usually caused by fungi, that lead to the degeneration of roots.

Rootstock. An underground stem of a perennial plant with its associated buds and roots.

Runner. A thin, creeping, horizontal stem that trails along the surface of the ground and gives rise to small plants.

Scape. A leafless stem bearing a cluster of flowers.

Scarification. Abrasion of the seed coat allowing the passage of water and oxygen into the seed, thereby enhancing germination in some species.

Seed coat. The outer protective covering of a seed.

Sepal. A modified leaf that forms the covering of a flower bud. Sepals are attached to the outer margin of the receptacle and are usually green. However, in some species the sepals are brightly colored and resemble petals.

Shoot. The aboveground or stem portion of a plant that bears leaves, buds, and flowers.

Shoot bud. A bud that develops into stem and leaf tissue.

Short-day plant. A plant that flowers in response to the long nights of fall or early spring.

Simple flower. A solitary flower borne on a single stem.

Slip. An old-fashioned name for a cutting used for propagation.

Softwood cutting. A propagation technique of cutting green, rapidly growing portions of stems while they are pliable.

Spadix. A fleshy, spindle-shaped column bearing flowers in members of the arum family.

Spathe. A large, leafy bract that frequently envelops the spadix in members of the arum and other plant families.

Stamen. The male sexual part of a flower consisting of an anther and a filament.

Stigma. The top surface of a pistil upon which pollen grains are deposited.

Stolon. A thin, underground runner.

Stratification. Chilling seeds to enhance their germination.

Style. The portion of the pistil connecting the stigma and the ovary.

Taproot. A thick, strongly vertical root, usually extending to considerable depth, for example, the carrot.

Tender annual. An annual plant whose seedlings are killed by spring frosts.

Tender perennial. Perennial plants that are permanently damaged or killed by subfreezing temperatures.

True root. The descending, underground portion of a plant that is specialized to provide support and absorb water and nutrients. True roots usually lack buds.

Tuber. A rootstock formed by a fleshy, swollen tip of a stolon.

Vernalization. The cold treatment needed by some fall-germinating plants to promote flowering the following spring.

Weed. Any plant that grows where it is not wanted.

Wildflower. An herbaceous plant capable of growing, reproducing, and becoming established without cultivation.

Winter annual. An annual plant that usually germinates in the fall, overwinters as a seedling, and flowers the following spring.

Woody. Having hard, tough tissues that persist from year to year and are capable of producing shoot or flower buds. Woody plants also have the capacity to increase in diameter from year to year.

Index

Boldface numbers, such as **55**, indicate that illustrations or tables appear on that page.

Coneflower. *See* Mexican hat
Container gardening, 9–10
Copa de oro. See California poppy
Coralbells, 8, **24**, 146–147, **147**
Coreopsis lanceolata, 104–105, **105**. *See also* Lance-leaved coreopsis
Corms, **17**, 22
  division, 48–49, **49**
Corn lily. *See* Yellow clintonia
Cornus canadensis, 106–107, **107**. *See also* Bunchberry
Corolla, 16
Cosmos, **4**, 108–109, **109**
Cosmos bipinnatus, 108–109, **109**. *See also* Cosmos
Culver's physic. *See* Culver's root
Culver's root, 248-249, **249**
Cutflower garden, **4**
Cypripedium acaule, 110-111, **111**

D

Day length, effect on flowering, 25
Deadheading, 25
Deer, 44
Deergrass. *See* Meadow beauty
Desert baileya. *See* Desert marigold
Desert hollyhock. *See* Desert mallow
Desert mallow, 9, 236–237, **237**
Desert marigold, 8, 9, 86–87, **87**
Desmodium canadense, 112–113, **113**. *See also* Showy tick trefoil
Dicentra cucullaria, 114–115, **115**. *See also* Dutchman's breeches
Dichelostemma pulchellum. See Blue dicks
Disc flowers, **15**, 16
Dodecatheon clevelandii, 116–117, **117**. *See also* Western shooting star
Dodecatheon media, 118–119, **119**. *See also* Eastern shooting star
Dogtooth violet. *See* Eastern trout lily
Doll's eyes. *See* White baneberry
Dormancy, 32
Douglas's iris, 8, 154–155, **155**
Douglas's lupine. *See* Sky lupine
Douglas's wallflower, 7, **13**, 126–127, **127**
Drummond's phlox. *See* Annual phlox
Dry soil, wildflowers for, 9. *See also* Soil, moisture conditions
Dutchman's breeches, 8, **41**, 114–115, **115**
Dwarf cornell. *See* Bunchberry
Dwarf sunflower. *See* Mule's ears

E

Eastern columbine, 7, 8, 9, **10**, 70–71, **71**
Eastern shooting star, **24**, 118–119, **119**
Eastern trout lily, 128–129, **129**. *See also* Fawn lily
Eastern woodland garden, **41**
Echinacea purpurea, 120–121, **121**. *See also* Purple coneflower
Ecotypes, 25, 28
Edible garden, 7–8
Elephantheads, 9, 194–195, **195**
Elephantella. *See* Elephant heads
Elevation, effect on flowering, 24–25
Elk grass. *See* Bear grass
Eriophyllum conferiflorum, 122–123, **123**
Eryngium yuccifolium, 124–125, **125**. *See also* Rattlesnake master
Erysimum capitatum, 126–127, **127**. *See also* Douglas's wallflower
Erythronium americanum, 128–129, **129**. *See also* Fawn lily
Erythronium grandiflorum, 130–131, **131**. *See also* Fawn lily
Eschscholzia californica, 132–133, **133**. *See also* California poppy
Escobita. *See* Owl's clover
Euphorbia marginata, 134–135, **135**. *See also* Snow-on-the-mountain
Evening star. *See* Blazing star

F

False dragonhead, **4**, 208–209, **209**
False Solomon's seal, 7, **13**, 234–235, **235**
Farewell-to-spring, 9, 96–97, **97**
Fawn lily. *See* Eastern trout lily; Yellow fawn lily
Fibrous roots, **17**
Field lupines. *See* Sky lupine
Filament, **15**, 16
Fir needles, 41
Flame lily. *See* Wood lily
Flaming poppy. *See* Wind poppy
Flats, 47
Florets, 16
Flower
  color, 16, **18–19**
  disc, **15**
  height, 16, **20–21**
  parts, 15–16, **15**
  ray, **15**

Flower *(continued)*
  sexual parts, 15–16
  single disc, **15**
  stalk, 15
Flowering progression, **26–27**
Flowering season, 23–28
  extending, 25–28
Fragrance garden, **13**. *See also* Perfume garden
Fritillaria biflora, 136–137, **137**

G

Gaillardia. *See* Blanketflower
Gaillardia aristata, 138–139, **139**. *See also* Blanketflower
Garden
  butterfly, 7, **9**
  cutflower, **4**
  eastern woodland, **41**
  edible, 7–8
  hummingbird, 7, **10**
  natural, 8–9
  perfume, 7, **13**
  rock, 8, **24**
  themes, 7–9
  West Coast grassland, **28**
  midwest prairie, **47**
Gardening, container, 9–10
Gaultheria procumbens, 140–141, **141**. *See also* Wintergreen
Gayfeather, **4**, 8, **47**, 164–165, **165**
Genetic factors, effect on flowering, 25
Gentian. *See* Closed gentian
Gentiana andrewsii, 142–143, **143**. *See also* Closed gentian
Giant evening primrose, 188–189, **189**
Gilia coronopifolia. See Standing cypress
Gilia rubra. See Standing cypress
Glacier lily. *See* Yellow fawn lily
Glade lily. *See* Missouri evening primrose
Goatsbeard, 8, 76–77, **77**
Godetia. *See* Farewell-to-spring
Golden stars, 8, 88–89, **89**
Golden yarrow, 122–123, **123**
Goldfields, 8, **28**, 158–159, **159**
Gooding's verbena. *See* Southwestern verbena
Ground covers, 8, **14**
Ground limestone, 41
Groundnut, 7, 8, **13**, 66–67, **67**
  planting, 47–48
Growing degree days, 23–24

Growing wildflowers
outside native range, 9
reasons for, 3–5
Gypsum, 38-39, 41

H

Hardiness zones, 29–32, **34–35**
(map), 33
Hedges, 8
Height, 16, **20–21**
Heliotrope. *See* Purple heliotrope
Hepatica acutiloba, 144–145, **145**. *See also* Sharp-lobed hepatica
Herald-of-summer. *See* Farewell-to-spring
Heuchera sanguinea, 146–147, **147**. *See also* Coralbells
Holding bed, 49–50
Hooker's evening primrose. *See* Giant evening primrose
Hot water treatments, 46
Houstonia caerulea, 148–149, **149**. *See also* Bluets
Hummingbirds, garden for attracting, 7, **10**
Hymenoxys grandiflora, 150–151, **151**. *See also* Old-man-of-the-mountain

I

Indian basket grass. *See* Bear grass
Indian blanket. *See* Blanketflower
Indian pink, 7, 8, **10**, 228–229, **229**
Indian turnip. *See* Jack-in-the-pulpit
Information, sources of, 13–14
Innocence. *See* Bluets; Chinese houses
Insects, 44
Ipomopsis rubra, 152–153, **153**. *See also* Standing cypress
Iris, 9. *See also* Douglas's iris; Larger blue flag
Iris douglasiana, 154–155, **155**. *See also* Douglas's iris
Iris versicolor, 156–157, **157**. *See also* Larger blue flag

J

Jack-in-the-pulpit, 8, **41**, 74–75, **75**
changing sex, 4

K

Kalo, Inc., 48

L

Lacy phacelia. *See* Purple heliotrope
Lady's slipper. *See* Pink lady's slipper
Lamb's tongue. *See* Yellow fawn lily
Lance-leaved coreopsis, **4**, 8, 9, 104–105, **105**
Large-flowered linanthus. *See* Linanthus
Large-flowered trillium. *See* White trillium
Larger blue flag, 8, 156–157, **157**
Lasthenia californica, 158–159, **159**. *See also* Goldfields
Lasthenia chrysostoma. *See* Goldfields.
Lawn, planting wildflowers in, 9
Layia platyglossa, 160–161, **161**. *See also* Tidy tips
Leadplant, 8, **47**, 60–61, **61**
planting, 47–48
Legumes, planting, 47–48
Lepachys columnaris. *See* Mexican hat
Lewisia rediviva, 162–163, **163**. *See also* Bitterroot
Liatris pycnostachya, 164–165, **165**. *See also* Gayfeather
Light conditions, 29, **30–31**
Light or dark treatments, 46
Lilium philadelphicum, 166–167, **167**. *See also* Wood lily
Lilium umbellatum. *See* Wood lily
Lily. *See* Chocolate lily; Eastern trout lily; Wood lily; Yellow fawn lily
Limestone, 41
Linanthus, 8, 168–169, **169**
Linanthus grandiflorus, 168–169, **169**. *See also* Linanthus
Linum lewisii, 170–171, **171**. *See also* Blue flax
Little bluestem, **47**
Little pink elephants. *See* Elephantheads
Live plants, buying, 11
Lobelia cardinalis, 172–173, **173**. *See also* Cardinal flower
Local conditions, effect on flowering, 24–25
"Long-day" plants, 25, 280
Long-stemmed eriophyllum. *See* Golden yarrow
Lupines, 7. *See also* Purple annual lupine; Sky lupine
planting, 47–48
Lupinus nanus, 174–175, **175**. *See also* Sky lupine
Lupinus succulentus, 176–177, **177**

M

Mandrake. *See* Mayapple
Marianas. *See* Baby blue-eyes
Mayapple, 8, 210–211, **211**
Meadow beauty, 7, 9, 218–219, **219**
Meadows, planting wildflowers in, 9
Mentzelia lindleyi, 178–179, **179**. *See also* Blazing star
Mertensia virginica, 180–181, **181**
Mexican hat, **4**, 216–217, **217**
Midland shooting star. *See* Eastern shooting star
Midwest prairie garden, **47**
Mission bells. *See* Chocolate lily
Missouri evening primrose, 8, **24**, 190–191, **191**
Missouri primrose. *See* Missouri evening primrose
Mitchella repens, 182–183, **183**. *See also* Partridgeberry
Moccasin flower. *See* Pink lady's slipper
Moisture conditions, 9, 32–39, **36–37**
Monarda fistulosa, 184–185, **185**. *See also* Wild bergamot
Mountain iris. *See* Douglas's iris
Mountain phlox. *See* Linanthus
Mulch, effect on flowering, 24–25
Mule's ear wyethia. *See* Mule's ears
Mule's ears, 250–251, **251**

N

National Council of State Garden Clubs, 5
National Forests, 14
National Wildlife Refuges, 14
Native plants, restoration programs, 5
Natural gardens, 8–9
Nature Conservancy, 14
Nemophila menziesii, 186–187, **187**
New England aster, 7, 8, **9**, 82–83, **83**
Nitragin Company, 48
Nitrogen, 39
Nodding wild onion, 8, **47**, 56–57, **57**
Nursery beds, 47, 49–50

O

Obedient plant. *See* False dragonhead
Oenothera hookeri, 188–189, **189**
Oenothera missouriensis, 190–191, **191**. *See also* Missouri evening primrose
Old-man-of-the-mountain, 8, **24**, 150–151, **151**

Y

Yarrow. *See* Golden yarrow
Yellow adder's tongue. *See* Eastern trout
    lily
Yellow clintonia, 7, 8, **14**, 100–101, **101**

Yellow fawn lily, 130–131, **131**. *See also*
    Fawn lily
Yellow yarrow. *See* Golden yarrow
Yucca moth, 4
Yucca whipplei, 254–255, **255**. *See also*
    Our Lord's candle

Henry W. Art is chairman of the biology department at Williams College and director of the Hopkins Memorial Forest, part of the college's Center for Environmental Studies. He received a doctorate in Forest Ecology from Yale University, and is affiliated with numerous scientific organizations. He is the author of *Ecological Studies in the Sunken Forest, Fire Island, New York,* as well as articles for *Science* and *Natural History* magazines. He and his wife, Pam, have three sons.

A. Wood lily *(Lilium philadelphicum)*
B. Lance-leaved coreopsis *(Coreopsis lanceolata)*
C. Sharp-lobed hepatica *(Hepatica acutiloba)*
D. Colorado columbine *(Aquilegia caerulea)*
E. Pasture rose *(Rosa carolina)*
F. New England aster *(Aster novae-angliae)*
G. Tidy Tips *(Layia platyglossa)*
H. Black-eyed Susan *(Rudbeckia hirta)*